BUILDING THE CHURCH IN AMERICA

BUILDING THE
CHURCH IN AMERICA

Studies in Honor of Monsignor Robert F. Trisco

on the Occasion of His Seventieth Birthday

MELVILLE STUDIES IN CHURCH HISTORY

Joseph C. Linck, C.O., and Raymond J. Kupke, editors

The Catholic University of America Press

Washington, D.C.

The paper used in this publication meets the minimum requirements of
American National Standards for Information Science—Permanence of
Paper for Printed Library materials, ANSI Z39.48–1984.
∞

Building the Church in America: Studies in Honor of Monsignor Robert F. Trisco
was designed and composed in Meridien Roman by Kachergis Book
Design, Pittsboro, North Carolina; and printed on 60-pound
Glatfelter Natural Smooth and bound by Braun-Brumfield, Inc.,
Ann Arbor, Michigan.

Library of Congress Cataloging-in-Publication Data
Building the church in America : studies in honor of Monsignor Robert
F. Trisco on the occasion of his seventieth birthday / Joseph C. Linck and
Raymond J. Kupke, editors.
    p.   cm. (Melville Studies in Church History)
    Includes bibliographical references and index.
    1. Catholic Church—United States—History.   2. United States—
Church history.   I. Trisco, Robert Frederick.   II. Linck, Joseph, 1964– .
III. Kupke, Raymond J.   IV. Series
BX1406.2.B854 1999
282'.73—dc21
99-25225
ISBN 0-8132-0953-6

CONTENTS

FOREWORD

This *Festschrift* pays well-merited and appropriate attention to Monsignor Robert F. Trisco with papers of exceptionally solid scholarship. The volume thus reflects the approach to history Monsignor Trisco has championed in the classroom, in his writing, in his editing the *Catholic Historical Review,* and in directing the dissertations of more than a generation of scholars at The Catholic University of America.

His former students have joined other distinguished scholars in contributing readable, well researched, and occasionally even controversial findings to this publication. They thus give fitting recognition to Monsignor Trisco, a dedicated historian and at the same time a faithful priest whose early-morning celebration of the Eucharist at the Basilica of the National Shrine of the Immaculate Conception has touched in a pastoral way so many at the Catholic University campus.

The papers treat of such disparate matters of American Church History as preaching in our early days, slavery and the Catholic Church, disciplinary and administrative issues, and higher education.

These fascinating glimpses into our past illumine various aspects of the relationship between Church and civil society. They also instruct us on how human gifts and sometimes even human foibles, blessed by faith and the special circumstances of freedom and challenge in the United States of America, enrich our humanity and help us respond more completely to the insistent call to discipleship that Jesus offers through the Church.

Cardinal William H. Keeler
Archbishop of Baltimore

vii

ACKNOWLEDGMENTS

Many years ago a sign was placed outside a North London Church: "Wanted: Workers for God (Plenty of Overtime)." This anecdote fittingly reflects on the life of Monsignor Robert F. Trisco, who has put in countless hours of "overtime" in his life as a scholar, teacher, editor, and priest. During our studies at Catholic University, it was a common occurrence for us to encounter Monsignor working after hours in the library, researching entries for the *Catholic Historical Review* or organizing the books for review that have been layered on his desks in perilous stacks for as long as anyone can remember. Nor was it unusual, if one was up that early, to meet him on his way to his daily celebration of the early Mass at the National Shrine, bordering the University campus. Monsignor Trisco is truly one who has labored extensively for the kingdom, and in the process he has won the admiration and respect of those who know him, especially his students and colleagues. As we set about to prepare this volume, the unanimous response of those who were contacted was: "What a fitting tribute; no one is more deserving of it." It is, then, with gratitude and esteem that this collection of essays is presented to him, on the occasion of his seventieth birthday.

In the process of assembling this volume, many individuals and organizations have provided generous assistance and encouragement, and we would like to offer them our appreciation and gratitude. First we would like to thank Professor Nelson H. Minnich, Chair of the Department of Church History at The Catholic University of America, for his constant support and encouragement from the first moment this project was set on foot, in May of 1995. Without his wise and helpful guidance, our best efforts would have floundered; that this work has been brought to a successful conclusion is due in large part to him.

We are grateful as well for the generous assistance of Dr. David J. McGonagle of The Catholic University of America Press. He has shepherded the project along with expert advice and much needed support. Our thanks to him for helping us to meet our goal of completing the volume in time for Monsignor's seventieth birthday. Further thanks to the Press's hardworking and helpful staff, especially to Susan Needham for her wise and sympathetic editorial assistance.

Of course, without the scholarly contributions from the authors of this collection, we would have had nothing to publish. We appreciate their good-natured willingness to meet deadlines and make revisions. Their articles, which offer both wide-ranging as well as fascinating insights into the history of the Catholic Church in America, are a fitting tribute to Monsignor Trisco, whose life has been spent in the service of that history. Our thanks go out in a special way to His Eminence, Cardinal William Keeler, for contributing his gracious Foreword.

Despite the quality of our contributions, they would never have seen the light of day without generous financial assistance from a number of benefactors. The American Catholic Historical Association, under then President Dr. Ute-Renate Blumenthal, provided a substantial donation from the Anne M. Wolf Fund in gratitude for the decades that Monsignor Trisco has spent as Secretary of the Association and as Editor of the *Catholic Historical Review.* The Department of Church History at The Catholic University of America, under then Chair the Reverend Jacques M. Gres-Gayer, also contributed a major subsidy from its Annabelle Melville Fund. Support for publication was further increased by financial contributions from two of Monsignor's former students: Monsignor Timothy M. Dolan and the Reverend Fergus M. O'Donoghue, S.J.

The priestly ministry, academic instruction, and scholarly endeavors of Monsignor Robert Trisco, carried out with the quiet grace that is his hallmark, have enlightened the lives of countless individuals. This volume is dedicated to him, in token of our appreciation for the ways in which he has manifested the kingdom of Jesus Christ.

Rev. Joseph C. Linck, C.O.
Rev. Msgr. Raymond J. Kupke
Feast of the Epiphany of the Lord 1999

BUILDING THE CHURCH IN AMERICA

Thomas J. Shelley

BIOGRAPHICAL SKETCH OF
MONSIGNOR ROBERT TRISCO

For forty years Monsignor Robert Trisco has been a familiar figure on the campus of the Catholic University of America, delivering his lectures and directing seminars in the classrooms of Shahan Hall and Caldwell Hall, celebrating Mass each morning at the National Shrine of the Immaculate Conception, administering the affairs of the American Catholic Historical Association and editing the *Catholic Historical Review* in Room 318 of the Mullen Library from behind a desk piled high with stacks of review books, and frequently returning to the library on Sunday afternoons to survey the latest acquisitions among the current periodicals.

Early Years and Education

Robert Frederick Trisco was born in Chicago, Illinois, on November 11, 1929, to Richard Edward and Harriet Rose (Hardt) Trisco. From 1943 to 1948 he attended Quigley Preparatory Seminary, the nonresident minor seminary of the Archdiocese of Chicago. The five-year course of studies consisted of four years of high school and the first year of college. In the fall of 1948 he entered the major seminary of the archdiocese, Saint Mary of the Lake Seminary, the showcase institution built by

George Cardinal Mundelein, which is located some thirty miles north of Chicago in the town renamed in honor of Mundelein. Young Robert Trisco spent the next three years there, from 1948 to 1951, completing his college education and earning the B.A. degree.

Instead of continuing his education for the priesthood with the rest of his class at St. Mary of the Lake Seminary, however, in the fall of 1951 Robert was sent to Rome for his theological studies. As a seminarian in residence at the North American College, he attended classes at the Pontifical Gregorian University, earning the S.T.B. degree in 1953 and the S.T.L. degree in 1955. In the meantime, in Rome, on December 8, 1954, he was ordained a priest of the Archdiocese of Chicago. After ordination, Father Trisco remained in Rome for another five years, finishing his licentiate in theology and pursuing graduate studies in church history from 1955 to 1959 at the Gregorian University, where he was awarded the degree of Doctor of Ecclesiastical History (Hist.Eccl.D.) in 1962.[1]

Teaching and Professional Activities

In the normal course of events, Father Trisco could have expected an appointment to teach church history at St. Mary of the Lake Seminary, perhaps after a brief stint as a curate in a Chicago parish. Instead, upon his return to the United States in 1959, he was appointed an instructor in the History Department of the Graduate School of Arts and Sciences of The Catholic University of America in Washington, D.C. That unexpected development was due to the intervention of Monsignor John Tracy Ellis, who explained later how it happened. "I had become aware of his superior talents," said Ellis,

> and of the highly effective way he employed them, several years before I met him. And I had been sufficiently impressed to launch a "conspiracy" to steal the prize student of my good friend, Monsignor Harry C. Koenig, former professor of church history in Saint Mary of the Lake Seminary at Mundelein, that is, to steal him from the Archdiocese of Chicago for the Catholic University of America, the *Review,* and the Association. As a matter of sober fact, the "con-

1. Information provided for the author by Msgr. Robert Trisco.

spiracy" profited from the assistance of Monsignor Koenig once he understood what we had in mind for Robert Trisco.

Once Ellis decided that he wanted Father Trisco in Washington, he went about getting him in characteristically aggressive fashion. Having obtained the permission of Monsignor Aloysius Ziegler, the chairman of the History Department, Ellis called on Samuel Cardinal Stritch, at his Chicago residence in May 1957 and asked Cardinal Stritch to release Father Trisco to teach at the university. The cardinal was agreeable but wished to discuss the matter with Father Trisco, who knew nothing about these maneuvers. Stritch and Trisco met that summer in Paris and Cardinal Stritch gave his consent.[2]

As a result, two years later, in September 1959, at the age of twenty-nine, Father Trisco joined the history department of the university with the rank of instructor. At the same time he was also appointed assistant secretary of the American Catholic Historical Association. In 1963, following the completion of his doctorate, he was promoted to assistant professor. He became an associate professor in 1965 and a full professor in 1975. In 1976 he was also made a full professor in the Department of Church History of the School of Religious Studies.

In addition to his teaching responsibilities, Father Trisco has filled several administrative posts at the university, serving as the director of the Department of Archives and Manuscripts from 1959 to 1962, as the vice-rector for Academic Affairs from 1966 to 1968, and as the chairman of the Department of Church History from 1975 to 1978. In the course of his forty years at The Catholic University of America, Father Trisco has served on numerous committees, either as a member or as the chairman. Perhaps his most important contributions to the university in this area have been his service for twenty-one years (1974–95) as the chairman of the Committee on Archives and Manuscripts and his service for almost thirty years (1967–96) as a member of the Editorial Committee of the Catholic University of America Press.

During the Second Vatican Council (1962–65), Father Trisco was appointed a *peritus*, serving as a member of the United States Bishops'

2. John Tracy Ellis, "Reflections of an Ex-Editor," *Catholic Historical Review* 50 (January 1965): 468.

Press Panel and as a staff member in the Rome office of the National Catholic Welfare Conference. Monsignor Ellis was as impressed with Father Trisco's performance in these roles as he was with his academic record. Indulging his own penchant for contemporary *petite histoire,* Ellis mentioned in print that "one of the *periti* of Vatican Council II, who is himself among the best informed priests of my acquaintance on the contemporary Church" told him that "during the daily meetings in Rome of the American bishops' press panel for the council, when a journalist's question about a minute point in theology, canon law, or church history was going about begging for an answer, it was Father Trisco who most frequently supplied the information."[3]

In the decade following the council, Trisco was a member of the NCWC's Committee for Ecumenical and Interreligious Affairs, serving first on the Subcommittee for Consultation with the American Baptist Convention (1966–72) and later on the Subcommittee for the Presbyterian/Reformed Consultation (1972–75). His other activities on behalf of the NCWC and its successor organization, the National Conference of Catholic Bishops, included membership on the History Subcommittee of the Committee on Priestly Life and Ministry (1968–71), membership on the History Subcommittee of the Committee for the Bicentennial of American Independence (1973–76), and membership on the History Subcommittee of the *ad hoc* Committee on the Observance of the Quincentenary of Evangelization in the Americas (1986–92). In April 1999 Edward Cardinal Cassidy, the president of the Pontifical Council for Promoting Christian Unity, appointed Trisco to the Mixed International Commission for Theological Dialogue between the Catholic Church and the Orthodox Church.

Father Trisco participated in the planning of the *New Catholic Encyclopedia,* serving as co-area editor for American church history in 1960–61 and as staff editor for American church history in 1962. He twice served on committees of the Canon Law Society of America. In 1969 he was a member of the Committee for the Study of the Legislation of the Plenary Councils of Baltimore, and in 1970–71 he was a member of the Commit-

---

3. Ibid., p. 469. Whenever Msgr. Ellis quoted one "who is among the best informed priests of my acquaintance in the contemporary Church," he was almost invariably referring to his close friend Msgr. George G. Higgins.

tee on the Selection of Bishops. He was also one of the first Catholics to serve as a member of the Council of the American Society of Church History, the leading American Protestant church history society. For almost a quarter century Trisco has also been associated with the International Commission for Comparative Church History, serving as liaison between the organization and the United States in 1975–77, as President of the American Subcommission in 1978–80, and as *assesseur* for the period 1980–2000. He was appointed a member of the Pontifical Committee for Historical Sciences in 1982 and reappointed in 1989. Since 1986 he has also been an honorary member of the Accademia di San Carlo of Milan.

Father Trisco has been the recipient of several papal honors. In 1957 he received the *Benemerenti* Gold Medal of Pope Pius XII and in 1989 he received the *Benemerenti* Gold Medal of Pope John Paul II. In 1992 he was also made an honorary prelate (Monsignor) to Pope John Paul II, and in that same year he received an honorary doctorate of humane letters from Belmont Abbey College.

Publications

In 1962 Father Trisco published *The Holy See and the Nascent Church in the Middle Western United States, 1826–1850*,[4] his doctoral dissertation from the Gregorian University. It received favorable comments from the two leading American Catholic church historians of that day, Father Thomas T. McAvoy, C.S.C., of the University of Notre Dame, and Monsignor Ellis. Father McAvoy hailed it as the first attempt to use the newly available materials in the archives of the Congregation de Propaganda Fide for the history of the Catholic Church in the Midwest. McAvoy paid tribute to Trisco's "careful scrutiny" of the material and said that it "will take preeminence" among studies of the American Catholic church from the perspective of Propaganda Fide. Ellis was equally positive, referring to the "uncommon thoroughness" with which it was written.[5]

4. Robert F. Trisco, *The Holy See and the Nascent Church in the Middle Western United States*, Analecta Gregoriana, vol. 125 (Rome: Gregorian University Press, 1962).
5. McAvoy, *Catholic Historical Review* 48 (January 1963): 522–23; Ellis, *Catholic Historical Review* 50 (January 1965): 469.

In 1971 Father Trisco contributed a lengthy essay, "Bishops and
Their Priests in the United States," to *The Catholic Priest in the United States,*
Historical Investigations, a volume edited by Monsignor John Tracy Ellis
and published under the auspices of the Committee on Priestly Life and
Ministry of the National Conference of Catholic Bishops. In 1976 Trisco
himself edited *Catholics in America, 1776–1976,* an attractive volume sponsored and published in both clothbound and paperback edition by the
National Conference of Catholic Bishops on the occasion of the bicentennial of American Independence. The book consisted of sixty short articles written by experts in American Catholic history and originally distributed on a weekly basis by the National Catholic News Service during
the bicentennial year. Monsignor Francis J. Weber said that it "ranks
among the most important and probably the most enduring projects
sponsored by the National Conference of Catholic Bishops to commemo-
rate the 200th year of the nation's independence."[6]

Six years later Father Trisco placed all American church historians
in his debt when he revised Monsignor Ellis's bibliography of American
Catholic history, which had first appeared in 1944. The revised edition, *A*
Guide to American Catholic History,[7] was more than twice the size of the
first edition. The book appeared under the joint authorship of Ellis and
Trisco, but (as Ellis was quick to point out) the annotations were solely
the work of Father Trisco, who on several occasions came close to em-
balming both a book and its author's reputation in one sentence.

Edward Gaustad welcomed it as a "Guide . . . that actually guides,
not simply lists." "For those weary of reading the same severely restricted list of platitudinous adjectives found in most other annotated bibliographies," said Gaustad, "these two church historians offer a breath
(gale?) of fresh air." As an example, Gaustad cited the evaluation of Andrew Greeley's survey of American Catholic history, *The Catholic Experi-*

---

6. Robert Trisco, "Bishops and Their Priests in the United States," in John Tracy
Ellis, ed., *The Catholic Priest in the United States: Historical Investigations* (Collegeville: The
Liturgical Press, 1971), pp. 111–292. It was reprinted as *Bishops and Their Priests in the*
United States (New York: Garland, 1988) with a new preface. Robert Trisco, *Catholics in*
America, 1776–1976 (Washington, D.C.: National Conference of Catholic Bishops,
1976). Francis J. Weber, *Catholic Historical Review* 63 (1977): 639–40.

7. John Tracy Ellis and Robert Trisco, *A Guide to American Catholic History,* 2d ed.
(Santa Barbara: ABC-Clio, 1982).

ence. "This selective survey," said Trisco, "hastily and poorly written by a sociologist of religion, while containing some original insights and provocative observations, suffers from numerous factual errors, unproved assumptions, and unacknowledged borrowings from the works of others." "Wow!" commented the usually dispassionate Gaustad, "Who ever said that bibliographies have to be dull?"[8]

In 1985 Father Trisco collaborated with two other colleagues in the Church History Department of the Catholic University of America, the late Robert B. Eno, S.S., and Nelson H. Minnich, to produce a handsome *Festschrift* for Monsignor Ellis, *Studies in Catholic History in Honor of John Tracy Ellis,*[9] on the occasion of Ellis's eightieth birthday. Father Trisco himself contributed a lengthy essay entitled "The Holy See and the First 'Independent Catholic Church' in the United States," pp. 175–238.

Father Trisco has also written several dozen articles for the standard American and European dictionaries and encyclopedias, among them the *Encyclopedia Britannica, Encyclopedia Americana, Dictionary of American History, New Catholic Encyclopedia, Dictionnaire d'Histoire et de Géographie Ecclésiastiques, Lexikon für Theologie und Kirche, American National Biography, Encyclopedia of the Reformation, Encyclopedia of Catholicism,* and *Encyclopedia of American Catholic History.* He also wrote the chapter entitled "The Countries of the English-Speaking Area," for the final volume of the ten-volume *History of the Church,* edited by Hubert Jedin, Konrad Repgen, and John Dolan, *The Church in the Modern Age* (New York: Crossroad, 1981), pp. 614–71.

Trisco's major field of interest, faithfully reflected in these publications, has been American Catholic history. The selection of bishops is a topic to which he has returned on a number of occasions, most notably "The Variety of Procedures in Modern History," in *The Choosing of Bishops,* edited by William W. Bassett (Hartford: The Canon Law Society of America, 1971), pp. 33–60; "Democratic Influence on the Election of Bishops and Pastors and on the Administration of Dioceses and Parishes in the U.S.A.," *Concilium* 77 (1972): 132–38; and "The Debate on the Election of Bishops in the Council of Trent," *The Jurist* 34 (1974): 257–91.

8. Edwin S. Gaustad, *Catholic Historical Review* 69 (January 1983): 93–94.
9. Nelson H. Minnich, Robert B. Eno, S.S., and Robert F. Trisco, eds., *Studies in Catholic History in Honor of John Tracy Ellis* (Wilmington: Michael Glazier, 1985).

Another enduring interest has been early modern church history. His contributions to this field have included "Reforming the Roman Curia: Emperor Ferdinand I and the Council of Trent," in *Reform and Authority in the Medieval and Renaissance Church,* edited by Guy F. Lytle (Washington, D.C.: The Catholic University of America Press, 1981), pp. 143–337; and, more recently, "Carlo Borromeo and the Council of Trent: The Question of Reform," in *San Carlo Borromeo: Catholic Reform and Ecclesiastical Politics in the Second Half of the Sixteenth Century,* edited by John M. Headley and John B. Tomaro (Washington, D.C.: The Folger Shakespeare Library; London and Toronto: Associated University Presses, 1988), pp. 47–66.

A personal interest, pursued intermittently over the years, has been the role of Amleto Cardinal Cicognani during his long tenure as Apostolic Delegate to the United States. Thus far, this interest has led to the publication of "Giovanni XXIII ed il card. Amleto Giovanni Cicognani," in *Giovanni XXIII: Transizione del Papato e della Chiesa,* edited by Giuseppe Alberigo (Rome: Edizioni Borle, 1988), pp. 79–104; "Building a New Home for the Apostolic Delegate in the Decade of the Great Depression," *U.S. Catholic Historian* 12 (Spring 1994): 107–29; and "Archbishop Cicognani, Apostolic Delegate, Apostle of the Word Spoken and Printed," in *The Church's Mission of Evangelization* (Steubenville: Franciscan University Press, 1996), pp. 371–86.

American Catholic Historical Association

When Monsignor Ellis "stole" young Father Trisco from the Archdiocese of Chicago, he said that he hoped to secure his services not only for the Catholic University of America, but also for the American Catholic Historical Association and its scholarly quarterly, the *Catholic Historical Review.* Trisco's association with the ACHA began shortly after his arrival at the university in January 1960, when he was appointed assistant secretary of the association. A few months later he replaced Father Alfred C. Rush, C.Ss.R., as associate editor of the *CHR.* In 1961, when Ellis resigned as secretary for reasons of health, Trisco succeeded him in that office and has held it to the present day. In 1963, after Monsignor Ellis had left Washington to take a teaching position in the University of San

Francisco, Father Trisco succeeded him as the editor of the *CHR*, a position that he has also continued to hold to the present day. Reflecting in 1965 on Trisco's performance as his successor, Ellis commented: "The *Review* and the ACHA of the past two years are the most eloquent witnesses to his competence. . . ."[10] In addition to his other responsibilities, in 1983 Trisco also assumed the office of treasurer of the ACHA.

More than any other individual, he has been responsible for the endurance of the ACHA as the country's most important professional Catholic historical organization and for the high scholarly standards of its official journal. As such he inherits the mantle of Monsignor Peter Guilday, one of principal editors of the *CHR* from its founding in April 1915 until February 1941, and of Monsignor John Tracy Ellis, who was editor from February 1941 until February 1963. Trisco has served as editor for a longer period than either of his predecessors, in fact, for almost half the lifetime of the *CHR*. He has edited the journal with such meticulous care that at a recent session of the ACHA, none of the participants could recall a single instance when a typo or misspelling had escaped Father Trisco's eagle eye. A rare correction appeared in the January 1999 issue of the *CHR* (page 156), but it involved nothing more substantial than a corrected telephone number for a committee chairman of the ACHA.

Like Guilday and Ellis, Trisco has also played a crucial role in the ACHA as secretary since 1961, and as secretary-treasurer since 1983. The presidents of the ACHA are elected for an annual term and their duties are largely ceremonial. It is the secretary-treasurer who supervises the day-to-day activities of the ACHA, manages the finances, helps to organize the annual winter and spring meetings and (in the case of Trisco, as with Guilday and Ellis) edits the quarterly journal. Moreover, it has all been done on an extremely tight budget and with a minimum of staff that has rarely exceeded the employment of more than one fulltime secretary.

A perennial problem for the ACHA has been its relatively small membership, which reached a peak of 1,333 members in 1961 and slipped to 1,109 members in 1998 during a period when the Catholic population of the United States grew from 44,000,000 to 59,000,000. It is

10. Ellis, "Reflections of an Ex-Editor," p. 469.

not a new problem. In the inaugural issue of the *CHR* in April 1915, the editor-in-chief, Thomas J. Shahan, the rector of the Catholic University of America, confidently but naively expressed the opinion that "an interest in historical studies and the fashion of viewing actions and events in their historical relations are the natural inheritance of Catholics."[11]

Fifty years later John Tracy Ellis demurred. After spending two decades trying to enlarge the membership of the ACHA, he concluded sadly that Shahan was wrong in claiming a natural American Catholic interest in history. "Natural inheritance there may well be," said Ellis, "in the sense that the Church to which Catholics belong takes a long range view of human events through her nearly 2,000 years in this world." However, he added, "to reason that her spiritual offspring in this country have, therefore, been conspicuous in manifesting this implied interest in a practical way, would be a decided *non sequitur.*" "American Catholics," he complained, "still leave much to be desired by way of active and practical evidence of their interest and support of historical enterprises such as this *Review* and the Association of which it is the official organ."[12] Unfortunately it is a criticism that is still applicable to the American Catholic community in 1999.

If the membership of the ACHA and the circulation of the *CHR* have remained perennial problems, the financial condition of the association has been a considerably happier story during Monsignor Trisco's stewardship. In the 1960s when Monsignor John K. Cartwright, the rector of St. Matthew's Cathedral in Washington, D.C., was the treasurer of the ACHA, in his annual financial statements he regularly listed as income such items "50¢" and "33¢" from "exchange on foreign checks." Total investments amounted to little more than $16,000. By contrast, in 1999, the total investments amounted to a whopping $931,202.58 and was approaching one million dollars.[13]

---

11. Thomas J. Shahan, "Introductory: The Spirit of the Catholic Historical Review," *Catholic Historical Review* 1 (April 1915): 5. It should be pointed out that the circulation of the *CHR* was almost double that of the membership of the ACHA—2013 copies in 1998.

12. Ellis, "Reflections of an Ex-Editor," pp. 461–62.

13. *Catholic Historical Review* 48 (April 1967); *Catholic Historical Review* 85 (April 1999): 247. To be fair, it should be mentioned that Msgr. Cartwright served without compensation as the treasurer of the ACHA for thirty-three years.

The ACHA has never applied any religious test for membership in the association or for acceptance of manuscripts for publication in the *CHR*. On the contrary the *CHR* has adhered faithfully to the policy enunciated by Bishop Shahan in the inaugural issue when he declared that "it should serve as a means for diffusing the results of the labors of all who love American Catholic history."[14] In recent years, several distinguished non-Catholic historians, among them Martin Marty and Joseph Altholz, have been elected presidents of the ACHA. Nonetheless, the ACHA has unquestionably retained its Catholic identity. At the annual presidential banquet, the bishop or archbishop of the host city is always invited to give the invocation; a Mass is celebrated for deceased members as part of the winter meeting; and, in his annual report, the secretary-treasurer never fails to conclude the necrology with the traditional prayer that "their souls and the souls of all the departed members of the American Catholic Historical Association through the mercy of God rest in peace."

Monsignor Trisco's own initial contribution to the *CHR* dates back to April 1960 when he wrote a lengthy and favorable review of *Diario della Conciliazione*, the edited version of the diary kept by Francesco Pacelli, the brother of the future Pius XII, during the negotiation of the Lateran Treaties of 1929. Less fortunate than Pacelli was Father Joseph Brusher, whose popular history of the papacy, *Popes through the Ages*, was reviewed by Trisco shortly thereafter. It was a harbinger of things to come. Trisco spotted an "immense number of factual errors" which he proceeded to document in exhausting detail. A comparable history of the College of Cardinals, *The Papal Princes, A History of the Sacred College of Cardinals* by Glenn D. Kittler, received even rougher treatment at Father Trisco's hands and elicited the dry comment that "though this is not the author's thesis, he does prove one point, viz., that popularization should be attempted only by, or at least under, the guidance of, professional historians."[15]

14. Shahan, "Introductory," p. 12. Bishop Shahan's reference to "American Catholic history" reflects the fact that for the first six years the *CHR* was restricted to that field.

15. Robert Trisco, *Catholic Historical Review* 46 (April 1960): 65–68; 46 (October 1961): 325–28; 47 (July 1961): 206–8.

Mentor and Dissertation Director

Like Guilday and Ellis before him, Monsignor Trisco has made an important contribution to the historical profession by training future historians, especially through his direction of their doctoral dissertations. Since 1969 he has guided twenty-three doctoral dissertations to successful conclusion at the Catholic University of America, ten of them in the Department of History, and the other thirteen in the Department of Church History. Two of the dissertations had as their subject matter British and Irish history, and a third explored the work of the Sisters of Notre Dame de Namur in Japan. The other twenty dissertations focused on various aspects of American Catholic history such as the activities of the National Catholic Welfare Conference, the Catholic Interracial Council of New York, the role of American Catholics in the founding of the United Nations, the history of the Catholic Church in Puerto Rico, Catholic preaching in colonial America, and American Catholic attitudes to Italian fascism. Other dissertations have traced the contributions to American Catholicism of such significant figures as Martin Spalding, Michael O'Connor, Thomas J. Shahan, John O'Grady, Thomas A. Becker, Edwin Vincent O'Hara, Herman Heuser, James J. Norris, and Arthur Preuss. The full title of each is listed at the back of the book, in chronological order.

Joseph C. Linck, C.O.

1. "THE EXAMPLE OF YOUR CRUCIFIED SAVIOR"

*The Spiritual Counsel of Catholic Homilists
in Anglo-Colonial America*

Peter Bayley has written: "Preaching is a littérature engagée: it aims to convince men of certain ideas and move them to act in accordance with certain principles. It is a record of temperament, taste, and conviction, and an especially valuable record at a time when church-going is widespread, and mass-media unknown."[1] If this was true of the period that Bayley treated in his study (France of the early seventeenth century), it is an equally valid observation to make concerning the Catholic community of eighteenth-century Anglo-colonial America. While there is a lamentable scarcity of surviving material on which to base an extensive account of life in this community, the American Catholic Sermon Collection at Georgetown University comprises more than 400 homiletic manuscripts, which provide the researcher with many insights into not only the spiritual but also the social lives of the Catholics of colonial Maryland and Pennsylvania. Since it was primarily through their "spiritual counsel" that the homilists nourished the faith of their flock, and so

1. Peter Bayley, *French Pulpit Oratory, 1598–1650* (Cambridge: Cambridge University Press, 1980), 4.

provided for the stability and "building up" of the infant Church in America, it is to that spiritual advice that we will direct our attention, though in fewer words than can be found in even one colonial homily— so this can be considered only the most summary of treatments.

But first a brief word about the sermons themselves. They span the eighteenth century (though most date from 1750 to 1800), and represent the labors of over forty priests on the Maryland and Pennsylvania mission, the majority of whom were members of the Society of Jesus (or, after the suppression of the Jesuits in 1773, ex-members), most of these from the English province.[2] The sermons are typically eight pages in length, written out in their entirety (though some spoke from notes),[3] and were bequeathed from one priest to another (as the valued possessions they were). Stylistically, they can be described as being in the "plain style"; that is, using unadorned and intelligible language with the

2. Robert Emmett Curran, S.J., notes: "The large majority were Englishmen who came to British America fully expecting to serve in that mission for the rest of their lives." *American Jesuit Spirituality: The Maryland Tradition, 1634–1900* (New York: Paulist Press, 1988), 13. An examination of the sermon collection revealed that, while at least nineteen out of the forty-four priests hail from England, twelve are from the colonies and six from the Continent. For a treatment of the colonial-born clergy, see James Hennesey, S.J., "Several Youth Sent from Here: Native-Born Priests and Religious of English America, 1634–1776," in *Studies in Catholic History in Honor of John Tracy Ellis*, ed. Nelson H. Minnich, Robert B. Eno, S.S., and Robert F. Trisco (Wilmington, Del.: Michael Glazier, 1985), 1–26.

3. See, for example, American Catholic Sermon Collection (hereafter ACSC), Neal-8(a–d), Neal-10(g–h), Pi-8, Pi-9, Car-10, Car-12, Special Collections, Lauinger Library, Georgetown University, Washington, D.C. (all quotations from the sermons have been adapted with regard to spelling and punctuation). It seems fairly certain that the Anglo-Catholic missioners routinely preached from a written text, at least in the first three-quarters of the century. This can be established not only from the existence of the large number of manuscripts in the Collection, but also from comments such as the following by Ferdinand Farmer, a prodigious German Jesuit who labored in Pennsylvania: "I preach in German and English. However, in the latter, only on paper as the English-born do themselves" (Maryland Province Archives, Special Collections, Lauinger Library, Georgetown University, Washington, D.C. [hereafter MPA], 25, 5). It would seem that a more fluid homiletic style was demanded as the century neared its close, as witnessed by the following comment of Robert Molyneaux to John Carroll in 1785: "I am now near thirteen years at Philadelphia, and I find it harder to preach than formerly. I wish I had the talent of doing it ex tempore. To preach with a paper does not suit this place so well; and now from want of time and habit, I would find it difficult to speak without" (Thomas Hughes, S.J., *History of the Society of Jesus in North America, Text*, vol. 2 [London: Longmans, Green and Company, 1917], 514).

aim of educating those who heard them in the truths of the faith.[4] Arguments are supported by references not only to the Fathers of the Church and conciliar texts, but also to moralistic stories from classical and ecclesiastical history.[5] The overarching thrust of the sermons is to move those in the congregation to practice their faith and embody Christian virtues in their lives, frequently by offering practical examples of ways to achieve this.

While much evidence exists for considering the sermons to be highly derivative—oftentimes copied directly from homiletic works of such continental preachers as Bourdaloue, Colombière, and Darrell[6]—it must also be noted that the homilists felt free to digress from their sources, condensing material from a variety of texts, and they were not at all adverse to incorporating examples and exhortations tailored to their own congregations.[7] It is not at all unreasonable, then, to assume that the contents of the homilies authentically reflect, at least to some degree, the lives of the colonial Catholics.

The approach of the sermons has been described as practical, and indeed this was a hallmark of the seventeenth-century French homilists whom many of the missioners took as their models. Joseph de Guibert notes that the former "were manifestly men more preoccupied with their matter than their form . . . ," and rarely spoke "in abstract form about the matters of the interior life. Instead, what they pass on to us . . .

4. See Joseph M. Connors, S.V.D., "Catholic Homiletic Theory in Historical Perspective" (Ph.D. diss., Northwestern University, 1962), 43.

5. There are many instances of this, e.g., ACSC, Nea-1, which includes a story from Xiphilinus about Emperor Domitian inviting guests to a funeral banquet, and ACSC, Mat-4, which recounts Baronius's tale of Niceporus and Sapricius, in which the latter's refusal to forgive leads to God depriving him of the grace of martyrdom.

6. Louis Bourdaloue, S.J. (1632–1704), St. Claude de la Colombière, S.J. (1641–82), William Darrell, S.J. (1651–1721).

7. For example, James Beadnall makes use of Colombière's sermon on the Feast of the Circumcision of the Lord (New Year's Day) in his sermon for the day in question, but incorporates some examples familiar to his audience, e.g., speaking of the "old planter grown pale and wane," and the "poor slave both decrepit and old," ACSC, Be-3. For Colombière's sermon see *Oeuvres Complètes du Vénérable Père Claude de la Colombière*, 6 vols. (Grenoble: Imprimerie du Patronage Catholique, 1900), 1:179–201. For more on the homilists' selective borrowing and editing, see Joseph C. Linck, C.O., "Fully Instructed and Vehemently Influenced: Catholic Preaching in Anglo-Colonial America" (Ph.D. diss., The Catholic University of America, 1995), 62–88.

is above all the observations accumulated in their daily work amidst the most fervent Christians."[8] The Jesuits in particular stressed that a "direct struggle and a direct effort" were needed to "overcome defects and acquire virtues,"[9] and the regimen they prescribed to accomplish this was founded on the notion of the imitation of Christ and the saints, and included such spiritual practices as prayer, spiritual reading, penance, the sacraments, and concrete acts of charity. Such a regimen was considered indispensable, given the challenging circumstances under which the Catholics of colonial Maryland and Pennsylvania lived out their faith.[10]

The notion of "imitation" was truly a foundational theme in colonial homiletics. Again, this was not surprising considering that the preachers were formed in the spirituality of the Jesuits, in which "Jesus is above all the leader and model, the one to be loved, followed, and imitated. The examples of His mortal life make up the concrete ideal of the 'true life'; and this ideal is tirelessly kept before the eyes to guide and encourage the efforts at reformation."[11] We can see the embodiment of this theme of imitation in Bernard Diderich's exhortation to "follow then . . . the example of your crucified Savior. If we are like to Christ by penance, by crosses and afflictions, we may be sure to be in the way as to a happy eternity."[12] Bishop John Carroll would comment in a similar vein, "The life of Jesus, and the instructions contained in it, are the most useful book, and the most advantageous for meditation, to which we can resort. There are to be found the most perfect models of Christian virtue, and the best encouragements to practice them."[13] Indeed, the homilists considered the imitation of Christ, and especially his sufferings, as such an important element in the spiritual life that they dismissed any suggestion that it could be dispensed with, John Lewis noting:

8. *The Jesuits: Their Spiritual Doctrine and Practice*, ed. George E. Ganss, S.J., trans. William J. Young, S.J. (Chicago: Institute of Jesuit Sources, 1964), 569.

9. Ibid.

10. Readers seeking information on the life of colonial Catholics should consult John Tracy Ellis, *Catholics in Colonial America* (Baltimore: Helicon, 1965).

11. Ganss, 569.

12. ACSC, Di-27.

13. ACSC, Car-27. Also reprinted in *The John Carroll Papers* (hereafter *JCP*), 3 vols., ed. Thomas O'Brien Hanley, S.J. (Notre Dame: University of Notre Dame Press, 1976), 3:448–50. Other descriptions of the life of Christ as a pattern may be found in ACSC, Je-13, Neal-3(a).

Now [if] it was by sufferings that our Savior Christ entered into his glory, what other way can we pretend to go? I cannot do penance, says one; I cannot fast, I cannot endure affronts as people put upon me, says another; I cannot endure the least sickness and infirmity, I cannot undergo any mortification, I cannot suffer any kind of contradiction, says a third. Alas, Christ, who are we, that for us poor miserable sinners a new way to heaven must be found out?[14]

Though the missioners preached first and foremost the imitation of Christ, they did not ignore other sources from which Christians might receive instruction in virtue, namely, the vast company of the saints, and especially the Virgin Mary. The presence of the saints was perhaps even more important to the colonial Anglo-Catholics than to their Continental co-religionists, as their invocation was a witness to that which was distinctively "Catholic" in the midst of a society that was overwhelmingly Protestant. Lacking what might be termed a "sacralized landscape,"[15] excluded (except in Pennsylvania) from worshipping publicly for much of the century, the "family" of the saints was an invaluable means by which Catholic identity could be defended and substantiated.[16]

The sermons present the Mother of God as a particularly good example to imitate, since in their view Mary's great dignity was a result of the virtues she exemplified in her life, especially fidelity and humility. On the feast of the Assumption (August 15), Father William Hunter pointed out to his flock at the conclusion of his sermon: "Thus you see, Dear Christians, the means by which the Blessed Virgin Mary mounted to the happiness which she now enjoys. No other way is open to us. The same path which conducted her to glory, will also lead us thither. We shall be partners in her reward, if we copy her witness."[17] James Ashby, in dis-

14. ACSC, Le-17.

15. A thought-provoking examination of the relationship between geography and the sacred is provided by Belden C. Lane, *Landscapes of the Sacred: Geography and Narrative in American Spirituality* (New York: Paulist Press, 1988).

16. John Bossy argues persuasively that the cult of the saints in medieval Europe played an important role in the strengthening of social bonds among Christians. One imagines that this aspect of the veneration of the saints, if still as effective in the eighteenth century as in the fifteenth, would have been valued by the scattered Catholic flock of colonial America. See *Christianity in the West, 1400–1700* (Oxford: Oxford University Press, 1987), 11–13.

17. ACSC, Hu-4. For a more extended treatment of the role of Mary in the ser-

cussing the virtues that Mary exemplified in her life, recommends in a similar vein: "'Tis in our power to make use of the same by following her example. For we may be faithful as well as she to Almighty God's commands according to the measure of grace he has been pleased to offer us. We may obey his voice speaking interiorly to our hearts as she did. . . ."[18]

Looking to the homilist's views on the imitation of the saints, we will see that they are presented in terms quite similar to the imitation of Christ and his mother. Sylvester Boarman referred to them collectively as the "perfect model, by which we all may regulate our lives," able to "rouse the tepidity and animate the courage of the tepid and slothful to practice true sanctity."[19] Perhaps no saint was so lauded in this regard as Ignatius Loyola, the founder of the Jesuits; one who was said to address the colonial Catholics in the words of Saint Paul: "'Be ye imitators of me as I am of Christ.'"[20] George Hunter, after telling at length the wonders of Ignatius's life, concludes by urging his listeners: "Christians, let us . . . endeavor to copy in our own persons what we so much admire in his life and conduct. Let us then resolve from this time to be faithful in corresponding with all God's graces and inspirations as our saint did, and we may be sure almighty God will be faithful in seconding us on all occasions as he did our saint."[21]

In one instance, a missionary himself was presented as a worthy model of the Christian life. In a funeral sermon preached for his friend and fellow-worker in Philadelphia, Robert Molyneaux listed the admirable virtues that had made Ferdinand Farmer such a beloved pastor and concluded by exhorting the assembly: "It remains with us . . . care-

---

mons in the collection, see Michael Sean Winters, "Marian Spirituality in Early America," *American Catholic Preaching and Piety in the Time of John Carroll* (hereafter *ACPP*), ed. Raymond J. Kupke (Lanham, Md.: University Press of America, 1991), 87–105.

18. ACSC, As-4.   19. ACSC, Boa-5.
20. ACSC, Pu-1.

21. ACSC, Hu-2. Besides giving an excellent example of the way in which the homilists called on their flocks to be imitators of the virtues of the saints, this quotation also hints at the closeness the missioners felt to their founder, i.e., "our saint." That lay Catholics had a devotion to Ignatius may be inferred from the name's ubiquity among Catholic men of southern Maryland in the eighteenth century. Cf. Charles Metzger, S.J., *Catholics in the American Revolution* (Chicago: Loyola University Press, 1962), 189–90.

fully to follow in the steps he has traced out to us, by his bright and edi-fying example."[22] Thus even a noncanonized missioner could be held up to the community as an example worthy of imitation.

It should not be thought that the homilists were incapable of pro-viding concrete examples of what the imitation of Christ and the saints involved. On the contrary, they enumerated a number of spiritual prac-tices, to which we now turn.

Not surprisingly, frequent prayer was urged upon the colonial Cath-olics as a vital element in their spiritual lives, and not just in abstract and vague language. At a time when the nearest chapel might be so distant as to render it inaccessible on a regular basis, the priests were adamant in their insistence that everyone had the obligation to develop a regular, structured life of prayer. Indeed, when one realizes the infrequency with which organized liturgical prayer (especially the Mass) was available to the colonial Catholic community, it becomes obvious why the preachers stressed the cultivation of personal prayer, for only this would allow the faith to survive in such difficult diaspora conditions. Yet the Jesuits were aware that their counsels were routinely ignored, and they were quick to draw attention to this. Arnold Livers asks of those in his flock who protest that they have not the time for prayer: "What reasonable pre-tense can hinder them from daily saying the short office to our Blessed Lady, and the penitential psalms, with the long Litanies, besides a short half-hour devoted to their evening prayers?"[23] Charles Sewell argues the case for morning and evening prayer slightly more touchingly when he tells his congregation:

> At least, in the beginning of each day, when rising from that sleep
> which is the image of death . . . [how] shocking is our ingratitude,

22. ACSC, Mol-nn. Many copies of this printed sermon are extant. For more in-formation on Farmer's admirable life and ministry, see "Pioneer Missionary. Ferdi-nand Farmer, S.J.: 1720–1786," *Woodstock Letters* 75 (June, October, December 1946): 103–15, 207–31, 311–21.

23. ACSC, Li-4. This same text may be found in Manning's "Fifty-Fifth Enter-tainment" with one small change, namely that Livers omits Manning's recommenda-tion to spend "one half-hour at least in spiritual reading . . ."—perhaps because he feared presenting too onerous a regimen (certainly not because he disapproved of spiritual reading). Robert Manning, *Moral Entertainments on the Most Practical Truths of the Christian Religion* (Dublin: Richard Grace, 1839), 423.

if we neglect to pay a tribute of praise to that eternal Being, who stationed around us his blessed angels . . . to shield us during our slumbers. . . . Again, at the return of the night, is it not a shameful insensibility to retire . . . without looking back with grateful emotions on the blessings of the day past?[24]

Besides urging a prayer that was highly structured, the homilists also advocated that this spiritual exercise be performed in common, John Bolton encouraging his audience to imitate the disciples in the Cenacle at Pentecost by "setting an example of it in your families, praying together like apostles: father, mother and children, all with one voice and heart."[25] Joseph Mosley recommended that servants be included in these familial morning prayers, as did John Carroll, who, however, suggested that the evening was a more convenient time for these devotions. He wisely anticipates the objection that such pious practices will consume valuable time by arguing that through "a regular and constant method and time of gathering your family to prayers, you will suffer no loss, no diminution of labor."[26]

One particular prayer that was warmly advocated by the missioners was the rosary, perhaps precisely because it was seen to be, in Lewis's words (though here quoting Robert Manning): "a devotion suited to all capacities and states: for a traveler may perform it on the road, a laborer at his work, a tradesman in his shop, a gentleman in his walks . . . and a sick man confined to his bed."[27] John Bolton saw the particular excellence of the rosary to be in its ability to lead one's mind "through all the mysteries of man's redemption." He discounted any ideas that Marian prayer represented a greater confidence in Mary than in God, exclaiming: "No, God forbid, this is what we utterly abhor as blasphemy itself . . . [rather it shows] we have a greater confidence in her prayers than in our own."[28]

Another spiritual practice that was endorsed by the preachers was

---

24. ACSC, Se-4.   25. Bol-24.

26. ACSC, Mos-6, Car-55. The latter is reprinted in *JCP,* 3:436–43. For a set of "Evening Devotions for Families," see Richard Challoner, *The Garden of the Soul: or a Manual of Spiritual Exercises and Instructions* (Philadelphia: Joseph Cruikshank, [1774]), 167–83.

27. ACSC, Le-13; Cf. Manning, 412.

28. ACSC, Bol-9.

the familiar Jesuit technique of the "examen." This endeavor, which Guibert describes as a "direct and methodical labor for the reformation of [one's] life . . . ,"[29] was explained by Robert Harding as the method by which Christians "enter often into yourselves, to examen yourselves, in order to be acquainted with yourselves. . . . [It is] to know our obligations, the good we ought to practice and do not . . . the obstacles we meet with, the helps to salvation, with what progress we advance, and to what miscarriages we are liable."[30] Henry Pile spoke of it as a means by which Christians set about "to examine how far we practice what we know, and by constant endeavors never cease, till, by degrees, we reform in ourselves what we observe to be contrary to the maxims of Christian discipline, of justice and of truth."[31]

For the practice of the examen to be successful, though, the preachers insisted that it was important for the individual Catholic periodically to find some respite from the pressures of the world and its demands. John Lewis insists, "Retirement then is the only means to give us a clear prospect of our danger and leisure to find a way to avoid it."[32] Augustine Jenkins, in a sermon preached the Sunday after Easter, called upon his flock to "set apart some little time in the year, wherein renouncing all worldly distractions as much as possible, we might with more than ordinary recollection, employ ourselves wholly in heavenly things. . . ." This was important, even if only "a day in each month, or a few minutes every day. . . ."[33] That some people actively took this advice is indicated by a sermon manuscript from 1787 entitled "At a Retreat's Beginning," in which Father Charles Sewall endorses "at certain regulated times . . . a proper separation and a holy retirement from the world. For . . . it is only in this spiritual retreat from the noise and perplexity of temporal business, where we can find a repose of mind. . . . [At such times] we examine our past life, we regulate our present conduct, and look into futurity. . . ."[34] Though he admits the difficulty of finding time for such an

---

29. Guibert, 570. This author writes that for Ignatius "the examen was not a mere glance over the manner, more or less perfect, in which his actions had been performed, but also a humble search for faults that had escaped him." Guibert, 67. Ignatius practiced this exercise every hour and incorporated it into his Society.
30. ACSC, Ha-2. Cf. also Ro-13, and Pi-13.
31. ACSC, Pi-13.   32. ACSC, Le-3.
33. ACSC, Je-8. For other references to this practice, cf. Ne-2, Neal-10(e).
34. ACSC, Se-5.

exercise, nevertheless he insists that "it is in these little retirements from the noise of the world, that almighty God speaks to the heart, illuminates the mind, convinces us of our faults, [and] gives us a horror of vice and a love for the things of heaven."[35]

Closely tied to the development of a fruitful prayer life was the practice of spiritual reading, a discipline that the missioners strongly advocated both in word and in action. They often listed it as a component of the spiritual life, along with the practices mentioned above, as in James Ashby's query: "Is there a time set apart for prayer, spiritual reading, examination of conscience, and other devotions . . . ?"[36] Augustine Jenkins instructed his congregation that reading from some spiritual work was an indispensable part of Christian life, advising: "I would recommend a short lesson in some pious book every day. It is in the reading of pious books we draw wholesome lessons for our salvation, and do not easily lose the remembrance of them."[37] Henry Pile quotes an adage of the Church Fathers to the effect that "when we pray we speak to God, and when we read he speaks to us," though he worries about his audience becoming overwhelmed by a multiplicity of books. He suggests:

> Read not many books, but only a few well-chosen, which may be proper to stir you up to virtue . . . such as the Imitation of Christ by Thomas a Kempis, the Introduction to a Devout Life by St. Francis de Sales, the Guide to Sinners by Father Granada, the Christian Directory by Father Parsons, or some other according to the advice of your confessor. Read but little at a time and attentively; make some reflections upon what you read and endeavor to draw some good resolutions from thence, and beg of God the grace to put them into execution. Content not yourself with having read a book once over, but peruse it often.[38]

This last piece of advice made sense not only from a spiritual, but from a practical standpoint as well. Books, especially dealing with Catholic spirituality, were a rare commodity in colonial Anglo-America. The Jesuits,

35. Ibid. Another source for information about spiritual retreats, entitled: "A Spiritual Retreat for the use of Religious Persons," can be found in MPA, (Rev.) John Digges, Jr. Papers.

36. ACSC, As-3.   37. ACSC, Je-8.

38. ACSC, Pi-25. For other sermons in which the importance of spiritual reading is mentioned, cf. Hu-5, Le-6, Le-16, Li-1, Li-3, Di-21, Je-11, Boa-6, Se-1.

however, took an active role in procuring works of spirituality for the use of their flock, and they maintained lending libraries, which gave these works a wider circulation than would otherwise have been possible.[39]

The homilists also recommended more energetic spiritual practices, especially of the penitential kind, and particularly during the season of Lent. Henry Neale, missioned in Philadelphia, told his congregation on Ash Wednesday in 1748:

> By pampering the flesh, we only fatten a victim for death, and pre-pare a greater trophy for the grave. You are afraid of looking pale, and yet by and by this will be your only color. You have a horror of becoming lean; how fat will you be in the grave? Let not only ash-es be upon your forehead by way of ceremony, but . . . moderate your body with fasting, with praying, with watching, with hair cloth, and with other pious artifices of self-denial and abnegation.[40]

The reason most often given for such penitential activity was that the "flesh" constituted one of three enemies that sought to drive Jesus Christ out of the soul; however, the only "flesh that is able to hurt us," said James Walton, "is an unmortified flesh, a flesh whose passions are alive and always soliciting it to rebel against the light of reason and divine grace. . . ."[41] It will be observed above that this penance was seen to in-clude not only the somewhat conventional activity of fasting, but also the hair shirt. Peter Atwood, early in the century, even urges that a "sharp pointed chain" should "gore our sides till the blood spurts out."[42] In 1779 Ignatius Matthews speaks of the Holy Spirit prompting those in search of virtue to "put on the hair shirt, or chastise their flesh by whips

---

39. See Thomas Hughes's extensive comments in *Text,* 2:517 n. 7; and Curran, 15. A list of books at Newtown Manor ca. 1767, as well as books ordered for the laity (including Manning's *Sermons* and Challoner's *Think Well On't*), may be consulted in the Newtown "Memoranda Book," MPA, 3, 15. Father James Walton's diary records that he received a shipment of books including twelve copies of *Garden of the Soul,* lent out a book on Saint Aloysius and a catechism, and was given money to purchase books (and beads), MPA, 4, 2.

40. ACSC, Nea-1. It is hoped that Neale took his own advice, for three months later he would die himself at the age of only 45.

41. ACSC, Wa-5.

42. ACSC, At-1(b). Ignatius Matthews also mentions disciplining the flesh "by whips . . . to blood. . . ." Mat-5, as does Roels, Ro-1; and Walton speaks of "macerat-ing" the body, Wa-6.

and disciplines to blood. . . ."[43] Perhaps this should be understood mainly as figurative or at least rare, though, since later in the century Charles Sewall asks his audience, "Perhaps you'll say . . . must we must punish our bodies as the saints did theirs, must we make use of long and rigorous fasts, must we wear hair shirts, and discipline ourselves to blood . . . ?" He goes on to reassure his listeners:

> No, Christians, such austerities are not to be undertaken without a particular inspiration from almighty God. But this at least we must do, if we have a mind to conquer our grievous temptations. We must [illeg.] all our inordinate desires, we must deprive ourselves of all vain, superfluous and unnecessary pleasures, we must keep a strict guard over our senses, especially our eyes and tongue, and we must be moderate in our drink, temperate in our meals. . . .[44]

If the application for strict penances was limited, the sacramental life had a much more universal application and was an obvious component of the life of any Catholic, even in the straitened circumstances of the American mission. While confirmations and ordinations were unknown, and sermons were not always preached at baptisms and weddings, the sacraments of Penance and Eucharist made up the substance of the missioner's life, and hence they are the most frequently discussed in the sermons.

Confession was usually presented—not surprisingly—as the necessary preparation for the reception of Holy Communion, and since, as one priest noted "Everybody knows how to fall into sin, but very few know how to do penance for it . . ."[45] the preachers spent much time on the nature of confession and how one disposes oneself for it.[46] The homilists tried to inculcate in their flocks the necessity of having a true, interior sorrow for their sins, apart from a rote recitation of their prayer of contrition. For, as Leonard Neale observed "to read over an act of contrition, and to be truly contrite of heart, are two very different things." He adds comically that such rote reading of an act of contrition is "of no more service than if a parrot were to utter the same words."[47]

43. ACSC, Mat-5.   44. ACSC, Se-1.
45. ACSC, Bi-4.
46. See, for example, ACSC, Je-5, Le-5, Mat-3, Mol-1.
47. ACSC, Neal-C. Is it possible to detect here in the future Archbishop of Balti-

In regard to the actual confessing of sins, the main concern expressed by the clergy is that their flocks fail to approach the Sacrament often enough, either through shame or through indifference. John Bolton observes that many penitents try to find a "confessor that's both blind, deaf and dumb,"[48] while Henry Pile laments that some, after committing a sin, "instead of quickly raising themselves, and having recourse to the sacrament of Penance, yield to all occasions, neglecting to confess themselves, whether for fear, shame, remissness, or negligence of their salvation, until some great feast or indulgence obliges them. . . . This abuse is very common among you, and the cause that many fall back after their good resolutions. . . ."[49]

A great concern for many of the priests was the rapidity with which their people seemed to relapse into sin. Louis Roels uses the analogy of sin as a snake-bite, in that the confessor only "presses out the venom of your sins, so that the wound remains still wide open, and if no care is taken of it, will soon fester again." The moral he drew from this was that one should not "trust to present resolutions, without taking proper measures; no end can be obtained without proper means. Never make peace with flesh [and] blood and God almighty will give the peace of a good conscience in this world, and a happy eternity in the next."[50] Leonard Neale tried a different approach to convey the necessity of resisting the various temptations that will seek to lead the shriven penitent back to a life of sin. He notes, in another homespun analogy, that bad habits "leave behind them certain remnants, which are, with regard to the soul, much the same as old wounds, fractures and bruises are to the body." Just as the latter act up when the weather is bad, so the former, "when they are put to a stress by temptations, and especially by the presence of dangerous objects, then they will begin to throb and give pain, and perhaps the old sore will break out afresh, and bring death to the soul."[51]

The Eucharist, of course, was the great remedy for such spiritual

---

more (a man not normally given to humor) echoes of his contact with trained wildlife in Guiana while on mission there?

48. ACSC, Bol-3.

49. ACSC, Pi-25. Given the scarcity of confessors and opportunities for Confession, one wonders what alternatives the colonial Catholics often had.

50. ACSC, Ro-21.   51. ACSC, Neal-16.

maladies, if properly received. James Frambach describes its efficacy
when he declares: "This Divine Sacrament supports our spiritual life by
the abundance of graces which it furnishes for the food and nourish-
ment of our souls. [It is the bread] that gives us force against all temptations, that weakens our passions and concupiscences, that enables us to
grow daily in virtue. . . ."[52] Yet here too, the missioners were concerned
with the abuses they saw besetting the eucharistic practice of their congregations, not least of which was laxity in fulfilling the Easter Duty,
which required a yearly reception of the sacraments of Penance and
Holy Communion. John Carroll lamented: "Ah how many, contented
with public and notorious violation of this yearly salutary command-
ment of the Church, openly ridicule its observance, and without reason
or enquiry impute to ignorant simplicity the exalted acts of virtue and
religion? Such persons as these we may truly call the pests of a religious
society, the corrupters of Christian morality."[53] Others criticized the all
too prevalent view that a yearly Communion sufficed. For example,
Bernard Diderich taught: "Those who communicate very seldom or never are the worst portion of the church of God," whereas "those who
communicate often, are the most eminent for piety and religion, the
most regular in their lives and most virtuous. . . ."[54]

Father Mosley directed an interesting light onto church-going behavior when he critiqued the behavior of those who did come to Mass:
women for "admiring each new dress, considering every fashion that appears," as well as the "undevout tepid men. Do you think you hear
Mass, while you place yourself in some unbecoming posture, either seat-

52. ACSC, Fr-1. For a fuller description of the sermons' presentation of the spiritual effects of the Eucharist, see my "The Eucharist as Presented in the *Corpus Christi*
Sermons of Colonial Anglo-America," in *ACPP,* 27–53.

53. ACSC, Car-46, also in *JCP,* 3:403–4.

54. ACSC, Di-11. Jesuit spirituality strongly recommended frequent reception
of Communion, but would the colonial homilists actually have encouraged daily
Communion? Such a practice would have been unusual in the eighteenth century
(in the first half of the twentieth as well), and moreover the scattered nature of the
Maryland and Pennsylvania Catholic community and the sporadic opportunities its
members had to attend Mass would seem to argue against it. Augustine Jenkins
probably presents the "typical" approach when he says "no business ought to hinder
anyone from communicating at least once a month." ACSC, Je-7. This advice agrees
with the mainstream of thought for the Society of Jesus for most of its history up to
1773.

ed at your ease, or standing . . . or at best only one knee on the ground, while . . . you devoutly lean till you drop asleep? While you are at talk under a tree, or lolling in the shade . . . or carrying off two or three of your idle companions to divert yourselves at a spring and quench your thirst . . . ?"[55] He even admonished those who "can't hear Mass devoutly unless they read some prayer book, or say their prayers," observing that "one single part of the Mass ought to occupy an interior Christian with sufficient matter to meditate upon for whole years. . . ."[56]

In addition to stressing the importance of the frequent reception of the Eucharist and attendance at the sacrifice of the Mass, some homilists also encouraged their flocks to make visits to the Blessed Sacrament and to pray in the Lord's eucharistic presence. This should not be surprising, since even after the prohibition of public worship in 1715 (in Maryland), Catholics were still permitted to attend Masses celebrated in the chapels or rooms of private houses (whether those owned by the wealthy laity, e.g., the substantial chapel of the Carroll's at Doughoregan Manor, or the plantation residences of the clergy, e.g., the "Mass House" of Benet Neale at Deer Creek),[57] and it would be logical to assume that the Eucharist was reserved in at least some of these.[58] For example, during a discourse on Saint Mary Magdalene, Benet Neale (whose "Mass House" was just mentioned) asks his audience: "Why does this God-man reside personally upon our altars, but that I may have frequent access unto him and . . . may like Magdalene spend some time at least bathing his sacred feet with my penitential tears, [and] in conversing with him. . . ."[59] Yet the colonial clergy were aware that many of their flock had a difficult enough time coming to a chapel to attend Mass, let alone to spend time

55. ACSC, Mos-3.

56. ACSC, Mos-4. Sr. Marion Norman, I.V.B.M., comments that John Gother "gently deplored the habit of saying the rosary or 'getting in' one's breviary or other devotion during the Holy Sacrifice." "John Gother and the English Way of Spirituality," *Recusant History* 11 (October 1972): 311.

57. See John W. McGrain, Jr., "Priest Neale, His Mass House, and His Successors," *Maryland Historical Magazine* 62 (Sept. 1967): 254–84.

58. The clergy would at the very least have reserved the Eucharist for distribution as viaticum. A wooden tabernacle once used in the chapel of John Carroll's mother's plantation at Rock Creek, Maryland—where he carried out his priestly ministry upon his return from Europe in 1774—could be seen until recently in the museum of the Visitation Sisters School in Georgetown.

59. ACSC, Ne-7.

in eucharistic adoration, as a number of their sermons demonstrate. Charles Sewall, in describing the means that may be used to acquire a love of God, notes: "Many holy souls . . . make three visits a day to the most Blessed Sacrament with the intention of obtaining this love. But as it is not in your power to visit the chapels so often you may at least make the same petition in your private chambers, or when you are at work or walking about. . . ."[60] George Hunter offers similar advice: "Often adore, praise and glorify with all possible fervor the Sacred Heart by frequent visits to the Blessed Sacrament; devout meditations, pious aspirations in the presence thereof, or in your chambers or private oratories."[61] The focus of one's prayer was to be eucharistic, even if it could not be undertaken in the physical presence of the Blessed Sacrament.[62]

Finally, like the spirituality of the "English Way" in general, the colonial sermons emphasized the theme of social justice—especially as regards the necessity of aiding those in need—as an important element of the spiritual life.[63] Catholics of means, in particular, were warned: "As thou art rich and placed in a higher station than others, so thou art more strictly obliged to virtue. [You must] find work enough to manage your estate, to support your family, to defend the oppressed, to protect orphans and widows, to relieve the poor."[64] In reply to what must have been a common complaint that the means for such assistance were not

60. ACSC, Se-14.

61. ACSC, Hu-1. Hunter's reference to "private oratories" is imprecise; if it refers to domestic chapels or Mass rooms (as opposed to an alcove with a pre-dieu), then it indicates that some of these did not have the Eucharist reserved in them.

62. A document from St. Thomas Manor at Chapel Point, Charles County, Maryland, dated August 1768, lists the names of people who had pledged to participate in a "Perpetual Adoration of the Blessed Sacrament." The terms were as follows: "The subscribers oblige themselves to employ every month through the year, the half-hours to which their names are annexed, on their knees, in honor of the Blessed Sacrament, by meditating or saying of vocal prayers, either relating to the Blessed Sacrament or to the Sacred Heart." The roster provided for a half-hour, twice a month, and included members of Maryland's oldest Catholic families: the Neales, Brents, Boarmans, etc. I do not believe that the possibility should be ruled out that some of these families had access to the reserved Blessed Sacrament to carry out this adoration. MPA, 57, 2. See also John LaFarge, S.J., "Our Pioneer Adorers of the Blessed Sacrament," *Emmanuel* 35 (July 1929): 176–79.

63. For the importance of social justice themes in English spirituality of the eighteenth century, see Norman, "John Gother," 310.

64. ACSC, Le-6.

available, James Walton replied: "Shall we never try whether God will not prove more faithful, and whether our liberalities to the poor will not render him more favorable to our designs? I know not whether my eyes deceive me: I see on all sides ample fortunes ruined, families disgraced . . . and that by gaming, ambition, idleness, debauchery and prodigality. But I see nobody that is reduced to these deplorable circumstances by alms."[65] He asserts quite strongly: "All rich persons consequently must look upon themselves as the stewards of the poor appointed by God to supply their wants. . . ."[66] It should be noted that in preaching the duty of their flocks to care for the disadvantaged, the priests were but building on a tradition that stretched back to the early days of the Maryland Catholic community, which was known for its commitment to its weakest members. Through business and religious associations, and the dispositions of their wills, the early colonists sought to assure that the needy and marginalized among their number were cared for.[67]

While many other facets of colonial spiritual counsel could be discussed, it is hoped that this brief and fragmentary outline has been helpful in summarizing the main points of the catechesis offered by the priests of the Maryland and Pennsylvania mission. One will note how practical and pragmatic it was, shaped by the trying circumstances in which the Catholic community lived out their faith. The ideal of the *imitatio Christi,* lived out in a regimen of prayer, asceticism, frequenting of the sacraments, and charity, provided a solid, if conventional, foundation for colonial Catholics. This ideal was not only preached but lived out by those who ministered to them. Together these Catholic pioneers, in their deeds, words, and prayers, helped to build the Church in America.

65. ACSC, Wa-1.

66. Ibid. That this preaching had some effect might be inferred from the life of Richard Bennett, one of wealthiest Catholics of his day. Upon his death in 1749, his obituary praised him as a generous man, by whose death "the poor and needy have lost their greatest Friend and Benefactor." Quoted by Michael D. Coyne in "Richard Bennett, III," *The Origins and History of Saint Peter's Church,* ed. Edward B. Carley (p.p., 1976), 148–53, here 148. One could also point to the generosity that was practiced by the priests themselves, e.g., Joseph Mosley's records of money he gave in alms. Cf. MPA, 49, 2.

67. See James Michael Graham, S.J., "Lord Baltimore's Pious Enterprise: Toleration and Community in Colonial Maryland" (Ph.D. diss., University of Michigan, 1983), 85–102.

Robert Emmett Curran

2. ROME, THE AMERICAN CHURCH, AND SLAVERY

In December 1839 Pope Gregory XVI published an apostolic letter, *In Supremo Apostolatus,* in which he explicitly condemned the slave trade and seemed to condemn by implication the institution of slavery itself. "We consider it our pastoral duty," Gregory stated,

> to make every effort to turn the faithful away from the inhuman traffic in negroes, or any other class of men. . . . [W]e . . . do vehemently admonish and abjure in the Lord all believers in Christ, of whatsoever condition, that no one hereafter may dare unjustly to molest Indians, negroes, or other men of this sort; or to spoil them of their goods; or to reduce them to slavery; or to extend help or favor to others who perpetrate such things against them . . .

The pontiff forbade any Catholic to defend such practices "under any pretext or . . . excuse."[1]

The letter initially received little attention in the United States, either within or outside the Catholic community. The following year, however, it briefly became an issue in the presidential campaign. In an issueless election in which the Whigs were outJacksoning the Jacksoni-

1. Apostolic Letter, December 3, 1939, reproduced in E. George Read, ed., *Letters of the late Bishop England to the Hon John Forsyth, on the Subject of Domestic Slavery* (Baltimore, 1844), ix–xi.

ans in their exploitation of political symbolism ("Tippecanoe and Tyler Too"), a prominent Democrat, Martin Van Buren's Secretary of State John Forsyth, desperate to secure votes for Van Buren and not above using anti-Catholicism to smear William Henry Harrison, the Whig candidate, claimed the pope's letter as evidence that the Catholic Church was a promoter of abolition. Forsyth, speaking before a Georgian audience, was arguing that Harrison had been forced upon Southern Whigs by a combination of sinister forces that included anti-Masons, abolitionists, the British government and the pope, whom he implied had written his letter on slavery under the pressure of British influence.

Forsyth's published remarks occasioned a series of public letters from Bishop John England of Charleston to Forsyth in which he treated the history of the Church's position on slavery.[2] England argued that the present pontiff, Gregory XVI, had clearly distinguished between the slave traffic and domestic slavery as it existed in the United States. The latter, the bishop insisted, had not been condemned by Rome. England pointed out that at their triennial meeting in 1840, the American bishops, a majority of whom were from slave states, had formally accepted the pope's letter. If even one of them had found in it anything that he could not accept in conscience concerning the teaching of the Church regarding slavery, he would have been under obligation to raise a protest to the pontiff. But none did. If they had found in the letter anything contrary to the institution of slavery as it existed in the United States, they would have made it their duty to do all they could to eradicate the evils that the pope had identified. But none felt so obligated. Indeed the pope himself, England reported, in a private audience with the Charleston bishop had shown his awareness that the American South was heir to a system that had been saddled upon the region long before. American Southerners were not engaged in the kind of slave trafficking condemned in the apostolic letter. No American, he concluded, should think that any Catholic, including the pope, was an abolitionist. "Slavery," he informed Forsyth, "is regarded by that church of which the Pope is the

---

2. There were eighteen letters in all over a two-year period, all devoted to a historical exposition of the Church's teaching on slavery. England's death in 1842 prevented him from taking up the other two topics he intended to treat: the question of slavery in the New World and the condition of blacks in the United States.

presiding officer, not to be incompatible with the natural law, to be the result of sin by Divine dispensation, to have been established by human legislation, and, when the dominion of the slave is justly acquired by the master to be lawful, not only in the sight of the human tribunal, but also in the eye of Heaven . . ."[3]

Despite Forsyth's scare tactics, Harrison won the election (he even carried Georgia). Three years later *In supremo apostolatus* momentarily surfaced again when Daniel O'Connell, the Great Liberator of Irish politics, used it in a futile attempt to woo Irish Americans to the abolitionist standard.[4] But it had no lasting impact on American Catholic society. It was after all a letter that had been occasioned by European efforts to eliminate the international slave trade. Pope Gregory, who was deeply interested in the evangelization of Africa, was naturally attracted to such a goal. Moreover, the papal magisterium was still in the process of becoming the reality we take for granted. In the early nineteenth century the pope spoke rarely as a moral teacher. As it was, the American bishops continued to keep their peace about the issue that gradually polarized the country to the point of civil war. If the gag rule did not ultimately prevail in the United States Congress, within the American Catholic community, there seemed to be a self-imposed gag rule that was extremely effective. Catholics, like most other Americans, proved loyal to their respective sections, but the American Catholic church, unlike other churches, did not split over the issue. Still, in the American church's failure to face this dominant social question, there was a Roman factor—of which Gregory XVI's letter was the most dramatic manifestation—in which the Holy See proved a progressive force in the American church's confrontation with the slavery issue.

The American Catholic church and slavery had to a large extent grown up together in this country. During the colonial and early national periods, Catholics were even more confined to the South than slavery was. Only in the early nineteenth century, at the very time slavery was being abolished in the northern states, did mass immigration shift the center of the Catholic Church in America from southern plantations and

3. *Letters,* 19–21, 24.
4. Gilbert Osofsky, "Abolitionists, Irish Immigrants, and the Dilemmas of Romantic Nationalism," *American Historical Review* 80 (October 1975): 889–912.

farms to northern cities. But until the 1820s the largest concentrations of Catholics were in Maryland, Kentucky, and Louisiana. The two greatest churchmen of antebellum Catholicism, John Carroll and John England, were southern bishops. In 1840, the year of the Council of Baltimore that formally received Gregory's letter on slavery, the majority of Catholic episcopal sees were still located in the South. American Catholicism until that time was largely a southern phenomenon and the "peculiar institution" was an integral part of it.

Catholics easily accommodated themselves to slavery. The traditional moral theology of the Church held that slavery was not in itself evil so long as the mutual rights and duties of slaveholder and slave were respected. Even before the discovery of America, however, Pope Pius II denounced the enslavement of African natives. His successor, Leo X, in the early sixteenth century condemned the attempts of the Spanish and Portugese to enslave the Indians as something "not only the christian religion, but Nature herself cried out against . . ."[5] By the seventeenth century the papal strictures were in no common memory of French or English Catholics settling in Louisiana and Maryland. When slavery gradually became the dominant source of labor in the staple agricultural economies of the southern colonies, Catholic planters became slaveholders.

Nor was the practice confined to the laity. Priests, religious, even bishops held slaves. The Maryland Province of the Society of Jesus in the 1820s was one of the largest slaveholders, certainly in Maryland, if not in the South itself, with its work force of nearly four hundred slaves on its six estates. Originating in the need to support their ministries, the plantations acquired by the Jesuits had seldom returned enough profit to fulfill their initial purpose. As the tobacco economy of the Chesapeake region became increasingly stagnant in the first decades of the nineteenth century, the condition of the Jesuit properties continued to decline. In 1820 one Jesuit visitor from Ireland found them the epitome of "splendid poverty . . . so much apparent wealth & real poverty."[6] Such

---

5. Ludwig Pastor, *History of the Popes from the Close of the Middle Ages* VIII (St. Louis, 1908), 447, cited in Madeleine Hooke Rice, *American Catholic Opinion in the Slavery Controversy* (New York, 1944), 16.

6. Archives of the Maryland Province of the Society of Jesus (hereafter MPA), X T 1, "Temporalities," 1820. See Robert Emmett Curran, S.J., "'Splendid Poverty': Je-

appearances occasioned several controversies about the Maryland Jesuit plantations and their slaves that reached to Rome itself.

As early as 1788 a former Irish Catholic missionary to Maryland, Patrick Smyth, accused the Jesuit slaveholders of being the cause of the languishing condition of the Church in the area in which the Jesuits were working. Smyth reported in a pamphlet that the ex-Jesuits were "superbly lodged on the banks of the Potomack, or basking in the luxuriant climes of the Eastern Shore. . . . They have a prodigious number of negroes," many of whom they found it necessary to goad and whip and "almost flayed alive." The shame of it all, Smyth summed up, was that ministers themselves, the very people who should be sharing the sad burden of the African's afflictions, had become taskmasters.[7] John Carroll thought the charges serious enough, and liable to be believed in Rome where they were circulating, that he issued his own pamphlet to rebut Smyth.

Twenty-five years later, two other Irish priests raised the same question, not as publicly but in higher circles.[8] The Irish priests who brought the protest in 1814 were two Dominicans, William Vincent Harold and John Ryan, who had recently returned to Ireland from Philadelphia where they had served. John Carroll, prizing Harold's renown as a devoted missionary and outstanding preacher, had lamented his departure from the United States in 1813. A year later Carroll was doing everything to block Harold's appointment to the vacant see of Philadelphia. What turned him against the Dominican was an account he received in the fall of 1813 from a London friend about the reports Harold and Ryan were circulating in England and Ireland concerning clerical slaveholding in Maryland. The two were savaging the American Jesuits for holding great

suit Slaveholding in Maryland, 1805–1838," in Randall M. Miller and Jon L. Wakelyn, eds., *Catholics in the Old South* (Macon, 1983), 125–46.

7. *The Present State of the Catholic Mission, Conducted by the Ex-Jesuits in North America* (Dublin 1788), 17–18.

8. The prominence of the Irish on both sides of the question of slavery and Catholicism has to be noted. The Irish, of course, were involved in their own fight for freedom. Of those Irish who stayed in America, like John England, the Purcells, and the Kenricks, where they fell out on the matter depended very much on where they made their homes in America, whether in Charleston, for instance, or Cincinnati.

estates, trafficking in slaves, and being a scandal to slave and nonslave alike. Carroll himself they accused of being a great holder of slaves.[9]

Carroll, in his response to Archbishop John Troy of Dublin (where the two were at the time), admitted that slaveholding was widespread among the clergy in America. He noted with some contempt there was not yet in the United States "that enthusiasm for [the slaves'] emancipation," which had become so fashionable in England, the very country responsible for the introduction of slavery into its former colony. But he denied that the clergy ever engaged in the slave traffic. Harold and Ryan should have known, Carroll added, that the clergy they had attacked, the Jesuits in Maryland, were actually working out a program to emancipate their slaves gradually. As for himself, he pointed out that he had freed the slaves he had inherited and possessed none at all.[10]

Carroll was very sensitive about the slavery question. Like his cousin Charles Carroll of Carrollton and fellow Maryland Catholic Roger Taney, he regarded slavery as a social and economic affliction.[11] Taney and the Carrolls favored gradual emancipation as a solution. The two laymen were officers of the Colonization Society. What the three could not tolerate were the abolitionists, whom they tended to associate with the radical freethinkers of the French Revolution, in particular Rousseau and Raynal, both of whom had condemned slavery on moral grounds. In 1801 John Carroll had removed a priest, John Thayer, from Kentucky, who had, among other things, stirred up the people because of his opposition to slavery. Thayer was suspected of being a disciple of Raynal.[12]

9. Dale B. Light, *Rome and the New Republic: Conflict and Community in Philadelphia Catholicism between the Revolution and the Civil War* (Notre Dame and London, 1996), 75.

10. Thomas O'Brien Hanley, S.J., ed., *The Papers of John Carroll* (Notre Dame, 1976), Carroll to John Troy, Baltimore [1813], 3:312–13. Hanley dates this letter in 1815, but the extract in the archives of Propaganda Fide gives the date of 28 December 1813 (*Archivo di Propaganda Fide* [hereafter APF], *Congregationi Particulari*, 1814, vol. 146, folios 533r–536v).

11. Taney, the future Chief Justice of the Supreme Court, regarded slavery in 1818 as "a blot on our national character" (cited in John T. Noonan, Jr., "The Catholic Justices of the United States Supreme Court," *Catholic Historical Review* [July 1981]: 369–85).

12. Annabelle M. Melville, *John Carroll of Baltimore, Founder of the American Catholic Hierarchy* (New York, 1955), 188–89. Carroll had, to an earlier complaint from Thayer about the evils of slavery, assured him that he shared his uneasiness about

Harold and Ryan immediately answered Carroll. Ryan, writing for his fellow Dominican, perhaps because of Harold's episcopal ambitions, expressed surprise to Archbishop Troy that Carroll had not only defended slavery on abstract principles but condemned the opponents of the system as hypocrites. *Pace* Carroll, the Dominican informed the prefect, not all priests were slaveholders; indeed from Boston to Maryland there was not one. The problem was the Maryland Jesuits with their hundreds of slaves. The scandal was aggravated by the contiguity of Maryland to Pennsylvania, where slavery had been abolished by the efforts of the Quakers and others precisely on the grounds of its incompatibility with Christian social morality. Unlike New York and Pennsylvania, where the Irish had settled heavily in the past generation, the Church was declining in Maryland because of its association with slavery. The Jesuit mission at Bohemia was a stark metaphor of the condition of the Maryland church. Once a flourishing parish (according to Ryan) the chapel was now collapsing, the birds of the air circulating through the holes in the roof and leaving their droppings on its altar. The once large congregation now consisted of fifty adult slaves and their children.

Ryan also insisted that the Maryland Jesuits trafficked in slaves, if that term meant the buying and selling of individuals for various reasons, some of which, he admitted, were commendable, given their commitment to the system itself, such as the selling of a slave to keep families together. The real question, Ryan maintained, was not the theoretical justification of slavery according to traditional moral theology, but rather the actual scandal that de facto slaveholding by priests was giving in the United States to Catholics and non-Catholics alike. "Even tho the reverend gentlemen," he argued,

> could ever so triumphantly prove on abstract principles that their system is not a defrauding the labourer of his hire, a sin which is somewhere said to call to heaven for vengeance, yet if having the appearance of evil it render the Incorporated clergymen so many stumbling blocks in the way of their Quaker brethren and of thou-

"the treatment & manners of the Negroes. I do the best I can to correct the evils I see; & then recur to those principles which . . . influenced the many eminent & holy missionaries in S. America & Asia, where slavery equally exists" (Carroll to Thayer, Baltimore, 15 July 1794, in Hanley, *Carroll Papers*, 2:122–23).

sands besides among their fellow citizens: if metaphysical distinctions, and finedrawn casuistry be too subtle for the mental vision of
these blunt, honest folks:—and that labouring under the incapacity
of comprehending Doctor Carroll's reasoning on this subject they
identify the principles of the Catholic Religion with a practice on
the part of its ministers, so apparently uncharitable, they become
so prejudiced . . . as never to inquire *fairly* as to the truth of that religion . . .

Ryan claimed never to have heard anything about a plan of gradual
emancipation. If the Jesuits had a plan, he suggested, it was *in petto,* a secret one for some indefinite future which could not justify the losses to
the Church which their scandalous involvement with slavery was causing.[13]

Ryan in 1814 took their case to the Congregation for the Propaga-
tion of the Faith, the body responsible for the governance of the church
in America. He had heard that another Irish Dominican, John Connolly,
had been appointed Bishop of New York and he thought the time a particular good one to urge Rome to use the new prelate to investigate the
church's slaveholding in Maryland. He urged the cardinal prefect to
bring the matter to the attention of the pope himself.[14]

There is no evidence that Propaganda ever did anything about the
complaint of the Dominicans about the Jesuit slaveholding. Shortly after
he returned to the United States in 1820, Harold tried to put the best
face on their criticism of Carroll in a letter to the cardinal prefect: that
the archbishop of Baltimore was caught up in a system of which he did
not approve, as was demonstrated by his emancipation of the patrimonial slaves he had received.[15] It was as though Harold was trying to protect
his own fading episcopal possibilities. Whatever, Harold was appointed

13. APF, *Congregazioni Particolari,* 1814, vol. 146, fols. 533v–536v, Ryan to John
Troy, College of St. Thomas, Bloomfield, 20 March 1814.
14. APF, *Cong. Part.* 1814, vol. 146, folios 656(1)rv–657(1)v, Ryan to Rt. Rev. Dr.
Milner, 14 November 1814.
15. In 1821, seven years later, Harold finally wrote to Propaganda, explaining that he had not meant to denigrate Carroll and that the latter was caught up in
a system which he did not approve, as was demonstrated by his emancipation
of the patrimonial slaves he had received (APF, *Scritture Riferite nei Congressi America Centrale,* 1821–1822, vol. 7, folios 155–156v, Harold to Cardinal ?, 5 January
1821).

to no see and Jesuit slaveholding on a grand scale continued for another two decades.

Although Ryan and Harold were not privy to it, the Maryland Jesuits, through their legal body, the Corporation of Roman Catholic Clergymen, had in fact adopted a policy of gradual emancipation long before 1815. Some slaves had gained their freedom in that way. What seems noteworthy, however, is a resolution passed by the trustees of the Corporation, of which Carroll was one, in June of 1814, six months after Carroll had learned of the Dominicans' attack. The trustees resolved to hire out most of the slaves on their plantations for a set number of years, after which they would be free.[16] But the resolution was never carried out, to Carroll's "surprise and mortification." A month before he died in 1815, the archbishop protested the sale for life of several individuals on the White Marsh plantation.[17] There is record of only one slave being freed as a result of the resolution. It seems obvious that Carroll was the force behind the resolution and with his death, the impetus for the policy died as well. In 1820 the Corporation repealed the resolution with the explanation that "mature reflection" had convinced them that such a plan was "prejudicial."[18]

The reflection, no doubt, had two sources: the Superior General in Rome had told the Maryland Jesuits to delay any action involving the plantations. In addition the archbishop of Baltimore, Ambrose Maréchal, was contesting the Jesuits' claim to ownership of the property, including the slaves. That dispute was finally settled in 1828 with the Jesuits retaining their lands. The 1830s saw a new generation of leaders in the new Maryland Province, determined to sell the slaves and lease the property to tenant farmers. By that time, deferred emancipation had effectively become a social impossiblity in Maryland, so the Jesuits looked toward a mass sale. In October 1836 Father General Jan Roothaan approved the proposal, with the stipulations that they not separate families and that they make provision for the continuing spiritual care of the slaves.

16. MPA, Corporation Minutes, 14 June 1814.
17. Carroll to Francis Neale, Baltimore, October 3, 1815, in Hanley, *Carroll Papers*, 3:361.
18. MPA, Minutes of Corporation, St. Thomas, 22 August 1820.

More than two hundred and seventy slaves of the Maryland Jesuits were sold to two planters in Louisiana in 1838. The scale and nature of the sale sent shockwaves beyond the Catholic community. In the 1830s fewer than two percent of the slaves sold in Maryland left the state. But since the typical Maryland slaveholder had one slave and 90 percent held fewer than 15, the possibilities for a local sale of nearly 300 slaves without breaking up families were clearly extremely limited. Nonetheless the specter of Jesuits selling their slaves to the deep South, even to a heavily Catholic state like Louisiana, was one which scandalized many Jesuits and non-Jesuits alike. The European Jesuits in Maryland, who tended to romanticize the master-slave relationship as a superior form of feudalism, were most vocal in their opposition. Native Jesuits who were superiors of the plantations also strenuously objected to the sale and at least a few apparently managed to warn their slaves that the provincial and the sheriff were coming to collect them. Some of the blacks escaped to the woods to return later to the estates. Most were shipped south and some families were evidently separated. The resulting scandal, news of which reached Roothaan from outraged Jesuits and laity alike, forced the resignation of the Maryland provincial, Thomas Mulledy, and his exile to Europe.

All this, of course, happened before *In Supremo apostolatus,* and there is no evidence that it had any influence on the shaping of that document. Benedict Fenwick, the bishop of Boston and a Jesuit from Maryland, thought that his Maryland brethren might have sold their slaves as quickly as they did because they knew of the impending papal letter, but nothing survives to support Fenwick's suspicion.[19] It is, however, quite possible that Jan Roothaan knew of such a letter by the early part of 1839, and that it played a part in his sharp reaction to the sale.

With the sale of the Jesuit slaves the most visible example of Catholic slaveholding had largely disappeared, but Southern Catholics were by and large more committed to the institution in 1840 than they had been in 1820. It was virtually impossible to find a Southern Catholic like William Gaston, a justice of the supreme court of North Carolina, who as

19. Archives of the Archbishop of Baltimore, Benedict Fenwick to Eccleston, Boston, 11 March 1840.

late as 1832 termed slavery "the worst evil that afflicts the Southern part of our confederacy."[20] By that time Gaston, who even supported voting rights for free blacks, was dangerously out of step in the South. John England, who privately shared Gaston's abhorrence for slavery, nonetheless, as we have seen, defended it publicly. Catholics north and south opposed the abolition movement on several grounds. They identified it with nativism, perfectionism, and Great Britain. As John England put it, "I witnessed [in Ireland] the yearly display by the anti-slavery society of the preparation and presentation to parliament of two petitions; one for abolishing the slavery of the negroes in the West Indies, the other for riveting the chains of the white slaves in Ireland, by continuing to enforce the penal laws against the Roman Catholics."[21] But the American Catholic opposition to abolitionism went beyond its association with anti-Catholicism. The immediate abolition of slavery, Catholic spokesmen like Orestes Brownson argued, would be an injustice to the slaveholder and a disaster for the freedman. Then, too, they feared that the assertion of federal power that abolition involved would be a dangerous precedent for the federal government's interference in other areas, including the religious.

The nativism of the 1830s through the 1850s made the American church all too conscious of its status as an alien minority in America. By 1850 Catholics were still less than nine percent of the population, but having become the largest denomination in the country, were under stronger attacks than ever. Self-preservation became a priority. The bishops as a group concentrated on private behavior rather than social ethics. Except for the area of public education, the bishops foreswore any activity that could be deemed political. When the prelates held their first plenary council in Baltimore in 1852, they limited their remarks about slavery to the need to provide for the spiritual needs of the individual slaves. Francis Kenrick, successively bishop of Philadelphia and archbishop of Baltimore, lamented that the condition of slaves (he could have enlarged this to blacks in general) had deteriorated since the rise of

---

20. Rice, *American Catholic Opinion*, 134–15, citing *American Catholic Historical Researches*, VIII. 71.

21. *Letters*, 14–15.

the anti-slavery movement, but could only conclude that "such is the state of things, nothing should be attempted against the laws . . ."[22]

And what of Rome? Except for the apostolic letter of 1839 there was little said about slavery. Partly that was the result of the way in which Propaganda functioned. It tended to be reactive, responding to complaints brought or questions raised. And there were few of either regarding slavery. Those that did arise tended to come from foreigners, like Harold and Ryan. Thus in 1816 Charles Nerinckx, a Belgian priest working in Kentucky, raised several matters about which he was in doubt concerning Kentucky society. One was slavery. He seemed at sea about it. "What judgment must one make," he asked, "about the selling of slaves . . . ? What if they are sold to heretics, or at a public auction?" Propaganda forwarded it to the Holy Office, whose response was "non licere" ("This is not allowed").[23] Yet the selling continued, even, as we have seen, by religious themselves. In 1828 an immigrant Bishop Giuseppe Rosati of St. Louis sought guidance about the validity of clandestine marriages of slaves (in some states slave marriage was not allowed). The question once again was forwarded to the Holy Office, which assured the bishop that the ceremonies were indeed valid.[24]

American slavery in fact was no higher a priority for Propaganda than it was for the American church. When in January 1861 the Sacred Congregation was preparing a set of issues that it thought the American bishops should take up at their next plenary council, slavery and the evangelization of the blacks were not among them (the evangelization of Indians was).[25]

Rome, although aware of the slavery controversy in the United States that had brought that nation to the brink of war, was at the time

22. Kenrick, *Theologia Moralis*, I, tract V, Cap. V, translated in *U.S. Catholic Miscellany*, Dec. 9, 1843, quoted in Rice, 71.

23. APF, *Atti*, 1816, vol. 179, *Dubbi propositi dal Sig. Nerinckx*, 1 April 1816, 13 r, 24 v.

24. APF, *Lettere e Decreti*, 1828, vol. 309, fol. 758, Prop. Fide to Rosati, 25 October 1828.

25. APF, *Atti*, 1861, vol. 225, January 1861. *Ponente L'Eminentissimo e Reverendissimo Sig Cardinale Costantino Patrizi Ristrello con Somnario e Note Di Archivio Sul Metodo attualmente vigente nelle elezioni dei Vescovi per gli Stati Uniti d' America e sopra diversi inconveniente che occorono in quelle Diocesi*, 21 January 1861. Printed.

preoccupied with its own insurrection in the Papal States. Initially it had a common interest with the United States government in affirming the right of self-defense against rebellion. Finding itself increasingly isolated as a temporal power in the European sphere, certain papal officials, such as Giacomo Antonelli, the Cardinal Secretary of State, were looking to the United States as a rising power to foil Great Britain's supposed encouragement of *risorgimento* in the Italian peninsula (the United States and the Papal States had diplomatic relations at the time).[26] By the fall of 1862, however, this tilt toward the North began to shift. Ironically, the Lincoln administration's reluctant decision to make the abolition of slavery an implicit war goal in the form of the Emancipation Proclamation proved crucial in reversing the Holy See's previously favorable attitude toward the North's prosecution of the war. As the casualties in America mounted to horrifying numbers, the Roman perception grew that the Lincoln administration seemed intent not on using the measured force appropriate to a just war to restore the union, but on the complete submission of the South (the adoption of an unconditional surrender policy by the federal government only reinforced this attitude). The news of the Emancipation Proclamation was seen as a desperate measure to encourage slave rebellion in the South. The very government that had justified its call for volunteers on the grounds of putting down an insurrection now appeared to be consorting in servile insurrection. And that conjured up visions of slaves murdering defenseless women and children in the deep South. The Emancipation Proclamation in fact rekindled the prejudices and fears about the United States as a radical republic that the Holy See, like other European powers, had long harbored.

The North's commitment to abolish slavery seemed then, from Rome, to be cynically self-serving and hypocritical. As *L'Osservatore Romano* remarked in October 1862: "We are certain that [emancipation] will not come about from the benevolent initiative of the North." Instead the editors professed themselves ready to believe that the Confederates, once they gained independence, would work out a peaceful solution to the issue. "Will not the example of France and England," they concluded, "be imitated by a race which is intelligent and chivalrous, as the Con-

---

26. David J. Alvarez, "The Papacy in the Diplomacy of the American Civil War," *Catholic Historical Review* 69 (April 1983): 233–34.

federates of the South have always shown themselves to be."[27] Obviously the Confederacy was winning the propaganda war in Rome.

In part the southern influence upon the Holy See came from an American Catholic, Martin Spalding, the bishop of Louisville. In the spring of 1863 Spalding had written to Cardinal Alessandro Barnabò to protest the abolitionist position that three Catholic clerics of Cincinnati had taken: Archbishop John Baptist Purcell, his priest brother, Edward, editor of *The Catholic Telegraph*, and Purcell's auxiliary, Sylvester Rosecrans, the brother of the Union general. In a 23-page-letter Spalding defended the constitutional right of secession and reviewed the chief causes of the war, which he identified as the tariff and slavery. The bishop admitted—as he claimed all good and moderate men did—that slavery was a great inherited social evil. The important question was how to free the slaves without ruining the country and the blacks themselves. Spalding pointed out the dismaying plight of free blacks, especially in the segregated North, as well as the hypocrisy of the North, particularly in the refusal of several northern states to allow emancipated blacks to settle there. "Our philanthropists of the North," Spalding commented, "wish certainly to see the slaves freed, but they wish by no means to have them among themselves."[28] He castigated the Punic war aims of the Lincoln administration: confiscation of property, including blacks, and the arming of the freed blacks. He underscored the connection of abolitionism with anti-Catholicism among nothern religious and political leaders: "Down with slavery and popery."[29] As Spalding surveyed the American landscape after two years of bloody conflict, he saw an escalation of violence and bloodshed that promised nothing short of genocide in the South:

> Our miserable war, first begun to restore the broken Union, has now become a war of confiscation of property, of violent emancipation of the Negroes, of threatened and encouraged slave insurrection, of destruction and desolation of the vast and fair territory of the South, and finally of extermination of all the whites, and

27. *L'Osservatore*, 8 November 1862, quoted in Anthony B. Lalli, S.X., and Thomas H. O'Connor, "Roman Views on the American Civil War," *Catholic Historical Review* 57 (April 1971): 34.

28. David [Thomas M.] Spalding, C.F.X., ed., "Martin John Spalding's 'Dissertation on the American Civil War,'" *Catholic Historical Review* 52 (April 1966): 78.

29. Ibid., 79.

perhaps at the same time also of the Negroes themselves, if the revolt can not by any other means be suppressed. Such is at least the present spirit of our government.[30]

What should the Church do amidst such carnage and treachery? To Spalding it should simply stay out of the way. The passions that were killing hundreds of thousands of soldiers and maiming many more, destroying and plundering property, were surely not going to cease with the end of the slaughter. To identify in any partisan way with the struggle was to invite persecution of the Church after the war.[31]

Spalding's apocaplyptic account must have seemed prophetic when news came shortly afterwards of the draft riots in New York, at the heart of which were Irish Catholics. Significantly, Spalding's essay was published anonymously in serial form in *L'Osservatore* (in October). Six months later he was appointed archbishop of Baltimore.

While Spalding was attempting to get Propaganda to silence those prelates who were speaking out in favor of abolition, the Papal States' consul in New York City, Louis B. Binsse, was suggesting that the Sacred Congregation apply pressure in the opposite direction. In September 1863 Binsse addressed the tradition of silence about slavery within the American Catholic church. In the face of civil laws that denied natural rights to slaves, such as those connected with marriage and family, and the telling evidence that religion made little progress where slavery prevailed, Binsse wondered how much longer Roman authorities could be silent. He cited with approval the moral stand taken in Cincinnati against slavery. "I regret to say," he added, "that among the Catholic clergy, there are a good number, especially among those teaching in the colleges of the south, who favor the cause of separation and who are hostile to the cause of the government."[32] Binsse's source of concern about the need for the Church to take a stand about slavery was apparently Isaac Hecker. In January 1864 the consul was conveying to the cardinal prefect Hecker's conviction about the urgency of the question and

30. Ibid., 81.
31. Ibid., 83–85.
32. APF, *Scritture*, 1864–1865, vol. 20, folios 213r–214rv, Binsse to Barnabò, New York, 18 Sept. 1863.

the need for the Church to declare itself. "The question of the future so-lution of slavery is the question of the day for the United States," he in-formed Barnabò. Binsse confessed that he could not comprehend the thinking of those who opposed abolition, who were persisting in protect-ing the institution and ignoring its role "as the sole cause of our terrible civil war."[33]

The Holy See, as noted, not about to be party to the Lincoln policy on emancipation, indeed had begun to send signals that it favored the Confederacy. When Pius IX sent a letter addressing President Jefferson Davis as the head of the Confederate States, the Confederacy claimed this as evidence of the Holy See's recognition of its independence. This occasioned a protest from the new American minister to the Papal States, Rufus King, that the government of the Holy See should be the last one to sympathize with "the enemies of Human Liberty."[34] Pope Pius IX assured King that he could never sanction a system of slavery. His Secretary of State, Cardinal Giacomo Antonelli, subsequently admitted that, upon further study of the U.S. Constitution, the South's war for in-dependence seemed an illegitimate one. But real sympathies remained with the Confederacy. There was no attempt to communicate the Holy See's stated position on the war to the American hierarchy.

Late in the war Propaganda did finally examine the issue of slavery in connection with the American conflict. The occasion was the pastoral that the bishop of Natchitoches, Augustus Martin, had issued in August 1861. In his address to the people of northern Louisiana he defended as divinely ordained not only the de facto institution of slavery in the South but the very enslavement of Africans. For Martin "the will of God" was manifest in the exchange of the Africans' labor for the necessi-ties of life, both material and spiritual, which they received in slavery, no matter what "extravagant humanitarian utopians . . . [,] sentimental . . . English philanthropists[,] and northern Puritans thought."[35]

33. APF, *Scritture*, 1864–1865, vol. 20, folios 503rv–506rv, Binsse to Barnabò, New York, January 5, 1864.

34. Alvarez, "Papacy," 245.

35. APF, *Scritture*, 1864–1865, vol. 20, fols. 1207r–1213v. *Lettre Pastorale de Mgr. L'Eveque De Natchitoches A l'occasion de la guerre du Sud pour son Indpendance* (August 1861).

More than three years later, in the fall of 1864, the consultor of Propaganda, who was charged to examine the pastoral, a Dominican, Vincent M. Gatti, found Martin's position on slavery completely opposed to the teaching of *In Supremo Apostolatus* and predicated on some fallacious biblical assumptions, such as the blacks being the descendants of Canaan and subject to Noah's curse. Even if they had been, Gatti noted, all such ethnic distinctions were obliterated by Christ. Martin, he suggested, was really the sentimental one in imagining that slavers were somehow applying Adam Smith's invisible hand to the peculiar institution—that in pursuing their selfish ends through such violence, the greater good of the blacks was really being promoted. Even the blessing of Christianity was no "justification for the iniquity which such traffic" entailed.

Slavery, Gatti continued, was wrong because it was a violation of the natural right of liberty. He admitted that the Church had not condemned every form of slavery in the past, but it was certainly opposed to the kind that originated in the unjust deprivation of individual liberty, to the kind that was defended on the grounds of some intrinsic difference between whites and blacks. Original sin was something shared by all and was no excuse for perpetuating injustice. Education was the key to eliminating differences in human capacity. In serving as an apologist for the "peculiar institution," Martin, Gatti concluded, was contradicting the popes who had "condemned not only the enslavement of individuals, but the continued keeping of them as slaves."[36]

Gatti was making the distinction between the chattel slavery of the United States and the milder forms of slavery which the Church had traditionally legitimized. This was a distinction that the Holy Office itself fi-

---

36. APF, *Scritture,* 1864–1865, vol. 20, fols. 1199r–1205v. Gatti, Minerva, 25 November 1864. Gatti seems to have been influenced by the German moral theologian, Johann Sailer, Bishop of Ratisbon, whose *Handbuch der Christlichen Moral* (II, 1830–1841) developed the Pauline doctrine of equality in Christ in regard to slavery. "The state of slavery," Bishop Sailor wrote, "and any treatment of human beings as slaves, turns people who are persons into mere things, turns people who are ends in themselves into mere means, and does not allow the responsibility of people for what they do, or do not do, to develop properly, and in this way cripples them in their very humanity; hence it is contrary to the basic principle of all morality. . . ." (cited in John Francis Maxwell, *Slavery and the Catholic Church: The History of Catholic Teaching Concerning the Moral Legitimacy of the Institution of Slavery* [Chichester and London, 1975], 102–3).

nally promulgated in 1866. By that time of course, the Civil War was over, and the Thirteenth Amendment had abolished slavery not only in the areas in rebellion against the federal government but throughout the land.

During his controversy with Secretary of State Forsyth, John England confessed that many persons had asked him about his personal view about slavery: "whether I am friendly to the existence or continuation of slavery? I am not—but I also see the impossibility of now abolishing it here. When it can and ought to be abolished is a question for the legislature and not for me."[37] Slavery might be an evil, but it was out of the Church's domain to decide the practical means by which it was to be ended. The Church could enunciate the general principles but had to leave applications to those competent. So too Francis Kenrick: the slavery discussion pertained "to politics." Indeed, Kenrick was all too typical of the prelates who felt that the whole controversy over slavery was simply polarizing the country to the detriment of the slaves themselves.[38] In effect, in the question of slavery the American bishops were making a rigid separation between the private and public orders, making any public criticism of slavery unthinkable.[39] Such a separation, John Noonan has suggested, makes more understandable why a Catholic, Roger Taney, could have freed his own slaves and treated blacks as equals within the Church, yet still issued the Dred Scot decision in 1857. As a result the prelates kept their peace about even the worst evils of the system. *Pace* John England, they did not speak out against the evils, which were all too visible. To the extent that they defended the system, they created a fantasy that had little to do with the reality of slavery in the United States, and certainly had nothing to do with their own experience of the

37. Rice, *American Catholic Opinion*, 69.

38. See APF, Congress: Amer. Cent., Section XX, fols. 213v and 214rv, Kenrick to Barnabò, Baltimore, 11 May 1863.

39. In *A Vindication of The Catholic Church* Kenrick had written in 1855: "As regards political institutions, she is wholly independent of any, and suited to all. It is not her province to model or fashion them; but being indifferent to each particular form of social organization, she studies only to infuse the spirit and maxims of Christ, and thus to modify and mitigate whatever may be exorbitant and unjust" ([Baltimore, 1855], 332). By its persistent silence on the realities of American slavery by the 1850s, however, the Church in America was failing Kenrick's own moral standard.

institution. Not until January 1861 did a bishop speak out publicly on the evils of slavery: a southern bishop, Augustin Verot of St. Augustine. Verot defended the institution of slavery but called for significant reform if the new Confederacy was to endure.[40] Verot also was responsible for the topic of the freedman getting onto the agenda of the Second Plenary Council in 1866, but with no better results than came from his efforts to reform slavery.

The slavery controversy was occurring at the very time the Church in this country was under attack as an anti-American institution. The tendency to identify the abolitionist and nativist movements only reinforced the conviction that silence was the best policy for American church leaders. Ecclesiastical self-preservation and unity proved to take priority over even such a fundamental question of social ethics as slavery.

One historian has observed: "There was an element of unreality in any claim of North American Catholics to be loyal followers of the common Catholic teaching. For they must have been well aware that the form of slavery which existed under the inhuman slavery legislation in the slave-holding States was an extreme form of chattel-slavery."[41] The fact of the matter seems to have been that they were not. They were very much children of their culture and to that extent captives of it. Until the war itself, the persons who did look to Rome for guidance were all foreigners.

For its part Rome seemed reluctant to intervene. Although it would respond occasionally to *ad hoc* requests for solutions to dilemmas regarding slavery, there was no effort made to enunciate any overall teaching regarding slavery in the United States. It is significant that the letter from the Holy See that had the greatest impact in this country was written not for the United States but for Africa. Rome itself had more pressing concerns. The Church itself was still a much more decentralized institution than it would be by the end of the century. Only with Pius IX did the papal encyclical become a prominent means of exercising the magisterium. Catholics throughout the world, including America, did not tend to look

40. See Michael Gannon, *Rebel Bishop: The Life and Era of Augustine Verot* (Milwaukee, 1964), 31–56.
41. Maxwell, *Slavery and the Catholic Church*, 112.

to Rome as the center of authority the way they would after the First Vatican Council. Hence the role that the Holy See might have played in forcing American Catholics to transcend the chains of culture went largely unfulfilled. On the matter of the "peculiar institution" Rome respected the wisdom of the local church that survival dictated silence and conformity. That strategy worked but one can today wonder at the price that was paid.

Gerald P. Fogarty, S.J.

3. TWO VIRGINIA PRIESTS IN CONTENTION WITH THEIR BISHOP

The Problem of Incorporation of Church Property

One of Monsignor Robert Trisco's many significant contributions to our understanding of American Catholic history is his exhaustive treatment of clerical discipline, "Bishops and Their Priests in the United States," in Monsignor John Tracy Ellis's edited work *The Catholic Priest in the United States: Historical Investigations*.[1] It therefore seems appropriate to illustrate that account with the story of two priests who served in the Diocese of Richmond in the nineteenth century and who both had difficulties with their bishops. Richmond had been established as a diocese in 1820 before it had adequate resources to sustain itself. The first bishop, Patrick Kelly, arrived in Norfolk in 1821 but left within a year without ever visiting his see city. The diocese was then returned to the administration of the archbishops of Baltimore, who continued to supply priests to the struggling southern diocese. Two of these priests are the subjects of this essay, Timothy O'Brien, who virtually founded the church in Richmond in 1832, and Matthew O'Keefe, who was on loan from Baltimore from 1852 to 1888 and became synonymous with Catholicism in Norfolk.

1. Robert Trisco, "Bishops and Their Priests in the United States," in John Tracy Ellis, ed., *The Catholic Priest in the United States: Historical Investigations* (Collegeville, Minn.: St. John's University Press, 1971), pp. 111–292.

The difficulties of O'Brien and O'Keefe stemmed not from disobedience but from two other, separate issues. First, as Monsignor Trisco has noted, although dioceses had been established in the United States since 1789 with bishops having ordinary jurisdiction, technically speaking, there were no parishes until 1908. Priests enjoyed no tenure and could be transferred or removed from their "missions" at the will of the bishop. Only at the intervention of the Holy See in 1884 did the Third Plenary Council legislate that some missions would enjoy irremovability—their "rectors" were "quasi-pastors" and could not be removed without a formal trial.

The second issue stemmed from the peculiar law of Virginia that still in 1999 prohibits churches from being incorporated to own property. Priests frequently purchased property with their own funds and held it in their own names until any debt incurred had been paid off, at which time they transferred title to the bishop, who held it in fee simple. The bishop, in turn, had to write a will to the Archbishop of Baltimore or the next nearest suffragan and his successors. Only in the 1940s was the law altered, enabling the incumbent bishop to hold property still in his own name but as "Bishop of Richmond" to assure its being passed on to his successor. In the case of church property within the city of Richmond, the problem arose from a bequest of land made in 1818 by Joseph Gallego, a wealthy mill owner, to the "Catholic Community" of Richmond. Unfortunately, due to Virginia's laws prohibiting the incorporation of any church, the settlement of the Gallego bequest was contested for several decades, for there was no legal corporation of the "Catholic Community." An earlier priest had, nevertheless, built a small frame church on the property. O'Brien would not only have to conduct the litigation over the contested property but also build up the Catholic community.

Born in Ballina, County Mayo, Ireland, O'Brien volunteered for service in the Archdiocese of Baltimore, pursued his theological studies at St. Mary's Seminary in Baltimore, and was ordained in 1819. After a brief stint in the Jesuit novitiate in Maryland, he left to do pastoral work in the archdiocese, before being assigned to Richmond in 1832.[2] Even as

2. Clarence V. Joerndt, *St. Ignatius, Hickory, and Its Missions* (Baltimore: Publica-

he was accepting his appointment to Richmond, Archbishop James Whitfield was informing the Congregation of Propaganda in Rome of the dire situation of the Church in Virginia. Catholics numbered only 4,000 out of a population of 1,211,405. The archbishop had himself visited Richmond, but, of the four priests he had sent there, three had returned saying they saw little hope for any increase among the twenty-five Catholics then in the city. Yet, he was now confident that under O'Brien "our holy religion will flourish in those arid places." He had promised O'Brien financial support "if he would built a decent church of brick, for the Catholics have used up to now a small, humble church built of wood in a city where you will find the Protestant chuches, and even private homes, as often as not, outstanding for beauty and ornamentation."[3]

O'Brien was equal to the task of building a "decent church of brick." He was an indefatigable worker, as he indicated in July, 1832, in his first letter to Whitfield. Upon his arrival in May, he called a meeting of the trustees. Finding the religious education of the children "greatly neglected," he inaugurated "catechism at 4 every Sunday evening," followed by Vespers an hour later. He even discovered that "several protestants have been in the habit of attending the evening instructions & I am informed have been much pleased." But he remained concerned about title to the disputed property. He feared that, if the court ruled against him, the congregation would receive only "the value of the little church which will not amount to $600 though it cost nearly $2000." He was already seeking an alternative site for a church, but faced the difficulty of raising funds, for "there is but little sympathy for us & unfortunately we are a degraded caste in one of the most aristocratic dens in the world."[4]

O'Brien's first report to Whitfield outlined his agenda for the church

---

tion Press, 1972), pp. 385–93, has brief biographical sketches of both Todrig, O'Brien's predecessor, and O'Brien.

3. Archives of the Congregation of Propaganda Fide, ACTA, 197, 92–93r, Whitfield to Propaganda, Baltimore, June 14, 1832.

4. Archives of the Archdiocese of Baltimore (henceforth AAB), 23 P4, O'Brien to Whitfield, Richmond, July 3, 1832. For an account of Virginia laws pertaining to church property and the Gallego case, see Thomas E. Buckley, S.J., "After Disestablishment: Thomas Jefferson's Wall of Separation in Antebellum Virginia," *Journal of Southern History* 61 (Aug. 1995): 445-80.

in Richmond over almost the next twenty years. He had a sense of the role Catholics should play in the community, and this meant having a church in a prominent place. He concentrated on the catechetical instruction of all the people, but especially the children. He made a special appeal to Protestants and would soon see his approach bear fruit with the conversion of several prominent people, including the three daughters of Governor John Floyd, whose wife and son also later converted. And, whenever necessary, he paid bills out of his own personal money. His strong personality, when coupled with his personal expenditures for the church, however, led him into conflict with at least one bishop and caused him eventually to leave the city and diocese.

As Whitfield had reported to Propaganda, he had promised O'Brien financial support for building a proper church in Richmond—a promise he kept by building more churches in Virginia than in Maryland during his episcopacy.[5] O'Brien also had charge of Petersburg, south of Richmond. While he sought to build a church there, his main focus was Richmond. He wanted to make a statement both in terms of size and location. The dimensions he planned were modest enough, "namely 75 feet long by 45 in width, including a dwelling in the rear," but he wanted the "building [to] be put up in the neighborhood of the Capitol." If he could purchase the disputed Gallego property with its existing church and "convert it into an asylum under the guidance of the Sisters of Charity, with the impulse given to religion, we must I think succeed here." To procure the new site, however, "it will be necessary to transact that business through the agency of some person who may not be suspected as the idea of building a church would greatly enhance its value." He stressed that the new property would be vested in the archbishop.[6]

By August of 1833, O'Brien had obtained the prominent site he desired for his church, a lot "in the genteelist part of the city & within a few yards of the western gate of the Capitol." He paid $3,000 for the lot and another $7,500 for the construction of the "church 75 by 45 with a por-

5. Thomas Spalding, *The Premier See: A History of the Archdiocese of Baltimore, 1789–1989* (Baltimore: The Johns Hopkins University Press, 1989), p. 110.
6. AAB, 23 P5 O'Brien to Whitfield, Richmond, Feb. 19, 1833.

tico supported by 4 large pillars 2½ feet diameter & 25 feet high with a cupola surmounted by a cross." Behind the church, however, he retained a lot for himself. On it, an elderly benefactor built a house for him on the condition that he himself be allowed to live there until his death. This would be a major source of contention with Bishop John McGill.

Although O'Brien realized Whitfield might "be surprised at our boldness," he argued that he could construct a grand church "with as much ease as an inferior building." He hoped that "many will assist us with a view to ornament the city who under other circumstances would not give us a dollar. Indeed we had no alternative, the lot is too conspicuous to admit of an inferior building." He had already collected over $4,000 for the project and hoped to raise the remainder by begging in Philadelphia and New York. He and the trustees, who supported the endeavor, also calculated "on large aid from your grace, in proportion to the efforts that are being made. I hope we shall not be disappointed."[7] On May 25, 1834, Whitfield formally dedicated St. Peter's Church with the grandest Catholic ceremony Virginia's capital had ever seen.

In the meantime, on July 24, 1833, O'Brien had purchased the Gallego lot in his own name from Peter J. Chevallie, Gallego's last surviving executor, for $500. The deed to O'Brien and his heirs was formally recorded in the court of Hustings on September 2, 1833.[8] O'Brien's purchase of this lot at Fourth and Marshall Streets opened the way for him to invite the Sisters of Charity to open an orphan asylum in Richmond, but was another factor in his later difficulties with McGill.

On November 22, 1834, O'Brien welcomed the Sisters of Charity from Emmitsburg, who opened St. Joseph's orphan asylum and free school in the renovated wooden chapel. Five years later, the sisters replaced the frame house with a brick one.[9] Meanwhile, in June 1838, O'Brien had also engaged the sisters to provide nurses for the infirmary attached to the Richmond Medical College, an arrangement that ended in 1841.[10]

7. Archives of the Diocese of Richmond (henceforth ADR), O'Brien to Whitfield, Richmond, Aug. 13, 1833.
8. ADR, Deed of Lot 630, Gallego's executor to O'Brien.
9. Archives of St. Joseph's Provincial House, Emmitsburg, Md. (henceforth ASJPH), Richmond, Va., St. Joseph's Asylum and School.
10. ASJPH, "Richmond Villa," quoted in Sister Bernadette Armiger, "The Histo-

The Diocese of Richmond in the meantime had remained bereft of a bishop until the arrival of Richard Vincent Whelan in 1841. Rather than reside at the city's only church, which in fact became the cathedral, however, he purchased property for a seminary and lived there. In 1846, he departed Richmond for Wheeling, then in the state of Virginia, where he took up residence. Back in Richmond, O'Brien, with Whelan's approval, had also arranged for German-speaking Jesuits to begin a new parish, St. Mary's, for the city's increasing German population. Late in 1850, meanwhile, Whelan became the first Bishop of Wheeling and was succeeded in Richmond by Bishop John McGill.

In December 1850, however, McGill had hardly arrived in Richmond before he was in open conflict with O'Brien. The problem arose from there being no income for a bishop. When O'Brien offered to pay him the salary of an assistant pastor, McGill flatly rejected it. Within a week, O'Brien left Richmond to join his brother, John, in Lowell, Massachusetts. On the way, he passed through Georgetown.

A week after O'Brien's departure, McGill notified Ignatius Brocard, the Jesuit provincial, that he wished the Jesuits permanently to staff the German parish. He then narrated his difficulties with O'Brien and asked for a Jesuit to assist him at least for Christmas. He lamented "how difficult it is for a Bishop, *in the midst of Protestants,* and with very small Catholic congregations, to find worthy, zealous, and disinterested priests" to serve in such a mission. "My own position," he continued, "is sufficiently painful at present." He then narrated the source of his contention with O'Brien:

> I had no source of income certain, and I could not consent to remain in my cathedral church and congregation as a salaried assistant of one of my priests. Yet such is the lamentable state of things, that the Bishop may be said to have absolutely nothing. For the small church is in debt to someone several hundred dollars, and to Father O'Brien himself upwards of $7000 on his own representation. The house, which he values at $5000.00 he also claims. The establishment of the sisters, which he estimates at $14,000.00 he

ry of the Hospital Work of the Daughters of Charity of St. Vincent de Paul in the Eastern Province of the United States: 1823–1860," unpublished M.S. in Nursing Education, Catholic University of America, Washington, D.C., 1947, p. 18.

claims to be his own, and consequently is worth $26,000.00. The only property of the Bishop here is the unproductive buildings and grounds where Bp Whelan failed in his project for a seminary and college.[11]

McGill's letter to Brocard is the only extant description of the details of the dispute. He began a correspondence with Whelan on the issue, which, unfortunately, cannot be located, but McGill apparently accused Whelan of choosing to remain in Wheeling to avoid conflict with O'Brien.

In a lengthy letter to McGill, Whelan accused O'Brien of an "open attempt to plunder the Church" and declared his claims "base & groundless fraud." He further stated that he "would long since have removed from his position one who now manifests himself so unworthy of the confidence reposed in him," if O'Brien had ever hinted at such claims. Whelan argued that the property had been deeded to the Archbishop of Baltimore in such a way that "zeal & activity & prudent management of the revenues" would pay off any debt remaining.

Whelan then recommended that McGill take direct action against O'Brien, since

> the law gives Mr. O'Brien no right whatever even to the dwelling, which was put up without any permission or consent on my part. Therefore I should advise no compromise at all, but simply to eject him from the premises by legal force, if necessary; & have him to make good his claims at law. I should withdraw his faculties instantly, for his claim places him in my eyes in the attitude of a sacrilegious robber, & renders him undeserving of all consideration. For the past ten years he has been entrusted with the revenues of the Church for the purpose of meeting obligations due upon it & now to ask funds applied to that purpose to be returned is intolerable. I consider it however the scheme of an impudent extortioner to intimidate, or perhaps in the end by lowering his pretensions to secure an income with the merit of generosity. He is just the man for either. I am truly mortified that my successor should have been placed in so unpleasant a situation. Once more I assure you that I had not the slightest anticipation of any such difficulty; & that my

11. AMP, McGill to Brocard, Richmond, Dec. 17, 1850.

sole motive for selecting Wheeling was that here the church was un-encumbered with debt, & there was none comparatively. So I de-clared at the [Seventh Provincial] Council [of Baltimore in 1849].

Whelan's vituperative language in describing O'Brien provides some evidence that O'Brien's presence in Richmond was one reason for Whelan's original move to Wheeling.

Whelan, however, then became a bit more cautious on how McGill should proceed against O'Brien. Apparently McGill had also said O'Brien was claiming money for the St. Joseph's Asylum property. Whelan's recollection was that $4000 had been collected for it in Baltimore and that several hundred more were raised through fairs in Richmond. But here he became ambiguous as to the justice of O'Brien's claims. If O'Brien was "disposed to compromise for that, at a fair rate, say about $5000," he advised McGill, "I would do it. If not, I should bring suit in the name of the Catholics of Richmond for this amount (that is if he puts the Sisters out of the house or requires more than the interest of $5000 for rent)." He further suggested "$5000 as a fair annuity during his natural life, by way of compromise for all claims & for ceding without him (unless there are bona fide debts) all the property which stands in Mr. O'Brien's name in Richmond—$600 for the cession of all claims & demands whatever in the diocese." He reminded McGill that there was also a legacy of $3,000 owed to Petersburg. With these financial arrangements, he thought the "revenues of the church will be found sufficient with economy to support the Bishop & an assistant, including, I should think, the rent of the house or the portion allowed for it."[12]

In the meantime, McGill had procured a Jesuit for the German community but not one to replace O'Brien. In response to Brocard's suggestions about O'Brien, McGill assured him that "Father O'Brien must know that he left contrary to my request and repeated solicitations, so his return, *with a willingness to occupy his proper position,* would be acceptable to me." He begged Brocard to use his influence to have O'Brien come back. On a practical level, he needed to know if he should forward O'Brien's mail or keep it for his return.[13]

12. ADR, Whelan to McGill, Wheeling, Dec. 18, 1850.
13. AMP, 218M, McGill to [Brocard?], Richmond, Dec. 20, 1850.

McGill also sought the advice of his friend Bishop Francis P. Kenrick of Philadelphia, who recommended he submit O'Brien's claims to Archbishop Samuel Eccleston, but not pay any rent for the house, for "the presumption naturally is that it was built from public funds for the residence of the clergy." This, of course, is part of what O'Brien contested. If O'Brien retired, Kenrick continued, "it is his own fault. It is plainly his duty to stand by you, and give you every aid." If McGill immediately contacted Eccleston, "you may bring him [O'Brien] to his senses." Kenrick encouraged his younger colleague that "the difficulties with which you have to contend are not insurmountable, and great consolations will, I trust, follow."[14]

Even as McGill was corresponding with Kenrick, however, the male members of St. Peter's Church met in the basement on December 21. Recalling O'Brien's nineteen years of service that had lifted the church "up with the help of God from a feeble and languishing existence to its present condition," which "caused him to be esteemed not only in his own Church but by the community in which he lived without religious distinction," the committee recounted how O'Brien had built St. Peter's Church and St. Joseph's Female Orphan Asylum. Though "Catholics were few, . . . the prejudices against the Catholic Church were a serious obstacle in his path," but O'Brien had "brought the Church as it were 'through the Valley of the shadow of Death' to its present state of comparitive [*sic*] prosperity." He exercised "fatherly anxiety and kindness" as well as firmness "towards those whose spiritual welfare was under his guidance." During several epidemics, he had "remained in the city always faithful to his duty under the most trying circumstances of exposure and fatigue." Now, the committee continued, "to sever the connection between such a spiritual Father and the congregation which has been so long guided by him in the path of religious duty—many of them from childhood—is to afflict us with a grief which words are too feeble to describe."

The committee then submitted five resolutions to the bishop with the request that the petition be forwarded to O'Brien: that they heard "with deep and sincere sorrow" that O'Brien was severing "those ties

14. ADR, Kenrick to McGill, Philadelphia, Dec. 19, 1850.

which have so closely bound us to him"; that, while welcoming the new bishop, O'Brien's departure would deprive "him of the most valuable aid he can have in entering upon the solemn and responsible duties of his office"; that their expression of gratitude toward O'Brien might induce him to return; that McGill join with them in asking O'Brien's return; and that the committee give the petition to McGill and forward a copy to O'Brien.[15]

Whelan had heard from a Richmond source that "O'Brien himself is at the bottom of this project to bring him back to Richmond." He urged his Richmond colleague to "be firm & keep him away, or at least avail yourself of the opportunity to prescribe the conditions such as may keep him in his place." The petition should cause no apprehension, he continued, for "if Mr. O has some devoted friends, he has many more foes who would rejoice at his removal." Even the friends, he thought, "are not the men to give trouble; they are too conscientious." Whelan was certain that the deed for St. Peter's he himself possessed included the land on which the house stood, so he urged McGill to occupy the house, regardless of O'Brien's threats. If O'Brien contested any of these terms, he would recommend arbitration, either by Eccleston or by some ecclesiastical body.[16]

Whelan may have been certain that the deed he held included the residence and ground behind St. Peter's, but O'Brien also possessed a deed. McGill offered him $4,000 for the property and house. Instead, O'Brien sold both to a Halifax, N.C., merchant for $5,000. He had his money, so McGill then had to purchase the property back, if he wanted to live behind his cathedral.[17] But the case was far from settled.

In the meantime, Kenrick had been transferred from Philadelphia to become Archbishop of Baltimore. In May 1852, he was delegated by the Holy See to preside over the First Plenary Council of Baltimore. In the midst of their discussion of national issues, the bishops appointed a committee to investigate the McGill–O'Brien dispute. Under the chairman-

15. ADR, John Purcell and R. H. Gallagher Petition, December 21, 1850.
16. ADR, Whelan to McGill, Wheeling, Jan. 18, 1851.
17. ADR, A Statement of facts relating to the conditions of matters at Richmond and Petersburg with respect to claims of Rev. T. O'Brien. This seems to have been McGill's petition to the commission established by the First Plenary Council in May 1852.

ship of Bishop Michael Portier of Mobile, the committee consisted of Ignatius Reynolds of Charleston; Amadeus Rappe of Cleveland; Whelan;
Peter Paul Lefevere, coadjutor and administrator of Detroit; and John
Martin Henni of Milwaukee, who in fact arrived after the matter was
settled. McGill submitted his charges against O'Brien. The priest was
claiming a total of $33,903.30 in repayment for what he had spent on
the house and property at St. Peter's, debts on the church itself, the
property for the school and orphan asylum, and a lot for a church in Petersburg. McGill's list of charges was long, but his main argument was
that it was

> a fact notorious that Mr. O'Brien came to Richmond poor, without
> estate or means. If he has acquired any thing, he obtained it as
> priest and neither as merchant, trader nor speculator. But if he ac-
> quired what he obtained as priest, he received it as the representa-
> tive of religion and for the benefit of religion. He was ordained *ad
> titulum missionis*, and under this title and on consideration of his
> services the mission had to support him. The mission did support
> him. What money he put into the church he had received as priest,
> and that he put it into the church is proof that religion needed it
> and required it and it would be as reasonable for any subscriber or
> donor, who contributed to the church, to *reclaim his donation with in-
> terest*, as for Mr. O'Brien to reclaim what the necessities of his mis-
> sion and his particular church required him to expend for the good
> of religion, and which not only he had obtained from the public as
> priest, but which he could spare over and above his support.

McGill noted he had already paid $5,000 to regain the house and ground
at St. Peter's and an additional $2,000 for the land in Petersburg, when
he heard O'Brien might sell that.[18] From other evidence, however,
McGill's charge was false that O'Brien came to Richmond a poor man.
O'Brien seems to have paid his passage to the United States and for his
seminary education. He certainly paid for the purchase of the Gallego
property out of his own pocket, and his family would send three genera-
tions of priests to the American Church.

While the committee of bishops accepted McGill's arguments that

18. Ibid.

what O'Brien expended had in fact been given him for the purposes of
the church in Richmond and Petersburg, it nevertheless concluded, "In
view of the honest impression of Rev. T. O'Brien to the contrary, and of
his long, laborious, zealous and efficient ministry, . . . that the Bishop of
Richmond should meet his obligations given for the purpose of securing
said property, and that Rev. T. O'Brien may without molestation be allowed to enjoy and use for himself the said seven thousand dollars, *Provided* that he shall forthwith make to the Bishop of Richmond a legal
deed to all the property now held by him (said T. O'Brien) in the Diocese
of Richmond, and relinquish all other his said claims." The committee
report was formally submitted to the council, where it was unanimously
adopted.[19]

O'Brien, then living with his brother John in Lowell, Massachusetts,
responded to the decision of the council on May 17. "I must I suppose
bow in submission to the decision of the Prelates in my case," he wrote.
He would donate the asylum to the diocese, since that was his original
intention, never "thinking that I would have occasion to fall back on it."
He likewise relinquished any claim against the church, while "protesting
. . . before my God that it is a just claim, & that the money claimed by
me was my own and applied by me to the best of my judgement for the
good of Religion." His concluding words were sad:

> I am now in my old age. I am a cripple creeping along to my grave
> after having spent thirty-three years at the altar of Religion & it is
> hard, after so many years to be obliged to proceed to take an active
> part in the duties of the mission for my support. God's will be done.
> I have at all times confided in Him, & in Him I have put my trust.
> When I stand in his presence I hope & pray I will be judged with
> mercy.[20]

It was a tragic end for one of Virginia's most dynamic pastors. But
O'Brien fired one last parting shot. He had agreed to donate the asylum
to the diocese.[21] Instead, he signed the deed to the "Trustees of St.

19. ADR, Report of the Committee of Grievances on claims of Rev. T. O'Brien
against the congregation and Diocese of Richmond, Va., submitted to the national
council and approved. May 15, 1852.
20. ADR, O'Brien to Lynch, secretary of the council, Lowell, May 17, 1852.
21. ADR, Fitzpatrick to McGill, Boston, Sept. 21, 1852.

Joseph's Female Academy & Orphan Asylum of the City of Richmond."
When McGill protested, O'Brien replied that the institution was built
with the donations "of the poor workmen on the canal." He had to protect their orphans. He pointed out that the by-laws of the corporation
could be amended to provide for the bishop or pastor of St. Peter's to be
chairman, but, while he would surrender his own rights, he would not
"sacrifice" those "of the good Srs. of Charity & the orphans."[22]

Whether it was a case of a priest making poor financial judgments
or using his ministry to gain personal wealth or of a bishop whose personality could not allow competition for authority, the O'Brien–McGill
dispute cast a pall on the beginning of McGill's administration and ended
O'Brien's service to the church in Richmond that he had virtually founded. In Lowell, O'Brien took charge of the school his brother founded
and, in 1854, resisted demands of the local Know Nothings to inspect the
living quarters of the convent. Three years later, he died. Almost twenty
years later his brother John, who had briefly labored in Virginia (and incidentally patented "Father John's Medicine"), also died. Both are
prominently interred at the entrance of St. Patrick's Church in Lowell.
They founded what became known among Lowell Catholics as the
"O'Brien Dynasty" that lasted from 1848 to 1922, for John was succeeded by his nephew and he, in turn, by his cousin.[23]

Although O'Brien's departure from Richmond was not over clerical
discipline but over financial matters, both issues combined in O'Keefe's
case. Until 1884, priests did not enjoy tenure in office; they served only
at the will of the bishop. In 1855, the First Provincial Council of St. Louis
adopted a procedure for handling disputes between priests and bishops.
If a priest challenged his transfer or removal, the bishop or vicar general
was to appoint two consultors to hear the case. If the consultors upheld
the priest, the bishop was to appoint a third consultor. If all three upheld
the priest, appeal was to be made to the metropolitan or to the senior
suffragan, if the case originated in the metropolitan see. The decision of

22. ADR, O'Brien to McGill, Lowell, Sept. 22, 1852.
23. Joerndt, *St. Ignatius, Hickory,* p. 391; Brian C. Mitchell, *The Paddy Camps: The
Irish of Lowell: 1821–61* (Urbana and Chicago: University of Illinois Press, 1988), pp.
123–24, 138–39.

the metropolitan or senior suffragan was final, except for appeal by either the priest or bishop to the Holy See.[24] This procedure was then adopted by the Ninth Provincial Council of Baltimore in 1858 and was extended to the entire American Church by the Second Plenary Council of Baltimore in 1866.[25]

The Holy See, however, continued to receive appeals from priests. In 1878, the Congregation of Propaganda issued a new form of clerical discipline, according to which the bishop was to appoint, preferably in a diocesan synod, a commission of five or at least three priests, trained in canon law, to examine the evidence, collect testimony, and interrogate witnesses in order to assist the bishop in rendering his decision. If a priest protested his removal from a mission, the bishop had to have the advice of at least three members of this commission. In the event of an appeal, the metropolitan or senior suffragan was to proceed in the same manner and his investigating commission was to have access to the records of the trial in the first instance.[26] Under pressure from the Holy See, the bishops at the Third Plenary Council in 1884 reenacted this legislation and also provided for "irremovable rectors" of certain parishes. It was this legislation that shaped part of the dispute between Bishop John J. Keane and Matthew O'Keefe.

Two years after O'Brien left Richmond, McGill procured the loan of a priest from Archbishop Kenrick of Baltimore.[27] Born in Waterford in 1828, Matthew O'Keefe had taught Latin, Greek, and geometry for three years at St. John's College in Waterford (where Bishop Kelly, Richmond's first bishop, had been president), until he reached the canonical age for ordination. In 1852, he was ordained for Baltimore,[28] but almost immediately took charge of St. Patrick's Church in Norfolk. Although he would serve under three bishops in Virginia, he remained, by Kenrick's choice, a priest of the Archdiocese of Baltimore.[29] He immediately set

24. *Collectio Lacensis*, III, 308, 311–12.

25. *Concilii Plenarii Baltimorensis II. In Ecclesia Metropolitana Baltimorensi a die VII. ad diem XXI., Octobris A.D. MDCCCLXVI. Habiti et a Sede Apostolica Recogniti Acta et Decreta*, 2d ed. (Baltimore: John Murphy, 1894), no. 108, p. 75.

26. *Acta Sanctae Sedis*, 12 (1878): 88–89.

27. ADR, F. P. Kenrick to McGill, Baltimore, Sept. 6, 1852.

28. Archives of the Irish College, Rome, O'Keefe to Kirby, Norfolk, May 31, 1854; ADR, O'Keefe to Gibbons, Norfolk, July 30, 1874.

29. ADR, Kenrick to McGill, Baltimore, July 6, 1853.

about to place the church on the map. During the Yellow Fever epidemic of 1855, when others, including many ministers and doctors, fled, he heroically remained to tend to the sick. In anticipation of an ecumenical age, he entered a pact with a Protestant minister that if either should die of the fever, the other would conduct the funeral. Neither perished in the epidemic, but O'Keefe did conduct the funeral of his friend several years later. No sooner was the yellow fever epidemic over, however, than a new danger threatened. In Norfolk, O'Keefe had at least one encounter with the Know Nothings. Sometime between October and December 1856, when he also had charge of Portsmouth, two men knocked on his door to ask him to attend a dying man in Portsmouth. Dutifully, he responded, but with some caution. When his escorts reached the other side of the Elizabeth River, they said the dying man was further outside of town. He then took a pair of revolvers from his coat, placed the men under citizen's arrest, and marched them into Portsmouth, where he turned them over to the sheriff. They subsequently confessed they had been hired to assassinate him.[30] But O'Keefe had not heard the last of prejudice.

In March 1856, O'Keefe invited the Redemptorists to give a mission in Norfolk. The preachers on the occasion were Isaac Hecker and Clarence Walworth. It was the first time Hecker had aimed his preaching principally at non-Catholics.[31] But the mission and Father O'Keefe at St. Patrick's Church may have aroused hostility in their outreach to Protestants. Late in the evening of December 7, 1856, the church was burned after "an incendiary" set fire to a neighboring building. Only the walls remained standing.[32]

Whether the "incendiary" had St. Patrick's as the principal target is

30. Unsigned, "Chaplain Matthew O'Keefe of Mahone's Brigade," *Southern Historical Society Papers* 35 (1907): 180. The entry is dated Towson, Md., January 28, 1906, and was probably written by one of the associate priests at the Immaculate Conception Church that O'Keefe later founded in that Baltimore suburb.

31. John Farina, *An American Experience of God: The Spirituality of Isaac Hecker* (New York: Paulist Press, 1981), p. 104.

32. Richmond *Daily Dispatch*, Dec. 10, 1856, p. 2. McGill's diary says that Miss Herron had presented the painting of the Crucifixion and that Queen Amélie, wife of Louis Philipe of France, had given one of the Assumption. James Henry Bailey, *A History of the Diocese of Richmond: The Formative Years* (Richmond: Chancery Office, 1956), p. 121.

uncertain, but O'Keefe took immediate action. Almost every week, he took the steamship to Baltimore and then on to Philadelphia and New York to raise funds for a new church. By the weekend, he was back in Norfolk. On Monday, he paid the laborers for their previous week's work and took off again on his journey.[33] In July 1857, he described his progress for Tobias Kirby, rector of the Irish College in Rome. The burning of his church "on the morning of the 8th of December last," he wrote, was "a circumstance which I cannot fail to view as not without meaning & which I have endeavored to turn to account by raising to Our Blessed Mother of the *'Immaculate Conception'* an edifice worthy of Her, & which is not half finished. It is of Gothic structure, about 150 feet by 75 with clerestory. . . ."[34] O'Keefe was obviously intent on making a statement to those who had burned his church. The dedication of his new church on October 2, 1858, was designed to make sure Norfolk knew Catholics were there to stay. Bishop McGill consecrated the altars and dedicated the church, and Bishop Patrick Lynch of Charleston preached.[35] O'Keefe had made his statement. In 1991, Pope John Paul II would name St. Mary of the Immaculate Conception a minor basilica.

After the Civil War broke out, O'Keefe was named a brigade chaplain in the Confederate Army, a position that did not necessitate leaving his parish. When Union forces occupied Norfolk in May 1862, he refused to obey the orders of the notorious General Benjamin Butler to have all the church bells rung in honor of the Union victory. When the city settled down to Reconstruction, O'Keefe saw the opportunity of influencing the broader culture through the print media and lent money to Michael Glennon, an Irish immigrant, parishioner and Confederate veteran, to purchase the city's newspaper, *The Virginian*. He also enjoyed prominence in non-Catholic circles. On May 19, 1875, he officiated at the marriage of Mary Pinckney Hardy, daughter of a cotton merchant, and Captain Arthur MacArthur, U.S.A. Supposedly, no Protestant minister would officiate at the marriage of a Virginia woman and a Yankee of-

33. Cornelius M. Buckley, S.J., trans., *A Frenchman, A Chaplain, A Rebel: The War Letters of Père Louis-Hippolyte Gache, S.J.* (Chicago: Loyola University Press, 1981), pp. 62–63.

34. Archives of the Irish College, Rome, 1983: O'Keefe to Kirby, Norfolk, July 8, 1857.

35. ADR, McGill, "Record," pp. 13–14: Oct. 2–10, 1858.

ficer. For that matter, "Pinky's" two brothers, who had fought under Lee, likewise refused to attend.[36] O'Keefe seems to have had no difficulty in presiding at the marriage of two Protestants, whose son, Douglas, later achieved such great military fame.

Before the Civil War, O'Keefe had personally paid the tuition for two seminarians at the Irish College in Rome. After the war, he opened his own seminary in Norfolk. By 1872, he had been nominated as a bishop at least once. James Gibbons, who had become Bishop of Richmond in 1872, thought he would make a good successor to Bishop Whelan of Wheeling, because he was a "good financier," "his moral record is above suspicion," and "his natural sternness of character is calculated to inspire the clergy with more than affection for him."[37] It was precisely O'Keefe's financial acumen, however, that brought about his downfall.

Complaints against O'Keefe began surfacing just before Gibbons was transferred to Baltimore in 1877. Sister Mary Alice Thomas, superior of St. Mary's Orphanage in Norfolk, claimed O'Keefe was deflecting the orphanage collection of his parish to pay off the church debt.[38] Gibbons's seeming sympathy with her complaint ended his friendship with O'Keefe. When John J. Keane succeeded Gibbons in Richmond, yet other issues came to the fore. James Behan, a wealthy Irish-born businessman in Norfolk, had left property in Norfolk for the Jesuits eventually to build a college. The Jesuits, in turn, delegated O'Keefe to administer the property. Then a parishioner charged that, though the property should have been exempt because it was intended for a college, O'Keefe had failed to pay the taxes, and the city of Norfolk was about to take possession of it.[39] The Jesuit superior in Baltimore, however, assured Keane that the province paid any bills O'Keefe sent and that his "dealings with Fr O'Keefe have been satisfactory."[40] O'Keefe claimed that this particular accuser was Behan's cousin, R. Devereux Doyle, whose family had "squandered" what it had received from Behan's will and now relied on "the well-known hostility of the people of Virginia to the Jesuits" to ap-

36. Records of St. Mary's Parish, May 19, 1875. William Manchester, *American Caesar* (Boston: Little, Brown, and Company, 1978), p. 38. Manchester, unfortunately, does not mention the fact that a Catholic priest officiated at the wedding.

37. AAB, 41S5: Gibbons to Bayley, Richmond, July 22, 1874.

38. ADR, Diocesan Diary, p. 83: Jan. 20, 1879.

39. ADR, J. C. Carroll to Keane, Norfolk, Jan. 8, 1879.

40. ADR, McGurk to Keane, Loyola College, Baltimore, Jan. 9, 1879.

propriate the property for themselves by filing "suit in our Norfolk Courts."[41]

In the meantime, Sister Mary Alice had again protested that the asylum could no longer be maintained, because of O'Keefe's "indifference." In January 1879, Keane went to Norfolk personally to discuss the future of the asylum.[42] At this point, the issue seemed to be a personality conflict between Sister Mary Alice and O'Keefe. A solution to that problem seemed to be reached in March 1879, when Sister Euphemia, the superior of the Daughters of Charity in Emmitsburg, informed Keane that she was replacing Sister Mary Alice with Sister Mary Augustine Wilson, who, she trusted, "will succeed in pleasing Father O'Keefe."[43] At the end of May, the transfer took place, at which point, Keane recorded, Sister Mary Alice "astonished the community by putting off her habit."[44] Sister Mary Alice's removal now melded with the broader issue of O'Keefe's business practices.

A man of simple personal tastes, O'Keefe rented a room for himself and leased the rectory to two nieces of the late Archbishop Martin J. Spalding of Baltimore to pay the debt on his church. When they fell arrears in their rent, he evicted them. This prompted Doyle to tell Keane that it was a "sacrilege to say Father" in reference to O'Keefe. He linked together the eviction of the two nieces and "the removal of that noble Christian woman & refined lady, Sr Mary Alice," which had merely "intensified the bad feeling already entertained of him by the majority of the congregation." Doyle now demanded O'Keefe's removal.[45] Instead, Keane forwarded this correspondence to O'Keefe, who paid Doyle a visit accompanied by his lawyer and a friend. Doyle then demanded that Keane appoint an investigator or refer the matter to Gibbons. Moreover, since Keane had passed on his letter to O'Keefe, he now demanded to see O'Keefe's letters to the bishop.[46]

During the spring of 1879, the feud continued to heat up. O'Keefe dismissed Doyle's complaints with the comment: "I could not have be-

---

41. AAB, 81K7: O'Keefe to Keane, Norfolk, July 3, 1886 (copy).
42. ADR, Diocesan Diary, p. 83: Jan. 20, 1879.
43. ADR, Mother Euphemia to Keane, St. Joseph's, March 17, 1879.
44. ADR, Diocesan Diary, p. 89: May 30, 1879.
45. ADR, R. Devereux Doyle to Keane, Norfolk, April 5, 1879.
46. ADR, Doyle to Keane, Norfolk, April 17, 1879.

lieved that a being in the form of man such as he could have existed claiming a drop of Irish blood. <u>He has been proved a willful, self-convicted slanderer & base coward."[47]</u> At this juncture, and while the suit over the Jesuit property was pending, Keane paid a second visit to the warring parties to discuss all of O'Keefe's financial dealings. O'Keefe complained that he had to stand by in silence as the bishop listened passively to Doyle's unfounded charges about his financial activities. Instead of defending O'Keefe, Keane ordered him to sell his real estate within three years and cease his business activities. A further complication in the story: one of the Doyle women was married to the brother of Sister Isidore, director of St. Vincent's Hospital, which O'Keefe later claimed was the center of a conspiracy against him.[48] Keane, in the meantime, had succeeded in having all the Norfolk church property vested in his name.

O'Keefe seems to have tried to comply with Keane's orders to cease his business ventures, but he ran into difficulties. Early in 1882, he reported that a lien on his property prevented him from conveying it to a new purchaser within the three years he had promised.[49] Keane then granted the first of several extensions of time within which he was to sell his property. O'Keefe's principal difficulty seems to have been that he was using his own property as collateral to purchase property for the church or to pay off his church debt. But the attacks continued. In March 1885, Keane received an anonymous letter accusing O'Keefe of being engaged in "business" and of being the "real owner" of *The Virginian*. The priest again defended himself and pointed out that he had helped Michael Glennon financially in purchasing the newspaper. He now promised to do away with all "business" affairs.[50]

Keane's next action raised the controversy to a new level. On January 3, 1886, he transferred O'Keefe to St. Patrick's in Richmond, effective at the beginning of February. He added:

> In the meantime, you will put the business and accounts of the parish in good shape for your successor, Father [John] Doherty.

47. ADR, O'Keefe to Keane, Norfolk, May 3, 1879.
48. ADR, O'Keefe to Keane, Norfolk, May 6, 1879; AAB, 81K7: O'Keefe to Keane, Norfolk, July 3, 1886 (copy).
49. ADR, O'Keefe to Keane, Norfolk, Jan. 18, 1882.
50. ADR, O'Keefe to Keane, Norfolk, March 30, 1885.

Please give due notice to the present occupants of the pastoral residence, that it may be vacated for the use of the priests as early as
possible.

Father Doherty leaves St. Patrick's parish in very good condition. You will have an ample field for your zeal, can have a more
peaceful life than for years past, and will be near at hand to aid me
with your experience as one of my counselors.[51]

O'Keefe responded that he acquiesced "promptly & fully in your arrangements as regards Norfolk and shall be most happy to facilitate in
every way possible the entre of my esteemed friend Fr. Doherty on his
duties." In regard to being transferred to Richmond, however, he retort-
ed that "I beg leave to say that my future happiness must be consulted
on that point, and I now feel convinced that my future peace of mind
can be attained only by seeking occupation elsewhere." He planned on
applying to Gibbons for readmission to Baltimore, for which he had been
ordained, or, if refused, to apply elsewhere. He had, in the meantime,
ordered the tenants out of the residence.[52]

O'Keefe then visited Keane in Richmond. He argued that he could
not wind up his personal business by February "without occasioning
scandalous accusations." He therefore asked to postpone his departure
until September 1, at which point, as Keane recorded it, "he said he
would willingly leave the Diocese & return to the Archdiocese if accepted."[53] Keane then informed Gibbons that O'Keefe wished his departure
to be without notoriety in order "to represent his return to his own diocese as an act solely depending on his own volition and the kind good
will of his Archbishop as well as of the Bishop of the Diocese in which he
had been working."[54]

For more than thirty-four years, O'Keefe had been an admirable
pastor. In his annual report for 1885—which he did not send until May
of 1886—he listed 1,200 people in the parish with 6,000–7,000 com-
munions. His parish societies included the Living Rosary, St. Patrick's
Benevolent Society, St. Augustine's, Emerald Beneficent Society, and the

51. ADR, Keane to O'Keefe. Richmond, Jan. 3, 1886 (copy).
52. ADR, O'Keefe to Keane, Norfolk, Jan. 8, 1886.
53. Ibid., Keane's notation.
54. AAB, 80C6: Keane to Gibbons, Richmond, Jan. 16, 1886.

Children of Mary.[55] He did not, however, list Keane's favorite, the Sodality of the Holy Ghost.

In May 1886, yet another charge was made against O'Keefe. He had dismissed from his employ a woman he suspected of theft. She now complained to Keane that O'Keefe owed her money.[56] O'Keefe's reaction was strong. First, he was angry that Keane had basically charged him with "perjury" in regard to Doyle's earlier accusations. Now, he was bitter that Keane was accepting the accusations of a servant woman. Such actions, he thought, revealed Keane's true character, for "it is not the reptile who has been warmed by his benefactor that seeks to sting, but it is the poor worm that instinctively writhes when pressure makes the pain almost unendurable, in my case." He assured Keane that there was no danger of scandal, since he had given little cause for it for over thirty-four years.[57]

O'Keefe's departure from Norfolk was now becoming public and was jeopardizing the sale of his property. In early July, he reproached Keane that, within three weeks of their January meeting in Richmond, some Catholics were reporting he was being ordered to leave. In the meantime, word of his removal had spread beyond Virginia, and he had received letters from priests around the country pledging their support and from editors promising they "will make it hotter for you than during the Plenary Council." He was now appealing to Gibbons as the metropolitan for "redress from an unjustifiable aggression on these rights, beginning years ago, and culminating January of this year. This course is now forced on me."

He then narrated at length the painful history of his experiences with Keane as Bishop of Richmond, which seemed to denigrate his own heroic service during the Yellow Fever epidemic, his fight against the Know Nothings, his refusal to accept any salary until the debt on his church was paid off, and the support he had received from Archbishops Kenrick and Spalding and Bishops McGill and Gibbons.[58]

Gibbons, who had in the meantime been named a cardinal, now be-

55. ADR, O'Keefe to Keane, Norfolk, May 31, 1886.
56. ADR, Helen A. Schoenfeld to Keane, Norfolk, Richmond, May 4, 1886.
57. ADR, O'Keefe to Keane, Norfolk, May 10, 1886.
58. AAB, 81K7: O'Keefe to Keane, Norfolk, July 3, 1886 (copy).

came personally involved in the case. In July, he met with O'Keefe in Baltimore and recommended that Keane grant him another six months to put his affairs in order. He accepted O'Keefe's argument that the accusation that he was being ordered to leave Norfolk made it difficult to sell his property by September.[59] A week later, O'Keefe formally sought Gibbons's intervention and protection against Keane's "unjust and uncanonical proceeding." Sending Gibbons a copy of his earlier letter to Keane detailing his grievances, he pointed out that, other than three times Keane had received complaints from his creditors, he had never been charged with anything. His own property had been the basis of his credit and he had always used it for the good of the church. He therefore blamed Keane, for the demand to sell his property all at once had depreciated its value. He had vindicated himself in regard to the complaints of his creditors, but then Keane "by an arrogant assumption of authority over my private affairs, dictated an order which no law, human or divine could justify, but which has been to me ever since the bane of my life."[60]

The same day, O'Keefe wrote to Keane with further demands. Keane responded that at their last meeting a few weeks earlier, he had "expressed to you my surprise and sorrow that your approaching departure from Norfolk was already known & commented." He had himself heard it as far away as New York, but had "mentioned it to no one besides my vicar general & Fr. Doherty." O'Keefe had also demanded an ecclesiastical trial on the basis of the instruction of Propaganda in 1878 and threatened to take his case personally to Cardinal Giovanni Simeoni, prefect of the Congregation of Propaganda in Rome. To this, Keane replied:

> Your reference to . . . [the] *Instructio* [of 1878] is entirely outside of the question; it has no application to cases like the present, as you might have seen from the very first paragraph of the Responsio S. Congis. from which you also quote.
>
> Being fully assured, after careful consultation with the best authorities in Rome, that I have acted all along in entire accordance

59. ADR, O'Keefe to Keane, Baltimore, July 4, 1886.
60. ADR, O'Keefe to Gibbons, Norfolk, July 11, 1886.

with law, I am quite content to await his Eminence's decision on your appeal. Meantime, you will please bear in mind that the effect of such appeal is not *in suspensivo,* but *in devolutivo.* (See Third Plen. Council n. 286.)[61]

As the tension between Keane and O'Keefe was heating up, Gibbons' cooler counsel prevailed. On July 22, he summoned O'Keefe by telegraph to meet him in Baltimore. There, he told the priest he would not accept his appeal. O'Keefe "bore the disappointment with good grace," Gibbons informed Keane, as he recommended that O'Keefe be granted a further extension of a year, to July 22, 1887, to put his affairs in order. O'Keefe had, the cardinal continued, laid down "only one condition, or rather I should say injunction, because its breach though regrettable, would not in my judgment, destroy the compact, viz: that the arrangement be kept a secret. I promised on my part to observe it." Gibbons recommended that Keane accept the agreement, for "if you decline, my impression is that he might either ask a trial, or bring his case to Rome."[62]

Keane accepted Gibbons' arrangements "without comment." The delay in O'Keefe's departure, he thought, "is not too much to pay for peace." Since he would soon become rector of the newly established Catholic University of America, he wanted to avoid "future quibbling on his part, and to make the condition practicable for myself or my successor." He was only concerned that his telling Doherty to go to Norfolk and another priest to replace Doherty in Richmond "not . . . be construed into breach of [the] secrecy" that O'Keefe demanded. O'Keefe was, furthermore, not to use the alleged depreciation of his property as an argument for further delay and was not to make any derogatory statements about Keane.[63] O'Keefe acquiesced and told Gibbons that only necessity kept him in Norfolk.[64] The letter was "entirely satisfactory," Gibbons told Keane, congratulating him "on the successful termination of an unpleasant affair."[65]

61. ADR, Keane to O'Keefe, Fortress Monroe, July 16, 1886 (copy also sent to Gibbons).

62. ADR, Gibbons to Keane, Baltimore, July 22, 1886.

63. ADR, Keane to Gibbons, Fortress Monroe, July 25, 1886 (copy).

64. ADR, O'Keefe to Gibbons, Norfolk, July 31, 1886.

65. ADR, Gibbons to Keane, Baltimore, Aug. 3, 1886.

The painful episode ending O'Keefe's service to Norfolk ironically occurred just as Keane held the Second Synod of Richmond, which promulgated the decrees of the Third Plenary Council but did not yet establish which parishes would have irremovable rectors. Had St. Mary's in Norfolk enjoyed the right of irremovability, O'Keefe could not have been removed or transferred without a formal trial. But Keane was still worried that O'Keefe might appeal to Rome. Here, he relied on Denis O'Connell, priest of Richmond, rector of the American College in Rome, and Gibbons's protege. Ordained in 1877, O'Connell had extremely limited pastoral experience before Gibbons summoned him in 1883 to help prepare for the Third Plenary Council. After inquiring if Propaganda had received an appeal from O'Keefe, O'Connell informed Keane that Archbishop Domenico Jacobini, the secretary of the congregation,

> said "he [O'Keefe] will have to go to the Archbishop of Balto. first." Then he asked me about the particulars of the case and I informed him. "Oh pshaw!" he replied, "it is only about a transfer, he can do nothing." I hope Father O'Keefe for his own sake will not make the mistake, for I wish him well. It only shows how delusive were all hopes of his being able to alter his course in Norfolk. I hope your health is very good and that the priests are well.[66]

In a few years, O'Connell would play an active role in the restoration to the Church of Father Edward McGlynn, but his attitude then was not so much to support priests' rights as to embarrass Archbishop Michael A. Corrigan of New York.

From the end of October 1886 to early June 1887, Keane was in Rome working for the approval of the Catholic University and other issues. On July 12, 1887, he formally released O'Keefe from service in Norfolk to go to Baltimore.[67] O'Keefe was then fifty-nine years old, having begun work in Norfolk at the age of twenty-four. Although ten years later he again attempted to have himself restored to Norfolk so that he could voluntarily resign, he was to pass the remaining years of his life in Baltimore, where he was editor of *The Catholic Mirror* and later founded a parish on a hill in Towson, Maryland, a suburb of Baltimore. It was

66. ADR, D. J. O'Connell to Keane, Rome, Aug. 22, 1886.
67. AAB, 83B9, Keane to Gibbons, Richmond, July 12, 1887.

named the Immaculate Conception and was built in a French Gothic revival style, reminiscent of his beloved St. Mary's of the Immaculate Conception in Norfolk. He died in January 1906, the last surviving brigade
chaplain of the Confederate Army. The newspapers recalled his being
awarded the Legion of Honor by Emperor Louis Napoleon of France for
his care of men stricken with Yellow Fever on a French frigate in 1869.[68]
They also reported his frugal life to the end—he ate only one meal a day,
at noon. He was buried in his Towson church with the Confederate battle flag and the flags of Maryland and Virginia.[69]

Like the case of Timothy O'Brien in Richmond thirty-five years earlier, that of O'Keefe is ambiguous. Had he been so long in Norfolk that
he regarded himself as autonomous? Had he made bad financial
arrangements? Or was he the victim of false accusations about his business successes, over which Keane simply did not want to alienate one of
the most prominent families in Norfolk? O'Keefe's papers are, unfortunately, not extant, so there is no way accurately to determine the support he claimed to have. Unlike O'Brien, who had substantial docu-
mented support from Richmond's most prominent Catholics, no such
evidence for lay support exists in Keane's meager papers—Keane later
destroyed the bulk of his papers that could have included such material.
Nor did there seem to be any concern raised about him among the other
priests. Whatever the truth, O'Keefe's departure from Norfolk marked
the end of an era in Norfolk and a dark cloud over the end of Keane's
episcopacy in Richmond.

The two cases reported here are of course quite different, but they
bore striking similarities to each other. Both stemmed from Virginia's
laws regarding ownership of church property. Both O'Brien and O'Keefe
used their own personal wealth to purchase additional property for their
respective churches. From the available evidence, O'Keefe seems to have
taken this policy further by using his own property as collateral for the
purchase of more. Both were accused of accumulating personal wealth,
but the evidence does not substantiate this. Both are tragic cases, but that
of O'Keefe is more so: though he had once been considered an apt candi-

---

68. *Baltimore Sun*, editorial, Jan. 29, 1906, p. 6.
69. Ibid., Feb. 1, 1906, p. 14.

date for the episcopacy, his superiors—first Gibbons and then Keane—turned against him because of vague charges from his enemies. Both illustrate a forgotten aspect of American Catholic history—Irish priests who came to the United States not to make their fortune but to devote their wealth to the welfare of their people on the American mission.

Charles Edwards O'Neill, S.J.

4. JESUITS IN THE SOUTHERN USA

*Organizational and Structural Development of the
New Orleans Mission of the Society of Jesus*

Jesuits of the South did mission work as auxiliaries in support of planting the Church in the southeastern portion of the USA. In the nineteenth century the New Orleans Mission, studied here, drew its members mainly from France and Ireland; the locally born were a minority. Southern Jesuit missionaries taught at Grand Coteau and New Orleans in Louisiana, and at Spring Hill in Alabama. Jesuit activity, though, was more parish-oriented than the Society's service in other parts of the nation. The missionaries set up parishes where there were none, and they preached in established parishes where they were invited for parish missions. Outreach to the South's non-Catholic majority and to the Native Peoples was dreamed of, but the missionaries' preoccupation with Catholic immigrants and their descendants set limits to such ministry. In Atlanta, the South's large, pivotal city, the New Orleans Mission of the Society of Jesus never took root, but its parishes in smaller Georgia cities were long cared for by the New Orleans Province. This chapter will examine the history of the organizational and structural development of the Mission which helped in the building of the Catholic Church in America.

The Society of Jesus had hardly been restored by Pope Pius VII in

1814 when Louis-Guillaume DuBourg, the new bishop of New Orleans, asked the pope to help him get Jesuits for his diocese. The bishop, as Pius VII wrote to Superior General Tadeusz Brzozowski in October of 1815, "strongly hopes to establish in his diocese clerics of the Society of Jesus, and by their ministry bring the light of the gospel to the large number of infidels who inhabit the diocese." The pope explained that "to obtain this goal [Bishop DuBourg] would like to bring with him two priests of the Society and five or six novices so that by their work the Society can be spread there, and one or more colleges be established in the diocese."[1] Pius VII asked Brzozowski to grant DuBourg, if possible, members of the Society of Jesus who were judged apt and who were willing to dedicate themselves to this work. Obedience, however, faltered on the phrase *if possible*. The restored Society simply had no one to send with DuBourg. Then a decade later, in the summer of 1826, DuBourg, discouraged for various reasons, resigned the see of New Orleans and was soon after named to a see in France.[2]

Meanwhile, thanks to Sulpician DuBourg, Flemish Jesuits, who had entered the USA via Maryland, had reached the city of St. Louis in "Upper Louisiana," where Bishop Joseph Rosati, a Vincentian who succeeded DuBourg, preferred to live rather than in turbulent New Orleans. When the diocese was divided in two, Rome granted Rosati the see of St. Louis, but he had to administer the see of New Orleans on into 1830.

Jan Roothaan, elected superior general of the Society of Jesus in 1829, was convinced of the Louisiana idea by Antoine Blanc, who became bishop of New Orleans in 1835, and Pierre Ladavière, the Jesuit missionary who had experience in Louisiana. In 1836 Roothaan instructed François Renault, the Paris Jesuit provincial superior, to provide the personnel.[3] In reply Renault let Roothaan know that, to some who saw only the surface of things, it seemed as though the Roman order to send men to Louisiana would hurt apostolates already established;

1. Oct. 16, 1815, Castel Gandolfo, R. de Martinis, ed., *Ius Pontificium de Propaganda Fide*, Romae, 1891, IV, 533–34. Annabelle Melville, *Louis William DuBourg, Bishop of Louisiana and the Floridas, Bishop of Montauban, and Archbishop of Besançon, 1766–1833* (2 vols. w. contin. pag'n: Chicago, 1986), 341–43.

2. Melville, *DuBourg*, 730, 748.

3. Thomas H. Clancy, "The Antebellum Jesuits of the New Orleans Province, 1837–1861," *Louisiana History* 34 (1993): 328.

nonetheless, Renault reported, he had a group of four, picked out by mid-August of 1836. Two or three of them even knew a little English. With varying degrees of competence they could teach or prefect in a school. Among them, of course, was the valiant and valuable veteran La- davière, who had been with Blanc in Rome. In Renault's view, Nicolas Point should come down from Kentucky to be superior in Louisiana; as for Point himself, he would have preferred to go on mission to the Na- tive Peoples.[4]

When the little band of French Jesuits sailed into the port city of New Orleans and awaited the opportunity to set up their college in the countryside, they engaged in pastoral ministry, particularly among the sick in hospitals. In 1837 they established their school for boys on land given by the Smith family in Grand Coteau, Louisiana—between Lafayette and Opelousas—where the religious of the Sacred Heart of Je- sus had a school for girls. The selection of the site caused debate then and later among Jesuits; the new foundation did not begin easily.[5] Roothaan, after hearing the unanimous opinion of the Paris provincial superior and his Consultors, joined the French mission in Louisiana onto the Belgians' Missouri Mission. The Grand Coteau missionaries, even though their complaints had occasioned the change, were not happy with the superior general's decision. Yet they were responsible for it be- cause, few as they were, they had reported discord among themselves; for example, Father Rector Point, the future missionary to the north- western Native Peoples, was accused of asperity of manner.[6] The Grand Coteau Jesuits had furthermore insisted on their need of English-speak- ers, which in fact the Missouri Mission could provide. Superiors in Paris and Rome judged that the simplest solution to the problems was to join the little group in Louisiana to the more numerous Missouri Mission.

The union, however, did not engender harmony and efficiency. The

4. Joseph Burnichon, S.J., *La Compagnie de Jésus en France. Histoire d'un siècle*, 4 vols. (Paris, 1914-22), 3:301. [Conrad Widman S.I.], "Historia Missionis Neo-Aure- lianensis," [II] 49–51, Archives of the New Orleans Province of the Society of Jesus [henceforth ANOPSJ], A1.A2.H9/Z.1G. Cornelius M. Buckley, S.J., *Nicolas Point, S.J.: His Life & Northwest Indian Chronicles* (Chicago, 1989), 115.

5. [Widman], "Historia Missionis Neo-Aurelianensis," [II] 47, ANOPSJ, A1.A2.H9/Z.1G.

6. Buckley, *Point*, 136 and 164.

Missourians were mainly Flemish, who learned English readily. The Louisiana missionaries were French, whose language sufficed for their work in southwest Louisiana. The city of St. Louis, moreover, was the gateway to the West; so even though steamboats might go up and down the Mississippi River, it was hard for the Missouri superior to focus attention on bucolic Grand Coteau, the Deep South's only Jesuit center. Finally, in 1847, Roothaan, in response to further information and new appeals for Jesuit presence in the southern part of the USA, detached the southern states from Missouri's administration and confided the newly created New Orleans Mission to the newly created Lyons Province. Jean-Baptiste Maisounabe was chosen to be superior of the Mission; he was the intelligent rector of the scholasticate at Vals-près-le-Puy.[7]

Maisounabe, who entered the USA by the port of New York, was a vigorous personality. He quickly confirmed the arrangement worked out by another Jesuit with the Bishop of Mobile regarding Spring Hill College, although Maisounabe himself said he would not have drafted such a contract.[8] (The letter from Lyons saying to wait for Maisounabe arrived too late.) He accepted the given situation of the Mission but expressed unhappy surprise that his predecessors had ever chosen Grand Coteau as the site of their college; he acquired property in the city of New Orleans and launched a new collège. Aware of the need of English-speaking Jesuits, he begged insistently for recruits from the English Jesuit Province. Also Maisounabe formed the Louisiana corporation that continued to be the legal entity of the future New Orleans Province of the Society of Jesus.[9] As a zealous priest, Maisounabe wanted to minister to the victims of yellow fever. Disregarding the warnings of veterans as well as of the local bishop, he re-entered New Orleans in the dangerous season; he died in September of 1848 at the age of 43, a mere fourteen months after his arrival in the Mission. His successor was Father Visitor John Cambiaso.[10] While Louis/Aloysius Curioz was Mission superior, Felix Sopranis,

---

7. C. Boulanger to Roothaan, Nov. 22, 1834, Archivum Romanum Societatis Iesu [henceforth ARSI], Francia, 1003, x, p. 16. ANOPSJ, Maisounabe Diary, July 6, 1847. The diary lists the letters he wrote. Burnichon, 3:302.

8. ANOPSJ, Maisounabe Diary, Aug. 3, 1847.

9. ANOPSJ, Maisounabe Diary, Aug. 21, 1848, and Feb. 28, 1848.

10. ANOPSJ, Maisounabe Diary, Aug. 20, 1847, and Aug. 18, 1848. The last entry is Sept. 4, 1848, a week before he died. Burnichon, 3:302. Clancy, p. 330. [J. B.

who had been provincial superior of Rome and then Assistant for Italy, was sent as Visitor for the entire USA, and came to the South in the winter of 1860–61.

The secession of the southern states and the Civil War (1861–65) gravely worsened the problems of the still insecure New Orleans Mission. In 1862 when Union Navy Captain David Farragut threatened to bombard New Orleans and when Union Army General Benjamin Butler occupied the city, the French consul intervened in behalf of the thousands of French nationals and their property.[11] So the French Jesuit missionaries, like their compatriots, could fly France's tricolor over their church and school. But the Federal occupation of New Orleans cut off the Mission superior from Spring Hill College at Mobile in Alabama and from St. Charles College at Grand Coteau in Louisiana. The war blockade delayed the arrival of the letters of Father General Pieter Beckx; among them was the letter that granted Curioz's request for release from the Mission superiorship and named Antoine Jourdant his successor.[12] Subsequently Rome and New Orleans agreed that until the end of hostilities no effort should be made in regard to changes usually effected according to the customary terms of office of local superiors.

Missionaries of the New Orleans Mission ministered to the troops of the Confederate States of America. Darius Hubert, who had blessed the new flag at the declaration of Louisiana's secession, remained a Louisiana hero long years after the end of the war. In Baton Rouge the Union occupation authorities became suspicious of Father Frédéric Larnaudie and interned him. The superior of the Mission came to his defense. When Beckx was informed of the incident, he counselled prudence lest offense be given.[13]

The war prevented younger Jesuits in the CSA from pursuing their studies in the USA; indeed, the wartime battlefront and blockade of ports made all travel virtually impossible. A Jesuit Visitor had decided on

Goetstouwers, S.J.], *Synopsis historiae Societatis Jesu* (Louvain, 1950), cols. 633, 636, and 700.

11. Charles E. O'Neill, S.J., "The Fall of Confederate New Orleans," in Gerald J. Eberle, ed., *Loyola University Studies in the Humanities* (New Orleans, 1962), 7.

12. Beckx to Curioz, Jan. 18, 1862, ARSI, Mission. Assist. Gall., I, 15–16. Beckx to Jourdant, Aug. 30, 1862, ARSI, ibid., 77–78.

13. Beckx to Jourdant, Oct. 20, 1863, ARSI, ibid., 191.

the closing of the inchoate philosophate at Spring Hill College; the Mission superior repeatedly but in vain asked Rome to let it resume functioning. Right after the end of the war Mission Superior Jourdant shipped three scholastics off to France for their studies.[14]

In 1864, before the end of the war, the superior general approved a local house treasurer's proposal to exchange legally but at a great loss all the Confederate money he could. The end of the war brought relief but also financial disaster. Confederate paper money was worthless.[15]

When peace came, regular correspondence resumed. In 1865 Francis de Sales Gautrelet received his requested rest at the end of sixteen years as rector of Spring Hill College.[16] He got his replacement and a new job, but three years later he was named Mission superior; little did Gautrelet realize that he would hold that post for the next twelve years. In 1870 he went to his native France to beg for men and money. Not surprisingly for the time, he did not travel on to Rome. Anti-Jesuit feeling was so intense in Rome, capital now of the united Italian kingdom, that the Jesuit superior general and his aides moved to Fiesole near Florence in 1873.

By 1879 a diffused malaise was being felt in the New Orleans Mission of the Lyons Province Jesuits. Various complaints were being heard; for example, that the French missionaries and superiors in the Mission were too European and too Continental, were not open enough to cultural adaptation, and were too little American in mentality, policy, and comportment. Governance remained in the hands of those who were looked upon as forming an Old Guard. Mission Superior Gautrelet, who as was the custom doubled as rector of the New Orleans college, was 65 years of age and had been in the Mission for 32 years; he was generally esteemed, but he had been in office for 10 years. The two rectors—of St. Charles College in Grand Coteau, Louisiana, and Spring Hill College near Mobile, Alabama—were French missionary veterans in their fifties, but, given the briefer life span in mid-nineteenth century, the age of 50 seemed older then than it seemed in the late twentieth century. During 1877 and 1878 the number of scholastics and novices in the Mission had

14. Beckx to Jourdant, May 25, 1865, ARSI, ibid., 307–8.
15. Beckx to Abbadie, Aug. 16, 1864, ARSI, ibid., 249–50.
16. Beckx to Gautrelet, Sept. 22, 1865, ARSI, ibid., 326–27.

been decimated. The Mission's confidence in the future had been shaken by the recent dismissals, deaths, and departures. The quality of recruits, moreover, and the recruitment policy itself came under sharp questioning in the Mission and in Fiesole. Then too, the Mission in general was without financial resources, for the South's economic woes affected the Jesuit schools, where students were all too few.[17]

The French language had prevailed in the Mission, and the focus of attention had been fixed on New Orleans and French-speaking southwest Louisiana. Young English-speaking Jesuits, whether the few from the USA or the many from Ireland, felt that their presence and views were not attended to sufficiently; also, they thought ill of any missionary in the USA who was not fluent in English. Many of the Irish had done their studies in France, and hence knew both French and English. Nonetheless, as the French critics liked to point out, the Irish missionary had a brogue that marked him as a foreigner. If there was murmuring and dejection in the ranks, there was an air of *fin de régime* among superiors.[18] The Lyons Province, responding to the pope's request, was reinforcing its mission efforts in the Near East. Also, with zeal and élan French missionaries were heading for China and India, for Madagascar and the African continent.

Superior General Beckx, prompted by letters from the New Orleans Mission, especially by the superiors' and Consultors' letters of 1879, asked Gautrelet's reaction to alternative proposals: the sending of an English-speaking Visitor or the naming of an English-language superior for the Mission. Gautrelet and the provincial superior in Lyons both opted for the Visitation. Gautrelet asked Beckx (April 3, 1879) that, since the tension between French and Irish missionaries was one of the key problems, the Visitor be neither French nor Irish. Beckx agreed. He intended that his delegate, the Visitor, not enter New Orleans until after the annual yellow fever threat had passed; any time in October would be safe. Actually, it was only at the end of the year of 1879 that Beckx chose Thomas O'Neil, who had just completed six years as provincial superior of the neighboring Missouri Province. The superior general

17. Beckx to Benausse, June 17, 1868, ARSI, ibid., 489.
18. Beckx to Gautrelet, March 9, 1879, ARSI, ibid., II, p. 188.

thought, as he later explained, that he was naming a native-born Mid-westerner. What escaped his notice at the time was the fact that Thomas O'Neil, however many years he may have spent in the USA, had been born in Ballydavid, County Tipperary, Ireland.[19]

Once on the scene the Visitor heard the already mentioned complaints; it was probably easier for this English-speaking, Irish-born, resident Missourian to appreciate the viewpoint of those who were ill at ease under French leadership. As in many a Visitation in the history of the Society of Jesus, O'Neil changed superiors. Within a few weeks after his arrival in the Mission he had made his choices, and he obtained the superior general's approval. As Mission superior, Ireland-born Theobald Butler succeeded France-born Francis Gautrelet. Ireland-born John Downey succeeded France-born Dominique Beaudequin as rector of Spring Hill College. The French missionaries retained the other rectorship; in French-speaking southwest Louisiana, Jean Montillot became the head of St. Charles College. During a two-week period, April 28 to May 10, 1880, these rectors and the superiors of three small residences had been changed.[20] Thus O'Neil had made a clean sweep of superiors.

The Irish missionaries had won a victory, and some of them did not mind cheering.[21] The French, however, felt unappreciated, wounded, humiliated. Even the fine new rector of Grand Coteau, a veteran of thirty years in the Mission, felt so crushed that he asked the superior general's permission to return to France, but Beckx persuaded Montillot to stay on in the area and look to the future.[22] The Visitation was soon over, and Visitor O'Neil left, warned by Beckx to move out before the summer heat could hurt his health. (The mosquito was as yet unknown as the real fever-transmitter.)

Beckx, although he insisted on the need for the Visitation and the changes it effected, came close to apologizing to the French for the hurt caused by the reported tactlessness of his Visitor. The superior general

19. Rufus Mendizabal, S.I., ed., *Catalogus defunctorum in renata Societate Iesu* (Rome, 1972), p. 169, #9.396.

20. [Widman], "Historia Missionis Neo-Aurelianensis," [I], 285, ANOPSJ, A1.A2.H9./Z1.G. *Catalogus Sociorum et Officiorum Missionis Neo-Aurelianensis Societatis Iesu ineunte anno MDCCCLXXXII*, pp. 1, 7, 10, 14.

21. Holaind to Anderledy, April 29, 1886, ARSI, Miss. Neo-Aur. 1003, I-4.

22. Beckx to Montillot, Nov. 23, 1880, ARSI, Prov. Neo-Aur., I, p. 2.

encouraged the French missionaries to stay at their posts and to hope for the best. He counselled Mission Superior Butler "to pour balm on the wound made by the very painful amputation which, all things considered, had been judged necessary."[23]

What to do with the separated mission remained, however, a structural problem that had to be solved. The superior general in Fiesole and the provincial superior in Lyons leaned toward simply integrating it into the Missouri Province. Yet an alternative proposal was also on the table, namely, that the New Orleans Mission remain apart, with a Mission superior who would be subject to some American provincial, preferably Missouri's, but possibly Maryland–New York's. Missouri, recalling the lack of success of the 1838–1847 union, declined the proffered gift of the New Orleans Mission. Meanwhile Butler and his Consultors opted for a third plan, namely some form of independence. Since the weakness of the Mission precluded the status of province, the only alternative was an entity new to the Jesuit Order's structure, namely the "Independent Mission." The superior general granted this exceptional status in October of 1880; henceforward the superior of the New Orleans Mission would be directly responsible to the superior general. The Independent Mission passed out of the French Assistancy into the English Assistancy, where it joined the two USA provinces of the period, namely Missouri and Maryland–New York.[24]

Butler, the new Mission superior, came from an aristocratic family; as a boy, he had studied at Clongowes Wood, a Jesuit school frequented by the Catholic elite of Ireland. As a young Jesuit he had studied in France and knew French well. He had a reputation of being above the narrow national feeling that troubled the factions in the Mission. His well-mannered respect for the French veteran missionaries was indeed soothing balm on sore wounds.[25] During the eight years of Butler's governance the problem of nationalism abated greatly but did not disappear entirely.

A quite new crisis, though, arose when in 1887 Anton Anderledy asked the New Orleans Mission to accept the British Honduras Mission,

23. Beckx to Butler, Oct. 6, 1880, and Apr. 7, 1881, ARSI, ibid., pp. 1 and 5–6.
24. Beckx to Butler, Oct. 6, 1880, ARSI, ibid., 1.
25. Holaind to Anderledy, Apr. 29, 1886, ARSI, Miss. Neo-Aur. 1003, I-4.

which until then had been the responsibility of the English Province. (When Beckx, who was senile, died in March of 1887, Anderledy, elected in September 1883 as permanent vicar with right of succession, succeeded to the role of superior general. At the time the Society of Jesus did not have legislation that permitted a superior general to resign.) Butler, with the assurance of a superior who had seven years of experience, made a bold response. A mission like British Honduras, he wrote, required chosen men of exceptional fortitude and constancy. The English Province, it was known, had long wanted to get rid of that heavy load, and "to gain its point proposes that Belize be annexed to N[ew] Orleans because of the proximity of the two Missions." Butler continued in his letter to the superior general: "I firmly believe that if your Paternity had a thoroughly correct idea of the state of the question you would not for an instant listen to the proposal of putting an additional burthen on the shoulders of an already overburthened Mission." The Mission superior reported to the superior general that there was unanimous opposition roundabout, for "we are convinced that we have all we can possibly do to take care of ourselves," and that to take on Belize was beyond New Orleans' strength. If the proposal were to be carried out, Butler solemnly wrote to Anderledy, "we would lose all confidence in the Paternal government of the Society." As for the supposed closeness of the two missions, Butler pointed out, steamers left New Orleans for Belize only twice a month and took four or five days to get there. Jesuits in the southern states of the USA, he wrote, looked toward expansion in Texas, Mississippi, Alabama, Florida, Georgia, Tennessee and the Carolinas; they did not, Butler insisted, "take any interest in the European colonies of Central America." Butler bluntly asked Anderledy: "If England with all its resources of men and of money, its 540 members, its 245 Fathers, its rich foundations, its Novitiate, Juniorate & Scholasticate, its steady supply of subjects, &c cannot carry the Belize load, how in the name of good sense, of fair play and common justice can the poor struggling, overburthened Mission of N.O. with its very small number of formed men, its limited resources, without foundations, with very few vocations, with no natural attraction because of warm climate and frequent visits from yellow fever, be asked to assume this burthen?" Butler begged Anderledy in his paternal love not to risk the drowning of the

New Orleans Mission, and to avoid what would appear to be harsh and unfair treatment "merely for the sake of pleasing the English Province."[26] But Butler was worried; four days after the previous strong letter he wrote again to Anderledy on the same themes, for, he said, he feared that "England can exercise more influence at Fiesole" than New Orleans could.[27] (Be it recalled that English Father Robert Whitty was the Assistant in Fiesole for the English Assistancy, to which the New Orleans Mission belonged.)

The Mission Consultors, one by one, in their letters reinforced the Mission superior's plea. One of them, Father Anthony Free, went so far as to express the hope that the British Honduras matter came not from Anderledy himself but rather from some advisors who were aware of their affairs but not of those in the New Orleans Mission.[28]

Anderledy reacted sharply, indeed angrily, telling Butler that his letter on British Honduras was unworthy of a professed father of the Society of Jesus, unless perhaps Butler "had been constituted the judge of [his] superior." Butler was further told that his statements implicitly attacking the English Jesuit superiors were false. Then, after mentioning the word *English,* Anderledy, who had worked in the United States of America and who knew the English language, ordered Butler to remember henceforward the obligation to write to the superior general in *Latin.*[29] Anderledy probably felt he was killing two birds with one stone, for not only would the law be observed but Butler's feisty eloquence would be tempered.

Nevertheless, this storm which menaced New Orleans all during the summer of 1887 had blown over by wintertime. Butler had had his knuckles rapped but his Mission did not have to take on the British Honduras Mission. (Some years later the Missouri Province, which had not wanted the New Orleans Mission, took up organizational responsibility for British Honduras.) During that same summer of 1887 Fiesole directed Butler to separate his office of Mission superior from that of rector of the New Orleans college. When John F. O'Connor was named to that

---

26. Butler to Anderledy, June 20, 1887, ARSI, Miss. Neo-Aur. 1003, I-6.
27. Butler to Anderledy, June 24, 1887, ARSI, Miss. Neo-Aur. 1003, I-8.
28. ARSI, Miss. Neo-Aur. 1003, I-10, -7, -9.
29. Anderledy to Butler, Aug. 7, 1887, ARSI, Prov. Neo-Aur., I, p. 41.

rectorship, he became the New Orleans Mission's first native-born superior.[30] Since Butler was in his eighth year of office, Anderledy was searching for a successor as Mission superior, but he decided first to send a Visitor who could speak in person with all the members of the Mission. The superior general chose as his delegate John Baptist Lessmann, a member of the German Province, who had served ten years as superior of the Buffalo [New York] Mission, and who had just completed "with fruit and consolation" a Visitation of the Canada Mission.[31] Two decades earlier, moreover, Lessmann had made a three-year Visitation of the Missions of Bombay and Madura. Anderledy, who had confidence in Lessmann, also wanted a further report on the British Honduras question.

Lessmann arrived in the New Orleans Mission toward the end of 1887; he spent a few months visiting every house and listening to each individual. He reported that the New Orleans Mission was in better condition than at the time of the O'Neil Visitation. The fires of nationalism, he judged, were down to embers—"under the ashes." The Visitor found no individual who thought that he himself indulged in nationalistic partisanship, but many who reproved or suspected it in others. Lessmann chose never to speak against it in public, but treated the matter only in private. Since the general atmosphere had been improving, the Visitor felt that the spirit of nationalism would in time be extinguished.[32]

Lessman found that Mission Superior Butler was so widely respected and loved that there was no desire for change. Nevertheless, as the superior general pointed out, Butler had been in office for eight years; so it was time for a change. A broad consultation, particularly with veteran French missionaries, even with some who had returned to France, brought in a list of ten names, more therefore than the three needed for the customary *terna*. In the review of these prospects, one consultant mentioned that John O'Shanahan was good-hearted and talented, but criticized him as forgetful and "too Irish."[33] O'Shanahan did not figure among the shorter list of six recommended by Butler and his three Mis-

---

30. Anderledy to Butler, Sept. 24, 1887, ARSI, ibid., p. 43.
31. Anderledy to Butler, Oct. 25, 1887, ARSI, ibid., p. 43.
32. Lessman to Anderledy, Mar. 11, 1888, ARSI, Miss. Neo-Aur. 1003, I-16.
33. Holaind to Anderledy, Apr. 29, 1886, ARSI, Miss. Neo-Aur. 1003, I-4.

sion Consultors. Lessmann, though, ever since he had visited the recently accepted school and church in Galveston, Texas, had been favorably
impressed by the affable, 50-year-old rector O'Shanahan, who, the Visitor thought, gave promise of carrying out whatever the eventual *Memori-
ale* would prescribe. Lessmann, who distinctly prided himself on his rapid assessment of an individual's potential, pressed for the naming of
O'Shanahan. The pros and cons regarding the nominees came out in all
frankness during the official Consultors' meetings. In the end Anderledy
accepted Lessmann's nominee, and in turn O'Shanahan did receive the
support of the Consultors.[34]

Back in Buffalo, Lessmann advised Anderledy that because of circumstances the New Orleans Mission would on some points of the Society's Institute [Rule] "not be conformed easily or in a short time."[35] The
correspondence indicates that the Visitor had in mind the keeping of
parishes, the chaplaining of nuns, and the going out of the house without a fellow Jesuit as companion. Meanwhile Butler, the former superior
of the Mission, was sent to succeed O'Shanahan as rector in Galveston
and to struggle with the weak school he himself had accepted for the
Mission.[36]

O'Shanahan, who was expansive by temperament and in policy,
was ever ready to open a new school or residence. When the Bishop of
St. Augustine, Florida, wanted to give responsibility for south Florida to
the Society of Jesus, O'Shanahan opened the Tampa house in 1889.
When the Bishop of Nashville, Tennessee, proposed opening a school in
his see city, O'Shanahan was in favor. O'Shanahan considered opening
schools in Atlanta, Augusta, and Savannah, where the Georgia bishop
was a great friend of the Jesuits. O'Shanahan scraped up the money to
buy land in uptown New Orleans for further expansion of the Jesuit
apostolate in the namesake city of the Mission. He did, though, turn
down at least one proposal: he said "no" when Archbishop Michael Corrigan of New York offered the Bahama Islands to the New Orleans–based
Jesuits.[37] Meanwhile the superior general reined in the ebullient superi-

34. Lessman to Anderledy, Feb. 4, 1888, ARSI, Miss. Neo-Aur. 1003, I-13. Anderledy to Lessman, Mar. 28, 1888, ARSI, Prov. Neo-Aur., I, pp. 48–49.
35. Lessman to Anderledy, Sept. 9, 1888, ARSI, Miss. Neo-Aur. 1003, I-24.
36. Lessman to Anderledy, May 7, 1888, ibid., I-19.
37. Colman J. Barry, O.S.B., *Worship and Work: Saint John's Abbey and University*

or of the New Orleans Mission. Reports to Fiesole cried financial danger and implied financial imprudence on the part of O'Shanahan. No one denied his charm and graciousness, but continued complaints weakened the superior general's confidence in the judgment of the Mission superior. After only three years in office O'Shanahan received a brief letter from the superior general calling for a *terna* toward choosing his successor. When O'Shanahan sent off the *terna* in September 1891, he told the superior general: "I give you heartfelt thanks for relegating me again to the obscurity I deserve."[38]

To the surprise of the Mission at large, the new Mission superior was 49-year-old Father William Kennely, whom O'Shanahan had brought in as rector of St. Charles College, Grand Coteau, Louisiana. The reason for Kennely's promotion, murmurers claimed, was that he came from the same part of Ireland as O'Shanahan; some maintained that the two were distantly related.[39] Kennely, kind-hearted though he was, was never in good health and seemed unable to cope with the problems he faced. Strong rectors and Consultors judged him severely and thought him inept and unfit for office. His defenders saw him as hemmed in by opponents—for example, those same rectors and Consultors. The defenders also insisted that it was O'Shanahan who had run up the heavy debt, which Kennely was working to pay off at the very time the critics were mistakenly blaming Kennely for creating the debt. On his part, Kennely felt that his opponents in their prejudice and favoritism were blocking the appointments he judged best and would have preferred to make.[40]

As a result Kennely, who tended temperamentally to be morose, withdrew more and more from the struggle. He felt unwell, he got up late, he absented himself from community prayer and recreation. A

1856–1980 (Collegeville, 1980), p. 207. O'Shanahan to Anderledy, Dec. 28, 1888, ARSI, Miss. Neo-Aur. 1003, II-6. McKiniry to Anderledy, Jan. 1, 1891, ibid., II-12. Moore to Carriere, March 25, 1893, ANOPSJ, *Acta S. Sedis & Acta Pot. Eccl.*

38. O'Shanahan to Anderledy, Sept. 13, 1891, ARSI, Miss. Neo-Aur. 1003, II-16.

39. Brislan to Meyer, Feb. 9, 1893, ARSI, Miss. Neo-Aur. 1003, III-13. Arqué to Meyer, Feb. 18, 1893, ARSI, Miss. Neo-Aur. 1003, III-15. At this time Saint Louis–born Rudolf Meyer, of the Jesuit Province of Missouri, was the "English" Assistant to the superior general of the Society of Jesus.

40. Butler to Meyer, Feb. 13, 1893, ARSI, Miss. Neo-Aur. 1003, III-14. O'Connor to Meyer, Jan. 15, 1894, ibid., III-38.

heavy smoker, he did not eat well; for stimulus he took alcoholic beverages. Gossip and letters to authorities marked him as a heavy drinker
who was impeded by alcohol from accomplishing his tasks and improving his health. Although Kennely and others believed that the majority
of southern-USA Jesuits did or would have confidence in him, the constant criticism eroded his courage and self-confidence. So in early 1893
he begged the new superior general to change him and provide a successor as soon as possible.[41]

Neither O'Shanahan nor Kennely was able to provide unifying leadership. Father Alphonse Arqué, a veteran French missionary who returned to France about this time, archly described the New Orleans Mission as "arms and hearts—with no head." Arqué's tone showed that
even in 1893 the nationalism issue was not dead. The malaise, he maintained with mordant humor, was traceable to the Irish Home Rule theory in the Mission: "Every Superior will be Irish, and every Irishman will
be a Superior."[42] Since the majority of Mission members were by this
time Irish, Arqué's criticism shows also his own chauvinism. Arqué's esteem for Butler diluted his acid, but the very fact that the generalate was
inviting selected veterans to analyze the situation showed that, despite
growth in numbers and in apostolates, this mission that wanted to be a
province seemed as yet unable to take care of itself.

In this quandary the superior general again named a Visitor. (Anderledy died in January of 1892; after the election during the General
Congregation [Chapter] held at Loyola, Spain, later in 1892, Father General Luis Martín began moving the Jesuit generalate from Fiesole back to
Rome.) This time the Visitor was John Clayton, who had just completed
a six-year term as provincial superior of the English Province. Clayton
arrived in the New Orleans Mission in November of 1894; he soon began
to hear that, as had happened with previous Visitations, whatever orders
he might leave would not be carried out—in other words, only by stay-
ing could he hope to have them put into practice.[43] With such an idea for

41. Davis to Vic. Gen., June 27, 1892, ARSI, Miss. Neo-Aur. 1003, III-5. Kennely to Martín, March 28, 1893, ibid., III-22.

42. Arqué to Meyer, Feb. 18, 1893, ARSI, Miss. Neo-Aur. 1003, III-15.

43. Clayton to Meyer, Nov. 17 and Dec. 22, 1894, ARSI, Miss. Neo-Aur. 1003,
IV-2 and IV-3. Martin to Kenely, Oct. 4, 1894, ARSI, Prov. Neo-Aur., I, pp. 113-14.

a starter, Martín and Clayton settled down for a long Visitation. After a half year of observing and listening, Clayton urged the superior general to remove Kennely as soon as possible. So the Mission superior was gently eased out of his post for reasons of health, and was assigned to Grand Coteau. As of June 29, 1895, Clayton was made Mission superior as well as Visitor.[44]

At the end of a year in the area, Clayton had formally visited all of the houses. The conclusion he reached was that the Mission should no longer be independent but should be incorporated into the Missouri Province. On December 29, 1895, Clayton wrote for Martín his recommendation and his reasons: "This Mission is composed of very discordant elements. Its members come from nearly every nation of Europe and there will always be factions more or less. They will never pull together and they should be dispersed by being joined to another Province." As an example of the bias he had seen, Clayton cited an incident that had arisen during the process of choosing a rector for the college in New Orleans (now no longer the Mission superior). One Mission Consultor had vetoed every name on Clayton's list. If, as that Consultor had stated, there was no one in the Mission fit for the local superiorship, how, Clayton asked, could he hope to find any one fit to be superior of the entire Mission?[45]

The future, moreover, in the Visitor's view, promised to be like the past. The members of the Mission, recruited in the same way, would continue in their nationalistic prejudices and factionalism. There was no use, Clayton reasoned, in bolstering the Mission as an independent entity by helping it recruit from every nation under the sun. For, argued the Visitor-Superior, "there is really next to no opening for the Society here in the South. Outside of New Orleans, Spring Hill and Galveston, I see none." In the cities of consequence, Clayton wrote, the bishops or clergy do not want us; so, he said, we seize upon any place offered. Clayton admitted that the Missouri Province might object to the fusion, but it ought not to, for among the members of the Mission were good, intelligent,

44. Clayton to Meyer, May 12, 1895, ARSI, Miss. Neo-Aur. 1003, IV-6. Martín to Clayton, June 4, 1895, ARSI, Prov. Neo-Aur., I, 117.
45. Clayton to Meyer, Dec. 29, 1895, ARSI, Miss. Neo-Aur. 1003, IV-10.

useful men. To be effective, thought Clayton, they needed only to be dispersed. In the event of union, the Missouri Province could accept the good offers from the West that it was now obliged to turn down. "Why," he asked, "should the Society be wasting its energies over small Residences in the South when there are openings in the West that have to be refused?"[46]

Clayton also recognized the significance of finances. Although the New Orleans Mission had no *arca seminarii*, the legal fund for Jesuit students' education years, the Mission did own property that was worth money and could be sold. With the South's novices and juniors studying in the Midwest, the Missouri Province could, for example, sell the Mission's novitiate property in Macon, Georgia. In New Orleans, moreover, the Mission-owned property on St. Charles Avenue had been appraised at one hundred thousand dollars.

Then too, Clayton foresaw, the Missouri Province could send to British Honduras some of the New Orleans Mission members who spoke Spanish.[47] Martín did not react to Clayton's proposal. Nor did Clayton preside over the dissolution of the New Orleans Mission.

Another full year in the office of Visitor-Superior of the New Orleans Mission produced a major change in Clayton's view of the Deep South's Jesuits and their future. On the whole, after having visited every house twice formally and sometimes informally, Clayton reported to Martín: "I am exceedingly pleased with [the Mission]. . . . I think that [it] would compare well with any other Province or Mission in the Society." He seems to have had no doubt that his three years there had had a role in this improvement; he went beyond his usual prim style, and, begging pardon if he was going too far, shared with the superior general an idea that had "been simmering in [his] mind for a long time: I would suggest," he wrote, "that the Mission be made a Vice-Province by way of encouraging them. I think such a step would do much good."[48] Again the superior general did not react to the Visitor's proposal. Nor did Clayton preside over the promotion of the New Orleans Mission.

In the search for a successor (as Mission superior) to Clayton, who

---

46. Ibid.   47. Ibid.
48. Clayton to Meyer, Feb. 10, 1897, ARSI, Miss. Neo-Aur. 1003, IV-27.

was due to return to Europe in 1897, the consultors favored the newly ordained 39-year-old Michael Moynihan, who, like O'Shanahan and Kennely, was originally from County Kerry in Ireland. Clayton, however, preferred William Power, a 40-year-old Dubliner, who wound up in third place on the *terna*. Rome chose Power, the recognized intellectual leader of the New Orleans Mission, even though, as Clayton had admitted, the prospective Mission superior had no experience in local government. One Consultor felt that Power was too much needed on the Mission Band for him to be spared for Mission superior. (The Mission Band travelled from parish to parish, wherever it was invited, in order to preach renewal.) Power, the brilliant preacher, was chosen Mission superior in June of 1897, and Clayton left the area soon after. Power's linguistic gifts, knowledge of literature, and spellbinding preaching made him legendary. For nine years he served as superior of the Mission and led it to within one year of its becoming a province of the Society of Jesus.[49]

Power, though, was almost called to another post in the service of the Church. In the spring of 1899 he dutifully reported to the Jesuit superior general in Rome that the apostolic delegate in Washington, D.C., was considering him as a likely nominee for the bishopric of Havana, Cuba, a see that had recently been detached from Spain. Martín directed Power to come promptly to Rome, to leave as soon as possible and to bring the local documents prepared for the forthcoming Congregation [Chapter] of Procurators, the triennial (quadrennial, since 1994) review meeting of delegates from all over the Society of Jesus. Thus for the first time a New Orleans Mission superior came to have a face-to-face conversation with the superior general of the Order. A few months later the apostolic delegate in Washington gave up his pursuit of Power, who had, according to his Jesuit vow, avoided promotion to an ecclesiastical dignity.

At century's end the problem of nationalism seemed to have disappeared in the New Orleans Mission, but the Irish still had a relative majority in posts of government. A reverse effect of the longstanding issue occurred when Ireland-born William Tyrrell tried to avoid being named

---

49. *Missio Neo-Aurelianensis Societatis Iesu ineunte 1898 / . . . 1899 / . . . 1900 / . . . 1905.* The catalogs usually list the superior of the Mission on page 5.

rector of Spring Hill College; he represented to the superior general that, since he was Irish, he should not be chosen, lest the old pattern seem to be renewed. He was appointed nonetheless. For, in 1899, of the five rectors in the New Orleans Mission only two were Irish, including the newly appointed Tyrrell; one was German, one was French, and one was native-born. Some members of the Mission felt that the spirit of nationalism was indeed gone, but that what lingered was the suspicion of it. They were too optimistic, for reports of it continued into the twentieth century. The future disappearance of nationalism was foreshadowed by the fact that those who denounced the aberration were themselves Ireland-born, and they sought to put an end to the divisions.

In 1906 Power was succeeded as Mission superior by Savannah-born John F. O'Connor, who was the first native-born member to hold the office and who seventeen years earlier had been rather bruised and shunted aside.[50] The membership, however, remained predominantly foreign-born. Promotion of the Mission to be vice-province or province had long been discussed. Exuberant O'Shanahan, invoking the support of the Mission Consultors and all its professed fathers, had sought that status as early as 1890. Even the critical Clayton had rallied round, and at the end of his Visitation in 1897 he had favored the promotion of the Mission to vice-provincehood. In 1899 and again in 1902 the Mission Consultors unanimously agreed to ask the superior general for the status of vice-province or province.[51] In response Martín proposed to create a new Jesuit province that would combine a southern portion of the Maryland–New York Province with the New Orleans Mission. But the New Orleans Mission superior and Consultors, after considering that idea, expressed their strong, unanimous hope that the territory of the Mission as then constituted would become a province or a vice-province. If, however, that could not be done, they wrote, they preferred to keep the present status rather than be merged with a portion of Maryland–New York.[52]

When Martín died after a lengthy illness, the Twenty-Fifth General Congregation [Chapter] in 1906 elected as his successor Franz X. Wernz.

50. O'Connor to Meyer, Jan. 15, 1894, ARSI, Miss. Neo-Aur. 1003, III-38.
51. ANOPSJ, Consultations of Apr. 12–16, 1899, and Jan. 14, 1902.
52. ANOPSJ, Consultation of Dec. 20, 1902.

The congregation delegates expressed themselves in favor of granting province status to mature transatlantic missions—for the sake of greater union, they said. In response to the new superior general's question, the New Orleans Mission superior and Consultors again affirmed that the Mission was ready to become a province. Wernz was encouraging, but he instructed the Consultors to omit all discussion of the boundaries of the future province. That issue he reserved to himself.[53] Finally, on June 7, 1907, Wernz erected three full-right transatlantic provinces: Canada, New Orleans, and Mexico. Thus, along with Maryland–New York and Missouri the transatlantic Jesuit provinces totaled five; the three USA provinces and Canada were gathered within the Order's English Assistancy.[54] In 1907 the territory of the New Orleans Province included North Carolina, which was later attached to the Maryland Province, and Oklahoma, which was later attached to the Missouri Province. The State of New Mexico (when admitted to the Union) and the area around El Paso, Texas, were subsequently attached to the New Orleans Province.

One year later, in 1908, Pope Pius X removed the Church in the United States from under the jurisdiction of the Congregation de Propaganda Fide. Catholics in the USA had, as a body, come of age, and their nation was no longer to be considered a mission field. Almost a century had passed since Pope Pius VII had restored the Society of Jesus and commended to the superior general the plea of Bishop DuBourg to have Jesuits sent to Louisiana. Like the Church in the USA the Jesuits' New Orleans Mission had come of age.

53. ANOPSJ, Consultation of Feb. 14, 1907. Wernz to O'Connor, May 21, 1907, ARSI, Prov. Neo-Aur., I, p. 259.

54. *Acta Romana S.I.* (Rome, 1912), 1907, pp. 85–86. ANOPSJ, Consultation of July 14, 1907.

Thomas W. Spalding, C.F.X.

5. CATHOLICS IN THE LAND OF
BILLY THE KID

The Catholic church in the United States has been created by people who have received scant recognition for their efforts. This is particularly true of those early pioneers in the often spotty accounts of its westward progression, where the role of laypeople was crucial. It was, in fact, these dauntless migrants who determined where the church would go and in large measure the shape it would take. Different groups have been responsible for the development of four distinct Catholic frontiers: Maryland (English) yeomen, French-Canadian fur trappers, Irish miners, and German farmers.[1] Seldom credited for their efforts were the Mexican Americans and "Anglo" cattlemen, mostly Irish, who planted the Catholic church in unexpected places like the Pecos River valley of New Mexico, the land of Billy the Kid.[2]

It has generally been assumed that there was almost no Catholic activity in southeastern New Mexico until after that period of violence called the Lincoln County War, whose closure was marked by the death of Billy the Kid in 1881.[3] To a great extent John Baptist Lamy, bishop

1. See Thomas W. Spalding, C.F.X., "The Catholic Frontiers," *U.S. Catholic Historian* 12 (Fall 1994): 1–15.

2. See, for example, Carole Larson, *Forgotten Frontier: The Story of Southeastern New Mexico* (Albuquerque: University of New Mexico Press, 1993), who gives no attention to the religious development of the area.

3. Billy Charles Patrick Cummings, *Frontier Parish: Recovered Catholic History of*

and later archbishop of Santa Fe, was himself to blame. While he adjusted easily to the fur traders' frontier and the bustling communities of their merchant successors in the northern part of New Mexico, he evidenced little interest in, or concern for, the cattle country that came into existence in southern New Mexico after the Civil War.[4] Except for his passage through towns on the Rio Grande above El Paso, Texas, Lamy would seem to have visited the southern half of the Territory of New Mexico only twice before 1882. In 1863 he went to a military post under construction on the Pecos River, Fort Sumner, to oversee the establishment of a school for the Indians recently corralled onto a reservation called Bosque Redondo, and in 1866 he visited Fort Stanton on the Rio Bonito farther south, where Major Lawrence G. Murphy was commanding officer.[5] At the beginning of 1867 the first notice of a Catholic congregation in southeastern New Mexico appeared in the *Catholic Directory* as a mission of Manzano some 130 miles to the northwest: "Rio Bonito, chapel building."[6] But this item would disappear in the next *Directory*.

In May 1873 Major Murphy and Bishop Lamy would recommend to the Board of Indian Commissioners in Washington that William Brady be appointed agent for the Mescalero Apaches, for whom a reservation had been established south of Fort Stanton.[7] Lamy was thus well ac-

---

Lincoln County, 1860–1884, No. 4 in Studies Concerning the History of Lincoln County, New Mexico, and Its Environs (Lincoln, N. Mex.: Lincoln County Historical Society, 1995), p. vii. I am grateful to Peter Lysy of the archives of the University of Notre Dame for having called my attention to this work after I had begun this article and even more grateful to its author, Billy Cummings, for his invaluable help in its writing.

4. Paul Horgan in his magisterial work, *Lamy of Santa Fe: His Life and Times* (New York: Farrar, Straus and Giroux, 1975), leaves unremarked Lamy's failure to visit the southern half of New Mexico but notes an admonition of the cardinal-prefect of the Congregation of the Propaganda Fide, Alessandro Barnabò, in 1867 that Lamy's canonical visitations ought in general to be more often and more thorough (p. 399). Lamy was named vicar apostolic of the Territory of New Mexico in 1850, bishop of Santa Fe in 1853, and archbishop of the same in 1875.

5. Gerald Thompson, *The Army and the Navajo* (Tucson: University of Arizona Press, 1976), pp. 17–19, 82. The school ended with the closing of the reservation in 1868. For the visit to Fort Stanton, Cummings, *Frontier Parish*, p. 4.

6. *Sadlier's Catholic Directory, Almanac and Ordo* (New York: Sadlier's & Co., 1867), p. 160 (hereafter *Catholic Directory*).

7. Donald R. Lavash, *Sheriff William Brady: Tragic Hero of the Lincoln County War* (Santa Fe: Sunstone Press, 1986), p. 45, n. 20. The recommendation was not honored.

quainted with two of the leading citizens of Lincoln County. Before his untimely death in 1876 Father Anthony Lamy, the bishop's nephew, made two or three visits from Manzano to the Rio Bonito area.[8] The bishop would, therefore, have been well informed on conditions in southeastern New Mexico. What he knew of it may, in fact, have been a factor in his reluctance to direct his energies to that part of his vast diocese.

In 1874 Bonifacio Baca of the town of Lincoln, the county seat, wrote to a former teacher at Notre Dame in Indiana that he was unable to frequent the sacraments because there had never been a priest stationed in the county. "Yet we have asked for several but the Bishop has not listen[ed] to our petitions." He also added, "We cannot go one mile away from the towns without being armed with pistols and guns for fear of thieves. Such is the Paradise of New Mexico where nothing but the pure juice of the grapes and dark eyed Senoritas enliven our hearts."[9]

Lamy had succeeded in having the southernmost counties of New Mexico, Doña Ana and Grant, assigned to the vicariate apostolic of Arizona, created in 1868, and had apparently persuaded his friend John Baptist Salpointe, the vicar apostolic, to assume responsibility for Lincoln County, created the following year. A year after he became an archbishop in 1875, Lamy finally chose a pastor for the Catholics of Lincoln County, but it was not until 1880 that the *Catholic Directory* announced: "Lincoln, new parish, Rev. Joseph S. Tafoya, who attends also several new missions."[10] Neither the parish at Lincoln nor its surrounding missions were "new."

The task of planting the church in the southeastern quarter of New Mexico fell originally to those Mexican Americans who went down from the Hispano homeland surrounding Santa Fe.[11] Mostly from its south-

8. Two of Anthony Lamy's letters to his sister Marie (Sister Francisca) dated June 23 and November 3, 1875, recounting his visits to Rio Bonito, can be found in the archives of the Sisters of Loretto, Nerinckx, Kentucky.

9. Archives of the University of Notre Dame, Edwards papers, Baca to Edwards, Lincoln, December 9, 1874.

10. *Catholic Directory*, 1880, p. 160.

11. Richard L. Nostrand, *The Hispano Homeland* (Norman: University of Oklahoma Press, 1992), pp. 92–95. Between 1790 and 1900 the Hispano homeland grew from approximately 5,380 square miles around Santa Fe to 85,000 square miles, penetrating Colorado, Arizona, and Texas. See maps on pp. 40, 94, 111, and 160.

western rim near the town of Manzano, they went to found sheepherd-
ing villages near Fort Stanton, established in 1855 to control the Mescalero Apaches. The first was called La Placita del Rio Bonito, "The Little
Village by the Pretty River" (later the town of Lincoln), founded about
1855, perhaps by members of the frowned-upon fraternity, the *Penitentes*.[12] Other villages sprang up in this area, where the Bonito and Ruidoso rivers met to form the Hondo River, which then continued some
sixty miles east to the Pecos River.

Saturnino Baca, a Civil War veteran, was considered the father of
Lincoln County and until his death at age ninety-four the patriarch of
the Hispano community.[13] In 1868, as a member of the territorial legislature, he proposed that a county be created for southeastern New Mexico
and that it be named for President Lincoln, not for himself as many
wished. Erected 1869 and comprising some 27,000 square miles when
enlarged in 1878, Lincoln County encompassed a quarter of the future
state of New Mexico.[14] Baca would be elected to a number of offices, including sheriff, and act as a bridge between the Hispanos and the Anglos
who came in increasing numbers after the Civil War.

Juan Bautista Patrón was much younger and came to Lincoln much
later. He also served as a bridge but was more ambitious than Baca.[15] A
native probably of Santa Fe, where he was educated in the Christian
Brothers' college, he was but twenty-five when, as a representative of
Lincoln, Doña Ana, and Grant counties, all of southern New Mexico, he
was elected speaker of the territorial legislature in January 1878. As
speaker he was able to persuade the assembly to override the governor's

12. Larson, *Forgotten Frontier*, pp. 68–69; Cummings, *Frontier Parish*, pp. 10–11.
One of the best histories of the penitential brotherhood that practiced self-flagella-
tion, *La Fraternidad de Nuestro Padre Jesús Nazareno* is Marta Weigle, *Brothers of Light,
Brothers of Blood: The Penitentes of the Southwest* (Santa Fe: Ancient City Press, 1976).

13. Dan L. Tharp, ed., *Encyclopedia of Frontier Biography*, 3 vols. (Lincoln: University of Nebraska Press, 1988), 1:50; Frederick Nolan, *The Lincoln County War: A Documentary History* (Norman: University of Oklahoma Press, 1992), pp. 38–39, 443–44,
and passim.

14. Marc Simmons, *New Mexico: An Interpretive History* (Albuquerque: University
of New Mexico Press, reprint 1988), p. 161.

15. *Encyclopedia of Frontier Biography*, 3:1118–19; Nolan, *Lincoln County War*, pp.
49, 71–73, 478, and passim. Patrón was the first teacher in Lincoln County and
chairman of the first Board of County Commissioners.

vetoes of bills incorporating the Jesuits of New Mexico and providing public funding for St. Vincent's Hospital in Santa Fe.[16] As early as 1876 Patrón was apparently the instigator of a move to build a Catholic church in the town of Lincoln itself, a project finally brought to a halt by the Lincoln County War.[17]

By then private chapels or oratorios had been erected nearby by Hispano *patrones* (community leaders). The first, some six miles west of Lincoln, Nuestra Señora del Pueblito, was constructed by Antonio Torres, perhaps before 1860. Closer to Lincoln, at La Placita de Gendres, was a *morada* (chapel) of the *Penitentes*. At San Patricio, some seven miles away by mountain trail, a chapel of the same name was built by Anicito Lucero. Hispano laymen, in the *patrón* tradition, owned and maintained not only these church buildings but often the adjoining conventos (rectories) and cemeteries.[18] Patiently they awaited the priest they knew would come.

Lily Casey Klasner remembered: "Because there was no priest closer than Manzano, we went to church only when he made his semiannual trips to the country."[19] Not only was Manzano the closest parish, 130 miles away, but transplanted Catholics on the Rio Bonito looked to their former pastor there to visit them. As early as 1860 John Baptist Ralliere, pastor of Tome, of which Manzano was then a mission, performed six baptisms at Rio Bonito and one at Fort Stanton. After the Civil War he returned to perform seventeen baptisms at Rio Bonito and twelve at Tularosa.[20] From 1869 to 1876 Lincoln County would, as already noted, be

16. Billy Charles Cummings, "Patron, Axtell Fight over Jesuits," *Los Amigos*, Lincoln Heritage Museum Newsletter, July 1995. For Governor Samuel Axtell's antipathy toward the Jesuits see Harold Roberts Lamar, *The Far Southwest, 1846–1912: A Territorial History* (New Haven: Yale University Press, 1966), pp. 167–69. The act of incorporation was annulled next year by the United States Congress.

17. Cummings, *Frontier Parish*, pp. 38–40. Historians have assumed incorrectly that an unfinished building in Lincoln at the time of the Lincoln County War was for a Presbyterian church planned by Alexander McSween, who will appear later.

18. Ibid., pp. 9–15, 69.

19. Lily Klasner, *My Girlhood among Outlaws*, ed. Eve Ball (Tucson: University of Arizona Press, 1972), p. 50.

20. Cummings, *Frontier Parish*, pp. 2–3, 5. These earliest records are preserved at Santa Rita's, Carrizozo. The 1860 census revealed a little more than 190 residents in what would become Lincoln County, all Hispanos but 17 from Missouri and 11 from (French) Canada.

served by priests of Salpointe's vicariate. In 1876 Lamy sent (or perhaps allowed) Father José Sembrano Tafoya to establish residence near the Rio Bonito apparently to take charge of the church planned by Juan Patrón and its dependent missions. In Lincoln County he was called Padre Sambrano.[21] A former pastor at Manzano, Padre Sambrano had friends and relatives in and around the town of Lincoln. In 1878, with Francisco Vigil, husband of his niece, he purchased 160 acres he called El Rancho del Padre. There he would raise sheep and build an oratorio he named Santo Niño. His ranch adjoined that of the widow of Robert Casey, cattleman.

Much of the growth of the church in southeastern New Mexico after the Civil War was due to an infusion of "Anglo" cattlemen. A great number of these Anglos were Irish. Some came up from Texas, like Robert Casey and Patrick Coghlan. Some were mustered out of the army in New Mexico at the end of the Civil War, like Lawrence G. Murphy and William Brady, already noted, and James J. Dolan, their associate. An even greater number, perhaps, were Anglos who married Hispanas and converted or allowed their children to be raised in the Catholic faith. John B. Wilson, George W. Peppin, George Kimbrell (or Kimball), and Hugh Beckwith, all prominent in the Lincoln County War, were Catholics, a fact ignored by, or unknown to, the host of historians of that war.[22]

The coming of the Anglos to the Pecos River valley had its beginnings with the erection of Fort Sumner in 1863–64 as military guardian of the ill-fated reservation called Bosque Redondo, the site of Lamy's short-lived (1864–68) Indian school. The need to supply this and other nearby forts and their reservation Indians with beef spurred the beginning of the cattle industry in New Mexico. The Goodnight-Loving trail was blazed up the Pecos from Texas in 1866. An associate of Charles Goodnight was John S. Chisum, who would become "Cow King of New Mexico," for a time owner of the largest herd of cattle in America.[23] Per-

21. Cummings, *Frontier Parish*, p. 28. Father Sembrano usually signed himself, or was recorded as, Sambrano. He was one of the native-born priests who did not rebel against Lamy.

22. Except for the Murphy-Dolan associates, the religion of these participants would remain largely unknown if not revealed in the parish registers examined by Cummings.

23. Simmons, *New Mexico*, p. 158.

haps the first Catholic cattleman was Robert Casey, a friend of Chisum in Texas.

Robert Casey drove a herd up to Fort Sumner in 1867 and soon after purchased a mill on the Hondo River near the juncture of the Bonito and Ruidoso rivers. The Caseys, according to daughter Lily, were "devout 'fighting Irish' Catholics."[24] Robert Casey also opened a store and a school. One of his clerk-teachers, Marshall Ashmun Upson, the future ghostwriter of *The Authentic Life of Billy the Kid*, declared in 1872 that Casey was the wealthiest of the rancheros on the Hondo. With a store and grist mill, 600 acres under cultivation, hundreds of head of stock, and a fine, healthy, handsome family, he was "one of Nature's noblemen."[25]

On 1 August 1875 at a convention in Lincoln, Robert Casey challenged the political, and by implication the economic, stranglehold that Major Lawrence Murphy and his associates had on Lincoln County. The same day a man named William Wilson, whom many believed was Murphy's henchman, shot Casey. The widow, unaware of any complicity on Murphy's part, asked him to conduct the funeral services in the absence of a priest. Murphy had often boasted of having been a seminarian. Wilson was tried and hanged, the first public execution in Lincoln County. Father Anthony Lamy visited him in jail and attended him on the scaffold.[26]

Lawrence G. Murphy, Irish born, rose in the Civil War to the rank of major.[27] Mustered out in 1866, he became the sutler (storekeeper) at the fort he had commanded, Fort Stanton, and there established the firm of L. G. Murphy & Co. In 1873 he moved to Lincoln, made clerk James J. (Jimmy) Dolan a partner, and erected the largest civilian structure in the

24. Klasner, *Girlhood,* p. 13. Ellen (Shellenbarger) Casey, the mother, was originally an Episcopalian. Robert Casey, born in Lowell, Massachusetts, joined the U.S. Army and served on the Texas frontier, where he took up ranching. There is some confusion as to when the Caseys came to New Mexico. Besides Klasner see also James D. Shinkle, *Robert Casey and the Ranch on the Rio Hondo* (Roswell, N. Mex.: Hall-Pourbaugh Press, 1970), and Nolan, *Lincoln County War,* pp. 67–71.

25. Nolan, *Lincoln County War,* p. 68, but see also p. 534, n. 11, where Susan McSween would accuse the Caseys of murder and theft, "well founded" allegations according to Nolan.

26. Klasner, *Girlhood,* pp. 125–36; Nolan, *Lincoln County War,* pp. 69–71.

27. *Encyclopedia of Frontier Biography,* 2:1035; Nolan, *Lincoln County War,* pp. 32–55, and passim.

county. The firm, in effect a commodity brokerage with a monopoly on government contracts, was known as "the House." Murphy was also a banker, saloon-keeper (himself the saloon's best customer), and rancher. That he was a fairly conscientious Catholic, however, may be inferred from the fact that he sent a son of Saturnino Baca, Bonifacio, to the college called Notre Dame in Indiana to be educated.

The House was singularly disliked for its extortionate practices. In 1876 John Henry Tunstall, a cultured Englishman, came to Lincoln at the invitation of Alexander A. McSween to create his own cattle empire. With McSween, whose services as a lawyer had been valued by Murphy, Chisum, and others since his arrival in Lincoln in 1875, Tunstall opened a store and bank in Lincoln. Chisum was a silent partner. It was more than economic rivalry. McSween, an ardent Presbyterian, asked the Presbyterian Board of Home Missions in 1877 to send a minister to open a church. Dr. Taylor F. Ealy, in a letter to a Presbyterian editor soon after his arrival in 1878, characterized those associated with the House as "a dirty set of Irish cut throats and you know what their religion is. They drink whiskey, gamble and nothing is too bad for them."[28]

In 1877 Murphy passed control of the House to his partner Jimmy Dolan and in 1878 went to St. Vincent's Hospital in Santa Fe to die, the result of alcoholism.[29] Dolan, like Murphy Irish born and a Civil War veteran, had decided to carve a career in Lincoln County.[30] As single-minded in the pursuit of profit and power as Murphy, he was even more ruthless. With conflict inevitable, Tunstall hired a band of gunslinging "ranchhands" to protect his interests. Among them was a young drifter who called himself Billy Bonney. Others called him "the Kid."

Though the origins of Billy the Kid are "shrouded in mystery," as Robert Utley, one of his best biographers, warned, the *Encyclopedia of Frontier Biography* states unequivocally that he was Henry McCarty, son of Patrick and Catherine (Devine) McCarty, baptized September 28,

28. Robert Utley, *High Noon in Lincoln: Violence on the Western Frontier* (Albuquerque: University of New Mexico Press, 1987), pp. 51, 65.

29. One of Murphy's enemies would claim that his death was hastened by "the Sisters of Charity [who] would not let him have whiskey, and that cut his living off." Utley, *High Noon*, pp. 163–64.

30. *Encyclopedia of Frontier Biography*, 1:411–12; Nolan, *Lincoln County War*, pp. 455–56, and passim.

1859, at St. Peter's Church, Barclay Street, New York, while a more recent study of his boyhood says with equal assurance that William Henry
McCarty was "born and raised in southern Indiana."[31] In any case, the
fatherless family wandered west, the mother remarrying in the Presbyterian church in Santa Fe in 1873. After her death in 1875 in a mining
town in southwestern New Mexico, Henry progressed from petty larce-
ny to the murder of an Irish bully in Arizona. With a gang of bandits he
returned to New Mexico with a new name, William Bonney.

Irish he doubtless was, but Billy Bonney evidenced no religious
commitment. He was, however, most at home in the Hispano communities of the Rio Bonito and Pecos River valleys. Sista Salas, a member of
the family with whom he first took refuge after his last escape from jail
in 1881, would later recall that upon his leavetaking, he asked the blessing of the parents, as all good Hispano boys would do. She always believed that Billy was "a good Catholic."[32]

Governor Miguel Otero would, in his *The Real Billy the Kid*, quote extensively a number of people who knew him well. Though Susan Mc-
Sween Barber, the widow of Alexander McSween, would claim with
some exaggeration that he was "universally liked," she would insist that
"the native citizens, in particular, loved him because he was always kind
and considerate to them and took much pleasure in helping them and
providing for their wants." She would also remark that he was a "grace-
ful and beautiful dancer" and in the company of women "a perfect gentleman."[33] Otero himself judged Billy "a man more sinned against than
sinning."[34]

Several times Billy would indicate a desire to make a fresh start,

---

31. *Encyclopedia of Frontier Biography*, 1:112; Jerry Weddle, *Antrim Is My Stepfa-
ther's Name: The Boyhood of Billy the Kid* (Phoenix: Arizona Historical Society, 1995), p.
1. Nolan, *Lincoln County War*, pp. 3–6, offers the best summation of conjectures. For
reliable lives of Billy the Kid see Robert M. Utley, *Billy the Kid: A Short and Violent Life*
(Lincoln: University of Nebraska Press, 1989); Joel Jacobsen, *Such Men as Billy the Kid:
The Lincoln County War Reconsidered* (Lincoln: University of Nebraska Press, 1994); and
Jon Tuska, *Billy the Kid: A Handbook* (Lincoln: University of Nebraska Press, 1983).

32. Cummings, *Frontier Parish*, pp. 61–62. According to the Cummings correspondence in the Rasch papers at the Lincoln County Historical Society, many of the
oldtimers around the 1920s believed Billy was a Catholic.

33. Miguel Antonio Otero, *The Real Billy the Kid: With New Light on the Lincoln
County War* (New York: Rufus Rockwell Wilson, 1936), pp. 113–14.

34. *The Real Billy*, p. 179. The battle lines have long been drawn between the

only to be thwarted on each occasion. In the fall of 1877, when the Widow Casey decided to return temporarily to Texas, he asked to go with her. Ellen Casey wanted to repossess the cattle she had been constrained to sell at auction to John Tunstall at far below the going rate and drive them to Texas. There she wished also to give her children a better education. Daughter Lily would be enrolled in the Ursuline Academy in San Antonio. Lily recalled Billy's request to accompany them. The mother turned him down.[35] He was then hired by Tunstall, for whom he apparently developed an immediate admiration. He found himself among more genial companions and planned, with one of the Tunstall band, to take up ranching. The oldest Casey boy remembered Billy as a "bum" when he had asked to go to Texas but a "gentleman" after he had been taken on by Tunstall. In the spring of 1878, however, Tunstall was killed by Dolan men and Billy swore vengeance.[36]

With Tunstall's death what had been mostly a legal contest became a shooting war.[37] Alexander McSween assumed control of the Tunstall hands, who called themselves "the Regulators." When Sheriff William Brady, Murphy's friend, was gunned down by a band of Regulators, Billy was singled out as the assassin. The Lincoln County War climaxed in July 1878 in a five-day battle, in which the McSween followers were bested and McSween killed. Dr. Ealy, caught in the middle of the battle, decided to build his church elsewhere.

News of the anarchy in Lincoln County reached all the way to Washington and a new governor was sent out, Lew Wallace, later famous as the author of *Ben Hur*. Wallace promised Billy a pardon if he

---

proponents of the satanic and the saintly Billy, the latter achieving a virtual "deification" in the Aaron Copland ballet *Billy the Kid*. See Kent Ladd Steckmesser, *The Western Hero in History and Legend* (Norman: University of Oklahoma Press, 1997 paperback edition). Steckmesser leans toward the satanic, but his attempt at historical accuracy is itself flawed.

35. Klasner, *Girlhood*, pp. 147–70; Jacobsen, *Billy the Kid*, pp. 22–23; Nolan, *Lincoln County War*, pp. 166–68.

36. Utley, *Billy the Kid*, pp. 32–48.

37. Literature on the Lincoln County War is voluminous. For the best and most trustworthy accounts, besides Nolan, *Lincoln County War*, Jacobsen, *Billy the Kid*, and Utley, *High Noon*, already cited, see William A. Keleher, *Violence in Lincoln County, 1869–1881* (Albuquerque: University of New Mexico Press, 1957), and Maurice Garland Fulton, *History of the Lincoln County War*, ed. Robert N. Mullin (Tucson: University of Arizona Press, 1968).

turned state's evidence in a murder committed by Dolan. Billy testified, but there was no pardon.[38] He walked out of the jail at Lincoln to lead a desultory life as rustler, largely to stay alive.

In the meantime Padre Sambrano, who had lain low during the more turbulent months, ended up waging a war of his own. An eject-ment suit and countersuit were filed in May 1879 by Ellen Casey and Padre Sambrano, whose land claims overlapped. This was followed by the theft of some of Sambrano's valuable possessions by the widow and a son, for which the priest had the two arrested. On June 28 the widow and another son, with three accomplices, committed what Padre Sam-brano charged was assault with intent to murder. For this the Caseys and accomplices were finally tried in 1881 but acquitted.[39]

Archbishop Lamy would finally visit the chapels in Lincoln County in September 1882, a little more than a year after the death of Billy the Kid had brought a measure of calm. As directed, Padre Sambrano asked the Torres and Lucero families to deed their chapels to the archbishop. The former agreed; but when the latter refused, the parishioners gutted the family chapel and raised another nearby. Padre Sambrano retired in 1883 to devote full time to raising sheep but met an accidental death the following year. That same year his successor purchased and transformed the old courthouse and saloon, the site of so many confrontations in the Lincoln County War, into the town of Lincoln's first church.[40]

Increasingly thereafter churches would be built by priests with the permission, or under the direction, of the archbishop. Before then al-most all churches, or chapels, in southern New Mexico and the Pecos River valley were the result of lay initiative, raised with little or no con-sultation with church authorities. Most, as already indicated, were built by Hispano *patrones*, but some by devout or enterprising newcomers. One such newcomer was Maria de la Luz Beaubien Maxwell, widow of a remarkable entrepreneur originally a member of the French-speaking

---

38. Utley, *Billy the Kid,* pp. 111–21; Tuska, *Billy the Kid,* pp. 61–71.

39. Cummings, *Frontier Parish,* pp. 52–64, citing documents from the Lincoln County District Court. Lily Casey Klasner says nothing of all this in her *Girlhood* rem-iniscences, perhaps as an episode best forgotten.

40. Cummings, *Frontier Parish,* pp. 69–79; John P. Wilson, *Merchants, Guns & Money: The Story of Lincoln County and Its Wars* (Santa Fe: Museum of New Mexico Press, 1987), pp. 138–40. A new church, San Juan Bautista, dedicated in 1887, still stands, as does its *convento*, or rectory, the original church.

community of Missouri and nearby Illinois. She built at Fort Sumner. The other was a Pole, Alexander Grzelachowski. He, with a Hispano from Rio Bonito, built at Puerto de Luna. Both the widow and the Pole were more than casual acquaintances of Billy the Kid. The two favorite places for Billy and his small band of fellow rustlers to hide in the last two years of his life were in the upper Pecos River valley, at Fort Sumner and Puerto de Luna.

In 1871, three years after the abandonment of the Bosque Redondo reservation, the federal government had sold Fort Sumner, just above the Lincoln County line, to Lucien Bonaparte Maxwell. Despite his Irish background, Maxwell belonged to the Creole elite of the St. Louis area, not a few of whom had moved to Taos, New Mexico, to become a part of the fur traders' frontier.[41] There he married Luz Beaubien, daughter of Judge Charles Beaubien, and through her he inherited the Beaubien-Miranda land grant, the largest bestowed by the Mexican government before the Mexican War. With the collapse of the fur trade Maxwell went into ranching on the grant itself at Cimarron in northern New Mexico. There he lived in a truly baronial style, claiming 1,000 horses, 10,000 cattle, and 40,000 sheep. In 1870 he sold the grant for $660,000 (which was resold to English capitalists for $1,350,000) and moved his entire operation, with some forty families, mostly Hispanos, to Fort Sumner.

When he died in 1875, Señora Maxwell and son Pete, Pedro, or Pierre, depending upon the speaker, took over the operation. Pete managed the business side and his mother, it would seem, the religious side. Upon the death of her husband she created a mission at Fort Sumner, either at the fort itself or at a chapel a mile and a half away, where she moved her family. Perhaps both. It is certain that in 1876 Fort Sumner became a *visita,* a mission, of the parish of San José in Anton Chico some ninety miles north on the Pecos.[42] Between Anton Chico and Fort Sumner a number of chapels would then be built, mostly by Hispano *pa-*

41. Lawrence R. Murphy, *Lucien Bonaparte Maxwell: Napoleon of the Southwest* (Norman: University of Oklahoma Press, 1983); William A. Keleher, *Maxwell Land Grant: A New Mexico Item* (Albuquerque: University of New Mexico Press, 1984). Lucien was son of Hugh Maxwell, brought from Ireland to Missouri by his uncle, Father James Maxwell, a pioneer priest in Missouri, and Odile, daughter of Pierre Menard, the first lieutenant governor of Illinois.

42. Murphy, *Maxwell,* pp. 190–97; James D. Shinkle, *Fort Sumner and the Bosque*

trones.[43] It is not unlikely that the pastor at Anton Chico who visited them, Father Augustin Redon, would have met Billy Bonney at either Fort Sumner or Puerto de Luna. He is reported to have said, "Billy did not have a bad heart, really. Most of his crimes were crimes of vengeance."[44]

Fort Sumner was for a time the most popular gathering place in the Pecos valley, its weekly *bailes* (dances) attracting ranchers from fifty miles away and more. Billy attended with some regularity. Pete Maxwell's younger sister, Paulita, was one of his *queridas* there.[45] At Fort Sumner he felt safe. There are indications that in this period Billy thought again of going straight in either Texas or Mexico. John Chisum and other big-time cattlemen, however, decided that Billy must be captured and hanged as an example to the swarm of petty rustlers who roamed the Pecos. For the job they chose Patrick Floyd (Pat) Garrett, one-time gambling companion of the Kid at Fort Sumner, where Pete Maxwell had given Garrett his first job in New Mexico. As sheriff of Lincoln County, Garrett captured Billy in December 1880 not far from Fort Sumner. At the fort he was put in irons. Señora Maxwell begged that they be removed so that he might see her daughter Paulita privately for an affectionate farewell. Her request was denied.[46]

Billy was taken first to Santa Fe, where Sister Blandina Segale claimed to have visited him.[47] At Mesilla he was sentenced to be hanged

---

Redondo Indian Reservation (Roswell, N. Mex.: Hall-Poorbaugh Press, 1965), pp. 79–85; Leon C. Metz, *Pat Garrett: The Story of a Western Lawman* (Norman: University of Oklahoma Press, 1974), pp. 39–40. The first notice of a mission at Fort Sumner, but called initially Bosque Redondo, appears in the *Catholic Directory* that was published at the beginning of 1877. A pueblo developed around Señora Maxwell's home that took the name Fort Sumner, the second of three communities to do so. The present Fort Sumner is north of the old fort. I am indebted to Harry R. Parsons and Don McAlavy for enlightenment on a number of points about the communities of Fort Sumner.

43. Harry R. Parsons, ed., *Our Mid-Pecos History—Living Water* (Fort Sumner, N. Mex.: Mid-Pecos Historical Foundation, 1980), pp. 128, 238–40, 279; Fabiola Cabeza de Baca, *We Fed Them Cactus*, 2d ed. (Albuquerque: University of New Mexico Press, 1994), chap. 7 and pp. 133–34. Information also supplied by Betty Rosenberger.

44. Cummings, *Frontier Parish*, p. 80, n. 4.

45. Utley, *Billy the Kid*, pp. 126–27.

46. Ibid., pp. 160–61; Tuska, *Billy the Kid*, p. 88. For the *Las Vegas Gazette* of December 28, 1880, Billy declared: "Chisum got me into all this trouble."

47. The first two of three encounters described by Sister Blandina in her ac-

for the murder of Sheriff Brady and sent to Lincoln for the hanging. Despite all precautions he escaped in April 1881 by killing his two captors. As Garrett guessed, he returned to Fort Sumner to hide out. While Garrett was questioning Pete Maxwell in his darkened bedroom on July 14, Billy walked in and, sensing another presence, asked, "¿Qien es?" ("Who's there?")—his last words. The villagers assembled and placed candles around his body for an all-night wake. He was buried the next day in the military cemetery not far from Lucien Maxwell.

It may not have been entirely coincidental that the following year eighty-eight cattle companies were incorporated in the territory of New Mexico.[48]

The other Catholic who played a significant role in the development of the Pecos River valley, and who could be numbered among the close acquaintances of Billy Bonney, was Alexander Grzelachowski. It was a difficult name for both Anglos and Hispanos to pronounce. John Chisum called him "Chowski." The Hispanos called him Padre Polaco or Don Alejandro. Many had known him as a priest.

Polish-born and ordained in Europe, Grzelachowski was laboring in Ohio when he was recruited by Lamy to serve in his newly created vicariate. With Joseph Machebeuf, they made the perilous journey from Texas to Santa Fe in 1851.[49] He was assigned to the parish at Las Vegas on the Santa Fe Trail and then to three Indian pueblos before being sent in late 1857 to Manzano. From there he may have been the first priest to visit Rio Bonito. But he was under a cloud as early as 1852, when he was suspended at Las Vegas.[50] Lily Casey Klasner claimed that his undo-

count entitled *At the End of the Santa Fe Trail* (Columbus, Ohio: Columbian Press, 1932), pp. 81–83, 110–13, and 207–9, for geographical reasons appear highly unlikely, and the third is flawed by chronology.

48. Gerald Robert Baydo, "Cattle Ranching in Territorial New Mexico" (Ph.D. diss, University of New Mexico, 1970), p. 74. Only five had been incorporated the year before.

49. Francis C. Kajencki has published two versions of the life of Grzelachowski, "Alexander Grzelachowski: Pioneer Merchant of Puerto do Luna, New Mexico," *Arizona and the West* 26 (1984): 243–60 (hereafter "Pioneer Merchant"), and "Alexander Grzelachowski: New Mexico's 'Padre Polaco' and Pioneer Merchant," in Kajencki's *Poles in the 19th Century Southwest* (El Paso, Tex.: Southwest Polonia Press, 1990), pp. 79–104 (hereafter "Padre Polaco"). He is never mentioned in Horgan's *Lamy*.

50. Bruce T. Ellis, ed., "New Notes on Bishop Lamy's First Years in New Mexico," *El Palacio* 65 (1958): 74.

ing was "too many young black eyed girls."[51] He returned to Las Vegas, acquired land in 1859, and went into business. In 1860, nevertheless, he told the census taker that he was a Roman Catholic clergyman and in 1861 he volunteered as a military chaplain.[52] After the war he returned to his business career. About 1870 he took a common-law wife, Secundina Baca, and raised a family of nine children in the Catholic faith. He was never laicized.[53]

Padre Polaco prospered in Las Vegas. He won Army contracts and operated a general store. He became a close associate of Charles Ilfeld, a Jew and the largest merchandise wholesaler in New Mexico.[54] He also took a partner, Richard Dunn. About 1874 he moved to the hamlet of Puerto de Luna on the Pecos, originally settled in 1863 by Hispanos all the way up from Rio Bonito.[55] There he constructed a combination home, store, and warehouse that became the showplace of the area. He also went into farming and raised cattle, sheep, and horses on three different ranches nearby. Puerto de Luna soon surpassed Fort Sumner, some forty miles south, as a popular rendezvous.

Billy Bonney was a frequent visitor to his store in Puerto de Luna. On occasion he rustled some of Padre Polaco's cattle. Despite this they remained friends. Billy admired the merchant for his command of languages and knowledge of the world and often pressed him to speak Polish, Latin, or Greek or to tell him stories of far-away places. On his way to Santa Fe, after his capture in 1880, Billy enjoyed his last Christmas dinner, in shackles, at the well-provisioned table of Padre Polaco.[56]

Two people of note associated themselves with Padre Polaco in the

51. Klasner, *Girlhood*, pp. 281–82.
52. He was later credited with having played a crucial role at the victory at Glorieta Pass that saved New Mexico for the Union. Kajencki, "Pioneer Merchant," pp. 247–48.
53. For this reason he was buried outside the cemetery of Puerto de Luna. Later, however, a stone monument was placed at the site and the boundary of the cemetery extended to include it.
54. Nostrand, *Hispano Homeland*, p. 113.
55. Ibid., p. 95; Fabiola Cabeza de Baca, "Puerto de Luna," *New Mexico Magazine* 36 (1958): 20.
56. Kajencki, "Padre Polaco," pp. 91–92; Utley, *Billy the Kid*, pp. 140–41, 258, n. 29; Tuska, *Billy the Kid*, pp. 78, 87–88. Tuska's claim that Grzelachowski also ran a brothel is probably not true.

development of Puerto de Luna and the surrounding area. One was John B. Clancey, a former sea captain, who in 1877 brought from California to Puerto de Luna 3,000 sheep and $50,000 in gold. The latter he deposited in Grzelachowski's large store safe, the only one of its kind in New Mexico. The former was expanded to one of the largest sheep-raising enterprises in the territory. Captain Clancey married a young lady of Puerto de Luna and his son a daughter of Don Alejandro.[57]

The other associate was Juan Bautista Patrón, who in 1879 had been commissioned by Governor Wallace to form a militia to bring order to Lincoln County. A thankless task, Patrón soon moved to Puerto de Luna. Some said it was because he had too many enemies in Lincoln, but the more likely reason was that he saw greater opportunities in the prosperous little town on the upper Pecos. There he opened a hotel.[58] It was in the building of a church, however, that he cooperated with Don Alejandro. The church of Our Lady of Refuge was built in 1881 and dedicated in 1882. In 1896 it would become a parish church with Fort Sumner as one of its missions.[59] Patrón was killed in Puerto de Luna in 1884 in a bar, some say by a man hired by his enemies in Lincoln.[60] And some say he was the first person buried from the church he had helped build.

But it was Don Alejandro who played the most important role in the development of town and valley. One of his goals was to make Puerto de Luna a county seat. This he finally achieved in 1892. Having served as postmaster from 1876 to 1886, he also served as probate judge of the new county and donated land, while Captain Clancey contributed $2,500, for the courthouse and jail. But his leadership extended to the upper Pecos valley as a whole in matters that affected the social, economic, political, and religious life of the region. He led, for example, the struggle for irrigation projects along the Pecos River, helping to secure the people's water rights in the process.[61] During his fifty years in New Mexico, in fact, Alexander Grzelachowski contributed in no small way to an accommodation of diverse cultures—Hispano, Indian, and Anglo. All

57. Parsons, *Living Water*, p. 20; Kajencki, "Padre Polaco," p. 93.
58. Nolan, *Lincoln County War*, pp. 383–84, 478.
59. Cabeza de Baca, *We Fed Them Cactus*, p. 79; Cummings, *Frontier Parish*, p. 40.
60. Fulton, *Lincoln County War*, pp. 405–9.
61. Kajencki, "Padre Polaco," pp. 94, 102–4.

admired the genial merchant for his integrity and intelligence. Many young men served their apprenticeships in his store and later became prosperous merchants elsewhere in the territory.

In the end, however, Don Alejandro's great ambitions were never fully realized. A business deal with John Chisum and Pete Maxwell soured. He sued Chisum, but the case dragged on till after Chisum's death in 1884. Not long after, Don Alejandro found himself in other financial difficulties. He died in 1895 mired in debt. In 1900 the railroad bypassed Puerto de Luna for Santa Rosa on the Pecos eleven miles north. Santa Rosa would replace Puerto de Luna as the county seat and parish, while the formerly prosperous village declined to almost a ghost town. "Gone are the days," concluded Grzelachowski's biographer on a poetic note, "when Don Alejandro's orchards bloomed, fine horses pranced in his corrals, bands of sheep grazed in the fields, herds of cattle carrying the A.G. brand dotted his lands, and Billy the Kid came to visit Padre Polaco."[62]

62. Ibid., p. 104.

Philip Gleason

6. NEWMAN'S *IDEA* IN THE MINDS OF AMERICAN EDUCATORS

In doing research for a book on the history of American Catholic higher education, I was struck by how often reference was made to Cardinal Newman's *Idea of a University*.[1] That was hardly a surprise, for though it is universally regarded as a classic, Catholic educators of an earlier generation tended to think of it as distinctively their own and cherished toward it a definitely proprietary feeling. Eventually, however, the repeated allusions aroused my curiosity about what might be called the "reception" of the book. Just when did Americans first hear of *The Idea of a University?* Were Catholics the only ones impressed by it? Did it pass through seasons of favor and disfavor? Contrary to my expectation, I couldn't find answers to these questions in the vast literature on Newman. That being the case, I was emboldened to undertake the present study, although I am the merest sort of novice in the field of Newman scholarship. What follows is no more than a sketch, but I hope it will call attention to matters deserving of more extended investigation.

From the historian's viewpoint, tracing the resonance of Newman's *Idea* in the minds of American educators is worthwhile for its own sake.

1. For references to Newman in the book itself, see Philip Gleason, *Contending with Modernity: Catholic Higher Education in the Twentieth Century* (New York: Oxford University Press, 1995), pp. 7, 143–44, 151, 248, 252.

A slightly different version of this paper was given as the Archbishop Gerety Lecture at Seton Hall University, February 5, 1997.

113

But does such a study have anything beyond "merely historical" interest? Does it have any relevance to our understanding of present-day educational issues, or of Newman himself?[2] Whatever the answer to those questions, the record shows that many Americans have resorted to Newman for intellectual ammunition in controversy, or, in calmer circumstances, to buttress arguments they were advancing. That means lots of people have *thought* Newman was relevant to their situation. A look at this record, so rich in controversy, may perhaps shed some new light on Newman and his educational thought. But before inquiring into its reception, a few words of background about the book and the circumstances of its composition will be helpful.

The Idea of a University as we know it today dates from 1873 and consists of two parts.[3] Part I comprises nine "discourses" which set forth the basic theoretical principles of Newman's "idea" of university education.[4] Two of these principles stand out: (1) the crucial role of theology in university studies; and (2) the point that cultivation of the intellect, not mere acquisition of knowledge or preparation for a career, is the primary goal of university education. Part II of the *Idea* gives us ten essays on various aspects of university study that are intended to illustrate the general principles expounded in Part I. Some of the essays, such as "Literature" and "Christianity and Scientific Investigation," are frequently cited, but the nine discourses of Part I are what people usually have in mind when they speak of *The Idea of a University*.

2. John Coulson and A. M. Allchin ask this question of Newman's theological ideas in the introduction to the symposium they edited, *The Rediscovery of Newman* (London: Sheed & Ward and SPCK, 1966), p. xi.

3. The following discussion of the book, its background, and its publishing history, is based on Fergal McGrath, *Newman's University: Idea and Reality* (London: Longmans, 1951); McGrath, *The Consecration of Learning* (New York: Fordham University Press, 1962); A. Dwight Culler, *The Imperial Intellect: A Study of Newman's Educational Ideal* (New Haven: Yale University Press, 1955); and Ian T. Ker, "Editor's Introduction" to Ker's critical edition of *The Idea of a University* (Oxford: Clarendon Press, 1976). Other editions of *The Idea of a University* by George N. Shuster (Garden City, N.Y.: Image paperback, 1959), Martin J. Svaglic (New York: Rinehart paperback, 1960), and Frank Turner (New Haven: Yale University Press, 1996), contain useful useful commentaries.

4. For an extended discussion of the notion that a university could be dominated by a ruling "idea," see Sheldon Rothblatt, *The Modern University and Its Discontents: The Fate of Newman's Legacies in Britain and America* (Cambridge: Cambridge University Press, 1997), chap. 1.

The two parts existed independently and with different titles before being brought together in 1873 as the *Idea*. This fact—along with the existence of a third book by Newman called *The Office and Work of Universities*—makes for a rather confusing publication history. For our purposes it will suffice to observe that all three of these works derive from Newman's role as founding rector of the Catholic University in Ireland in the years 1851 to 1858. What became Part I of the *Idea* were lectures he gave when the university was still in the planning stage. They were published in Dublin in 1852 under the title *Discourses on the Scope and Nature of University Education;* a revised edition appeared in London in 1859, and Newman revised them again for the *Idea*. The essays that make up Part II of the *Idea* were composed by Newman for various academic occasions after the university got under way and were collected as a book entitled *Lectures and Essays on University Subjects.* That book appeared in 1859, the same year as the second edition of the original discourses. Three years earlier (i.e., 1856), the previously mentioned *Office and Work of Universities* came out. Though never part of *The Idea of a University,* this collection of Newman's informal sketches of university history was the first of his educational writings to reach these shores. And to confuse the picture further, *The Office and Work of Universities* was later re-issued as *The Rise and Progress of Universities,* and later still as *University Sketches.*[5]

So much for general background; we turn now to our subject proper: how Newman's *Idea* has been received in America. The story falls into four chronological phases, the first of which covers the period 1852 to 1890—that is, from the delivery of Newman's discourses in Dublin to the year of his death.

I. Early Impact

The phase of early impact was charged with controversy. At the broadest level, the Revolutions of 1848 heightened already existing tensions between the Catholic Church and liberalism and fueled bitter anti-clericalism on the Continent. In England and the United States, anti-

---

5. In addition to McGrath, Culler, and Ker, cited above, see the Introduction by Michael Tierney to John Henry Newman, *University Sketches* (Dublin: Browne and Nolan, n.d.), esp. pp. xv–xvi.

Catholicism reached almost hysterical levels in the early 1850s. In Ireland, the university question itself grew out of religious controversy that centered on education. More precisely, the issue concerned the so-called "mixed education" that was to be offered by the newly created schools called Queens Colleges, which were designed to be religiously neutral institutions open to Catholics as well as Protestants. Although this was an improvement over the existing discrimination against Catholics in higher education, many Irish remained deeply suspicious of English intentions—especially since the British government seemed indifferent to Irish suffering in the Great Famine that struck just as the Queens Colleges plan was broached.

But despite their long-standing grievances against England, the Irish bishops could not present a united front on the question of mixed education.[6] Several opposed the idea vigorously; others, however, thought the Queens Colleges were the best they could hope for, and most middle-class lay Catholics agreed with the latter view. Since they couldn't come to any conclusion among themselves, the bishops referred the question to Rome for a solution. There Pope Pius IX saw in "mixed education" an example of the liberalism against which he meant to do battle. The Irish bishops, he said, should set up their own strictly Catholic university.

This was the institution to which Newman was called as rector. Although a stranger to Irish affairs, he knew very well he was stepping into a potential minefield. He therefore shaped the *Discourses* he gave to initiate the project with an eye to the disagreements existing among his listeners in Dublin. In stressing the crucial role of theology in university studies, Newman addressed the concerns of those who rejected the Queens Colleges. But by referring to his Oxford experience, and by insisting that cultivation of the intellect would be the new university's primary goal, he reassured lay Catholics that it would not be a strictly clerical school. This careful attention to the divergent expectations of his audience helped make Newman's lectures a great hit in Dublin. However,

6. It is worth noting that in 1850 the chief Irish opponent of mixed education, Archbishop Paul Cullen of Armagh and later Dublin, inquired of various American prelates what their experience had been in respect to "mixed colleges and mixed education in general." See John P. Marschall, "Francis P. Kenrick, 1851–1863: The Baltimore Years" (Ph.D. diss., Catholic University of America, 1965), p. 106.

they were interrupted when he had to rush back to England to defend himself in a libel suit that grew out of the religious polemics set off by the restoration of the Catholic hierarchy in 1850. The sensational nature of this affair perhaps obscured Newman's other activities, for when the Dublin *Discourses* were published a few months later, they passed almost completely unnoticed in England.[7]

Non-Catholics in this country were similarly unaware of his *Discourses*. So far as I have been able to discover, only two nineteenth-century Protestant educators even alluded to Newman's work.[8] Among American Catholics, however, the situation was quite different. They knew about the Irish university project from the beginning, and the example it furnished, along with Newman's writings, played a significant role in the establishment of the Catholic University of America, which opened its doors the year before Newman died.

We have the very best kind of evidence that American Catholics knew about the Irish university—namely, the fact that they gave a lot of money to help get it started.[9] This came about because the promoters of the university dispatched two priests who spent well over a year canvass-

---

7. Only the first five of the *Discourses* were actually delivered by Newman in Ireland; the remainder were written in England while he was still harried by the libel suit. According to Ker, "Introduction," xxviii–xxix, a "chilling silence" greeted their publication, with only the *Rambler*, a Catholic quarterly, taking any notice of the first version, and only the *Dublin Review*, also Catholic, commenting on the *Idea* when it appeared in 1873. An excerpt from the *Rambler's* review appeared in the *Metropolitan* (Baltimore) 2 (Feb. 1854): 17–21.

8. The only non-Catholic references to Newman I have found are: F. H. Hedge, "University Reform," *Atlantic Monthly* 18 (Sept. 1866): 301; and Daniel Coit Gilman, *University Problems in the United States* (New York: Century, 1898), p. 185. Gilman does not cite *Office and Work of Universities* by name (as Hedge did), but the passage he quotes is taken from that book. Hedge's mention of Newman, incidentally, provides the only index entry to Newman in Richard Hofstadter and Wilson Smith, eds., *American Higher Education: A Documentary History*, 2 vols. (Chicago: Univ. of Chicago Press, 1961), 2:563. John S. Brubacher and Willis Rudy, *Higher Education in Transition* (New York: Harper, 1958), pp. 280–81, suggest that Noah Porter had probably read Newman, but the passage they cite in Porter's *The American Colleges and the American Public* (New Haven: C. C. Chatfield., 1870), pp. 262–68, makes no mention of Newman. An article about Newman in *Notre Dame Scholastic* 17 (May 10, 1884): 553–55 complained that he was entirely overlooked in the most recent work on English literature published in the U.S.; however, the author of this article did not include *The Idea of a University* in his own discussion.

9. My information about this campaign comes from the *New York Freeman's Journal* (hereafter *NYFJ*), which also printed the text of Newman's first Dublin Dis-

ing for contributions from the eastern seaboard to the Mississippi River. These "Rev. Delegates," as they were called, appealed to ethnic feeling as well as to religion, by portraying the Queens Colleges as an English plot to rob the Irish of their nationality and proclaiming that the new university would restore "Ireland's ancient unrivalled fame in letters." They usually preached in churches, but also appeared before humble groups like the Quarrymen's Union Benevolent Society of New York. The Quarrymen could afford to give only $110, but the total amount raised was impressive: about $40,000 by 1853, a sum that does *not* include contributions made to help Newman defray the costs of his libel suit.[10]

Nationalism entered the picture more disruptively when Newman invited the great American convert, Orestes A. Brownson, to join the faculty of the new university. This occurred at the very height of American nativism, and the problem was that Brownson had just published two highly controversial articles on that subject. Although critical of Know-Nothing bigotry, Brownson acknowledged that the behavior of Irish newcomers gave some cause for complaint, and he agreed with the nativists in urging immigrants to become Americanized. To Irish Catholics hard-pressed by external enemies, this was treason most foul. Great was their outrage and report of it carried across the Atlantic. In Ireland it reinforced the suspicions of nationalists who had never been enthusiastic about having an Englishman—and a recent convert to boot—at the head of their university. To defuse the situation, an embarrassed Newman had to withdraw the invitation to Brownson.[11]

A less dramatic but far more important kind of ideological conflict

---

course (*NYFJ*, June 26, July 23, 1852), the text of his sermon "The Second Spring" (*NYFJ*, Sept. 4, 1852), and many news items about Newman's libel trial. *NYFJ* editor James A. McMaster converted to Catholicism as part of the American version of the Oxford Movement, was a great admirer of Newman, and had visited him at Littlemore shortly before Newman himself entered the Catholic Church. See Mary Augustine Kwitchen, *James Alphonsus McMaster: A Study in American Thought* (Washington, D.C.: The Catholic University of America Press, 1945), esp. pp. 33–38, 58–61.

10. The $40,000 figure comes from a letter written to the *NYFJ* several years later (issue of Jan. 10, 1857); for the nationalistic reference and Quarrymen's contribution, see *NYFJ*, Jan. 24, 1852; for other references, see *NYFJ*, Dec. 20, 1851; Jan. 3 and March 6, 1852; May 21 and Aug. 4, 1853.

11. See McGrath, *Newman's University*, pp. 187–88, 216–18; and Thomas R. Ryan, *Orestes A. Brownson: A Definitive Biography* (Huntington, Ind.: Our Sunday Visitor, 1976), chaps. 30, 31, and 33.

shaped the campaign to establish Catholic universities in both Ireland and the United States. It arose from the growing realization among Catholics in the mid-nineteenth century that the real threat to faith came, not from formal heresy or from traditional Protestant foes, but from the "deep, plausible skepticism" that permeated modern thought. Newman himself painted a dismaying picture of the accelerating tendency toward atheism and analyzed its workings in the learned world with stunning acuity. Indeed, he devoted Discourse IX of *The Idea of a University* to showing that, without the effective presence of the Church as a counter-influence, higher education tended inevitably to reinforce the drift toward atheism.[12] In this context, it is hardly surprising that American Catholics felt that they too needed a Catholic University, that the Irish initiative served as an early stimulus, and that Newman's writings figured prominently in the campaign to bring one into existence.[13]

Brownson, who had long believed Catholic education needed thorough reform, took note of Newman's writings in the 1850s, and after the Civil War virtually everyone who promoted the establishment of the Catholic University of America paid homage to *The Idea of a University* as a "classic which [the world] will not willingly let perish."[14] That was especially the case with Bishop John Lancaster Spalding of Peoria, whose

12. Newman, *Apologia Pro Vita Sua,* Modern Library ed. (New York, 1950), pp. 242, 256–58; Newman, *Idea of a University,* Discourse IX, "Duties of the Church Towards Knowledge"; see also "A Form of Infidelity of the Day," which is Lecture V of Part II of the *Idea.* As the leading promoter of the Catholic University of America put it, the "real issue . . . [is] not between the Church and the sects, but between the Church and infidelity." John Lancaster Spalding quoted in C. Joseph Nuesse, *The Catholic University of America: A Centennial History* (Washington, D.C.: The Catholic University of America Press, 1990), pp. 18–19.

13. John Tracy Ellis, *The Formative Years of the Catholic University of America* (Washington, D.C.: American Catholic Historical Association, 1946), is the standard work; for his rather hesitant comments on Newman's possible influence, see pp. 29–31; see also Nuesse, *Catholic University,* chap. 1. For the influence of "impoverished Ireland's" example, see "Shall We Have a Catholic Congress?" *Catholic World* 8 (Nov. 1868): 227; and Herman J. Heuser, "American Catholics and the Proposed University," *American Catholic Quarterly Review* (hereafter *ACQR*) 10 (Oct. 1885): 637.

14. *Brownson's Quarterly Review* 16 (Oct. 1859): 552, 554–55; ibid., 17 (July 1860): 320–23; quotation from Brother Azarias [Patrick F. Mullany], "The Catholic University Question in Ireland and England," *ACQR* 3 (Oct. 1878): 585. Thomas A. Becker's influential articles on the subject, "Shall We Have a University" and "A Plan for the Proposed Catholic University," *ACQR* 1 (April, Oct. 1876): 230–53, 655–79, used Newman's writings as their springboard. See also *Catholic Mirror* (Baltimore),

persistent agitation was the single most important factor in persuading his brother bishops to commit themselves to the creation of such an institution.[15] This was a major commitment, for though it was to begin with a theological faculty only, the Catholic University of America was designed from the beginning to be a real graduate-level university—and that would make it an altogether different kind of institution from the existing Catholic colleges, which might call themselves universities, but were essentially high schools.

Like other Catholics, Spalding looked upon a university as the best means of meeting the threat of infidelity, and he echoed Newman in asserting that "the great intellectual work of the church in our day is to show that theology . . . is the essential and central point of union of the whole scientific group [of universities studies]."[16] Yet he did *not* want an institution designed to turn out "profound theologians, or learned exegetes, or skillful metaphysicians or specialists of any kind." Like Newman, he wanted a university that would "impart not professional skill but cultivation of mind," that would strengthen and refine the intellect rather than storing the memory.[17] Not only did Spalding refer to and quote from Newman to buttress his argument, his line of reasoning and even his prose itself followed Newman's so closely as to border occasionally on plagiarism. Consider the following example:

> The education of which I speak is expansion and discipline of mind rather than learning; and its tendency is not so much to form . . . [scholarly specialists] as to cultivate a habit of mind, which, for want of a better word, may be called philosophical; to enlarge the intellect, to strengthen and [make] supple its faculties, to enable it

Sept. 19, 1885; John J. Keane, "The Roman Universities," *Catholic World* 46 (December 1887): 313–21; and Thomas Bouquillon, "Theology in Universities," *Catholic University Bulletin* 1 (1895): 25, 31.

15. Spalding's earliest remarks on the need for a university date from 1871 and 1873; he followed up with more elaborate statements in 1881, 1884, 1885, and 1888. See Ellis, *Formative Years*, 51–54, 56–57, 67–80, 85–86; Nuesse, *Catholic University*, 10–19; and David F. Sweeney, *The Life of John Lancaster Spalding, First Bishop of Peoria, 1840–1916* (New York: Herder, 1965), pp. 127-39, 157-58, 166-70.

16. J. L. Spalding, *The Life of the Most Reverend M. J. Spalding, D.D., Archbishop of Baltimore* (New York: Christian Press Association, 1873), pp. 315–17.

17. J. L. Spalding, *Lectures and Discourses* (New York: Catholic Publication Society, 1882), pp. 127–60, esp. p. 150.

to take connected views of things and their relations, and to see clear amid the mazes of human error and through the mists of human passion.[18]

Though this Newmanian vision inspired Spalding's drive to bring it into being, it did not shape the university's functioning once it was established. On the contrary, the Catholic University of America accepted the research emphasis sweeping through American higher education at the time and bent its efforts toward producing the learned specialists of whom Spalding spoke with near disdain. Even more ironically, Spalding, too, was by that time moving away from Newman, but not in the direction of Germanic *Wissenschaft*. In his last major statement on the subject—an address given at the cornerstone-laying of the university's first building—Spalding, in his enthusiasm for modern progress, left Newman far behind. But while he hailed the achievements of modern science and scholarship, he still insisted that the university should "make culture its first aim." Now, however, Spalding's understanding of "culture" owed more to Matthew Arnold than to Newman, for he invested it with quasi-religious value. "Mind," he proclaimed in his loftiest rhetorical flight, "is Heaven's pioneer making way for faith, hope, and love, for higher aims and nobler life . . ." To be human "is to be intelligent and moral, and therefore religious. . . . He who believes in culture must believe in God; for what but God do we mean when we talk of loving the best thoughts and the highest beauty."[19]

II. *The Modernist Interlude*

The Catholic University's developing along conventional research-university lines, and Spalding's turn toward Arnold, presaged a period in

18. J. L. Spalding, *Means and Ends of Education* (Chicago: McClurg, 1895), p. 209.
19. The lecture quoted here drew unfavorable notice from Rome; it is reprinted in Spalding's *Education and the Higher Life* (Chicago: McClurg, 1890), chap. 8, esp. pp. 197, 199, 203–4. For discussion, see Sweeney, *Spalding*, pp. 182–87. Spalding's Arnoldian turn is of special interest because he had earlier (*ACQR* 4 [July 1879]: 389–414) written an article critical of culture's being elevated to religious status, and also because David J. DeLaura argues persuasively that Newman strongly influenced Arnold; see DeLaura, *Hebrew and Hellene in Victorian England: Newman, Arnold, and Pater* (Austin: University of Texas Press, 1969), esp. pp. 39, 43ff., 79, 100–101.

which Newman's *Idea of a University* dropped into relative obscurity. This second chapter in our story, which we can call "The Modernist Interlude," extends from the 1890s to the First World War. During that epoch, other aspects of Newman's thought received much more attention than the *Idea,* and Catholic educators had their hands full dealing with practical issues on which Newman's book shed no very useful light. Both of these shifts involved a great deal of controversy, but the circumstances had changed greatly since the 1850s.

The most intense controversy centered around the movement called Modernism, which Pope Pius X condemned as a heresy in 1907. The condemnation resulted from the pope's conviction that the liberals were watering down essential Catholic doctrine in the vain effort to make it acceptable to modern thinkers. Modernism was really a European phenomenon, but it bore a clear family resemblance to the Americanism of the 1890s, and it had faint but audible echoes in the United States at the time of its condemnnation.[20] In recent years, Catholic scholars have largely rehabilitated the Modernists. But in the days when it was held to be an undoubted heresy, anyone who exhibited the least tendency toward Modernism was suspect. To a certain extent, that happened to Newman, for though he died before the movement took shape, he was often called its precursor.

While he never accepted the "liberalism" that emptied religion of its objective and dogmatic elements, Newman did oppose the extreme rigorism of ultramontane Catholicism as it developed after the proclamation of papal infallibilty in 1870. In that sense, he was a liberal and the later Modernists admired him for it. But his writings were even more important in establishing Newman's stature among the Modernists. Not, however, his *Idea of the University.* The key works for them were the *Essay on the Development of Christian Doctrine,* which accorded with their historicism and conviction of the need for change, and *An Essay in Aid of a Grammar of Assent,* with its subtle analysis of the psychology of religious belief. The first of these books inspired several articles by Alfred Loisy,

20. See Marvin R. O'Connell, *Critics on Trial: An Introduction to the Catholic Modernist Crisis* (Washington, D.C.: The Catholic University of America Press, 1994); R. Scott Appleby, *"Church and Age Unite!" The Modernist Impulse in American Catholicism* (Notre Dame, Ind.: University of Notre Dame Press, 1992).

the most important of the Modernists. Another Modernist, Henri Bremond, wrote one of the earliest biographies of Newman as an essay in religious psychology.[21]

Modernist admiration for Newman was not unqualified, for they knew he would never have gone as far as they thought necessary. But their sympathy for his general approach and their many references to his writings were enough to make the *Development of Christian Doctrine* and the *Grammar of Assent* suspect during the anti-Modernist reaction that followed condemnation of the movement. On the whole, however, American Catholic educators did not seem to pay much attention to these matters. Indeed, I can recall encountering only one cautionary reference to these books, and that came from a person very favorably disposed toward Newman.[22] As previously noted, Catholic educators were much more concerned with practical problems in the early years of the twentieth century. Yet there is a different kind of link with Newman here—one associated with what was coming to be known in the those days as "the Newman movement."

Newman Clubs, as those of a certain age will remember, were organizations designed to provide pastoral care for, and opportunities for social interaction among, Catholic students on the campuses of non-Catholic colleges and universities. In the early days of their organization, not all of these "Catholic clubs" took Newman's name, but by World War I it was firmly attached to the movement. *The Idea of a University* did not, however, play the same role in inspiring this movement as it did in the campaign to found the Catholic University of America. Such Catholic

21. O'Connell, *Critics on Trial*, pp. 178–81 (for Loisy), 285–86 (for Bremond); chap. 10, "The Ghost of Newman," is relevant throughout. There is no index entry for *The Idea of a University* in O'Connell's book. There is only one in Mary Jo Weaver, ed., *Newman and the Modernists* (Lanham, Md.: Univ. Press of America, 1985); it occurs (on p. 7) in Paul Misner's contribution, "The 'Liberal' Legacy of Newman," which follows a biographical method in tracing the shifting emphases of Newman's thought.

22. For this cautionary note, which occurs in a teachers' guide to Newman published in 1930, see Arnold Sparr, *To Promote, Defend, and Redeem: The Catholic Literary Revival and the Cultural Transformation of American Catholicism, 1920–1960* (Westport, Conn: Greenwood Press, 1990), p. 66. A leader of the Newman movement later recalled that some bishops "thought 'Newmanism' smacked of heresy." See John Whitney Evans, *The Newman Movement: Roman Catholics in American Higher Education, 1883–1971* (Notre Dame, Ind.: University of Notre Dame Press, 1980), p. 87.

clubs were, in fact, closer in spirit to Newman's later concern for getting Catholic students admitted to Oxford and providing for their pastoral needs—a shift of emphasis one scholar interprets as showing that, after his disappointments in Dublin, Newman changed his mind about whether a strictly Catholic university should be the goal.[23]

Be that as it may, the rapid spread of Newman Clubs in the years after 1900 was extremely disturbing to those in charge of Catholic colleges. For though they had to admit that students on non-Catholic campuses needed pastoral care, they didn't want to encourage attendance at such institutions. Since they feared that elaborate provision for Catholic centers at state universities and other "secular" schools would do just that, they regarded the Newman movement with considerable uneasiness. In fact, they tried in 1907 to get the bishops as a body to *mandate* attendance at Catholic colleges just as they had mandated attendance at parochial schools. That didn't work (although individual bishops later issued such orders locally), but the "drift" of Catholic students to secular institutions dramatized the weaknesses of Catholic colleges and sparked a movement of organizational and curricular reform that dominated the landscape of Catholic higher education from 1900 to 1920.[24]

The general tendency of these reforms was *away from* concentration on the classical languages, the study of which Newman endorsed in the *Idea*, and *toward* the professionalism he deprecated. It is therefore understandable that the leading promoters of the reform movement had little to say about Newman.[25] But the changes they pushed through were highly controversial, and it is surprising that the conservative opposition

23. Evans, *Newman Movement*, esp. pp. 19–21, 46–47, 53, and 55. John Coulson argues that Newman did indeed change his mind about a Catholic University: see Coulson, "Newman's Idea of an Educated Laity—the two versions," in Coulson, ed., *Theology and the University* (Baltimore: Helicon, 1964), pp. 47–65, and Coulson, *Newman and the Common Tradition* (Oxford: Clarendon, 1970), pp. 156–64. I. T. Ker takes the opposite view in "Did Newman Believe in the Idea of a Catholic University?" *Downside Review* 93 (Jan. 1975): 39–42; and in Ker, ed., *Idea of a University*, pp. 585–86n.

24. There was an abortive effort to revive the episcopal mandate idea in 1931–32. For both of these efforts, see Gleason, *Contending with Modernity*, pp. 24–25, 186; for the reform movement, ibid., chaps. 1–4.

25. It is revealing, for example, that James A. Burns, C.S.C., the main sparkplug of the reform movement, did not mention Newman in his *Catholic Education: A Study of Conditions* (New York: Longmans, 1917).

failed to enlist Newman in its defense of the old ways. One reason may have been that the Jesuits were the most prominent opponents of reform, and they were so married to their particular version of the classical liberal arts curriculum that they didn't see the relevance of Newman's book until very late in the game.[26]

Of course it was not altogether overlooked in those days. On the contrary, we can safely say that all Catholic educators venerated Newman in a general way, and quite a few made passing reference to *The Idea of a University*.[27] In 1914 a speaker at the Catholic Educational Association's annual meeting called the book "certainly a standard work," adding that anyone who dealt with the subject of liberal education could hardly avoid "fall[ing] into the phraseology of Newman." The same speaker, incidentally, was the first to make a point echoed by many later commentators, viz., that Newman's "university" is really what Americans would call a liberal arts college.[28] But despite this kind of attention, the Modernist interlude was a period of neglect compared to the epoch that followed.

26. The first Jesuit I found making purposeful use of Newman in criticizing the new trends was Francis P. Donnelly in "The Principles of Standardization," *Catholic Educational Association Bulletin* (hereafter *CEAB*) 16 (Nov. 1919): 144; and Donnelly, "The Fashion and Folly of Vocational Education," *America* 22 (Jan. 24, 1920): 309. Donnelly, however, was a strict classicist who valued Newman primarily as an ally in that cause. Thus most of the citations to Newman in his *Jesuit Education in Practice* (New York: Kenedy, 1934) refer to Cicero's influence on Newman or link the two in some other way.

27. See Brother Azarias [Patrick F. Mullany], *Phases of Thought and Culture* (Boston: Houghton Mifflin, 1892), pp. 17–23, 52, 75; John Talbot Smith, *The Training of a Priest* (New York: William H. Young, 1897), pp. 128, 189, 191, 193, 270; *Report of the First Annual Conference of the Association of Catholic Colleges . . . 1889* (Washington, D.C.: Catholic University of America, 1899), pp. 29–30, 44–45; *CEAB* 10 (Nov. 1913): 193; *CEAB* 14 (Nov. 1917): 57. As a student at Louvain—where he was, incidentally, suspected of being a Modernist—the future historian Peter K. Guilday was very devoted to Newman, calling him "My holy patron" and "my gentle heavenly protector." For Newman, see Guilday's diary, epilogue for 1907 and entry for February 25, 1908; for Modernism, entry Jan. 19 and 24, 1908, in Guilday papers, Archives of the Catholic University of America.

28. Augustine Stocker, O.S.B., "Liberal Education," *CEAB* 11 (Nov. 1914): 72, 73, 79–80, 82; on p. 84 the commentator on Stocker's paper also mentioned Newman.

III. The Golden Age of Newman's Idea

That third epoch, which extends from World War I to 1960, was the
golden age of Newman's *Idea*. In what follows, I will first sketch the evidence that justifies calling it that, and then suggest some reasons why
The Idea of a University had such visibility and influence in that era.

One thing that added to its visibility was the fact that non-Catholic
educators finally started paying attention to it. In 1915 the London *Times*
observed that although Newman had "not been accepted as a great educational writer, except by Roman Catholics of the intellectual type," his
work was actually well worth reading.[29] In the 1920s, the earlier praise
of Walter Pater, who called the *Idea* "the perfect handling of a theory,"
and of Sir Arthur Quiller-Couch, who held it up as a model for writers,
reached American audiences. Quiller-Couch added, incidentally, that its
earlier neglect was partly explainable by Newman's association with "a
religion still unpopular in England."[30]

The first significant non-Catholic voice in this country was that of
Charles F. Thwing, the president of Western Reserve University and a
prolific writer on higher education, who called the *Idea* "that precious
book," and quoted from it at length on the eve of World War I.[31] In the
1930s, Abraham Flexner and Robert M. Hutchins cited it in their cri-
tiques of American higher education, and the president of the University
of Minnesota was said to keep a copy on his desk and dip into it to "re-

29. Cited by Timothy Corcoran, S.J., "Liberal Studies and Moral Aims: A Critical
Survey of Newman's Position," *Thought* 1 (June 1926): 55. Several years earlier, a
British writer had in fact called the *Idea* a "universally-accepted masterpiece . . . the
first reading of which is always an epoch in every university man's life." See Alexander Whyte, *Newman: An Appreciation in Two Lectures* (Edinburgh and London:
Oliphant Anderson, & Ferrier, 1901), p. 122. For later citation of this judgment, see
below, note 35.

30. Pater's often-quoted comment is from his essay, "Style," first published in
1889; my citation is from Pater, *Essays on Literature and Art*, edited by Jennifer Uglow
(Totowa, N.J.: Rowman & Littlefield, 1973), p. 67. Arthur Quiller-Couch, *On the Art of
Writing* (New York: G. P. Putnam's Sons, 1916), p. 37. For Newman's possible influence on Pater, see DeLaura, *Hebrew and Hellene*.

31. Charles F. Thwing, *The American College* (New York: Platt and Rich, 1914),
pp. 2–3, 132; Thwing, "Education According to John Henry Newman," *School & Society* 3 (Feb. 12, 1916): 217–29. See also Harriet W. Handschy, "The Educational Theories of Cardinal Newman and John Dewey," *Education* 49 (Nov. 1928): 129–37.

fresh his spirit . . . whenever a free moment presented itself."[32] But the real breakthrough in respect to mainstream academic interest took place only after World War II. Then—almost a century late, one might say—came three major events: the chapter on the book in the 1945 study of Newman's thought by Charles F. Harrold of Ohio State University; the same author's edition of *The Idea of a University* in 1947; and the appearance in 1955 of *The Imperial Intellect,* a brilliant and widely noted study of Newman's educational thought by A. Dwight Culler of Yale.[33]

Among Catholics, the first stirrings of a veritable explosion of interest made themselves felt in the 1920s. Newman Clubs multiplied on non-Catholic campuses and began to take greater notice of their patron's educational ideas.[34] On Catholic campuses, students began to hear that reading *The Idea of a University* should mark an "epoch" in one's intellectual life, and a 1924 survey showed that their teachers gave it first place among the ten best Catholic books in the English language.[35] The young lay scholar George N. Shuster had already devoted three chapters to Newman in his *Catholic Spirit in Modern English Literature* (1922), and another lay professor was guiding the Catholic Literary Club of Pittsburgh in its exploration of Newman's writings.[36] The Jesuits, however, seized

32. Abraham Flexner, *Universities: American, English, German* (New York: Oxford, 1930), p. 3; Robert M. Hutchins, *The Higher Learning in America* (New Haven: Yale, 1936), pp. 62–63, 103. For the president of Minnesota, see William F. Cunningham, C.S.C., "Priorities in Higher Education," *Bulletin of the Educational Conference of the Priests of Holy Cross* 16 (June 1942): 36–37.

33. Charles F. Harrold, *John Henry Newman: An Expository and Critical Study of His Mind, Thought, and Art* (New York: Longmans, 1945), chap. 5; Harrold's edition of the *Idea* was published by Longmans in 1947. For Culler's work, see note 3, above. Though not about the *Idea,* Walter E. Houghton, *The Art of Newman's* Apologia (New Haven: Yale University Press, 1945), was also a significant landmark in American academic recognition of Newman.

34. On this point, see Evans, *Newman Movement,* 86–87, and Evans, "Was Newman Ever Our Patron?" *Campus Ministry Report* [published by the Department of Education, U.S. Catholic Conference] vol. 2, no. 6 (Feb. 1976): 1–8. I am grateful to Fr. Evans for giving me a copy of this paper.

35. Daniel M. O'Connell, S.J., "Newman and Catholic Culture," *America* 30 (Oct. 20, 1923): 21–23, cites the "epoch" quotation from Whyte, *Newman;* Svaglic cites it without identifying the source on the first page of his edition of the *Idea* (see above, note 3). A writer in *Notre Dame Scholastic* 54 (Feb. 5, 1921): 251–53 said that reading the *Idea* "ought to be one of the greatest delights of every student." For the survey of college teachers, see Francis X. Talbot, S.J., "Results of the College Vote," *America* 30 (Feb. 2, 1924): 380–81.

36. George N. Shuster, *Catholic Spirit in Modern English Literature* (New York:

the lead in promoting the great English cardinal. His most enthusiastic champion was Daniel M. O'Connell, S.J., of Xavier University in Cincinnati, who wrote a half-dozen articles urging college study of Newman's writings—which he piquantly described as "a veritable eureka" for Catholics. To assist this program in a practical way, O'Connell edited versions suitable for classroom use of *The Idea of a University, The Present Position of Catholics in England,* and the *Apologia Pro Vita Sua.*[37]

Evidence that O'Connell's campaign was having its effect is furnished by the following course description, which appeared in several Jesuit college catalogues:

> NEWMAN: His commanding position in the religious intellectual life of the nineteenth century; life and associations at Oxford; Catholic life; his philosophy of education in The Idea of a University; his controversial, apologetic and homiletic works; the great Christian protagonist in the warfare of modern rationalism; the acknowledged perfection of form in his prose.[38]

By 1930, two teachers' manuals to accompany such courses had already appeared, and a much broader study that came out in 1935—*The Catholic Literary Revival,* by Calvert Alexander, S.J.—greatly accelerated their development. Alexander portrayed Newman's conversion as the initial spark in a great revival of Catholic intellectual life that was still going on.

Macmillan, 1922), chaps. 3–5; for the Pittsburgh group, see *America* 30 (March 8, 1924): 498.

37. The O'Connell article cited in note 35 (from which the "eureka" quotation comes) later appeared with little or no change as "Cardinal Newman and Catholic Culture" in *American Ecclesiastical Review* 72 (May 1925): 467–73. His other articles are "Newman and the Catholic Colleges," *America* 30 (Dec. 29, 1923): 265–66; "Teaching Newman," ibid. 30 (Feb. 9, 1924): 409–10; and "A Newman Centenary," ibid., 80 (April 1929): 391–402 (the centenary was of Newman's appointment as vicar of St. Mary's, Oxford, in 1829). O'Connell's editions, all published by Loyola University Press in Chicago, were *Present Position of Catholics* (1925); *Idea of a University* (1927); *Apologia Pro Vita Sua* (1930). See also Raymond J. Gray, S.J., "The Literary Genius of Cardinal Newman," in Jesuit Educational Association, Mid-West Division, *Proceedings of the Fourth Annual Conference . . . 1925* (Chicago, 1925), 84–90.

38. The course description was originally drawn up as part of a major Jesuit curricular reform. For discussion of the reform, see Gleason, *Contending with Modernity,* pp. 57–58; for the original text, see *Report of the Committee on the Course of Studies, June, 1920* (copy in Woodstock Archives, Georgetown University); for its appearance in college catalogues, see Sparr, *Promote, Defend, and Redeem,* p. 66.

His book inspired scores of college courses on the revival that featured Newman prominently, and quite a few that were devoted exclusively to his writings.[39] I myself took one of the latter sort at the University of Dayton in the late 1940s. It wasn't very demanding, I'm afraid—all I can remember reading was *The Idea of a University*.

But interest in Newman was not confined to the college classroom. The centenaries of the Oxford Movement in 1933; of Newman's conversion in 1945; and of his Dublin *Discourses* in 1952 attracted much attention. Catholics marked these occasions with conferences, symposia, articles, and books, the most notable of which was *Newman's University: Idea and Reality*, by Fergal McGrath, S.J., a major contribution to scholarship.[40] And of course Catholics who participated in the midcentury discussion of liberal education made frequent mention of Newman. Two works that deserve special mention in this connection are Leo R. Ward's *Blueprint for a Catholic University* (1949), which devoted an entire chapter to analayzing the contemporary relevance of the *Idea*, and Justus George Lawler's *The Catholic Dimension of Higher Education* (1959), a book steeped in Newman's thought and published by a press named after him.[41] By

39. I. Q. Semper, *Questions and Exercises to Accompany Newman's* Idea of a University (Chicago: Loyola University Press, 1929); Edwin Ryan, *A College Handbook to Newman* (Washington, D.C.: Catholic Education Press, 1930); Calvert Alexander, *The Catholic Literary Revival* (Milwaukee: Bruce, 1935). A survey of Catholic colleges in 1940 reported 25 courses on the Catholic Literary Revival, 10 on Modern Catholic Writers, and 14 on Newman as such. See Franciscan Educational Conference, *Report of the Twenty-Second Annual Meeting . . . 1940* (Washington, D.C.: Capuchin College, 1940), 397–98. For discussion, see Sparr, *To Promote, Defend, and Redeem*, pp. 64ff., 101–4.

40. For a prize-winning essay on the 1933 centenary, see Thomas F. Coakley, "The Oxford Movement as a Stimulus to Catholic Education," *American Ecclesiastical Review* 89 (Dec. 1933): 597–603; for 1945, see John K. Ryan and Edmond Darvil Benard, eds., *American Essays for the Newman Centennial* (Washington, D.C.: The Catholic University of America Press, 1947), which reprints 13 representative essays and provides a 16-page listing, "Newman Centennial Literature"; for the third centenary, see Victor R. Yanitelli, S.J., ed., *A Newman Symposium: Report of the Tenth Annual Meeting of the Catholic Renascence Society . . . 1952* (New York: Fordham, n.d.), which concentrates on the *Idea* and educational issues. Although McGrath was an Irishman and his book (cited above, note 3) appeared in England, it attracted much attention in the U.S.

41. Leo R. Ward, C.S.C., *Blueprint for a Catholic University* (St. Louis: B. Herder, 1949), esp. chap. 15; Justus George Lawler, *The Catholic Dimension of Higher Education* (Westminster, Md.: Newman Press, 1959), has over 60 index entries to Newman. William F. Cunningham, C.S.C., *General Education and the Liberal College* (St. Louis: B.

the end of our third phase in 1960, interest in his educational ideas was lively enough to justify two new paperback editions of the *Idea*. One appeared in Doubleday's Catholic series called Image books; the other, expertly introduced and annotated by Loyola University's Martin J. Svaglic, took its place among the "Rinehart Editions," a series aimed at the general college market.[42]

So much for the evidence showing that this was the *Idea*'s golden age. Now we must try to account for the phenomenon. One explanatory factor—the three centenaries that focussed attention on Newman and his works—has already been touched upon.[43] Another—the continuing growth of American higher education—was relevant in at least three ways. It permitted the development of scholarly specialties like Victorian literature, in which Professors Harrold, Culler, and Svaglic worked. It enlarged the potential student audience for Newman's writings at the graduate as well as undergraduate level. And it enhanced the importance of, and public interest in, questions of educational policy such as those dealt with in *The Idea of a University*. The third of these considerations was especially relevant in the post–World War II years, in which a revival of religion coincided with a marked renewal of concern for liberal or (as it was often called) "general" education.

This brings us to ideological factors, for the postwar interest in religion and liberal arts had a definitely conservative coloration, and so too did the Newman of the *Idea*'s golden age. In fact, Russell Kirk included a lengthy discussion of Newman in his *Conservative Mind*, the best known work of the so-called New Conservatism of the 1950s.[44] Among Catho-

---

Herder, 1953), also treats Newman as a standard and still relevant authority. For discussion of the background of this book, see Gleason, *Contending with Modernity*, pp. 246–50.

42. The Image edition (Garden City, N.Y.: Doubleday, 1959) had an introduction by George N. Shuster; both it and the Rinehart Edition (New York: Rinehart, 1960) included all the essays comprising Part II of the *Idea*, but Svaglic also provided numerous notes for Part I. Three years later another paperback of Newman's writings appeared in the "Mentor-Omega" series: see Vincent Ferrer Blehl, S.J., ed., *The Essential Newman* (New York: New American Library, 1963).

43. According to Harrold, *Newman*, p. vii, as many as 10,000 books and articles were published to mark the centenary of the Oxford Movement in 1933.

44. Russell Kirk, *The Conservative Mind*, 7th rev. ed. ([1953] Chicago: Regnery, 1986), pp. 279–94.

lics, the ideological factor was the real key to the Newman revival, but it emerged in the 1920s and in a way harked back to the Newman of the 1850s.

The most obvious parallel between the two eras is found in O'Connell's re-issue of *The Present Position of Catholics in England,* a masterpiece of controversy in which Newman excoriated the No-Popery of his day. O'Connell stressed the relevance of this work to the latter-day anti-Catholicism of the 1920s: here readers would find that every wild charge "flung upon the gale" by the contemporary Ku Klux Klan had been demolished by Newman seven decades earlier.[45] But beyond the level of crude prejudice, there was a deeper parallel—in both eras, Newman stood forth as the champion of Catholic truth, Catholic learning, and Catholic culture against the irreligious spirit of the age. *The Idea of a University,* with its insistence on theology, its exaltation of intellectual cultivation, and its serene assurance that faith and knowledge are compatible, was the classic statement of this ideal of Catholic culture. That explains why O'Connell put out his classroom edition of the *Idea* in 1927, and why the book remained a central feature of the intellectual and cultural revival that dominated the American Catholic landscape for the next quarter century.[46]

This consideration also helps us understand why Newman's work found a wider audience after World War II. Six years of horror and devastation, followed by the brooding threat of nuclear destruction, confirmed his insight that mere human knowledge and human reason could never contend successfully "against those giants, the passion and the pride of man." In the ensuing "age of anxiety," religious faith regained some of its former intellectual respectability, and literate readers were

45. O'Connell, "Teaching Newman," and "Editor's Apologia" in O'Connell, ed., *Present Position of Catholics.* The phrase "flung upon the gale" is adapted from what J. M. Cameron calls "a wonderfully boisterous passage" of this book (pp. 57–58 of O'Connell's edition). See Cameron, *John Henry Newman* (London: Longmans, 1956), pp. 23–24. The editor of *Commonweal* adapted Newman's title in discussing anti-Catholicism in the year Al Smith ran for president; see "The Present Position of Catholics in the United States," in Michael Williams, *Catholicism and the Modern Mind* (New York: Dial Press, 1928), pp. 95–128.

46. For the Catholic revival in general, see Gleason, *Contending with Modernity,* chaps. 5–7, 11–13; for Newman's role, Sparr, *To Promote, Defend, and Redeem,* pp. 64–71.

drawn to what one Newman scholar called "the morally serious in literature."[47] In that spiritual climate, *The Idea of a University* struck a more resonant chord among Americans than it ever had before.

But besides the nice fit between its theological emphasis and this broad *cultural* conservatism, *The Idea of a University* stood for a type of *educational* conservatism that was making a strong comeback, namely, the revival of the traditional ideal of liberal education. This revival came about as a delayed reaction to turn-of-the-century curricular reforms—especially the widespread introduction of the elective system—which, according to devotees of the liberal arts, rendered American higher education both superficial and incoherent. Robert M. Hutchins, president of the University of Chicago, who struggled to replace the frivolities of "athleticism," "collegiatism," and "vocationalism" with the metaphysics of Aristotle and Aquinas, led the fight in the 1930s. After the war, he was joined by a host of others convinced that the crisis of the age demanded a revitalization of humanistic culture that only the liberal arts could provide. Catholics, who regarded themselves as the special champions of liberal education, endorsed the goals of this movement wholeheartedly, and often invoked "the great name of Newman." Justifiable as that was, it must also be said that some who did so were such rigid traditionalists that they helped discredit his authority by wrongly making it seem that *The Idea of a University* ruled out higher education's serving any kind of practical or vocational purpose.[48]

IV. Eclipse and Reappearance

Moving now from the conservatism of the 1950s to the radicalism of the sixties, we enter upon the final chapter of our story, which I am calling "Eclipse and Reappearance." Since it comes all the way to the present, we lack the perspective on this epoch that only time can give,

47. Martin J. Svaglic, "Newman: In Our Time," in Yanitelli, ed., *Newman Symposium*, p. 110. The Newman quotation is from the *Idea*, Discourse V, sect. 9.

48. For Catholics' grappling with these issues, see Gleason, *Contending with Modernity*, pp. 246–56; for the broader American context, see Bruce A. Kimball, *Orators and Philosophers: A History of the Idea of Liberal Education*, expanded version (New York: College Entrance Examination Board, 1995), chap. 6, esp. pp. 191ff.

which means that any judgment about it must be regarded as provisional. Even so, it seems clear that *The Idea of a University* lost ground in the tumultous decade of the sixties; began to regain its cultural standing as those storms abated; and has very recently been linked once again with cultural and religious conservatism.

First as to its losing ground in the sixties. Older readers will recall those days of "campus unrest," as it was euphemistically called—protests, strikes, sit-ins, buildings occupied and even bombed, police "busts" and bloodied victims. In that febrile atmosphere, few thought it worthwhile to take up Newman's ancient text. And though the student rebels professed to be animated by humanistic idealism, their passion for "relevance," for ideas that could be put to work immediately in "changing the system," was quite alien to Newman's dedication to knowledge that had no end beyond itself. And how would Newman's "gentleman" have fared in those days? Is it not pathetic as well as comical to picture him at the Berkeley of the "filthy speech movement," utterly out of place with his "cultivated intellect . . . delicate taste . . . candid, equitable, dispassionate mind . . . noble and courteous bearing in the conduct of life"?[49]

It is true that some representatives of the hated "establishment," such as Clark Kerr and Jacques Barzun, alluded to *The Idea of a University.* But that did little to redeem it in the eyes of the reformers. Besides, Kerr cited it primarily to dramatize the contrast between the modern "multiversity" and what Newman had in mind.[50] It didn't rate a single mention in a major history of American higher education published in 1965; three years later, an authoritative study of the ongoing academic revolution took passing notice of "Newman Societies," but nothing more. Even Father Hesburgh of Notre Dame, who venerated Newman and reaffirmed the crucial role of theology in the university, emphasized the re-

49. Quotation from *The Idea of a University,* Discourse V, sect. 9.
50. Clark Kerr, *The Uses of the University* (Cambridge: Harvard University Press, 1963), pp. 1–3; Jacques Barzun, *The American University: How It Runs, Where It Is Going* (New York: Harper & Row, 1968), p. 210. In a personal communication to me (March 3, 1997), Sheldon Rothblatt emphasizes that, by introducing the notion that a university should have a ruling "idea," Newman furnished an organizing principle for much of the post–World War II discussion of higher education, and he adduces Kerr's book as an illustration of this phenomenon, which can be discerned even in works where "Newman is not mentioned by name."

moteness of his vision from contemporary realities.[51] Aside from using the passage about the mind's need for elbow room as a proof-text in the campaign for academic freedom, Catholics rarely referred to *The Idea of a University* in the sixties. I know of only one substantial effort to relate it to the current scene—and that was made by George Shuster, whose admiration for Newman dated back to the 1920s.[52]

But this does not mean that Newman was forgotten by Catholics. What happened was a virtual replay of the Modernist Interlude, for as the *Idea* faded into the background, the Newman of the *Development of Doctrine*, the *Apologia*, and the *Grammar of Assent* took center stage once more. The catalyst of this "rediscovery of Newman," as a volume published in 1967 put it, was the Second Vatican Council, of which Newman was often called the spiritual father. And though one may doubt that very many of the prelates in attendance were directly influenced by him, the Council certainly moved in directions that Newman had anticipated, not just in respect to the idea of development, but also in ecclesiology, ecumenism, and the role of the laity.[53]

This opens up many important questions on which much has been written, but it would be out of place to enter upon these matters, even if I were competent to discuss them. For our purposes, the main point is simply that the Newman of the *Idea* was, for a number of years, quite overshadowed by a different Newman—a more liberal, anti-authoritarian Newman. Indeed, some commentators betrayed a hint of embarrassment about the Newman hailed in preconciliar days as a hero of Catholic

51. Laurence R. Veysey, *The Emergence of the American University* (Chicago: University of Chicago Press, 1965); Christopher Jencks and David Riesman, *The Academic Revolution* (Garden City, N.Y.: Doubleday, 1968); Theodore M. Hesburgh, C.S.C., "Looking Back at Newman," *America* 106 (March 3, 1962): 720–21.

52. George N. Shuster, "Reflections on Newman's *Idea*," in Neil G. McCluskey, ed., *The Catholic University: A Modern Appraisal* (Notre Dame, Ind.: University of Notre Dame Press, 1970), pp. 104–17. Shuster had also written an introduction to the 1959 Image paperback edition of the *Idea*.

53. Coulson and Allchin, *Rediscovery of Newman*, contains 37 index entries for the *Apologia*; 27 for *Development of Doctrine*; 25 for *Grammar of Assent*; but only 5 for *Idea of a University*. See also Ian T. Ker, "Newman and the Postconciliar Church," in Stanley L. Jaki, ed., *Newman Today* (San Francisco: Ignatius Press, 1989), pp. 121–41; and various essays in Ian Ker and Alan G. Hill, eds., *Newman After a Hundred Years* (Oxford: Clarendon, 1990), esp. Nicholas Lash, "Tides and Twilight: Newman Since Vatican II," pp. 446–64.

culture—the Newman who opposed "mixed education" and derided Protestant prejudice so scornfully. Catholics of the ghetto era had, according to one writer, taken a very narrow view of Newman, admiring him for the wrong reasons; another suggested that in later life Newman himself had come around to favoring mixed education at the university level.[54]

But as we all know, the fervor of the sixties did not last. Things would never be the same as they had been before, in the Church or in American society—and that most definitely included higher education! Yet over the next two decades, a more conservative spirit reasserted itself. One of its manifestations was the growing fear that Catholic colleges and universities were losing—or had already lost!—their Catholic character. In these circumstances, the Newman who steadfastly opposed religious liberalism and championed the dogmatic principle began to attract attention once again.[55] On the broader scene of American higher education, challenges stemming from the 1960s, as well as growth and change since then, had the effect of revitalizing debate over the kind of basic issues dealt with in *The Idea of a University.* These ideological factors gave added impetus to scholarly interest in Newman, already reawakened by the Council and given an additional boost by the centenary of his death in 1990.

Ian T. Ker's authoritative and fully annotated edition of *The Idea of a University,* which appeared in 1976, was a major event on the scholarly front. Soon thereafter, J. M. Cameron, who had earlier said that modern educational thinking was little more than "a series of footnotes" to Newman, used the *Idea* as his point of departure for reflections on higher education in the present.[56] The same approach was carried much further by

54. See Sparr, *To Promote, Defend, and Redeem,* pp. 66–67; Christopher Hollis, *Newman and the Modern World* (London: Hollis & Carter, 1967), p. 216; and the Coulson-Ker exchange cited in note 23, above.

55. Even a liberal like Nicholas Lash observes that "development," which was "the buzzword [of the 1960s] and was widely seen as Newman's gift," has "had its day" adding: "It is not the solution to a problem, but simply a name for it . . ." Lash, "Tides and Twilight," p. 454.

56. For citation to Ker, see above, note 3. Sheldon Rothblatt's review essay of Ker in *History of Education Quarterly* 12 (Fall 1977): 327–34 refers to footnotes-to-Newman as "a phrase now commonplace." It comes from Cameron, *Newman,* pp. 24–25. Cameron's *On the Idea of a University* (Toronto: University of Toronto Press,

Jaroslav Pelikan in his *The Idea of the University: A Reexamination,* which came out in 1992. Although far from uncritical, Pelikan found Newman a rewarding partner in a "dialogue" on the nature and purpose of higher education, and his must surely be the most audacious effort on record to use a book more than a century old as the prism for analyzing the current scene.[57] Yale professor Frank Turner's 1996 edition of the *Idea* brings Newman even more directly into confrontation with the present. Besides supplying "questions for reflection" and other helps to the reader, Turner's edition includes five "interpretive essays" by leading scholars who range from an advocate of religion in higher education, through a representative of postmodernism, to a visionary of the "electronic university." Most recently, Sheldon Rothblatt's *The Modern University and Its Discontents* (1997), a dazzling collection of essays on the history of higher education, carries the subtitle, "The Fate of Newman's Legacies in Britain and America."[58]

A few months after Frank Turner's edition appeared, a militantly conservative student publication at Notre Dame published a review of it entitled "Newman's Dangerous *Idea.*" Although heartened by its appearance, the reviewer felt that neither Turner nor the other commentators went far enough in expounding what he called the *Idea*'s twofold thesis—"first, that a university must serve intellectual truth as its immediate end; and second that, intellectual truth being a good in itself but not the highest good, a university must serve the Church as its ultimate end."[59] This is but one of an increasing number of instances in which the antiliberal Newman has been enlisted by conservatives in our currently rag-

---

1978) reflects his deep admiration for Newman, but his discussion indicates that he would agree with Rothblatt's review, which argues that Newman's work is pertinent mainly by reason of the contrast it offers to the contemporary university.

57. Jaroslav Pelikan, *The Idea of the University: A Reexamination* (New Haven: Yale University Press, 1992). By contrast, a scholar-administrator with experience at the University of Southampton and Oxford finds relatively little of current value in Newman. See J. M. Roberts, *"The Idea of a University* Revisited," in Ker and Hill, *Newman After a Hundred Years,* pp. 193–222.

58. Frank M. Turner, ed., *The Idea of a University* (New Haven: Yale University Press, 1996); Rothblatt's book is cited above, note 4.

59. *Right Reason,* September 1996. *Common Sense,* another independent student/faculty publication at Notre Dame, several years older than *Right Reason,* is the latter's militantly liberal counterpart.

ing ideological wars. The earliest example I have come across is a 1988 symposium more or less explicitly dedicated to reclaiming him from "fashionable Catholic theologians" who "previously made a sport of setting up Newman as a *peritus* in theological relativism . . ." Not all of the contributors to this collection struck quite so polemical a note, but the one who dealt with "Newman's Idea of a Catholic University" was harsh in his treatment of Catholic educational leaders who sold out to "the senile decrees of a dying liberalism."[60]

In 1993 the conservative trend institutionalized itself in the "Cardinal Newman Society for the Preservation of Catholic Higher Education." This body, which held its first annual meeting in Washington in October 1996, encourages publications like Notre Dame's *Right Reason,* has its own web-page, and publishes a newsletter whose title, *The Turnaround,* epitomizes the society's understanding of its mission. Indeed, it claims to have made a difference already by creating a counter-voice to that of the Catholic higher education establishment, thereby helping to stave off the *"total defeat"* of orthodox Catholicism in respect to the application to the United States of *Ex Corde Ecclesiae.*[61]

Concluding Remarks

On that embattled note we conclude our survey of Newman's *Idea* in the minds of American educators—or, more accurately, Americans concerned about education. It is, perhaps, disheartening to find it still enmeshed in ideological controversy. But such has always been the case with Newman's broader legacy, which opposing factions have claimed and put to contradictory uses.

To my mind, this pattern of usage confirms the perennial relevance of Newman's thought. But does it not also raise a question about his intellectual consistency? If both liberals and conservatives can legitimately claim him as an ally, may we not infer that he simply vacillated— couldn't make up his mind where he stood? Though misguided, the

60. Jaki, *Newman Today,* pp. 9, 11, 111.
61. *"Total defeat"* quoted from a letter soliciting support sent out by Msgr. George A. Kelly and dated December 20, 1996; the other information from *Turnaround* 2 (Dec. 1996).

question is plausible enough to require an answer. And it can be answered in a way that not only vindicates Newman's consistency but also illuminates his educational ideal.

The terms "liberal" and "conservative" are, of course, far too vague, capacious, and flexible to serve as the criteria for determining consistency. But even if they designated something more definite, the same point would apply to them that Newman applied to the "leading ideas" of "scientific men"—whatever truth such ideas embody, it is not the *whole truth;* they must always be "compared with other truths." Indeed, the capacity to compare, contrast, and juxtapose ideas, to view them from different perspectives, is the distinguishing mark of that "philosophical habit of mind" which Newman holds out as the *beau ideal* of liberal education. It is the mark of the mind "which has learned to leaven the dense mass of facts . . . with the elastic force of reason"; which "cannot be partial, cannot be exclusive, cannot be impetuous," but which has attained a "clear, calm, accurate vision and comprehension of all things, as far as the finite mind can embrace them, each in its place, and each with its own characteristics upon it."[62]

Possessed himself of this balanced and comprehensive vision, Newman could never be doctrinaire about anything, least of all religion. On the contrary, he understood that Catholic doctrine was in reality an ensemble "of separate propositions, each of which, if maintained to the exclusion of the rest, is a heresy."[63] From this it follows that circumstance has a great deal to do with what aspect of Catholic teaching one ought to stress. Under certain conditions, vindicating papal authority might take priority; in another set of circumstances, defending the claims of individual conscience could be the need of the hour.

This consideration in itself suffices to explain what might appear to be inconsistencies in Newman's stance—especially when we recall that his writings span a half-century of rapid and far-reaching change. But there is more, for Newman realized that sincere and intelligent Christian believers would *disagree* about what a given situation required, and he

---

62. Quotations from *Idea of a University,* Discourse IV, section 12; Disc. III, sect. 4; and Disc. VI, sect. 6.

63. Newman, *Development of Christian Doctrine* ([Harrold ed.] New York: Longmans, 1949), p. 14.

regarded the resulting controversy as natural, necessary, and beneficial. Speaking precisely of the "awful, never-dying duel" between authority and "private judgment" *within* the Catholic Church, he did not hesitate to call it "warfare" and to pronounce it "necessary for the very life of religion."[64] Taking into account this conflict theory of religious truth, as we may call it, along with Newman's appreciation for the multifaceted nature of religious truth and the role of circumstance in determining priorities, and remembering that most of his writings were, as he himself attested, responses to specific occasions—taking all this into account, need we wonder that at different times he stressed different points, or need we be perplexed that both liberals and conservative lay claim to his heritage?

But none of this was merely opportunistic. For just as Newman discerned a "continuity of principles" underlying the changes by which Christian doctrine "developed," we can be confident that an analogous kind of principle underlay any outward difference in the positions he took at one time and another.[65] To say what those principles were, and to speculate on how our grasping them would help us to deal with the problems of our own time, would require another essay—and another essayist as well! Let me conclude this one by stating my firm belief that our efforts to identify and apply those principles would be amply repaid, and that it would help us greatly in doing so if we could attain the philosophical habit of mind Newman describes so beautifully in *The Idea of a University.*

64. Newman, *Apologia Pro Vita Sua* ([Modern Library ed.] New York: Random House, 1950), p. 249.

65. Newman, *Development of Christian Doctrine*, pp. 165ff.

7. PRIEST, CHAPLAIN, SOLDIER . . . SPY?

Father Franz J. Feinler and the Experience of German American Catholics during World War I

"No Vacancy"

Perhaps Father Franz J. Feinler was surprised by Archbishop Michael J. Curley's response. Certainly he was disappointed by the arch-bishop's brief reply to his request for a chaplaincy or a pastorate some-where in the Archdiocese of Baltimore, which at that time, September 1926, still encompassed almost all of Maryland as well as the District of Columbia. Of course, Father Feinler was already familiar with Archbish-op Curley's matter-of-fact style. The priest's earlier requests for "tempo-rary work" and for ministerial faculties in the archdiocese had been ac-knowledged in an equally terse fashion. Although on those occasions at least Feinler's requests had been granted.[1]

The archbishop's response that "there is no vacancy for a Chaplain" and that "appointment to a parish is out the question for one who does not belong to the Diocese" seemed a sharp rejection of Father Feinler's offer of services.[2] After all, Father Feinler had been well received in

1. Archbishop Michael J. Curley to Rev. Franz J. Feinler, October 13, 1925, and February 12, 1926. Archives of the Archdiocese of Baltimore.
2. Archbishop Curley to Rev. Franz Feinler, September 10, 1926. Archives of the Archdiocese of Baltimore.

Washington by the pastor of St. Matthew's Church, Monsignor Edward Buckey, who was grateful to have the assistance of a priest confessor who could speak several languages. Feinler had also been welcomed at St. John's College, Washington's Catholic military academy, which employed him for his skills as an instructor in mathematics.[3] As the fifty-five-year-old priest read the archbishop's letter it would have been only natural for him to wonder if the stigma that he carried made Curley reluctant to accept his services on a permanent basis. Perhaps granting an official position to an ex–military chaplain convicted by a court-martial for having "willfully attempted to cause insubordination among the troops of the United States of America" invited more controversy than even the usually implacable Archbishop Curley would be willing to face. The archbishop may have been especially reluctant to take such a step if he knew that Feinler had come to Washington for the specific purpose of lobbying Congress for his exoneration.

German-American Catholics

Undoubtedly, one of the most important elements in building the Church in America were the millions of German-speaking Catholic immigrants and their descendants who, with Catholics of Irish descent, formed the largest components of American Catholicism at the turn of the twentieth century. An estimated 1.6 million German-speaking Catholics had flooded into the United States between 1820 and 1920, with the high point of emigration occurring during the 1880s.[4] Their numbers and their comparative wealth and education vis à vis other immigrant Catholics guaranteed that they would have a prominent role in shaping the Church in America. However, like other immigrant groups, the German-speaking Catholics who came to America had to struggle for acceptance not only in American society but also within the Catholic Church in the United States. Many of the English-speaking members of the Church in America, who themselves were recent immigrants from

3. Joseph Schifferli to Arthur Preuss, September 13, 1926. Arthur Preuss Papers. Reel 6. Archives of the Central Bureau of the Catholic Central Union, St. Louis, Mo. (hereafter APP).

4. Jay Dolan, *The American Catholic Experience: A History from Colonial Times to the Present* (Garden City, N.Y.: Doubleday, 1985), 130.

Ireland, feared that the "foreign" ways and language of their German co-religionists would undermine the effort of Catholics to find acceptance in American society.

For nearly twenty years, from the 1880s until the first years of the new century, German- and English-speaking Catholics were embroiled in disputes over the ethnic composition of the hierarchy, "national" parishes and schools, and the role of the Church in "Americanizing" its immigrant members.[5] By 1910, with the tide of German-speaking immigrants subsiding and the inevitable process of Americanization succeeding, German Catholics had come to a modus vivendi in American society and in an English-speaking Church. However, the onset of the Great War in Europe undermined the position of German-Americans in the United States and caused many of them to question all over again the level of their acceptance within the Church they had helped to build. The ordeal of Army Chaplain Father Franz J. Feinler indicates just how defenseless individuals and the Church itself were, once the forces of ethnic hatred had been set in motion by the war.

An Immigrant Priest

Franz Joseph Feinler was born in Gissigheim, Grand Duchy of Baden, on March 28, 1871. The son of Franz Carl and Maria Magdalena (Schmitt) Feinler, Franz received his education in local schools and in 1892 graduated from the Gymnasium at Tauberbischofsheim, Baden. He then entered the seminary at Freiburg, where he remained one year before transferring to the Collegio Urbano di Propaganda Fide in Rome. After four years at this institution, whose specific purpose was to train priests for mission lands, Feinler was ordained to the priesthood at the Basilica of St. John Lateran on June 12, 1897, for the Diocese of Sioux Falls, South Dakota.[6] Upon his arrival in the Diocese of Sioux Falls on

5. Colman J. Barry, O.S.B., *The Catholic Church and German Americans* (Milwaukee: Bruce Publishing Company, 1953). Philip Gleason, *The Conservative Reformers: German-American Catholics and the Social Order* (Notre Dame: University of Notre Dame Press, 1968). Rory T. Conley, *Arthur Preuss, Journalist and Voice of German and Conservative Catholics in America, 1871–1934*, New German-American Studies, vol. 16, ed. Don Heinrich Tolzmann (New York: Peter Lang, 1998).

6. Robinson, *The History of South Dakota*, vol. 2 (1905), 1681. Personnel File for Franz J. Feinler, Archives of the Diocese of Sioux Falls.

September 14, 1897, Feinler worked for a time as the secretary to Bishop Thomas O'Gorman.[7] Feinler's first parish assignment was as pastor of St. George's Church in Hartford, South Dakota, and, between 1898 and 1902, he served this church as well as Catholic congregations in the rural communities of Parker, Ipswich, and Del Rapids, South Dakota. From 1902 to 1905, Feinler was pastor at St. Peter's Church in White Lake. During his tenure at White Lake, Feinler's parents, brother and sister immigrated from Germany and joined him in South Dakota.[8] Feinler's assignment at White Lake was followed by two more, first at Ss. Peter and Paul in Starr (1905–7) and then at St. Lawrence Church in Milbank, South Dakota, in 1908.[9]

Army Chaplain

In December 1908 Feinler applied to the United States Army for an appointment as a chaplain. Two months later he was accepted and on March 2, 1909, received his first military posting to Vancouver, Washington, with the rank of first lieutenant.[10] Feinler remained at his station in Vancouver for nearly three years. In addition to his chaplain's duties, Feinler assisted at the church of St. James and St. Augustine in Vancouver.

Prior to the First World War, the United States maintained only a small standing army, and, apart from those officers trained at West Point, career soldiers enjoyed little of the prestige that would later be accorded American military officers. Military chaplains received even less honor. The military chaplaincy had a long and respected tradition within the American armed forces. However, most chaplains were political appointees, who in many cases had been less than successful in serving local churches. In the decade immediately preceding World War I, the reputation of military chaplains had become tarnished, as between 1898 and 1918 four chaplains were either courtmartialed or resigned to avoid

7. Personnel File for Franz J. Feinler, Archives of the Diocese of Sioux Falls.
8. Robinson, *The History of South Dakota*, vol. 2, 1681.
9. Assignments as listed in the *National Catholic Directory* for pertinent years.
10. File for Franz J. Feinler, Adjutant General's Office Document File (hereafter AGODF), Records Group (hereafter RG) 94. National Archives (hereafter NA) Number 1469251, December 31, 1908, February 15, 1909, and March 2, 1909.

trial. This was the largest proportion of the chaplaincy ever disciplined in such a brief time span. The situation of military chaplains was further complicated by their ambiguous status within the military, which treated them as being unimportant. Chaplains were discriminated against in rank, poorly paid, and in the words of General John Pershing, "often relegated . . . to the status of handy men who were detailed to write up boards of survey or operate libraries."[11]

The apparent ambivalence of the military authorities toward its chaplains merely reflected the attitudes of the churches from which they came. For the most part, both Protestant and Catholic church officials displayed little interest in either the appointments or the ministry of chaplains. It was only in 1905, at the instigation of Archbishop John Ireland, himself a chaplain in the Union army during the Civil War, that the American Catholic bishops began to address the problem. Shortly afterwards, the bishops created the Catholic Army and Navy Chaplains' Bureau to represent the hierarchy before the War Department in matters relating to the appointment of chaplains. However, during peacetime the military maintained few places for chaplains and showed little concern for their ministry. Thus, it is not surprising that when the United States entered World War I, there were only thirty-four Catholic military chaplains; sixteen were with the army, eight in the navy and ten were attached to National Guard units.[12]

Given such circumstances one wonders what motivated Father Franz Feinler to join the Army and for that matter, why the bishop of a "priest poor" diocese like Sioux Falls would have let him go. Perhaps, as a well-educated immigrant, he found the rural isolation of South Dakota too much for him. Unfortunately for the historian, the enlistment papers that Feinler filed for the U.S. Army did not require that he disclose the reasons for his application. During his initial posting at Vancouver, Feinler was expected to run educational and entertainment programs for the men in addition to providing religious services for the soldiers. According to the monthly reports that he was required to file, Feinler fulfilled his educational duties by providing such motivational lectures for the

11. John F. Piper, Jr., *The American Churches in World War I* (Athens: Ohio University Press, 1985), 107–8.
12. Ibid., 108.

soldiers as "How to make the Most of Ourselves."[13] Feinler also sought to address one of the principal problems of the soldiers, drunkenness. Periodically, Feinler gave lectures on the virtue of temperance and "gave the pledge" to a number of men.[14]

After his posting in Vancouver, Feinler's military assignments took him ever westward to army posts in the Pacific. In December 1912, Feinler was assigned to duty with the 13th Infantry in Manila.[15] There, responding to what was apparently an epidemic in the American army, Feinler added lectures on venereal disease and "social purity" to his repertoire.[16] Fifteen months after his posting to Manila, Feinler was assigned as an attaché at the American Embassy in Tokyo. This assignment was a result of Feinler's excellent abilities as a linguist. Having begun the study of Japanese in April 1911, Feinler was utilized at the embassy in Japan as a translator. While there, he worked on a producing a textbook for the study of Japanese.[17] It was during Feinler's three years in Tokyo that he received his promotion to the rank of captain in June 1916, after having completed the seven years of service required of chaplains.[18] Feinler's assignment in Japan ended in May 1917, a month after the U.S. entered the war against his native Germany.

"Vicious Spies . . . Among Us"

The America to which Father Feinler returned in November 1917 was much different from the country he had left just four years before. The United States was at war with Feinler's native land, Germany. One of the most notable aspects of American participation in the First World War was the rapidity with which the previously neutral nation was mobilized to meet the exigencies of modern, total warfare. Equally striking,

---

13. January 31, 1910. AGODF RG 94 1469251. NA.
14. March 31, 1910, August 31, 1910, and November 30, 1910. RG 94.1469251 F. J. Feinler. NA.
15. December 26, 1912. AGODF RG 94 1990454 NA.
16. June 30, 1913. January 31, 1914. AGODF RG 94 1469251 NA.
17. April 17, 1911. AGODF RG 94 1771651. November 10, 1913. AGODF RG 94 1990454. April 15, 1914, AGODF RG 94 2148527. December 31, 1914. AGODF RG 94 1469251 NA.
18. June 10, 1916. AGODF RG 94 1495374 NA.

and distressingly so, was the willingness of American government at all levels to suppress the basic civil rights of American citizens in order to enforce adherence to its policies. Through the use of modern methods of propaganda, the United States government, under the direction of the Wilson administration, succeeded in establishing almost universal support for a war which many thoughtful citizens, at least privately, found objectionable. To establish this widespread conformity, the government legitimated traditionally abhorrent "vigilance committees," severely restricted the freedom of the press, and participated in the harassment of its own citizens who happened to be of German descent.

This campaign to enforce conformity began even before war was declared. In late March 1917, in preparation for hostilities with Germany, Thomas Gregory, Attorney General of the United States, obtained President Wilson's approval to use volunteers to gather information on "suspected aliens and disloyal citizens."[19] These volunteers were to report their findings to the Justice Department, which would then oversee follow-up investigations. What was particularly disturbing about this employment of vigilantes was that in the process the government specifically designated a "superpatriotic" organization, the American Protective League, as a semi-official auxiliary of the Justice Department's Bureau of Investigation. Based in Chicago, the American Protective League had been formed in March 1917 by a private businessman. Its membership quickly swelled to over 200,000 members. These zealous but untrained "detectives" immersed themselves in hundreds of thousands of investigations. Armed with badges issued by the League, APL "agents" began by spying on suspect aliens, but they soon included their fellow citizens suspected of disloyalty. Foreign-born applicants for government positions had their private lives investigated by League members. Persons with German names or accents, regardless of their citizenship, were targets of suspicion. Predictably, since the American Protective League was a nativist organization founded to fight foreign subversion, they routinely raised fears of sedition, although they failed to discover a single German spy.[20]

19. Frederick C. Luebke, *Bonds of Loyalty: German-Americans and World War I* (DeKalb: Northern Illinois University Press, 1974), 211.
20. Ibid., 211–12.

Another mechanism authorized by the Wilson administration to galvanize support for the war effort was the Committee on Public Information. This committee, which Wilson created by executive order, in April 1917 sought to capture "the minds of men, for the conquest of their convictions."[21] As chairman of the Committee on Public Information, Wilson appointed his young protégé and former journalist, George Creel. Once appointed, Creel so dominated the activities of the committee that it came to be known popularly as the "Creel committee." As a government agency, the Creel committee was quite innovative in its methods. Employing all the techniques of modern advertising at a time when such techniques were still new, the Creel committee effectively mobilized public opinion in support of "Wilsonian idealism and wartime notions of patriotism."[22]

Although the Committee on Public Information took a positive approach in its propaganda efforts, "It contributed immeasurably to the climate of intolerance." The program of the Creel committee effectively defined patriotism as conformity of thought. Those who dissented from the Wilson administration's definition of patriotism were labelled as disloyal. The Creel committee also accentuated the popular hostility directed at all things German by feeding fears of German subversion. In the vision of the Creel committee, Americanization meant Anglicization, as the characteristics of English culture became the definition of culture itself.[23]

The activities of the Justice Department and the Creel committee spawned similar programs on the state level. The so-called "Councils of Defense" established in many states at the specific request of President Wilson were in many instances a real menace to civil liberties and vehicles for ethnic hatred. In some states these councils were merely panels of prominent citizens who acted as advisors to governors on issues related to the war effort. However, in the Midwestern states, where suspicion of German Americans ran deep, the state councils of defense were frequently given wide powers to combat perceived threats to national unity. In some states the councils of defense used vigilante methods in their

21. Secretary of War, Newton D. Baker cited in Mark Sullivan, *Our Times: The United States, 1900-1925,* 5 vols. (New York: Scribners, 1933), 423.
22. Luebke, *Bonds of Loyalty,* 212.
23. Ibid., 213.

pursuit of "slackers" and "Kaiserism." German-American citizens were regularly accused of disloyalty by secret informers and their free speech was limited by an atmosphere of intimidation and violence.[24]

By the summer of 1917 it had become increasingly dangerous to voice open opposition to the war. German Americans in particular had need to be cautious, as their perceived lack of enthusiasm for the cause was coming under attack from the president on down. On June 17, 1917, Flag Day, President Wilson had lent his office to baiting German Americans as a suspect group.

> The military masters of Germany filled our unsuspecting communities with vicious spies and conspirators and have sought to corrupt the opinion of our people [they have] spread sedition among us and sought to draw our citizens from their allegiance.[25]

George Creel's Committee on Public Information distributed seven million copies of Wilson's speech in the midst of a concurrent rise in anti-German feeling. Up until this time, much of the German-language press had continued to express its reservations regarding U.S. policies. Now the backlash set in. In July and August 1917 the popular magazines *Atlantic Monthly* and *Outlook* featured articles entitled "The Disloyalty of the German-American Press," and "The Menace of the German-American Press." In September, the magazine *Current Opinion* carried an essay detailing the growing demand for the suppression of the German-American press. These articles represented and stimulated the increasing distrust directed at German Americans.

"Not a Fit Language"

While such badgering may have caused the German-language press to reconsider their views concerning American involvement in the war, government restrictions quickly silenced all dissent. The Espionage Act passed by Congress in June 1917 empowered local postal inspectors to revoke second class mail permits for publications they deemed seditious.

24. Ibid., 214–15.
25. Quoted in Luebke, 234.

The German-language press was specifically targeted in October 1917, when a new law required their publishers to provide postal inspectors with English translations of any articles they published which referred to the government or the war.[26] The burden of these restrictions forced the German-language press to avoid controversial topics or to take on the expense of providing translations. Consequently, the content of the papers deteriorated. Furthermore, since simply reading German papers was considered offensive to some Americans, the circulations of such papers declined dramatically. Many of the smaller German-language papers were put out of business.[27]

As the first anniversary of the American declaration of war neared with no end in sight, public hostility toward Germans and German Americans intensified. A two month long Senate investigation of the National German-American Alliance begun in February 1918 heightened the rage against "Teutonism" by perpetuating the myth of German-American disloyalty. Acts of discrimination and violence against German Americans continued on the upsurge. German Americans were denied promotions and hounded for their supposed lack of support for the Liberty Loan drive. Throughout the Midwest, mobs forced individual German Americans into humiliating displays of "patriotism" by demanding that they kiss the flag or denounce the Kaiser.[28]

By this time the agitation against the use of the German language had reached a fever pitch. Numerous articles appeared in national publications calling for a complete ban on the use of German in America.[29] The American Defense Society, which claimed Theodore Roosevelt as its honorary president, made the outlawing of German a priority and led the campaign to eliminate German place names. One of its pamphlets asserted that "any language which produces a people of ruthless conquistadors such as now exists in Germany, is not a fit language to teach clean and pure American boys and girls."[30] The States began to legislate against the use of German in both private and public schools as an obsta-

---

26. Luebke, *Bonds of Loyalty,* 241–42.

27. Carl Wittke, *The German Language Press in America* (Frankfort: University of Kentucky Press, 1957), 264–72.

28. Luebke, 244–45, 273–80.   29. Ibid., 251.

30. Ibid., 216–17.

cle to "100% Americanization" of immigrants. The state of Missouri established an "honor roll" for churches, schools, and associations that
eliminated the use of German. German books were burned in "patriotic
rituals" across the country, while in South Dakota and Iowa the state
governments banned the use of German over the telephone or in gath-
erings of three or more people. Even the use of music written by German composers was banned in many places.[31]

The Plight of the "Church Germans"

One of the ironies of this hysteria directed at all things German was
that "church Germans," the German Americans who associated German
culture with their religious practice, but not with their politics, suffered
most. Those German-American organizations which had proudly associated themselves with German national interests in the period of American neutrality had by this time made an about-face and had readily disassociated themselves from the German language. "Church Germans"
on the other hand, because they had never associated themselves with
German war aims, saw no need to be apologetic about their continued
use of the German language, and so became the targets of the anti-
German backlash. German-speaking Mennonites and Hutterites were
especially abused because of their pacifism. Two Hutterites died in federal custody after four months in solitary confinement, where they were
required to stand all day with their hands chained above their heads.[32]
German Lutheran congregations also suffered from the terrorism. Their
churches were burned and some pastors were assaulted.[33]

German Catholics were generally more fortunate. The "superpatri-
ots" considered them to be foreign, but more Roman than German. Also,
the public pronouncements of Catholic bishops supporting the war effort
enhanced the patriotic image of the Catholic Church.[34] However, the
growth in anti-Catholicism that accompanied the popular xenophobia
led federal officials in June 1917 to search German-Catholic churches in
Milwaukee for weapons.[35] This particular "insult to every Catholic" was

31. Ibid., 248–53.   32. Ibid., 257–59.
33. Ibid., 15 and 281.   34. Ibid., 291–92.
35. "Notes and Gleanings," *Fortnightly Review* 34, no. 11 (June 1, 1917): 172.

simply the most blatant example of the anti-Catholic sentiment that was cropping up as a result of the war.[36]

Regrettably, the plight of German Catholics at this time evoked little sympathy within the Church at large. Some Catholics in America joined the assault on the use of the German language by protesting its use in sermons. Allegations from the 1880s and '90s that German Catholics actively promoted Pan-Germanism were revived and reopened the old wounds of ethnic division in the Church. With little regard for their German co-religionists, the Catholic press joined in the general chorus of "Hun" baiting. And in the view of some, the American bishops' rush to enlist the Church in Woodrow Wilson's war efforts left Catholics of German descent to fend for themselves against the increasingly shrill attacks on their ethnic and cultural heritage.

"Being Worked On"

It was into this environment of hostility and suspicion toward everything German that Father Feinler returned in November 1917. Feinler may have forebodings concerning his status in wartime America, since, when Feinler was ordered to return home in May 1917, he requested an assignment at the army post at Tientsin, China. This request was denied.[37] Once Feinler made it back to the U.S., he was posted to New York and shortly afterwards embarked for France. However, after only about a two months' stay, he received orders to return to the United States. In its 1927 discussion of Feinler's case, the *Fortnightly Review* reported that at the time of Feinler's prosecution a Honolulu newspaper circulated "the nonsensical statement" that Feinler was sent home from France because "he was detected making signals to the enemy." An ac-

---

Fortnightly Review (1894–1935) was a Catholic journal edited by a German-American layman, Arthur Preuss (1871–1934).

36. "Notes and Gleanings," *Fortnightly Review* 24, no. 12 (June 15, 1917): 186–87. "Notes and Gleanings," 24, no. 22 (October 15, 1917): 341.

37. May 4, 1917, AGODF RG 94 2589743. May 22, 1917, AGODF RG 94 1469251 NA. Feinler's military records for the period following American entry into the war, including those for his court martial, are no longer extant. The National Personnel Records Center stated on March 19, 1999: "No record located. If on file here on July 12, 1973 it may have been destroyed in a fire on that date."

count of this event in the *New York Times* stated that Feinler was returned from France for "showing German sympathies."[38] However, reported the *Review,* the real reason for Feinler's being sent home from the front, along with other American soldiers with German surnames, "at least as attributed to General Pershing by a Honolulu newspaper, was that the latter 'had to consider the feelings of the French.'"[39]

Having returned to the United States in early 1918, Feinler was once again posted to Hawaii. Passing through Washington on his way there, Feinler learned from a source at the War Department that his recall had been ordered because of his German birth. Not long after his arrival in Honolulu, on Feb. 28, 1918, Feinler was suddenly placed under house arrest without warrant or explanation. On March 5, formal charges were preferred against him.

On the same day that Feinler was arrested, a friend and recent visitor of his, who was "an American Monsignor," was arrested on suspicion that he was a German spy as he disembarked in San Francisco. The monsignor's papers were searched and he was detained until the authorities were satisfied that he was a priest in good standing in his home diocese. "This coincidence tends strongly to show that they were both victims of the wave of suspicion which swept this country and, even more so, its dependencies, during the war."[40]

There were four main charges leveled against Father Feinler. First, he was accused of violating the 95th Article of War by requesting that Battalion Sergeant Major Matthew Wright "surreptitiously obtain" for his inspection a confidential letter relating to the chaplain's record. Second, Feinler was charged with making "disloyal utterances" in connection with a lecture he had given to the Y.M.C.A. of Honolulu on January 10, 1918. Third, Feinler was accused of making statements to at least three other soldiers by which "he willfully attempted to cause disloyalty in the military forces of the U.S.A." Finally, Feinler was also accused of "using disrespectful language about the President, the Secretaries of War

38. *New York Times,* June 29, 1921. 1:2 "President Pardons Franz J. Feinler."
39. "A True Atrocity Story," *Fortnightly Review* 24, no. 11 (June 1, 1927): 229–31.
40. Ibid.

and Navy, about Congress, and his superior officers." The *Fortnightly Review* noted that the Espionage Act, under which Feinler was charged on this last count, "was not amended to take in 'incitement' and 'language' until two months *after* the chaplain's trial, that is, May, 1918."[41]

The courtmartial proceedings against Father Feinler lasted only a few days. As the transcripts published in the *Fortnightly Review* indicate, Feinler's defense against the charges was based on a very simple thesis. Feinler contended that because of his German origins, he was immediately under suspicion upon his arrival in Honolulu by his superior officer, Colonel Bolles. Bolles's unwarranted suspicion of Feinler led him to recruit other officers under his command to "entrap" the chaplain.

To sustain its case the defense elicited from the officers called as prosecution witnesses against Feinler a number of facts. First of all, Feinler's alleged efforts to "surreptitiously obtain" a confidential letter resulted wholly from an attempt by Colonel Bolles, commander of the Second Infantry Battalion, to entrap Feinler. Bolles had ordered a sergeant to approach Feinler on the pretext of needing some counseling and while with the priest to mention that Colonel Bolles had received a "confidential letter" from headquarters concerning the chaplain. The sergeant also offered to obtain a copy of the letter for Feinler. The court transcript discloses that while Feinler initially expressed an interest in seeing the letter, later the same day the priest told the sergeant, "Never mind about the letter," when the latter once again offered Feinler the possibility of procuring it. The transcript also indicates that the "confidential letter" was a complete fiction, concocted by Col. Bolles as bait for Feinler.[42]

As for Feinler's supposed "willful attempt" to "cause disloyalty," this charge was also the result of the fact that, as one of the priest's accuser's put it, "The Chaplain was being worked on . . ."[43] Col. Bolles sent other officers to Father Feinler for the specific purpose of sounding him out on subjects ranging from the competence of the French army to stories about German atrocities against Belgian civilians. Not only were these officers instructed to take notes on Feinler's responses, other officers were posted in the next room to listen in on these conversations and in

---

41. Ibid.   42. Ibid., June 1, 1927: 230.
43. Ibid.

one instance, Feinler's statements were transmitted to a waiting eaves-
dropper by way of a "dictaphone."[44]

Finally, concerning Feinler's "disloyal utterances" before an audience at the Y.M.C.A., which apparently were the catalyst for Col. Bolles's
campaign against him, the defense closed by reading an article published
in the *Army and Navy Journal* of 1914 concerning the danger of believing
propaganda about an enemy. It was this article which Feinler himself
had cited at the Y.M.C.A. meeting. When Feinler was asked at that meeting about German atrocities in Belgium, he had quoted the editor of the
Army and Navy Journal who had written that invading armies are always
accused of atrocities and that the German army was not the only army
guilty of such acts. In concluding, the defense argued that making such
an obvious statement of fact could not be interpreted as "disloyalty" and
"insubordination."[45]

Convicted

Despite the defense efforts, the court declared Father Feinler guilty
of the charge relating to the alleged confidential letter and also guilty of
violating the 95th Article of War by "willfully attempting to cause disloyalty in the military forces of the United States." Father Feinler was sentenced to fifteen years' hard labor in the federal penitentiary at McNeil
Island, Washington.[46]

Feinler's court martial could perhaps be attributed to his own imprudence. However, given the atmosphere of anti-German hysteria at
the time it is highly doubtful that he received a fair trial. Indicative of
this anti-German hysteria was the lynching of a German laborer by a
mob on April 5, 1918, in Collinsville, Illinois, just as the government was
making its case against Feinler. Unlike Feinler's trial, the murder of
Richard Praeger became widely known and was greeted in many places
with outrage. However, a jury refused to convict the admitted perpetra-
tors and in the surrounding communities of Illinois and Missouri the
murder was followed by several more acts of violence against German
Americans.[47] Commenting on the Praeger lynching, and reflecting wide-

44. Ibid., June 15, 1927: 250.   45. Ibid., July 1, 1927: 273.
46. Ibid., July 15, 1927: 274.   47. Luebke, *Bonds of Loyalty*, 3–25.

spread attitudes regarding the rights of German Americans, the *Washington Post* declared, "Enemy propaganda must be stopped even if a few lynchings may occur."[48] Nor was Feinler the only Catholic priest to feel the sting of wartime "justice." On April 10, 1918, the Rev. J. D. Metzler, pastor of St. Boniface in Edwardsville, Illinois, was threatened with tar and feathering after allegedly making pro-German remarks. Father Meztler was forced to leave his pastorate of twenty years.[49]

"A Grievous Injustice"

In the fall of 1919, after eighteen months of incarceration, and nearly a year after the war with Germany ended, Feinler's sentence was commuted to four years. He was paroled February 8, 1920, almost two years to the day of his initial arrest. From the moment of his release, Feinler began working for an official reopening of his case. In April 1921, Congressman Bourke Cochran of Missouri, who had taken up Feinler's case, wrote to the Secretary of War that Feinler's conviction was "a grievous injustice to a man of pre-eminent intellectual attainments, and spotless character." Cochran also stated that the prosecution of Feinler displayed "singular moral obtuseness" on the part of the officers involved "under pressure and excitement caused by war." He concluded by noting that "entrapments are always odious . . . but to plan an entrapment such as this was, is . . . without any precedent."[50] Through Cochran's efforts, Feinler was "pardoned" on May 18, 1921, by President Warren Harding and Feinler's case was made public on June 29, 1921.[51] But a presidential pardon would never be enough for Father Feinler. Feinler wanted a full exoneration both for himself as an individual and as a Catholic priest.

However, Feinler's case was never reopened by the Army. Apparently, the closest he came to a rehearing was in August 1921 when Senator Sterling introduced a resolution in the Senate providing for an in-

48. *Washington Post*, April 12, 1918.
49. Luebke, *Bonds of Loyalty*, 15.
50. Quoted in *Fortnightly Review*, July 15, 1927: 294.
51. *Washington Evening Star*, June 29, 1921. 2:2 "Army Chaplain Paroled, Receives Full Pardon." *New York Times*, June 29, 1921. 1:2 "President Pardons Franz J. Feinler."

vestigation of Feinler's case. But this resolution was squelched by the Senate Sub-Committee on Military Affairs.[52] Perhaps the senators on the sub-committee had read the vitriolic and subtly anti-Catholic editorial published by the *New York Times* the day after Feinler's pardon was announced. Under the title, "His Pardon Beyond Comprehension," the *Times* editors asserted that many people disagreed with the actions of the President and the Secretary of War in pardoning Feinler and "that the number of protestants is vastly larger than that of the people who think what they did was wise." The *Times* also warned that "it is doubtful that the liberation of a criminal like Feinler either wins or retains a single vote, but it is sure to cost the loss of a lot of them."[53]

Feinler continued to lobby various congressmen for assistance and this effort was evidently the main reason for his presence in Washington in 1925 and '26. Other avenues were approached as well. The articles on his case that appeared in the *Fortnightly Review* in 1927 were the direct result of his appeals to Catholic journalists of German-American background for assistance.[54] As the *Fortnightly Review* article on his case noted, until Feinler received a fair hearing Catholics would be subjected to such taunts as that in a 1927 newspaper article which stated that, while the record of military chaplains during the war was excellent, it "remained for the Catholic Church to furnish a Benedict Arnold!"[55] Feinler's "last determined effort to vindicate the Catholic priesthood" came in May of 1930, when he obtained assurances of help from Congressman Francis Sieberling of Ohio.[56] But this too came to nothing.

"A Life of Vagrancy"

One of the more interesting questions about Feinler's case concerns his apparent inability to enlist significant support from Catholic Church officials in his efforts to receive exoneration. To some German Catholics

52. *Fortnightly Review,* July 15, 1927: 294
53. *New York Times,* June 30, 1921. 16:6. "His Pardon Beyond Comprehension."
54. Joseph Schifferli to Arthur Preuss, September 13, 1926. APP.
55. *Fortnightly Review,* July 15, 1927: 294.
56. Franz J. Feinler to Bishop James A. McFadden (auxiliary bishop of Cleveland), May 7, 1930. Archives of the Diocese of Cleveland (hereafter ADC).

it was just another instance of the hierarchy's unwillingness to support them.[57] One prominent German Catholic leader, Frederick P. Kenkel, director of the Central Verein, writing in 1918, gave voice to their sense of abandonment. "We have been so discriminated against even by our co-religionists that we have but scant reason to feel overly friendly toward them." Kenkel added that he would never forget that the American hierarchy had not defended German Catholics "at a time when every wretched Knownothing in this country considered it brave and honorable to vent his spleen on all Americans of German blood."[58]

The official history of Catholic chaplains who served during World War I concludes its account of Feinler's wartime service by stating simply that he was discharged on April 20, 1918.[59] What it does not say is that this was the day that Feinler began his prison sentence at McNeil Island. Father Feinler's case was evidently an embarrassment. The Church in the United States, through official bodies such as the bishops' National Catholic War Council and the Knights of Columbus, had made an enormous effort to prove to the country that Catholics were at least as patriotic as other Americans. The publication of an official history of Catholic chaplains during the war is just one small example of this effort. Mounting an official, and necessarily public, campaign for the vindication of a priest convicted of disloyalty may have seemed imprudent to those who were in a position to help. The bishops and politicians to whom Feinler appealed perhaps wished that Feinler would simply accept his presidential pardon and go home. But that was another of the priest's problems. After nine years in the military and two years in prison, Feinler apparently had no home.

From the time of his parole in February 1920, Feinler appears to have spent the next several years wandering around the country in search of vindication. The June 1921 *New York Times* account of his pardon stated that at that time Feinler was living with the Paulist Fathers in Washington, D.C. The *National Catholic Directory* has no postwar listing for Feinler until 1923, when it described him as being "on leave" the previ-

---

57. Joseph Schifferli to Arthur Preuss, September 13, 1926. APP.
58. Gleason, *The Conservative Reformers*, 172–73.
59. *United States Catholic Chaplains in the World War* (New York: Ordinariate Army and Navy Chaplains, 1924), 97.

ous year. It is only with the 1924 *Directory,* which covered 1923, that Feinler appears back in his home diocese of Sioux Falls at St. John's Hospital in Mitchell, South Dakota. But he must not have been there for long, as in the next issue he was listed as being in Port Townsend, Washington, in 1924 serving at St. John's Hospital. Feinler's correspondence with Archbishop Curley indicates that he was back in the nation's capital by October 1925 and that he stayed at least until September of the following year. Peripatetic priests have long been the bane of the American bishops so Feinler's wandering probably did little to engender their support for his cause. The one bishop who was at least willing to write a letter on Feinler's behalf was Bishop Joseph Schrembs of Cleveland.[60] It was to Schrembs, who was himself a native of Germany, that Feinler had turned to in the fall of 1926 after his overtures to Archbishop Curley were rebuffed.

Despite his acceptance into the Diocese of Cleveland, Feinler appears to have had difficulty finding his niche there. At one point, Feinler himself would write to the chancellor of his "life of vagrancy, altogether involuntary on my part."[61] From October 1926 until April 1929 Feinler was the chaplain at the Rosemary Home for Crippled Children. There followed three assignments as an "administrator" of small, struggling, ethnic and rural parishes over the next eighteen months. Then, from October 1930 until October 1932, Feinler was on "leave" as a faculty member of the Catholic University of Peking. Upon his return to the Diocese of Cleveland in October 1932, Feinler was assigned as pastor of St. Peter's parish in Loudonville, Ohio.

Here, for a time at least, Feinler appears to have settled down. Within a year he had paid off the parish's debt to the diocese and he also began to take an interest in the Catholic Rural Life movement, attending some of its national meetings.[62] Still, his "checkered" past apparently left him insecure. In January 1934 he complained to the chancellor, Bishop James McFadden, "I wrote two weeks ago about my canonical status in

60. Bishop Joseph Schrembs to Hon. Francis Sieberling, May 21, 1930. ADC.

61. Franz J. Feinler to Bishop James A. McFadden, September 26, 1929. ADC.

62. Franz J. Feinler to Bishop James A. McFadden, October 31, 1933; August 13, 1934; September 11, 1934. Franz J. Feinler to Bishop Joseph Schrembs, October 12 and November 24, 1934. ADC.

the Cleveland Diocese, referring in particular to the predicate 'pro tempore' after my name in the Christmas number of the *Universe Bulletin*.
Will 'p.t.' appear in the 1934 edition of the *Catholic Directory?* Do not,
please, withhold the whole truth, even though it should be unpalat-
able." Bishop McFadden wrote back to assure Feinler this was a mistake
that would not be repeated.[63]

More trouble followed. From 1934 to December 1935, Feinler was
involved in a protracted dispute with the pastor of a parish where he had
once been pastor. Feinler's sister had been employed there and his successor as pastor, Father Edward Sullivan, borrowed $1,000 from her that
he was unable to repay in the agreed-upon period. As chancellor, Bishop
McFadden attempted to mediate the dispute between the two priests but
with no success.[64] During the course of this dispute, Feinler's adversary,
Father Sullivan, brought up the old accusation, ". . . when an Army Officer, particularly a Chaplain, is court martialed and dishonorably discharged from the Army . . . the Army has enough evidence to hang him
if they saw fit to do so."[65]

Feinler's frustration that the Diocese of Cleveland refused to take his
part in his conflict with Father Sullivan, coupled with the collapse of the
parish church in Loudonville while it was undergoing renovation, led
him to abruptly resign his pastorate of St. Peter's on December 31,
1935.[66] The sixty-five-year-old priest also requested to be allowed to "retire to a warmer climate." From 1937 until July 1941, Feinler served as
administrator of St. Ann Parish in Grant's Pass, Oregon. On July 10,

63. Feinler to Schrembs, January 23, 1934. Bishop James McFadden to Franz J.
Feinler, February 10, 1934. McFadden wrote in response to Feinler's complaint, "No
one has regretted more than I that your name had p.t. behind it. It will not appear in
the present directory."

64. Franz J. Feinler to Bishop James A. McFadden, March 8, 1934. Bishop
James A. McFadden to Franz J. Feinler, March 10, 1934, and June 4, 1934. Bishop
James A. McFadden to Edward F. Sullivan, March 10, 1934. Edward F. Sullivan to
Bishop James A. McFadden, May 21, 1934, and December 18, 1934. ADC.

65. Rev. Edward F. Sullivan to Bishop James A. McFadden, May 21, 1934. ADC.

66. Franz J. Feinler to Bishop Joseph Schrembs, October 24, 1935. Bishop
James A. McFadden to Franz J. Feinler, October 25, 1935. Franz J. Feinler to Bishop
James A. McFadden, December 31, 1935. Bishop James A. McFadden to Franz J.
Feinler, January 4, 1936. Franz J. Feinler to Bishop James A. McFadden, January 22,
1936. ADC.

1941, Father Feinler died of a heart attack while attending a regional labor conference at the University of Portland. Father Feinler's funeral was held at St. Mary's Cathedral in Portland, with Archbishop Edward Howard offering the Pontifical Requiem Mass. Father Feinler was seventy years old.[67]

Whatever flaws Father Franz J. Feinler may have had as a man and as a priest, it is evident that he was the victim of a terrible injustice. His case is also illustrative of the general plight of German Americans during World War I. Just as Feinler's nine years of honorable military service could not protect him from contrived evidence and false accusations, the overwhelming loyalty of German Americans during the war did not shield them from government suspicion and the hostility of their fellow citizens. Father Feinler's case, particularly his unsuccessful effort to be exonerated, also exemplifies the wartime experience of German Catholics within the American Church. Despite their enormous contributions to building the Church in the United States, when they came under attack because of their ethnicity, many German Catholics felt that they were abandoned by the Church's leadership, who seemed more concerned with demonstrating their patriotism than with living out their catholicity.

67. "Father Feinler, Once Diocese Priest, Buried," *Universe Bulletin* (Cleveland), July 18, 1941.

Douglas J. Slawson

8. WINE FOR THE GODS

Negotiations for the Sacramental Use of Alcohol during Prohibition

The "Noble Experiment" of Prohibition had deep roots, extending back to the pre–Civil War era. Nineteenth-century temperance movements had attempted, with modest but impermanent local success, to banish the sale, though never the production, of alcoholic beverages. Not until the foundation of the Anti-Saloon League (ASL) in 1893 did the dry crusade have an organization capable of carrying the nation. Serving as the political arm of evangelical Protestantism, especially Methodists, Presbyterians, and Baptists, the ASL initially concentrated on the enactment of state laws preventing the sale of drink. By 1912 it had secured the passage of prohibition legislation in six states, measures rendered porous by an earlier Supreme Court ruling that had upheld the right of citizens in dry states to import alcohol for personal use, thus giving rise to a mail-order booze industry. In early 1913, Congress took steps to close this loophole by passing the Webb-Kenyon Act, a flawed law that took interstate commerce in liquor out of federal hands, thereby enabling dry states to enforce their own laws, without, however, providing penalties for violation. Worse, for nine months, Congress failed to fund the Webb-Kenyon Act. Encouraged, nonetheless, by the amount of congressional support for this half-hearted measure, the ASL attempted national prohibition by constitutional amendment. The League made a concerted effort to elect dry congressmen in 1914 and then pressed for

161

the passage of a prohibition amendment, which, though winning an absolute majority of votes in the House of Representatives, failed to secure
the two-thirds necessary for passage. Redoubling its effort in the 1916
elections, the League convinced voters to return an overwhelming majority of drys to both houses of Congress.[1]

The task of prohibition actually became easier with America's entry
into World War I in 1917. First, the husbanding of foodstuffs took on increased importance. An enormous amount of grain could be conserved
by preventing its distillation into hard liquor or its brewing into beer.
Second, because many brewers were men of Teutonic ancestry, their
loyalty became suspect and their industry came to symbolize Germanism
and intemperance. In September 1917, Congress passed the Food Control Act, which shut down the hard-liquor industry while leaving the
prohibition of wine and beer to the discretion of the president, an exemption forced by a threatened filibuster of the bill. Three months later,
Congress sent to the states for ratification the Eighteenth Amendment,
which prohibited "the manufacture, sale or transportation of intoxicat-
ing liquors . . . for beverage purposes." Wet congressmen went along
with the measure only after the inclusion of two qualifications: the first,
a seven-year time limit for ratification—a period considered too short for
winning over the requisite thirty-six states; the second, a grace period of
one year for the liquor industry in the event of ratification. Contrary to
the wets' expectation, the amendment breezed through the states in
thirteen months, becoming fundamental law of the land in January
1919. Meanwhile, in November 1918, even though the war had ended,
the anti-drink forces in Congress had secured passage of the War Prohibition Act, extending the ban on hard liquor through the period of de-
mobilization and adding beer and wine to the list of forbidden beverages,
thus abolishing the entire liquor industry and robbing it of the year of

1. Herbert Asbury, *The Great Illusion: An Informal History of Prohibition* (Garden
City, N.Y.: Doubleday and Company, Inc., 1950), 121–29; Edward Behr, *Prohibition:
Thirteen Years that Changed America* (New York: Arcade Publishing, 1996), 7–61; Sean
Dennis Cashman, *Prohibition: The Lie of the Land* (New York: Free Press, 1981), 6–15;
John Kobler, *Ardent Spirits: The Rise and Fall of Prohibition* (London: Michael Joseph,
1973), 198–206; Charles Merz, *The Dry Decade* (Garden City, N.Y.: Doubleday, Doran
& Company, Inc., 1931), 1–24; Andrew Sinclair, *Era of Excess: A Social History of the
Prohibition Movement* (New York: Harper Colophon Books, 1964), 63–82.

grace it was to have enjoyed under the amendment. The Anti-Saloon League had accomplished its goal of making the nation dry.[2]

In outlawing beverage alcohol, prohibitionists never intended to interfere with the use of wine for sacramental or other religious purposes. The ban on liquor, however, necessitated that the federal government regulate sacramental wine to ensure that it did not go astray. Non-evangelical religious bodies—Catholics, Episcopalians, Lutherans, and Jews, who used fermented rather than unfermented grape juice in celebrating the Eucharist and the Shabbat—now had to submit to government oversight of the procurement of wine. The purpose of the present study is to recount the negotiations of the Catholic Church with the federal government for acceptable regulations, a subject that to this date has escaped historical investigation. For Catholics (and for Jews), who had suffered a history of religious bigotry in the United States, the issue took on added significance because the core sacramental experience of their faith was now in some way subject to the control of outsiders, who might or might not be friendly. This article will show that despite a resurgence of anti-Catholicism, and despite a desire of some prohibitionists for the most stringent regulations, the church and the government managed to negotiate common ground that, while not ideal, was at least acceptable. Of necessity, this story must be told largely from the vantage of Catholic sources because Congress authorized the destruction of all but a small sampling of Prohibition documents in the National Archives.

American Catholics by and large had opposed prohibition. To be sure, there had long been a Catholic temperance movement, which boasted prominent names, notably Archbishop John Ireland of St. Paul, Archbishop John Keane of Dubuque, and Bishop John Lancaster Spalding of Peoria, Illinois. Most Catholic temperance crusaders favored moral suasion over prohibition. There were, however, a few prominent Catholic prohibitionists, like Senator Thomas J. Walsh of Montana.[3] Yet the

2. Henry Steele Commager, ed., *Documents of American History*, 9th ed., 2 vols. (Englewood Cliffs, N.J.: Prentice-Hall, Inc., 1973), 2:814 (the quotation is from here); Asbury, *Great Illusion*, 129–34; Behr, *Prohibition*, 63–75; Cashman, *Prohibition*, 15–23; Kobler, *Ardent Spirits*, 206–12; Merz, *Dry Decade*, 24–42; Sinclair, *Era of Excess*, 116–28, 152–66.

3. Joan Bland, S.N.D., *Hibernian Crusade: The Story of the Catholic Total Abstinence Union* (Washington, D.C.: The Catholic University of America Press, 1951); Marvin R.

bulk of the Catholic population tended to be wet. For many Irish, German, French, Italian, and Polish Catholics, alcohol was an accepted if not
customary beverage. Although Cardinal James Gibbons of Baltimore,
the premier Catholic churchman in America, favored "local option," that
is, prohibition at the city or county level, where passage clearly represented the will of the majority in the community, he considered prohibition by amendment to be unenforceable and viewed it as a "national catastrophe," the very "denial of self-government" and an "infringement
of personal liberty."[4] The Knights of Columbus agreed. The law simply
made criminals of honest men and spawned an entirely new illegal industry: bootlegging.[5]

Beyond concerns about self-government and personal liberty, some
Catholics feared the use to which the amendment might be put, a fear
born of long-standing prejudice against them. The dominant Protestant
majority had always suspected Catholics of divided loyalties, of being
more devoted to Rome than to America. The latest wave of bigotry began in 1910 when *Watson's Magazine* (Georgia) and *The Menace* (Aurora,
Missouri) warned of the Catholic peril to the nation's liberty. The chief
target of both publications was the Knights of Columbus, whose members were allegedly sworn to make relentless war on Protestant America.
By 1914 there circulated through the mail a multidimensional constitutional amendment that proposed to bar Catholics from public office, to
prevent them from either teaching in public schools or serving on their
boards, to expel Jesuits from the land, to abolish convents, and finally, to
compel Catholic clergymen either to marry or to undergo castration as a
means of protecting women from mischief in the confessional.[6] Al-

---

O'Connell, *John Ireland and the American Catholic Church* (St. Paul: Minnesota Historical Society Press, 1988), 105–14; Patrick Henry Ahern, *The Life of John J. Keane: Educator and Archbishop, 1839–1918* (Milwaukee: Bruce Publishing Company, 1954),
48–49, 112–14, 126–27, 325–32, 360.

4. *New York Times*, April 29, 1917, VIII, 5; ibid., February 6, 1918, 9; John Tracy
Ellis, *The Life of James Cardinal Gibbons, Archbishop of Baltimore, 1834–1921*, 2 vols. (Milwaukee: Bruce Publishing Company, 1951), 2:535–39.

5. *New York Times*, December 19, 1920, I, 4.

6. Christopher J. Kauffman, *Faith and Fraternalism: The History of the Knights of
Columbus, 1882–1982* (New York: Harper and Row, 1982), 169–78; John Higham,
Strangers in the Land: Patterns of American Nativism, 1860–1925 (New York: Atheneum,
1975), 178–82; Gustavus Myers, *History of Bigotry in the United States*, ed. and rev. by

though the nation briefly pulled together to make the world safe for democracy, the superheated patriotism of wartime America heightened xenophobia, soon spilling into anti-Catholicism. Even though the Prohibition Amendment was not aimed at Catholics, some of them worried about how it might be used.

During 1919, the negotiations over the regulation of sacramental wine occurred in two separate spheres: the Treasury Department and Congress. The War Prohibition Act of November 1918 authorized the commissioner of the Internal Revenue Service (IRS) to devise regulations for the manufacture, sale, and distribution of sacramental wine. Because the machinery for the enforcement of both this law and the Eighteenth Amendment required special legislation, Congress too had to be involved in regulation. First to act was the Treasury Department. In February 1919, IRS Commissioner Daniel Roper ruled that a priest, pastor, or rabbi could procure a three-month supply of sacramental wine by presenting to the winery, warehouse, or dealer a sworn affidavit declaring himself to be the minister of a specific congregation in need of a specified amount of wine. The clergyman further had to swear to "undertake to the best of my ability to see that none of this wine is used for other than sacramental uses." The affidavit was to be in quadruplicate, one copy kept by the minister, one retained by the vendor, one sent to the revenue collector in the vendor's district, and the last sent to the revenue collector in the purchaser's district.[7]

While these regulations were certainly not onerous, Bishop Thomas Hickey of Rochester, New York, entered into negotiations with Roper for even more lenient rules. Having inherited the O-Neh-Da vineyard and sacramental winery from his predecessor Bishop Bernard McQuaid, Hickey had an obvious interest in seeing that wine for Mass was easy to obtain. Following his suggestions, Roper redesigned the regulations "to afford the most convenient method suitable to the needs of the parish priests and other clergy for sacramental wine."[8] Accordingly, the new

---

Henry M. Christman (New York: Capricorn Books, 1960), 192–99, 211–13; "A Burning Shame!" *America* 111 (1914): 328 (where the amendment is reproduced in full).

7. U.S. Treasury Department, Bureau of Internal Revenue, T.D. 2788, February 6, 1919, National Archives (hereinafter cited as NA), RG 287, box T228.

8. Daniel Roper to Cardinal James Gibbons, July 24, 1919, Archives of the Archdiocese of Baltimore (hereinafter cited as AAB), 127L3 (B); Roper to Bishop

rules, issued in July 1919, effectively gave a bishop complete oversight of the distribution of wine from church-run wineries like O-Neh-Da. In such instances, where wine was produced and distributed under clerical supervision, sworn affidavits were no longer necessary for procurement. Instead, a priest simply had to fill out two copies of an application naming his parish and the amount of wine needed; he would then submit the forms to the bishop for approval. Once approved, a copy of the application was to be returned to the priest, and the other forwarded to the winery, which would deliver the wine. While a liquor tax had to be paid, revenue agents were out of the picture altogether. For purchases made from wineries not under church control, Roper "preferred," but did not demand, that the earlier regulations be followed. Deputy Commissioner N. M. Gaylord considered the new rules a "simple and rational procedure." "We have endeavored," he declared in announcing them, "to cut out all 'red tape' and have made the regulations easy for bona fide organizations to follow."[9] With this new Treasury ruling, the Catholic community heaved a collective sigh of relief.

There were, however, a few voices of warning. On the basis of information received from a liquor merchant, Father Bernard McNamara, an army chaplain from the Archdiocese of Baltimore, cautioned that, while priests might experience less red tape in acquiring wine, there might be little wine to get. In the absence of regulations governing how dealers were to procure wine from manufacturers, and in the face of mounting incidents of theft during shipment, retailers were increasingly unwilling to stock wine.[10] In fact, Roper was refusing dealers permission to procure more wine "because of the uncertainty as to whether the new prohibition law, still in Congress, would permit any persons except druggists and Church officials to deal in sacramental wines." He wanted to spare

---

William Russell, July 28, 1919, Archives of the Diocese of Charleston (hereinafter cited as ADC), 106-R1; Robert F. McNamara, *The Diocese of Rochester, 1868–1968* (Rochester, N.Y.: Christopher Press, 1968), 238 and 322.

9. U.S. Treasury Department, Bureau of Internal Revenue, T.D. 2888, July 14, 1919, enclosure with Roper to Gibbons, July 24, 1919, AAB, 127L3 (C); N. M. Gaylord to J. Gibbons, August 1, 1919, AAB, 127O8 (the first quotation is from here); Buffalo *Catholic Union and Times*, July 31, 1919 (the second quotation is from here).

10. Bernard J. McNamara, "The Sacramental-Wine Question Again," *America* 21 (August 30, 1919): 513–14.

merchants the burden of having wine they might not be permitted to sell.[11] Ominously, McNamara reminded readers that the Treasury regulations could be changed at will by the commissioner of internal revenue. Worse still, although the Volstead bill, then under consideration by Congress for the enforcement of the Eighteenth Amendment, contained an exemption for sacramental wine, a subsequent Congress could repeal it. "These facts lead one to feel," concluded McNamara, "that there is some other reason . . . sinister and . . . anti-Catholic" behind the Prohibition movement.[12]

Church officials watching over congressional legislation worried less about a sinister movement than about ensuring that the law left the procurement of sacramental wine as unencumbered as possible. Both Bishop Hickey and Bishop William Russell of Charleston worked behind the scenes on Catholic congressmen, though Hickey's role has all but disappeared from the historical record. No novice at lobbying, Russell had, during his eight years as a pastor in Washington, represented Cardinal Gibbons before the government. When America went to war in 1917, Russell became one of four bishops on the Administrative Committee of the National Catholic War Council, an organization established to mobilize the Catholic community. At the time Congress was considering the Volstead bill, he and the Sulpician provincial, Father Edward Dyer, were pressing hard for the foundation of a new national Catholic organization to succeed the War Council and to care for the church's interests, particularly those with the government.[13]

The original version of the Volstead bill, one of four alternatives under consideration for the enforcement of Prohibition, contained only the following general exemption for churches: ". . . wine for sacramental purposes may be manufactured, purchased . . . and used as herein pro-

11. Roper, Memorandum [to Bishop Hickey], September 11, 1919, AAB, 128D2.

12. McNamara, "The Sacramental-Wine Question Again," 513–14.

13. Ellis, *Gibbons*, 2:208; Douglas J. Slawson, *The Foundation and First Decade of the National Catholic Welfare Council* (Washington, D.C.: The Catholic University of America Press, 1992), 47–57. On the War Council, see Elizabeth McKeown, *War and Welfare: American Catholics and World War I* (New York: Garland, 1988); Michael Williams, *American Catholics in the War: National Catholic War Council, 1917–1921* (New York: Macmillan, 1921).

vided." Yet the bill made no further provisions.[14] Russell considered that measure, along with its three companion proposals, to be "of the most drastic character in regard to altar wine." Through Father Peter O'Callaghan, C.S.P., a close friend of the ASL's Legislative Superintendent Edwin Dinwiddie, Bishop Russell requested the ASL to incorporate a series of amendments into the several bills for enforcement. The amendments (1) exempted the manufacture, sale, and transportation of sacramental wine from the measures; (2) authorized the head of a diocese or conference to endorse applications entitling priests, ministers, or rabbis to obtain sacramental wine; (3) empowered the head of a diocese or conference to appoint a minister to supervise the production and distribution of sacramental wine; and (4) permitted common carriers to deliver such wine "at any place by any of its agents" when a minister or rabbi presented a copy of a validly endorsed application. "Thus," commented Russell, "a priest can obtain by these provisions as much wine as he desires for sacramental purposes, as often as he desures [sic], to be delivered when he pleases, provided his application to any dealer is endorsed by the chancellor or any one else the bishop may appoint." Initially, Dinwiddie wanted to leave these matters to the discretion of the prohibition commissioner, a position allegedly to be created by the legislation. Russell objected because he feared that the person appointed the new commissioner might be a Protestant minister, perhaps even Dinwiddie himself, who was a former Lutheran pastor. Such an appointment would place the church in a "humiliating position" because the commissioner "would determine when, where, how, or how much, altar wine we should get. The Catholic Church in the United States would be under the censorship of a Protestant minister in regard to the Holy Sacrifice."[15]

14. U.S. Congress, House of Representatives, H.R. 6810, 66th Cong., 1st sess., ADC, uncataloged.

15. Russell to J. Gibbons and Bishop Peter Muldoon, about June 12, 1919, copy, ADC, 106-D2. The dating of this letter is troublesome. There are two copies in ADC, one hand-written dated June 11 and the typed copy, used here, dated "about June 12th." Muldoon replied to this letter, however, on June 10, 1919, which would suggest that both dates are incorrect. Other external evidence (beyond the Muldoon reply) as well as internal evidence suggest an earlier date, perhaps June 7 or 8. For further indication of Russell's thinking on the above matter, see Russell to Peter O'Callaghan, June 7, 1919, ADC, 106-A6. For the Volstead bill (U.S. Congress, House, H.R. 6810, 66th Cong., 1st sess.), see ADC, uncataloged.

Distrusting Dinwiddie, Russell and Father John Fenlon, S.S., secretary of the War Council's Administrative Committee, approached Senator Walsh of Montana, a member of the Judiciary Committee. Walsh agreed with Russell that the bills needed amending and jotted down a few clauses, which, on later reflection, Fenlon considered "very unsatisfactory," leaving the church "subject to many annoying regulations." Though acceptable wording of the amendments would have to be found, the senator's willingness to work on the church's behalf heartened the two lobbyists. Informed of Walsh's support of the amendments, Dinwiddie pledged to cooperate with the senator in every way.[16] Covering all bases, Russell sent Fenlon and Walter Hooke, a War Council functionary, to ask Representative Joseph Walsh, a Massachusetts Catholic on the House Judiciary Committee, to ensure that the bill was amended according to Catholic wishes. Congressman Walsh recommended, however, that the church confine its efforts to the Senate. "The temper of the House is prohibition-mad," noted Fenlon, "and the work had better be done quietly." Even so, there seemed little cause for the kind of alarm expressed by McNamara in *America* magazine. "Neither [of the Walshes] is apprehensive," concluded Fenlon.[17] Similarly, O'Callaghan informed Russell, "I do not see any tangible ground for suspicion of anyone connected with the prohibition forces in the present effort to formulate acceptable legislation."[18]

In late June 1919, Senator Walsh gathered three of Russell's four amendments into a single paragraph to be included in the Volstead bill:

Nothing herein contained . . . shall be held to apply to the manufacture, sale, importation, possession or distribution of wine for sacramental purposes, but this exception shall not extend to [permits, record-keeping, or penalties] . . . No person to whom a permit may be issued to manufacture, import or sell wine for sacramental

16. John Fenlon to Russell, June 9, 1919, ADC, 106-C2 (the quotation is from here); Russell to Gibbons and Muldoon, about June 12, 1919, ADC, 106-D2; O'Callaghan to Russell, June 5, 1919, ADC, 106-A4; Edwin C. Dinwiddie to Senator Thomas J. Walsh, June 2, 1919, copy, ADC, 106-A3.

17. Fenlon to Russell, June 9, 1919, ADC, 106-C2 (the quotations are from here); Russell to Gibbons and Muldoon, about June 12, 1919, ADC, 106-D2.

18. O'Callaghan to Russell, June 5, 1919, ADC, 106-A4; O'Callaghan to Russell, June 12, 1919, ADC, 106-D3.

purposes shall sell, barter, exchange or give any such to any person not a rabbi, minister of the gospel or priest, nor to any such except upon an application, duly subscribed by him and indorsed by an official specially designated for such purpose, by the head of the conference or diocese . . . which application shall be filed and preserved by the seller. The head of any conference or diocese . . . may designate any rabbi, minister or priest to supervise the manufacture of wine to be used for sacramental purposes, and the person so designated shall be entitled to a permit . . .

Absent from the amendment was Russell's clause regarding the shipment of sacramental wine, a matter that would not escape the bishop's notice. Before Senator Walsh submitted the amendment to Wayne Wheeler, the ASL's legal adviser, from whom he anticipated no objection, he sent the proposal to Russell for comment.[19]

Russell's recommendations regarding the amendment were few. He wanted the church authorized to supervise not only the manufacture but also the distribution of sacramental wine. Thus, a bishop could purchase a bulk load at a cheap rate and monitor the amount each priest received. More important, the amendment should include the following injunction: "Common carriers shall deliver wine for sacramental purposes in the same manner in which they distribute other general merchandise"—the absent clause regarding shipment. Russell explained that in the dry states of the South, officials required priests to appear in person to pick up a delivery of wine. Routinely, the depot was "a mean and low place and the one in charge is often an ex-minister," thereby rendering the experience demeaning and humiliating. Because sacramental wine was legal, there was no reason why it "should not be delivered as any ordinary merchandise."[20] Neither of Russell's suggestions appeared in the final version of the amendment. The absence of the clause regarding delivery would return to haunt the church in the mid-1920s.

On July 8, 1919, the House Judiciary Committee reported the Vol-

19. Walsh to Russell, June 24, 1919, with enclosure, ADC, 106-G5.
20. Russell to Walsh, June 29, 1919, copy, ADC, 106-H5. The issue of delivery greatly concerned Russell. See Russell to Gibbons and Muldoon, about June 12, 1919, ADC, 106-D2; and Russell's handwritten notes on the back of Senate Bill 555, 66th Cong., 1st sess., ADC, 105-P3.

stead bill without amendments and debate followed immediately. Although official church involvement in the legislative process halted (or at least disappeared from the historical record), Catholic interests had a voice. About two-thirds of the way through the debate, Representative Richard McKiniry, a Catholic from New York, delivered an impassioned plea against the bill as a violation of personal liberty, states' rights, and the separation of church and state. "One of the most dangerous and subtle provisions of this act," he concluded, "is its interference with the exercise of his religious duties by a minister or priest . . . It places in the hands of a governmental official the control of the sacramental use of wine. . . . Hence I must protest, even if in vain . . . so that the public may be informed as to the real and substantial danger and threats hidden under a cloak of reform."[21] McKiniry's words stirred the waters. Two days later, the bill's sponsor, Representative Andrew Volstead of Minnesota, asked unanimous consent to return to a consideration of the section that regulated the manufacture and distribution of alcohol for non-beverage purposes, which included the clause promising provisions for sacramental wine without, however, making any. "There has been some question as to what ought to be done in regard to the power to provide wine for sacramental purposes," said Volstead. "Various parties have been consulted, and we have agreed on a provision that ought to be inserted if there is no objection." These words leave little doubt that Volstead had conferred with Wayne Wheeler, Senator Walsh, and Representative William Igoe of St. Louis, leader of the minority that opposed the Volstead bill, for Igoe introduced the amendment drafted by Walsh, with the addition of a superfluous proviso, namely, that the exemptions contained therein would not apply to any minister or rabbi unwilling to comply with the terms of the amendment. The House gave unanimous approval.[22]

The amendment failed to calm the fears of *America* magazine. Associate editor Paul Blakely, S.J., echoed McKiniry's criticisms of the bill and warned that "the Holy Sacrifice of the Mass will be offered, if tolerated at all, only by grace and favor of some political underling in the Treasury

---

21. *Congressional Record,* 66th Cong., 1st sess., 1919, vol. 58, pt. 3, 2893–94.
22. Ibid., 2968.

Department. . . . The Eighteenth Amendment provides a ready weapon against the Catholic Church, which will not be forgotten, if the unfortunate day ever dawns upon a Congress ruled by bigots."[23] A week later, an editorial dismissed Igoe's amendment by noting that a permit was still required to procure wine. In the view of some prohibitionists, cautioned the editor, this seemed "to mark the beginning of the era in which the celebration of the Holy Sacrifice of the Mass can be made to depend on the favor of an internal revenue officer."[24]

Despite the magazine's foreboding, there seemed little cause for fear. The Senate Judiciary Committee altered the Igoe-Walsh amendment to make it even easier to obtain wine. The committee dropped the requirement that a minister's application for purchase be endorsed by a bishop or other ecclesiastical superior. It further broadened the wording to include wine "for sacramental purposes or like religious rites," thus securing the widest possible interpretation of ceremonial use. Finally, the committee trimmed off the meaningless proviso added by the House. These alterations were but several of the nearly three hundred recommended by the committee, recommendations the Senate accepted virtually without debate. Because of the many differences between the House and Senate versions of the legislation, a conference committee was appointed to iron them out.[25]

While the act was in conference committee, Bishop Hickey met with Commissioner Roper to seek further adjustments to Treasury regulations. As mentioned above, the commissioner had forbidden dealers to stockpile wine. Moreover, he had issued a new regulation limiting churches to the procurement of no more than a year's supply. Hickey found the commissioner eager to cooperate in every way. Roper permitted the church to designate specific wine merchants in various parts of the country whom the Treasury Department would allow to stock more wine, this despite the fact that the Volstead Act did indeed grant only retail druggists permission to sell alcohol for non-beverage purposes. The

23. Paul Blakely, S.J., "Prohibition or the Mass: Which?" *America* 21 (July 26, 1919): 400–401.

24. "Federal Prohibition and the Mass," *America* 21 (August 2, 1919): 428.

25. *Congressional Record,* 66th Cong., 1st sess., 1919, vol. 58, pt. 5, 4833, 4836–4908.

commissioner explained that he had limited parishes to a year's supply of wine simply to avoid criticism if the amount were left open-ended. He assured Hickey that the Internal Revenue Service would question no application for a greater volume if it was duly authorized by a bishop or his appointee. Though this ruling appeared only in memorandum form— never as an official Treasury document—it remained in force for a year and a half.[26]

Shortly after these new negotiations with the Treasury Department, a momentous event occurred for American Catholicism, one that altered its shape. In mid-September 1919, ninety-five bishops met at the Catholic University of America in Washington for the first annual meeting of the American hierarchy. The assembled prelates decided that the hierarchy in annual assembly would become the National Catholic Welfare Council (NCWC), a voluntary organization whose decisions were to be executed by an Administrative Committee of seven bishops, elected annually and charged with supervising a five-department secretariat in the national capital, including a Legislative Department to care for the church's legal interests. Each department was chaired by a bishop on the Administrative Committee, while its daily functions were handled by an on-site director.[27] Following the creation of the NCWC, Hickey explained all the regulations issued by the Treasury Department. Unlike *America*, Hickey pronounced the amendment on sacramental wine in the Volstead Act "most satisfactory." With gratitude for all work done, Cardinal Gibbons appointed both Hickey and Russell a committee of two to continue to watch over the church's interests regarding sacramental wine.[28]

The appointment of this committee was an understandable inconsistency. Although the hierarchy had just established an organization to look after Catholic legal interests, namely, the NCWC and its Legislative Department, Gibbons assigned a significant legal issue to an ad hoc committee. Without doubt, he did so automatically because the two prelates

26. Roper, Memorandum [to Hickey], September 11, 1919, AAB, 128D2; Hickey to Gibbons, September 17, 1919, 128E6.

27. Slawson, *National Catholic Welfare Council*, 62–83.

28. *Minutes of the First Annual Meeting of the American Hierarchy, September 1919*, pp. 10–11, Archives of The Catholic University of America (hereinafter cited as ACUA), NCWC General Secretary files.

had been handling negotiations with the government. Still, it seems that the aged cardinal, whom Russell and Dyer had had to coax and cajole into backing the plan for the creation of the NCWC,[29] failed to grasp the collegial and structural shift embodied in the new organization and continued to operate out of the model of church that had developed between 1887 and 1919 in which he functioned as de facto primate and assigned bishops various tasks. This action by the cardinal would complicate future negotiations with the federal government.

Within weeks of the establishment of the NCWC, the congressional conference committee reported its recommendations concerning the Volstead Act. Regarding sacramental wine, the committee adjusted the law to restore greater control over distribution to the commissioner of Internal Revenue. As mentioned, the Senate had scrapped the need for a bishop's endorsement of an application, thereby permitting a seller to dispense sacramental wine simply "upon an application duly subscribed by him [the priest, minister, or rabbi]." The conferees altered the wording to read "upon an application duly subscribed by him, . . . *authenticated as regulations may prescribe.*" Again, in both the House and Senate versions of the act, a bishop could appoint a cleric to oversee the manufacture of wine, and "the person so designated shall be *entitled to a permit, to be issued by the commissioner."* The conferees changed this to read "the person so designated *may, in the discretion of the commissioner, be granted* a permit."[30] While the wording of both the House and Senate versions gave the church absolute control over the distribution of church-manufactured wine, the new wording made that control conditional upon the commissioner. Both houses accepted these recommendations, and then overrode President Woodrow Wilson's veto to enact the law.[31]

Crafted by Wheeler, the Volstead Act was designed to ensure his control over Prohibition. He lodged enforcement of the law in the IRS, partly because that agency had always overseen the liquor traffic and partly because the overworked commissioner could not possibly handle the new task, thus necessitating the establishment of an enforcement di-

29. Slawson, *National Catholic Welfare Council*, 49–56.

30. *Congressional Record*, 66th Cong., 1st sess., 1919, vol. 58, pt. 5, 6432. Emphasis added.

31. Asbury, *Great Illusion*, 134; Kobler, *Ardent Spirits*, 241.

vision over which Wheeler hoped to exercise influence. As expected, in 1920 the Secretary of the Treasury created a Prohibition Unit within the IRS. Within eighteen months, Wheeler succeeded in securing the appointment of a pliant protégé to head the new division.[32] A byproduct of Wheeler's tinkering was the multiplication of jurisdictions. Although the commissioner of Internal Revenue retained the authority to make regulations, the new commissioner of Prohibition had a voice in their design. The Department of Justice, wherein enforcement should have rested, had the power both to interpret the law and to prosecute violations. This division of authority would lead to complications in negotiating for the distribution of sacramental wine. These complications would not, however, have to be faced in the near term. Shortly after passage, Commissioner Roper issued new regulations under the Volstead Act. Insofar as they pertained to sacramental wine, the rules remained unchanged, simply restating those already agreed upon with Hickey.[33] There would be no tightening of control while Roper held the reins.

The tightening came a year and a half later, after Roper's departure from the IRS, leading to a new and lengthy round of negotiations. In January 1921, Secretary of the Treasury David F. Houston, perhaps acting at the request of William M. Williams, Roper's successor in the Wilson administration, sought a ruling from Attorney General A. Mitchell Palmer on whether or not the IRS commissioner's power to issue permits for the sale of sacramental wine was limited to manufacturers and wholesale druggists. On February 2, 1921, in the waning days of the lame-duck administration, Palmer decided that under terms of the Volstead Act, indeed only manufacturers and importers could dispense sacramental wine.[34] Harry M. Daugherty, Harding's attorney general, agreed with the ruling. This interpretation put out of business the specially designated dealers approved by Roper, something that would

32. Sinclair, *Era of Excess,* 191; Laurence Schmeckebier, *The Bureau of Prohibition: Its History, Activities and Organization* (Washington, D.C.: Brookings Institution, 1929), 7.

33. U.S. Treasury Department, Bureau of Internal Revenue, T.D. 2940, October 29, 1919, NA, RG 287, box T228.

34. A. Mitchell Palmer to David F. Houston, February 2, 1921, and Statement by Commissioner William M. Williams in a Press Release, ACUA, NCWC Legal Department files.

make it very difficult for priests in rural areas to procure wine. To complicate matters further, the Catholic community widely misinterpreted the ruling to mean that sacramental wine could be obtained not only from manufacturers and importers but also from wholesale druggists, something that was untrue.

Although aware of the new ruling, Father John J. Burke, C.S.P., general secretary of the NCWC, could do little about it because Cardinal Gibbons had delegated the matter of sacramental wine to Bishops Hickey and Russell, the ad hoc committee of two. When complaint inevitably came, however, it went, not to Hickey or Russell, but to the NCWC. In late March 1921 Bishop Joseph Busch of St. Cloud, Minnesota, informed Burke that the E. M. Lohman Company of St. Paul was no longer empowered to distribute sacramental wine. Suspicious that non-Catholic druggists might tamper with the purity of wine, and fearing that they would be "extortionate in their prices," Busch urged that the NCWC Legislative Department find some way to have the law amended. "Otherwise," he warned, "priests will not have much confidence in the department & may even include the N.C.W.C. generally."[35] In fact, criticism of the NCWC was already in the air and would soon come to a head in a near-mortal attack on the organization by certain high prelates, an attack with which Busch sympathized.[36]

Like the federal government, the church had overlapping jurisdictions regarding sacramental wine. Although Hickey and Russell were the ad hoc committee in charge of the matter, the NCWC had a Legislative Department to watchdog the church's legal interests, among them Prohibition concerns. Fortunately, in addition to being one of the two bishops on the sacramental-wine committee, Russell belonged to the Administrative Committee of the NCWC. On April 6, 1921, that body sent him to the Department of Justice about the issue. Guy Goff, assistant attorney general to Daugherty, recommended that Russell propose a plan to outgoing Prohibition Commissioner John F. Kramer. The bishop delegated

35. Joseph Busch to John J. Burke, Thursday [either March 24 or 31, 1921], ACUA, NCWC General Secretary files; Buffalo *Catholic Union and Times*, April 14, 1921.
36. See Busch to Edward Hanna, March 28, 1922, Archives of the Archdiocese of San Francisco (hereinafter cited as AASF), NCWC files; Slawson, *National Catholic Welfare Council*, chap. 5.

William Cochran of the NCWC Legislative Department to craft a proposal. This action marked the beginning of a gradual transfer of the care of sacramental wine to the NCWC. Until the transfer was completed, however, Burke would complain, "Our interests have been complicated and handicapped by having a separate committee of two bishops who of course cannot be here [in Washington] to look after the matter."[37]

The NCWC threw itself into the negotiations as representative of the two bishops. The goal was the retention of the former system of distribution through specially approved dealers. Both Burke and William Cochran, director of the NCWC Legislative Department, met with a troika of government officials representing both the new and old presidential administrations: Goff, Kramer, and outgoing Assistant Attorney General Annette Abbott Adams, the author of the Palmer ruling. Both Kramer and Adams steadfastly maintained that the Volstead Act permitted clergymen to purchase wine only from manufacturers or importers, and that neither of the latter could appoint dealers as their agents to sell their products. Despite this setback, Burke did secure a tentative agreement that a bishop could designate one or several priests to function as diocesan brokers to negotiate with manufacturers for the purchase of wine that was to be shipped directly to individual parishes in quantities of not less than five gallons.[38]

Unwilling to let the matter rest there, Burke went over the conferees heads and asked Secretary of the Treasury Andrew Mellon to request a new ruling by Attorney General Daugherty. Mellon replied that rules consistent with Palmer's decision would be prepared by David Blair, the new commissioner of the IRS, once he entered office. "It is believed," stated Mellon, "that such regulations can be so framed as to provide for the convenient distribution of sacramental wines without undue hardship to the clergy, importers, manufacturers or their agents." He assured

37. Burke to Hanna, May 3, 1921, AASF, NCWC files; Minutes of the Administrative Committee, April 6, 1921, ACUA, NCWC General Secretary files.

38. Conference with Colonel Goff, Assistant Attorney General, John F. Kramer, Commissioner of Prohibition, and Mrs. Adams, Assistant to the Attorney General, April 22, 1921, ACUA, NCWC General Secretary files; Burke to Russell, April 22, 1921, copy, ACUA, NCWC General Secretary files; Memorandum from William Cochran to Burke, regarding suggested letter to the NCWC Administrative Committee about sacramental wine, April 27, 1921, ACUA, NCWC General Secretary files.

Burke that the NCWC would be granted a hearing before the new rules
were finalized, and, in the event that they proved unsatisfactory, Mellon
agreed "to take up further the matter of requesting reconsideration by
the Attorney General."[39]

Mellon's mention of the word "agents" hinted at the direction the
government was moving. Indeed, in mid-July Goff asked Cochran to
verify with Bishop Russell if an acceptable solution would be the distribution of sacramental wine through dealers who became the appointed
agents of manufacturers. When the new regulations embodying the solution outlined by Goff were unveiled at a hearing on July 18, 1921, officers of the NCWC's legislative department, representing both Bishops
Hickey and Russell, made no objection. Issued on August 3, 1921, the
regulations were to take effect on the fifteenth of that month. Because
the intervening time would prove too short for dealers to have themselves named the agents of manufacturers, Burke secured an additional
month of grace. Thus, the matter seemed to have been arranged, leaving
the status quo virtually unchanged.[40]

This neat settlement of the matter immediately unraveled. Dealers
protested the regulations because they now had to seek to become agencies of wineries or importers; manufacturers protested because legal title
to the wine remained with them, even though the wine might be in the
possession of dealers, thus placing wineries at risk for the actions of distant agents. In the face of these new protests, the Treasury Department
referred the question to the attorney general "for a specific ruling as to
whether permits to sell and distribute wines for sacramental purposes
may legally be issued to wholesale dealers such as are now in the business of supplying the clergy." Pending that decision, Burke secured from

39. Burke to Andrew Mellon, May 6, 1921, copy, ACUA, NCWC General Secretary files; Mellon to Burke, May 18, 1921, ACUA, NCWC General Secretary files.

40. Cochran to Russell, July 12, 1921, copy, ACUA, NCWC General Secretary
files; James R. Ryan to Hickey, July 15, 1921, copy, ACUA, NCWC Legal Department
files; Hickey to J. R. Ryan, telegram, July 17, 1921, ACUA, NCWC Legal Department
files; Boston *Pilot*, July 23 and 27, 1921; *New York Times*, July 24, 1921; Burke to Edmund Gibbons, August 29, 1921, Archives of the Diocese of Albany (hereinafter cited as ADA), NCWC files; "Report of the Chairman of the Department of Laws and
Legislation," *The National Catholic Welfare Council: Reports of Administrative Committee
and Departments Made at the Conference of the Hierarchy of the United States, Washington,
D.C., September 21–22, 1921* (Washington, D.C.: NCWC, 1921), 23–24.

the Treasury Department an indefinite suspension of the regulations that were to have gone into effect on September 15.[41]

Attorney General Daugherty scheduled a hearing for November 8, 1921, and invited the NCWC to participate. The invitation set in motion the transfer of this matter from the ad hoc committee of Hickey and Russell to the NCWC. Acting as general secretary in place of the ailing and absent Burke, Father James H. Ryan asked the two bishops if they wished to attend the hearing on behalf of the church. At this point, Hickey, who disliked the non-pastoral aspects of his episcopal office, turned the entire issue of sacramental wine over to the NCWC Legislative Department, chaired by Bishop Edmund Gibbons of Albany. Unable to attend the hearing, Russell too deferred to the Legislative Department. The NCWC now had complete charge. Archbishop Edward Hanna of San Francisco, chairman of the Administrative Committee, wanted Gibbons himself to appear before the attorney general, rather than send an underling. "I think Bishop Gibbons should give the question his personal attention," wrote Hanna to the Washington headquarters; "his presence and his position [as chairman of the Legislative Department] would make our argument triumphant."[42]

Hanna had already established the line of argument. When the dealers and manufacturers had protested the new regulations, he had fired off a lengthy telegram to Mellon, Blair, and Prohibition Commissioner Roy A. Haynes urging them to amend the rules to grant the half

41. Burke to James Cantwell (chancellor of Archdiocese of San Francisco), telegram, September 7, 1921, AASF, NCWC files; "Report of the Chairman of the Department of Laws and Legislation," 23–24; T.D. 3231 in Arthur W. Blakemore, *National Prohibition: The Volstead Act Annotated and Digest of National and State Prohibition Decisions* (Albany, N.Y.: Matthew Bender and Company, 1923), 588. The federal government considered the sale of sacramental wine to priests, ministers, and rabbis to be wholesale rather than retail—even though a retailer conducted the transaction— because the wine was to be used for professional purposes rather than for personal consumption (T.D. 3208 in Blakemore, *National Prohibition*, 583–84).

42. James H. Ryan to Edmund Gibbons, October 20, 1921, ADA, NCWC files; J. H. Ryan to Russell, October 27, 1921, copy, ACUA, NCWC General Secretary files; Russell to J. H. Ryan, November 5, 1921, copy, ACUA, NCWC General Secretary files; William J. Cochran to E. Gibbons, October 29, 1921, ADA, NCWC files; William Kerby to E. Gibbons, November 3, 1921, ADA, NCWC files (the quotation used in the text is quoted in this letter); Hickey to James R. Ryan, November 3, 1921, ACUA, NCWC Legal Department files (a copy in ADA, NCWC files).

dozen ecclesiastically approved wine dealers around the country the same status as wineries and importers, namely, the ability to buy, blend, and distribute wine from their own bonded warehouses.[43] At the hearing, conducted by Mable Walker Willebrandt, assistant attorney general in charge of prohibition prosecutions, Gibbons quoted the Volstead Act to show that the law exempted "the manufacture, sale, transportation, importation, possession, OR DISTRIBUTION of wine for sacramental purposes" from the provisions of the law, except with regard to penalties and permits. Given that exemption, he reiterated Hanna's argument for amended rules that would give ecclesiastically approved dealers equal status with wineries and importers.[44] Father William Kerby reported that the bishop came away "quite confident that the outcome will be satisfactory."[45]

Gibbons's confidence was unwarranted, for the church had no legal leg to stand on. A narrow reading of the Volstead law, which the act itself mandated, left no room for maneuver. The section of the legislation regarding permits specified that only druggists could be issued one to sell retail. Thus, wine dealers were out; only wholesalers, like wineries and importers, qualified for permits to sell. Besides this legal straightjacket, Gibbons had no inkling of Willebrandt's negative attitude toward issuing such permits. It would take time, however, and a considerable amount of wrangling before the church's loss of the argument would become clear, because the federal government was being pulled in opposite directions by forces from within and without.

Externally, while the Catholic Church attempted to keep the rules as loose as possible, the Jewish community tried to have them tightened. Jewish leaders were concerned about the traffic in bootlegged wine resulting from bogus rabbinical wine permits. According to Treasury regulations, rabbis were authorized to withdraw up to ten gallons of wine a

43. James Cantwell (chancellor of Hanna) to Burke, telegram, September 7, 1921, ACUA, NCWC General General Secretary files. This telegram quotes in its entirety the one sent to Mellon, Blair, and Haynes.

44. E. Gibbons, In the Matter of the Sale and Distribution of Sacramental Wine: Statement of the National Catholic Welfare Council Representing the Hierarchy of the Catholic Church in the United States, November 8, 1921, copy, ACUA, NCWC Legal Department files (emphasis in original).

45. Kerby to Hanna, November 10, 1921, AASF, NCWC files.

year for each family in a congregation for use in the weekly Shabbat and seasonal rituals. Because of fake rabbinical permits, much wine had gone astray. In order to end abuses, Louis Marshall, president of the American Jewish Committee, urged IRS Commissioner Blair to revise the prohibition regulations. Divergence in religious practice within the Jewish community, however, made it difficult to design appropriate rules. Some Jews used no wine in their ceremonies, others used very little, and still others used only unfermented grape juice. Because many rabbis held that such grape juice would satisfy for ritual purposes, prominent eastern newspapers rumored that the Treasury Department planned to outlaw sacramental wine altogether. In response to an NCWC inquiry, Blair dismissed as "preposterous" any such plan. Likewise, the New York State ASL announced that it had "never proposed and will never support any legislation which does not make full and fair provision for the obtaining of sacramental wine. . . ." As comforting as these denials were, the problem of designing satisfactory regulations remained.[46]

Internally, the federal government was divided between officials who wanted the tightest possible regulations and those who sought to make them convenient for the churches. Principal advocate of the former position was Willebrandt, who had conducted the hearing. A moderate dry, she was less concerned about prohibition enforcement for its own sake than for what it meant to the entire system of law. Fearing that flagrant violations of the Volstead Act might lead to lawlessness in general, she believed that Prohibition was doomed to failure until the government halted its liberal policy of issuing permits for the sale of non-beverage alcohol. "I urged, literally begged, prohibition officials yearly since 1922," she later commented, "to *refuse* applications [for permits] and let the applicants sue."[47] When, in early December 1921, the NCWC learned

46. *New York Times*, November 7 and December 23, 24, 25, and 28, 1921 (the ASL quote appears in the last mentioned); *Boston Herald*, December 24, 1921; Washington *Post*, December 24, 1921; David Blair to NCWC, December 27, 1921, ACUA, NCWC Legal Department files; Roy A. Haynes, *Prohibition Inside Out* (Garden City, N.Y.: Doubleday, Page & Company, 1923), 210–12; Sinclair, *Era of Excess*, 290.

47. Mabel Walker Willebrandt, *The Inside of Prohibition* (Indianapolis: Bobbs-Merrill Company, 1929), 41–61 (the quotation is on 51); Thomas M. Coffey, *The Long Thirst: Prohibition in America, 1920–1933* (New York: W. W. Norton and Company, Inc., 1975), 164–69.

that she was preparing a decision adverse to the one proposed by Gibbons, J. H. Ryan urged Goff to review the case before a final verdict was rendered. Confidentially, he warned William Burns, director of the FBI, that Willebrandt's position "would be fatal to the present Administration" because the Catholic Church "would have to fight this decision in the courts and in our Catholic papers," resulting in a great deal of animosity toward the Republican party. "For the sake of the President," said Ryan, "I do not wish to see this come about." Professing the greatest confidence in Goff (but "very little in Miss Willebrandt"), he asked Burns "to drop a hint to Colonel Goff that we would appreciate very much his reviewing this case." Immediately, Burns conferred with Goff, who promised to give the matter "his personal consideration before it is finally acted on."[48]

Division within the executive branch continued into early 1922. In mid-January a confidential source informed the NCWC that Willebrandt still opposed any relaxation in the regulations concerning sacramental wine, a position apparently not favored by her superiors.[49] Two weeks later, a Washington law firm ominously warned that the government was "not advancing the agency proposal in good faith" but was doing "everything in its power to discourage the granting of agencies in the hope of forcing the wineries to establish branch houses." The firm urged Bishop Gibbons to see Goff personally as soon as possible.[50] Before Gibbons could act, Goff summoned both him and Archbishop Hanna to inform them that "regulations concerning sacramental wine would be made, whereby the wine could be secured from authorized agents and not only manufacturers." The NCWC Administrative Committee considered this arrangement satisfactory if indeed the government carried it out.[51]

48. J. H. Ryan to Guy Goff, December 8, 1921, copy, ACUA, NCWC General Secretary files; J. H. Ryan to William Burns, December 8, 1921, copy, ACUA, NCWC General Secretary files; Burns to J. H. Ryan, December 9, 1921, ACUA, NCWC General Secretary files; Goff to J. H. Ryan, December 13, 1921, ACUA, NCWC General Secretary files.

49. Cochran to E. Gibbons, January 14, 1922, ADA, NCWC files.

50. Edmond Maher to E. Gibbons, January 25, 1922, ADA, NCWC files.

51. Minutes of the Administrative Committee, January 26, 1922, ACUA, NCWC General Secretary files.

Unfortunately, that was not to be the case. The government, in fact, tightened regulations on agencies. Commissioner Blair ruled that no permits for the establishment of an agency would be granted "unless it clearly appears that it is necessary to accomplish adequate and economical distribution in the locality." Because some wineries had established agencies "without thoroughly appreciating the liabilities and responsibilities thereby incurred," he spelled out that the responsibility for the business conduct of the agent "shall always be upon the manufacturer," and that title to the liquor in the agent's possession "shall remain with the manufacturer until title is transferred to a purchaser." As if the foregoing were not detailed enough, Blair continued: "The manufacturer must accept the risks of the business done through an agent. . . . The sale price must be controlled by the manufacturer and the agent's compensation must be definitely fixed by contract . . . The agent must be liable to the principal [i.e., the manufacturer] only for collections actually made. The agent must not guarantee collections. While collections may be made by the agent, invoices must always be in the name of the manufacturer . . . The agent must forward daily to the manufacturer for examination a complete report showing the details of all transactions of the agent."[52] Although Cochran reported that these new regulations were meant simply to forestall price gouging by dealers (for which there was apparently some evidence) and that the government would probably relax the rules once Attorney General Daugherty had rendered his decision,[53] the severity of them and the strictness of Willebrandt would seem to have argued against casting them in such a favorable light.

On learning of the new regulations, Hanna felt betrayed. Because few wineries would want to risk the appointment of an agent on "such [an] unreasonable and unbusinesslike basis," the rules were tantamount to the elimination of agencies altogether and served as a hindrance to the legitimate distribution of sacramental wine. Hanna urged Bishop Gibbons to protest against the regulations and seek to have them

52. U.S. Treasury Department, Bureau of Internal Revenue, T.D. 3300, March 10, 1922, ACUA, NCWC General Secretary files.
53. Cochran to Burke, March 24, 1922, ACUA, NCWC General Secretary files. On price gouging, see Burke, handwritten memorandum re sacramental wine, undated [December 1921], ACUA, NCWC General Secretary files.

amended so as "to permit [the] appointment of some half dozen ecclesi-astically endorsed sacramental wine distributors," authorized to receive bonded shipments in a bonded warehouse maintained by the dealer himself. Hanna was convinced that "this method would eliminate abuse, protect [the] Government, and facilitate legitimate distribution."[54] Gibbons handed the negotiations off to Burke—still recuperating but back at his desk—who had to conduct them under trying circumstances both within and outside of the church.

From without, the Catholic Church suffered renewed hostility in the form of a campaign for "one hundred percent Americanism," a nativist movement that might best be described as a compulsion for conformity aimed at creating national homogeneity. Marked by racism, anti-Semitism, anti-Catholicism, and a wholehearted devotion to public schools, the drive was never so tidy as to be confined to a particular organization or locale, nor did every group embrace the entire program. Generally speaking, two that did were the Freemasons and the Ku Klux Klan. For the Klan, Catholicism was not just an idolatrous religion with a lascivious clergy; it also raised the specter of papal domination through a priest-ridden laity that manipulated the political process. Never as crude as the Klan, the Southern Jurisdiction of the Scottish Rite, the most combative branch of Masonry, comprising the thirty-three states below the Ohio River and west of the Mississippi, believed that parochial schools inculcated an intolerable dual allegiance—to Washington and Rome—and that Catholics were ultimately bent on undermining public education. Both the Southern Jurisdiction and the Klan sought to counter this threat by requiring compulsory public schooling. In addition to promoting public education, the Invisible Empire supported Prohibition. "In almost every state the Klan was a champion of the 'noble experiment' of Prohibition," notes David Chalmers, a historian of hooded Americanism. "Most of the things which the Ku Klux Klan stood for and those which it opposed became unified in their focus upon a common enemy, the outsider-alien, as symbolized by the Roman Catholic Church."[55]

54. Hanna to E. Gibbons, telegram, March 22, 1922, copy, ADA, NCWC file (punctuation added).
55. Higham, *Strangers in the Land*, 194–298; Lynn Dumenil, *Freemasonry and*

If the resurgence of anti-Catholicism made Burke's position as a negotiator delicate, a situation internal to the Church rendered it difficult. At the instigation of Cardinals William O'Connell of Boston and Dennis Dougherty of Philadelphia, two of the foremost opponents of the NCWC, Rome suppressed the organization in late March 1922. Acting quickly, the hierarchy appealed the decision and won a suspension of the decree during the process of appeal. Although the Administrative Committee managed to keep news of the suppression more or less under wraps, word of Rome's action eventually became known to the government, undermining to a degree Burke's ability to negotiate.[56]

On March 27, 1922, Burke went to Attorney General Daugherty to plead for the retention of wine dealers with a status equal to manufacturers and importers. Though sympathetic, Daugherty believed that the Volstead Act left no room in that regard. The only method of distribution was between the individual priest and the manufacturer directly. If the church wished another way, it would have to ask Congress to alter the law. Given the pressure that the Masons were then applying to Congress with regard to public education and the Catholic Church, Burke considered this avenue of approach completely out of the question. Daugherty agreed. Burke then convinced the attorney general that, because the Volstead Act gave a bishop the authority to supervise the manufacture of sacramental wine, it also granted to him the lesser right to supervise distribution and even delegate it to a priest. Daugherty accepted this argument in principle and so did the Treasury Department.[57]

American Culture, 1880–930 (Princeton: Princeton University Press, 1984), 120–26; "The Peril of Public Schools," *New Age* 26 (1918): 450; "Is the Parochial School the Place for Patriotism?" ibid. 28 (1920): 69–70; David M. Chalmers, *Hooded Americanism: The History of the Ku Klux Klan* (New York: New Viewpoints, 1976), 28–33, 66–67, 73–74, 78–79, 110–14, 284–85; Kenneth T. Jackson, *The Ku Klux Klan in the City, 1915–1930* (New York: Oxford University Press, 1967), 18–21; Douglas Slawson, "The Attitudes and Activities of American Catholics Regarding the Proposals to Establish a Federal Department of Education between World War I and the Great Depression" (Ph.D. dissertation, The Catholic University of America, 1981), 172–81. In addition to the Klan and the Masons, the Evangelical Protestant Society, organized in New York City in early 1922 by Protestant ministers, warned of a papal conspiracy to undermine the public school system. In the same year, the National Patriotic Council, an offshoot of the Evangelical Society, adopted a policy close to that of the Scottish Rite (*New York Times*, April 6, 1922; *San Francisco Monitor*, August 5, 1922).

56. Slawson, *National Catholic Welfare Council*, 123–44.

57. Burke to Harry M. Daugherty, In the Matter of the Sale and Distribution of

Burke's bargaining position soon became compromised by the action of at least fourteen bishops, who telegraphed the government to urge no change in the regulations at all, even though the NCWC had already conceded that a change must be made. Because of those telegrams, reported Burke, the NCWC was "constantly met with the charge that we do not represent the Catholic body of the United States or that the Catholics do not know what they want."[58] News leaks about Rome's suppression of the NCWC further weakened his position. Although he and Daugherty had reached agreement on sacramental wine in early April, no official word was forthcoming for more than two months. The decision was "mysteriously held up." An inveterate worrier and given to seeing the darker side of things, Burke confided to his friend Bishop Peter Muldoon of Rockford, Illinois: "The N.C.W.C. is [*sic* instead of as] an organization of the Catholic body of the country to care for Catholic interests is today ineffective. It is known (i.e. our condition) in all government circles. . . . We cannot get the authorities to move. We are still respected: listened to: but we are no longer what we were."[59]

Soon thereafter, however, the clouds parted on all fronts. Almost simultaneously Rome rescinded the decree suppressing the NCWC, and the Attorney General's Office announced the terms under which sacramental wine could be distributed. With regard to the latter, dealers were out. "The intent of Congress is clear to abolish the business of the mid-

---

Sacramental Wine: Supplemental Statement of the National Catholic Welfare Council Representing the Hierarchy of the Catholic Church in the United States, March 27, 1922, copy, ACUA, NCWC General Secretary files; Burke to Muldoon, April 15, 1922, ACUA, NCWC General Secretary files; Burke, "Report on Sacramental Wine," addendum to Minutes of the Administrative Committee, August 11, 1922, ACUA, NCWC General Secretary files; Slawson, "Federal Department of Education," 253–61, 266–61.

One cannot help but point out the hypocrisy of Daugherty's demanding that churches obey the letter of the law while he himself and the "Ohio gang," cronies of President Warren G. Harding, sold protection and pardons to bootleggers and peddled confiscated whiskey to thirsty patrons (Sinclair, *Era of Excess*, 185; Cashman, *Prohibition*, 136; Behr, *Prohibition*, 121–25).

58. Burke, "Report on Sacramental Wine," addendum to Minutes of the Administrative Committee, August 11, 1922, ACUA, NCWC General Secretary files.

59. Burke to Muldoon, June 9, 1922, copy, ACUA, NCWC General Secretary files. On Burke's tendency to worry, see Douglas J. Slawson, "John J. Burke, C.S.P.: The Vision and Character of a Public Churchman," *Journal of Paulist Studies* 4 (1995–96): 62–78 passim.

dleman or retail distributor in sacramental wines," declared Daugherty. "But the intent," he continued, "is equally apparent to permit the church, if it agrees to assume the responsibility through its duly authorized rabbi, minister or priest, full power to supervise the manufacture of altar wines, and the specific grant of the greater privilege of the supervision of the manufacture carries with it the lesser privilege of supervision of distribution." The Treasury Department began drafting new regulations whereby the government would issue a permit to a priest, delegated by the bishop, to oversee the distribution of altar wine. This did not mean, however, that the delegated priest could stockpile wine and act as an agent; the actual distribution was still to be done by wineries and importers. The priest supervisor was to function more like a broker who authenticated and forwarded a pastor's request to the manufacturer or importer, who would ship directly to the parish. Having obtained a draft of the new regulations, Michael Slattery, executive secretary of the National Council of Catholic Men, suggested that the NCWC seek to have them altered to allow bishops to appoint laymen as well as priests to oversee distribution.[60] Finding the proposed regulations "intolerable," Burke reported the situation to the NCWC Administrative Committee, which also pronounced the new rules "entirely unsatisfactory" and directed that "still further endeavor be made to secure just regulations, which would not make the procuring of sacramental wine onerous upon the bishops and priests."[61]

60. Boston *Pilot*, June 24, 1922; *New York Times*, July 17, 1922; Draft of Treasury Department regulations, undated, enclosure with Michael Slattery to Burke, July 26, 1922, ACUA, NCWC General Secretary files.

61. Burke to Slattery, July 28, 1922, copy, ACUA, NCWC General Secretary files; Minutes of the Administrative Committee, August 11, 1922, ACUA, NCWC General Secretary files. Claiming that Senator Walsh had promised to ensure that dealerships would be protected by the Volstead Act, Burke blamed him for the church's present predicament. Burke could have learned of the alleged promise only from Russell or Fenlon. As seen above, having reviewed Walsh's amendment to bill, Russell had suggested changes, but the protection of dealerships was not among them. This fact would seem to indicate that such protection had not been part of the arrangement made with the senator. Strange to say, although both Russell and Fenlon were present at this meeting where Burke made his allegation, neither corrected him, at least as indicated in the minutes ("Report on Sacramental Wine," addendum to Minutes of the Administrative Committee, August 11, 1922, ACUA, NCWC General Secretary files).

Burke sent Slattery and Cochran to reenter negotiations with the government. The two met with C. P. Smith, assistant IRS commissioner; E. L. Lloyd, head of the Interpretation Division; and Judge James Britt, legal counselor of the Prohibition Unit. They all reached an informal agreement that would permit a bishop to appoint a priest or layman to become the actual distributor of wine.[62] When the Treasury Department formulated the new regulations, however, the provision for laymen was omitted. The rules provided two alternative methods of distribution. First, manufacturers might sell their wares either directly to the clergy or through their own branch offices. Or, second, the bishop might appoint a priest to supervise the distribution of sacramental wine. In this instance, the clergyman would have to post bond to possess wine, while title to the product remained with the manufacturer until it reached its final destination. In either case, all applications for wine had to be authenticated by the bishop or his appointee before any wine could be distributed.[63]

The NCWC put the best face on the situation. "The new regulations, in view of the definite wording of the Volstead Act and the necessity of proper safeguards, are extremely liberal," Bishop Gibbons told the hierarchy, "and show that government officials are well disposed and eager to provide as convenient a distribution of sacramental wine as possible under the law."[64] To be sure, officials like Goff and even Daugherty had tried to make distribution as painless and as easy as they could. Still, there can be no doubt that the regulations marked a significant tightening of the reins, despite the fact that the church could retain considerable control over the process.

The distribution of wine among Catholics functioned smoothly under the new regulations for nearly three and a half years. In fact, the government expressed "not only satisfaction but admiration at the record of

62. Untitled Report on Conference of Slattery and Cochran with C. P. Smith, E. L. Lloyd, and James J. Britt, August 17, 1922, ACUA, NCWC Legal Department files.

63. U.S. Treasury Department, Bureau of Internal Revenue, T.D. 3391, August 25, 1922, ACUA, NCWC General Secretary files. A summary of these is presented in "Synopsis of New Government Regulations Covering Distribution of Sacramental Wine," *NCWC Bulletin* 4 (September 1922): 8.

64. E. Gibbons to Denis O'Connell (actually a circular to the hierarchy), October 11, 1922, Archives of the Diocese of Richmond, O'Connell Papers.

Catholic bishops and priests in the matter of distribution."[65] Such commendation for the handling of the distribution of wine by no means meant that all clergy kept the law. The historical record holds veiled and not-so-veiled references to clerical violations of the Volstead Act. In early 1921, for instance, Monsignor Edward A. Pace, vice rector of the Catholic University of America, planned a stopover in Terre Haute, Indiana, to confer with Father James H. Ryan, a member of the NCWC Department of Education, before both proceeded to a meeting in Chicago. "Please remember," Pace concluded the letter regarding his itinerary, "that I travel by the B and O; that it is a dusty road and that I have a very delicate throat."[66] It takes little reading between the lines to decipher his message. More forthright was Bishop Muldoon, a confidant of the teetotaler Burke. When Rome lifted the decree of suppression against the NCWC, the bishop wired to his abstemious friend: "This is a great big day in our calendar. If I were near by [sic] I would try to induce you to violate the 18th Amendment."[67] Whether or not Muldoon himself violated the law, it seems clear that others did. Historian Edward Behr reports that Hanna instructed the priests of his archdiocese to purchase their wine only from the Beaulieu winery belonging to his close friend Georges de Latour. "The amounts were so huge that it is clear that most of the priests must have been bootleggers as well," concludes Behr, "for the de Latour books show that all sorts of table wines were sold to the churches."[68]

Even nuns were brought into the act. John Grosso, an Italian gentleman living in Niagara Falls, New York, had a taste for Canadian Whiskey. Not a very religious person himself, he had a wife who was devoted to Our Lady of Mount Carmel. The family was also close to two sisters of St. Joseph of Carondelet, Thecla and Ursuline. In the summer of 1922 or 1923, on the feast of Our Lady of Mount Carmel, Grosso planned to take his family and the two nuns across the river into Canada to a Carmelite monastery, which hosted a picnic on the feast day. His

65. Report of the Chairman, Department of Laws and Legislation, NCWC, September 1925, ADA, NCWC files.

66. Edward A. Pace to J. H. Ryan, January 19, 1921, copy, ACUA, Pace Papers.

67. Muldoon to Burke, telegram, June 23, 1922, ACUA, NCWC General Secretary files.

68. Behr, *Prohibition*, 86–87.

motive for the trip was less religious than his wife's or the two sisters'. He knew that the U.S. customs agents would never search nuns for liquor. While across the border, he purchased six to eight bottles of whiskey and asked the obliging religious to hide them under the skirts of their habits. All went according to plan: the border agents searched no one. Grosso gave his two accomplices a bottle each for their trouble.[69]

If Catholic violations went undetected, the same could not be said for those of the Jewish community. New difficulties arose in late 1925 because of the amount of wine still going astray through fake rabbis. The 1922 regulations limited Jews to two gallons of wine per family member per year. Contrary to expectation, the volume of wine distributed for sacramental purposes increased from a total of 2.13 million gallons in 1922 to 2.94 million in 1924, owing partly to the ineptitude of Prohibition Commissioner Haynes. In April 1925, President Calvin Coolidge made a move aimed not only at redressing the problem but also at undercutting the enormous influence that Wheeler exercised over the Prohibition Unit through his lackey, Haynes. The president appointed retired General Lincoln C. Andrews assistant secretary of the Treasury with full authority over Prohibition, thereby reducing Haynes to a figurehead. In the fall of that year, Andrews cut the amount of wine allotted to Jews to one gallon per adult per year, not to exceed an annual total of five gallons for any one family. The government bound the rabbis to "personally receive, safeguard, and make delivery thereof" and further made them "personally responsible" for the storage and safekeeping of the wine until its distribution.[70] These directives had the desired effect. The total amount of sacramental wine distributed decreased from 2.25 million gallons in 1926 to 648,871 in 1927.[71]

Prior to issuing the new regulations, Andrews sought Burke's advice regarding them to ensure that they contained nothing "inconsistent with existing practices, so far as your church is concerned, or anything which

69. Interview with Aquilyn Maggio, daughter of John Grosso, March 16, 1997, Pacific Beach, California.

70. U.S. Treasury Department, Bureau of Internal Revenue, T.D. 3779, November 30, 1925, copy, ACUA, NCWC General Secretary files; Schmeckebier, *Bureau of Prohibition*, 9–10, and 98; Behr, *Prohibition*, 223; Coffey, *Long Thirst*, 169; Sinclair, *Era of Excess*, 185.

71. Schmeckebier, *Bureau of Prohibition*, 98.

you think would be a mistake for the Government to put out."[72] While it was understandable that he would consult with Burke about how the new rules might have an impact on the church, it was remarkable that he would do so about possible mistakes by the government. Because the original version of the new regulations would indeed have upset the distribution for Catholics, Burke met with Andrews and straightened the matter out. "Changes I made were o.k.," he reported to Muldoon. "So the waters are smooth again and sky is fair. (But don't tell the Methodists or the Fellowship Forum [a Ku Klux Klan newspaper] about this)."[73]

The sky was not as clear as Burke had thought. In early 1926, information reached the NCWC that James Jones, federal director of Prohibition, had sent word to parts of the country stating that in the future priests could procure application forms for wine only from district prohibition directors themselves and no longer from chancery offices or wineries. This unofficial directive apparently sought to stem a practice engaged in by some wineries, namely, the making of pirated copies of the application form with their own names and addresses printed in the appropriate place. These forms were distributed to the clergy almost as advertising. Burke took the matter up with Andrews, who assured him that such regulation was warranted and that the clergy could continue to secure application blanks from chancery offices and wineries.[74]

Nothing more came of the matter until Andrews took a European vacation in the summer. With Andrews out of the country, Jones informed Burke of his intention to issue a directive mandating that clergymen procure application forms from either the district director or the chancery office; wineries would no longer be permitted to issue them. As Charles Fay, vice president of the Beaulieu winery expressed it, "It would appear . . . that the mice begin to play as soon as the cat is away."[75] Burke went at once to complain to Jones that the new order vi-

72. Lincoln C. Andrews to Burke, October 31, 1925, ACUA, NCWC General Secretary files.

73. Burke to Muldoon, November 9, 1925, copy, ACUA, NCWC General Secretary files.

74. Circular from Burke to the hierarchy, March 26, 1926, copy, ACUA, NCWC General Secretary files.

75. Burke to M. J. Hoferer, July 10, 1926, copy, ACUA, NCWC General Secretary files; Charles Fay to Burke, July 15, 1926, ACUA, NCWC General Secretary files.

olated the understanding arrived at with Andrews. To be sure, there must have been some mixup or miscommunication, for Burke claimed that Keith Weeks, the federal supervisor of wine control, had assured him that, although abuses needed to be corrected, no changes would be made in the regulations until Andrews returned. Wineries could continue to dispense applications. Jones, on the other hand, contended that Weeks had informed him just before Andrews departed the country that wineries could no longer issue application forms. At length, both parties agreed that nothing would be changed for the moment and that another conference would be held at a later date to reach a final agreement.[76] In the meantime, Burke checked with the NCWC Administrative Committee to determine what regulations would be satisfactory. None of the members objected to the government's idea of refusing wineries permission to issue applications, and all expressed willingness to use chancery offices for the distribution of such forms in order to "help the government in the administration of the law." In mid-October, the NCWC gave Andrews official notice of its endorsement of the proposed change in regulations.[77]

At this juncture, a new complaint led to a complete reversal of government policy. In December 1926, St. Stanislaus Seminary in Florrisant, Missouri, which ran a winery, brought to Burke's attention that the Chicago office of the Beaulieu Winery was continuing to print and distribute its own version of the application form, complete with the Beaulieu name and address already in place. Burke took the matter to Weeks, the federal supervisor of sacramental wine, who stated that instructions had been issued to district administrators of Prohibition not to honor such preprinted forms. Unsatisfied by this response, Burke demanded that the Treasury Department forbid wineries from being given any blank application forms. "Unless this is made the common policy of the Department," he remonstrated, "injustice and favoritism will result. What is denied to one should not be permitted another."[78] Two months

76. Burke interview with James Jones, July 10, 1926, ACUA, Interview Book, NCWC General Secretary files.

77. Minutes of the Administrative Committee, September 13, 1926, ACUA, NCWC General Secreetary files; J. H. Ryan to Burke, memorandum, October 12, 1926, ACUA, General Secretary files.

78. H. Keith Weeks to Burke, December 6, 1926, ACUA, NCWC General Secre-

later, "after considerable discussion and giving this problem much thought," Weeks did an about face, sending a letter to all prohibition administrators that permitted them the discretion to furnish wineries with application forms. "It is felt that the wine situation is under such control at the present time, that the law enforcement agencies will not be annoyed by the problem of unfair solicitation as hitherto existed, and that the present policy will cause far less inconvenience to the legitimate permittee than privilegee in the distribution of Sacramental wine."[79]

While the negotiations regarding application forms were taking place, the NCWC was also working on a different matter: the delivery of sacramental wine—the issue Bishop Russell had tried to circumvent through his amendment. On taking office, Andrews tightened the screws on this matter. Previous regulations specified that only a bonded carrier could transport sacramental wine, and that each carrier was to receive an authenticated copy of the application for purchase. Thus, a priest in a rural area would have to know the route of the wine and the number of carriers that would handle it in order to fill out the requisite number of applications. Bonds ranged from $1,000 to $5,000. During Haynes's reign, these regulations were widely ignored and went unenforced. It was not uncommon for an unbonded parishioner to go to the train station and pick up a shipment of wine without ever receiving a copy of the application. Andrews, however, cracked the whip. He raised the amount of the bond to between $5,000 and $25,000 (in 1926 the average annual income was $1,450) and required an authenticated copy of the application for each carrier on every leg of the product's journey.[80] Since no parishioner could post such a sizable bond, the priest himself would, as purchaser of the product, have to pick up the wine.

The NCWC negotiated with the Treasury Department for more than a year before the matter was resolved to Catholic satisfaction. In October 1926, while Burke was again ill and absent, Father James Ryan suggest-

tary files; Burke to Weeks, December 7, 1926, copy, ACUA, NCWC General Secretary files.

79. Weeks to Burke, February 2, 1927, copy, ACUA, NCWC General Secretary files; Weeks to Prohibition Administrators, February 1, 1927, copy, ACUA, General Secretary files. The first quote is from the former, and the second quote from the latter.

80. William Montavon to E. Gibbons, February 5, 1926, ADA, NCWC files.

ed to the government a possible solution, namely, a special label to be attached to the container (bottle, jug, case) of wine. The chancellor of a diocese would have sole charge of these labels, sign them, and send them to the winery for attachment at the same time that he sent an application. At the end of the year, he would report to the government how many labels he had issued.[81] This label would replace the copy of the application that had to be given to each bonded carrier. In other words, the label served as an authenticated application form attached to the container, thereby obviating the necessity of multiple, authenticated application forms, one for each carrier along the route. William Montavon, who succeeded Cochran as director of the Legal Department, reported that Andrews and his people were "sympathetic" toward the Catholic position, but held that their regulations were "indispensable because of abuses which have been committed, in no case by Catholic Priests, but by clergymen of other denominations, especially Jewish."[82]

Apparently, persistence paid off. Unfortunately, no record exists of what occurred during the negotiations, only the resolution reached. The government approved a new label for wine. In essence, it was a blank form with gum adhesive on the back. Before distributing the labels to diocesan chancellors, the district prohibition administrator had to sign them. When the chancellor received an application for wine, he had to sign, number, and fill out the label, specifying the name and address of the priest to receive the shipment as well as the quantity, kind, and brand of wine being sent. When such labels were used, common carriers sufficed.[83] A pleased Burke reported that the new label would "decrease the number of certificates to be signed and do away with the necessity in rural places of a bonded carrier."[84] Thereafter, until the noble experiment ended in 1933, there were no further complications regarding the procurement of wine for divine purposes.

81. J. H. Ryan to Burke, memorandum, October 12, 1926, ACUA, NCWC General Secretary files.
82. Ibid.
83. J. M. Doran to Burke, February 4, 1927, with enclosures (blank label and copy of Andrews to Prohibition Administrators, February 1, 1927), ACUA, NCWC General Secretary files.
84. Burke to Muldoon, November 9, 1925, copy, ACUA, NCWC General Secretary files; Burke to E. Gibbons, November 18, 1926, ADA, NCWC files; Burke to E. Gibbons, February 10, 1927, ADA, NCWC files.

From the foregoing account, several things become clear. First, Catholic officials played a significant role not only in shaping the Volstead Act, as it pertained to sacramental wine, but also in formulating Treasury regulations relative to the carrying out of that law. Their objective was ever the same: to keep the procurement of altar wine an easy process. In this regard they ran up against a government that increasingly sought to tighten the process in order to stem the flow of liquor to the public through religious avenues. Second, despite the rampant anti-Catholicism of the time, government agents appear to have been almost wholly untouched by it. Indeed, church authorities always described them as cordial, sympathetic, and willing to be as helpful as possible. Evidence in the present investigation bears witness that government officials sought to be as accommodating to the church as the law and personal makeup permitted. The spectrum of cooperation ranged widely, with Commissioner Roper and Assistant Attorney General Willebrandt representing opposite extremes, the former bending over backwards to grant the church almost total control over sacramental wine, the latter seeking to hold the tightest possible government rein. Nothing indicates that the Eighteenth Amendment or the Volstead Act warranted the fear expressed by *America* magazine that Prohibition meant the doom of Catholicism. All government authorities—even Willebrandt, who developed a critical attitude toward northeastern Catholics and Jews and a soft one toward klansmen—recognized the legality of sacramental wine. Finally, the government always commended the Catholic clergy for their adherence to prohibition regulations in the matter of sacramental wine. The extent to which that praise might or might not have been merited has yet to be determined—but that is another study.

Earl Boyea

9. ARCHBISHOP EDWARD MOONEY AND THE REVEREND CHARLES COUGHLIN'S ANTI-SEMITISM, 1938–1940

Was Edward Mooney, the archbishop of Detroit, anti-Semitic? Is that the reason for his delay during the late 1930s in silencing the "Radio Priest," the Reverend Charles Coughlin? Archbishop Amleto Cicognani, the papal apostolic delegate in the United States, hoped that making "public all the elements in the case" would help "exonerate the Church and its officers from all fault and responsibility."[1] It has taken nearly a half-century for the ecclesiastical archives dealing with the Reverend Charles Coughlin to be open.[2] These papers do not exactly "exonerate" Coughlin's superior, Archbishop Edward Mooney. On the one hand, they evidence too much toleration for the priest's increasing anti-Semitism while, on the other, they also demonstrate the restraints within which Mooney could act. This article will examine only a brief period of their relationship which most clearly exemplifies this state of affairs.

1. Archives of the Archdiocese of Detroit (AAD), Mooney Administration Coughlin Collection (MACC), Box 2, File 4, Cicognani to Mooney, Washington, D.C., April 30, 1942.
2. Charles Edward Coughlin was born in Hamilton, Ontario, on October 25, 1891. He was ordained in Toronto in 1916 and incardinated into the Diocese of Detroit on February 26, 1923. In 1926 he was assigned to Royal Oak, Michigan, to establish the parish of Saint Theresa of the Little Flower. He began his broadcasting the same year. He died on October 27, 1979, in Birmingham, Michigan.

Much has been written about Father Coughlin.[3] Most of this material has been based on printed sources in the public forum. In the context of a general history of the Archdiocese of Detroit, Leslie Woodcock Tentler has presented a thorough but necessarily brief account of Coughlin using the Archives of the Archdiocese of Detroit. In Dr. Tentler's work the papers of Archbishop Edward Mooney are discussed for the first time. Donald Warren also uses some of these papers. This account will augment their presentations especially with some private letters they did not use. Archival materials will also be used to expose more clearly how Mooney's behavior was affected by his colleagues in the American episcopate as well as by the Vatican and its representative in the United States, the apostolic delegate.

Edward Mooney was the chairman (1935–40; 1941–45) of the Administrative Board of the National Catholic Welfare Conference (NCWC).[4] One of his tasks was to guide the process the American bish-

3. The best summary of Coughlin's life is contained in Donald Warren, *Radio Priest: Charles Coughlin, the Father of Hate Radio* (New York: Free Press, 1996), and Leslie Woodcock Tentler, *Seasons of Grace: A History of the Catholic Archdiocese of Detroit* (Detroit: Wayne State University Press, 1990); see Sheldon Marcus, *Father Coughlin: The Tumultuous Life of the Priest of the Little Flower* (Boston: Little, Brown, and Company, 1973); Charles J. Tull, *Father Coughlin and the New Deal* (Syracuse: Syracuse University Press, 1965); Alan Brinkley, *Voices of Protest: Huey Long, Father Coughlin, and the Great Depression* (New York: Alfred A. Knopf, 1982); James P. Shenton, "The Coughlin Movement and the New Deal," *Political Science Quarterly* 73 (September 1958): 352–73; and James P. Shenton, "Fascism and Father Coughlin," *Wisconsin Magazine of History* 44 (Autumn 1960): 6–11. Also see Earl Boyea, "The Reverend Charles Coughlin and the Church: The Gallagher Years, 1930–1937," *Catholic Historical Review* 81 (April 1995): 211–25; and "Archbishop Edward Mooney and Reverend Charles Coughlin: The First 'Silencing,' 1937–1938," unpublished typescript.

4. The NCWC was the conference of American Catholic bishops which met annually, usually in Washington, D.C. The NCWC had a standing secretariat, headed by a General Secretary. For the history of this organization see Joseph M. McShane, *"Sufficiently Radical": Catholicism, Progressivism, and the Bishops' Program of 1919* (Washington, D.C.: The Catholic University of America Press, 1986); Elizabeth McKeown, "Apologia for an American Catholicism: The Petition and Report of the National Catholic Welfare Council to Pius XI, April 25, 1922," *Church History* 43 (December 1974): 514–28; idem, "The National Bishops' Conference: An Analysis of Its Origins," *Catholic Historical Review* 66 (October 1980): 565–83; and idem, "War and Welfare, A Study of American Catholic Leadership, 1917–1922" (Ph.D. dissertation, University of Chicago, 1972); John B. Sheerin, *Never Look Back: The Career and Concerns of John J. Burke* (New York: Paulist Press, 1975); Earl Boyea, "The National Catholic Welfare Conference: An Experience in Episcopal Leadership, 1935–1945" (Ph.D. dissertation, The Catholic University of America, 1987); Douglas Slawson, *Foundation and First*

ops used to issue pastoral statements. The NCWC positions on anti-Semitism give a view of Mooney's own formal and public opinion on the matter. While these statements were few and should have been more, they do reveal a real concern, but one often as not more focused on Catholics in Germany than on the Jewish people.

The hierarchy's first statement on Central European events was a letter to its colleagues in Germany in 1937. American Catholics had been quite silent about the persecutions of both Jews and Catholics in Germany until Pius XI's March 1937 encyclical on the German situation, "Mit brennender Sorge." As a Jewish writer has observed, this "persuaded the Catholic hierarchy to direct attention to the German scene."[5] While the American prelates did not specifically mention the Jews, they condemned the Nazi attempts to exterminate religion. By its nature the missive was meant to encourage the German Catholic Church.[6]

The year 1938 saw strong Jewish support for the Loyalists of Spain, who appeared to Catholics to be trying to destroy the Church there.[7] There was also a notable rise in anti-Semitism in the United States in 1938, in no small part aided by Coughlin. In this context, the bishops condemned all systems and theories alien to democracy and Christianity and called for a Catholic educational crusade to form good citizens.[8] In April 1939, hailing this crusade, the churchmen particularly warned the faithful of the evils of bigotry: "For that very reason our people will be

Decade of the National Catholic Welfare Conference (Washington, D.C.: The Catholic University of America Press, 1992).

5. Haim Genizi, *American Apathy: The Plight of Christian Refugees from Nazism* (Ramat-Gan, Israel: Bar Ilan University Press, 1983), p. 139. This book also helps to see American Catholic silence in the context of the general United States apathy.

6. "Letter to the German Hierarchy," November 18, 1937, Hugh J. Nolan, ed., *Pastoral Letters of the United States Catholic Bishops*, 6 vols. [sixth volume is edited by Patrick Carey] (Washington, D.C.: United States Catholic Conference, 1984–98), 1:419.

7. See J. David Valaik, "In the Days before Ecumenism: American Catholics, Anti-Semitism and the Spanish Civil War," *Journal of Church and State* 13 (Autumn 1971): 466–67.

8. "On Christian Democracy," October 14, 1938, Nolan, *Pastoral Letters*, 1:426–29. Cardinal Dennis Dougherty of Philadelphia wrote to FDR shortly after the NCWC meeting on October 26, 1938: "I beg you to please use the influence of your high office to safeguard [the German Jews'] rights as far as it may be in your power." Cited by Genizi, *American Apathy*, p. 142.

on their guard against all forms of racial bigotry of which Pope Pius XI, speaking of a pertinent instance, said: 'It is not possible for Christians to take part in anti-Semitism.'"[9] Yet, even this declaration was made only after "considerable discussion as to [its] advisability."[10] The churchmen were reluctant to venture into controversies.

Archbishop John T. McNicholas of Cincinnati, Mooney's close colleague in the NCWC, authored the 1941 episcopal statement "Crisis of Christianity," which affirmed: "We cannot too strongly condemn the inhuman treatment to which the Jewish people have been subjected in many countries."[11] In a very sympathetic letter to Norman M. Littell, the secretary of the National Committee Against Nazi Persecution and Extermination of the Jews, McNicholas in 1944 was even more adamant in his condemnation of "the inhuman Nazi persecution of the Jews which brutally violates imprescriptible human rights and disregards the divine dignity of every person." He fervently prayed that God would "bring to a speedy end the rule of these human monsters. . . ."[12]

The evils being inflicted upon the Jews having been condemned in the 1941 pastoral, they were again censured in 1942. In the context of general persecution, this paragraph, probably attributable to Mooney's influence, read:

> We express our deepest sympathy to our brother bishops in all countries of the world where religion is persecuted, liberty abolished, and the rights of God and of man are violated. Since the murderous assault on Poland, utterly devoid of every semblance of humanity, there has been a premeditated and systematic extermination of the people of this nation. The same satanic technique is

9. "On Bigotry," April 19, 1939, Raphael M. Huber, ed., *Our Bishops Speak* (Milwaukee: Bruce Publishing Company, 1952), p. 323.

10. Archives of the National Catholic Welfare Conference, General Secretary Files (ANCWC), Minutes of the Administrative Board, p. 406, April 19, 1939; Mooney, with Jewish and other Christian leaders, had also issued a December 25, 1938, condemnation of the Nazi persecution; see *Catholic Action*, January 1939, p. 12.

11. "Crisis of Christianity," November 14, 1941, Nolan, *Pastoral Letters*, 2:31–32; also see Paul E. Czuchlewski, "Liberal Catholicism and American Racism 1924–1960," *Records of the American Catholic Historical Society of Philadelphia* 85 (September–December 1974): 149, 156.

12. Archives of the Archdiocese of Cincinnati, McNicholas Administration (AACi), Cooperation, [McNicholas] to Littell, [Norwood], May 5, 1944, copy.

being applied to many other peoples. We feel a deep sense of revulsion against the cruel indignities heaped upon the Jews in conquered countries and upon defenseless peoples not of our faith. . . .[13]

The bishops as a body issued no other statements on the Holocaust, even when, as a Jewish scholar has asserted, by "1944 informed Americans knew, in broad outline, of the existence of a Jewish catastrophe."[14] Though these statements were important, there is a wonder that the bishops were not more forceful in their condemnation of the horror of the Holocaust. While Mooney would not have been able, single-handedly, to force stronger and more frequent statements, it is very probable that he was no less content with their output than his brother bishops were.

Certainly, one arena in which he could have demonstrated a stronger opposition to anti-Semitism, if such were his opinion, would have been to curb Coughlin.[15] Coughlin had established a large radio and press audience by the time Mooney arrived in Detroit as its first archbishop in 1937. The priest had found his relationship with the previous bishop of Detroit, Michael Gallagher, very cordial and sympathetic. It was due to their basic agreement on social issues that the priest was allowed a relatively free rein in expressing his views. Gallagher was even able to defend the priest and fend off opponents who wished him silenced.

Mooney's arrival marked a very significant change. Detroit now had an ecclesiastic with national stature who also was in basic disagreement with many of Coughlin's views. Mooney's diplomatic temperament was also in sharp contrast to the more flamboyant and exuberant Coughlin.

Mooney's first run-in with Coughlin, during the fall of 1937, was over the priest's attacks on the Congress of Industrial Organizations and on President Roosevelt. Coughlin tested Mooney's persistence by quitting the air-waves, letting the blame for this fall on Mooney, and orches-

13. "Victory and Peace," November 14, 1942, Nolan, *Pastoral Letters*, 2:41.
14. Esther Yolles Feldblum, *The American Catholic Press and the Jewish State* (New York: Ktav Publishing House, Inc., 1977), p. 56. See David S. Wyman, *The Abandonment of the Jews: America and the Holocaust, 1941–1945* (New York: Pantheon Books, 1984), pp. 19–58.
15. See Warren, *Radio Priest*, pp. 129–60, for a summary of Coughlin's anti-Semitism.

trating an avalanche of protest against his own archbishop. In the end, Mooney found himself alone to handle the matter. Fearful of stimulating a stampede of the priest's followers out of the Church, Mooney bided his time. Coughlin then manuevered his way back into official good standing as well as onto the air in early 1938. In that situation, Mooney's diplomatic nature, his desire to go slowly, fed his reticence to curb Coughlin on his own authority. This served as the background for Mooney's response to Coughlin's foray into anti-Semitism during 1938.

Coughlin had been expressing anti-Semitic remarks all during the 1930s, especially accusing Jewish bankers of being the cause for the Depression. These remarks, however, were usually so couched that he easily evaded being clearly labeled an anti-Semite. Still, many Jewish groups and individuals requested that Mooney curb his priest.

Mooney's answer to these groups was always the same. For example, responding to Dr. Leo M. Franklin, a Detroit rabbi, who had thanked the Catholic bishops for their 1939 statement, Mooney explained his caution, saying that religious leaders must make injustice known without sacrificing "the rather vaguely defined but priceless heritage of free speech. . . ." He added:

> Unfortunately, at times, our practical choice is between two evils and it may be necessary to counter the lesser evil indirectly rather than precipitate the greater by hasty action even on a good impulse.[16]

Mooney claimed that the greater evil was the loss of a priest's right to free speech, something neither Franklin nor many Jews would have accepted. Mooney's rationale was possibly just a means to disarm his correspondent. For, clearly, had Coughlin spoken against some theological doctrine of the Church, his right to free speech would not have prevented a swift action by Mooney. Then one must ask, how, objectively, Mooney could consider prejudice against Jews, which had a practical expression in the Nazi Holocaust, the lesser evil? Perhaps, Mooney simply did not consider anti-Semitism a problem of equal gravity. This could explain the archbishop's tolerance of Charles Coughlin.

16. AAD, Mooney Administration (MA), Box 21, File 7, [Mooney] to Franklin, [Detroit], May 17, 1939, copy.

However, there are some signs that this concern about freedom of speech was sincere. For Mooney was not alone in enunciating this right. Archbishop McNicholas attacked the "so called liberal forces here in Cinti [*sic*]" for wanting Coughlin silenced. He found that those "who talk loudest about free speach [*sic*] for subversive activities insist that the free speach of Coughlin be shut off."[17] Certainly, hypocrisy on the part of Coughlin's opponents should be confronted, but did not McNicholas, and perhaps Mooney as well, fail to see how morally subversive the Radio Priest's views could be?

Regardless of Coughlin's supposed right to free speech, Mooney was moved to act by two events. First of all, the apostolic delegate wrote Mooney on November 16, 1938, six days after *Kristallnacht* in Germany, noting that Jewish groups had been complaining to him about a series of articles appearing in Coughlin's *Social Justice* magazine in the summer of 1938 which "were deeply anti-Semitic in tone."[18] Secondly, Coughlin was publishing the "Protocols of Zion," which he acknowledged to be fiction but which he then treated as fact as he outlined a world-wide conspiracy of Jews.[19] Coughlin's November 20, 1938, broadcast of anti-Semitic materials, which had previously appeared only in print, also raised the affair to a new level and required Mooney's response.[20]

Mooney explained to the delegate that he could not stop the articles because there was nothing "manifestly wrong" with them. He reminded the delegate that, in fact, the articles were censored but that they "were

17. AAD, Mooney Administration Uncatalogued (MAU), Box 15, McNicholas to Mooney, Norwood, August 7, 1939.

18. Tentler, *Seasons of Grace,* p. 335; also see Mary Christine Athans, "The Fahey-Coughlin Connection: Father Denis Fahey, C.S.Sp., Father Charles Coughlin, and Religious Anti-Semitism in the United States, 1938–1954" (Ph.D. dissertation, Graduate Theological Union, 1982), p. 159, who has found the basis of Coughlin's strident anti-Semitism in teachings of Denis Fahey: "One name began to emerge, however, in the summer of 1938, whom Coughlin quoted as an authority in his controversial writings and speeches. That author was Denis Fahey, C.S.Sp." She has noted that the first citing of Fahey in *Social Justice* was on August 8, 1938. Also see Brinkley, *Voices of Protest,* pp. 269–83.

19. Warren, *Radio Priest,* p. 150: Coughlin "crossed the Rubicon of political anti-Semitism by identifying himself with the *Protocols.*"

20. Ibid., p. 155: Couglin appeared to justify Nazi hatred of Jews, who were blamed for the Versailles Treaty and the rise of Communism. Only after this sort of invective did the priest then lament the persecution of the many innocent Jews.

so artfully gotten up, contained so many disclaimers of anti-Semitic feeling and put forward the communistic issue so cleverly that it was impossible to take issue with them to the point of refusing to pass the articles." Mooney recognized that neither Coughlin's broadcasts nor his Social Justice were "productive of real good to the Church." However, he still spoke in terms of the lesser evil,

> between allowing the thing to go on while making it clear that he speaks for himself and not the Church as well as restraining him from making statements which are manifestly wrong, or, on the other hand, stopping him by a use of authority which may not be clearly understood and may thus raise difficulties in the minds of many indiscriminating people.

After mentioning how intractable Coughlin was, Mooney concluded that he was "chary of pronouncing a definite 'non licet' except in a case where the law is clear and the facts obvious."

This was the dilemma. Could not Mooney see that, in fact, the promotion of anti-Semitism by a Catholic priest was the greater evil? If he could not, could he not at least see that what Coughlin was doing was "manifestly wrong"? In this letter, Mooney expresses a fear of a public misperception of the use of ecclesial authority. He also seems to have found Coughlin's attacks on Communism somewhat excusing for the rest of his attitudes. Mostly, however, the anti-Semitism does not seem to have been evident or serious enough to warrant his action.

Mooney also noted that the November 20 broadcast, which portrayed German persecution of Jews as merely a defense mechanism against Communism (itself a Jewish movement), had passed, with modifications, the censorship of his auxiliary bishop, Stephen Woznicki. On this basis, the station manager had pointed out that Coughlin's comments had the approval of his superiors. Mooney related that he had publicly clarified the matter of censorship pointing out that Coughlin was not an authoritative exponent of Catholic teaching, nor did permission to broadcast an address imply approval of its contents.[21] If Mooney was concerned that the use of ecclesiastical authority to curb Coughlin

21. AAD, MACC, Box 1, File 6, [Mooney] to Cicognani, [Detroit], November 26, 1938, copy.

would cause problems for non-discriminating minds, surely he must have seen that this last distinction would be no clearer.

Yet, Coughlin was clever enough, as Mooney explained to Father Michael Ready, General Secretary of the NCWC "to say and unsay a thing in almost the same breath." That duplicity not only got the priest's articles past the diocesan censor but also allowed Coughlin the opportunity to claim he had not said what everyone knew he had said. Mooney also noted that many in America were harboring anti-Semitism and that Coughlin was merely exploiting that. Mooney's best advice to any Jews who would complain about Coughlin's activities was to ignore the priest and thus deprive him of publicity.[22] Here, it seems, Mooney was merely wishing the issue away. As the leader of the American hierarchy and privy to much information about the situation in Germany, he chose to be too tolerant of the anti-Semitism in his own country.

Critical in this whole episode was that all Coughlin's broadcasts linking the Jews (especially New York bankers) and Communists (November 20–December 11, 1938) had been approved by diocesan censors. The statements of the NCWC would seem to indicate that Mooney was not anti-Semitic. Yet his tolerance of Coughlin's antics calls this into question.

Were there other reasons, perhaps, in addition to the protection of freedom of speech, which made the Detroit archbishop reluctant to stop his priest, reasons that might mitigate a charge of anti-Semitism against Mooney? Leslie Woodcock Tentler has indicated that Mooney also feared the reaction of certain rightist groups in the country to any attempt on his part to silence Coughlin completely.

In addition, Mooney did not see that he had any real "grounds in canon law" to "act against Coughlin." The archbishop also deeply believed that his priest could create a schism in the Church if he were placed under more severe episcopal sanctions.[23] Finally, Mooney was not at all certain that he would find great support among his fellow bishops

22. AAD, MACC, Box 1, File 6, [Mooney] to Ready, [Detroit], December 2, 1938, copy.

23. Warren, *Radio Priest*, p. 220, states that Mooney's aim was to harass Coughlin without making him a martyr; also see pp. 213–15 for some anecdotal information regarding the danger of a schism.

for a complete silencing of Coughlin.[24] Given all these factors, Mooney did no more than try to eliminate what was "manifestly wrong" in Coughlin's talks and articles.

On the other hand, Mooney, trusting Coughlin's respect for the pope, chose to work behind the scenes. He asked Cicognani "for some word from Rome" that would guide Coughlin away from the scope of his recent broadcasts. Mooney would "use it privately . . . to give him further needed evidence that the judgment of his superiors reflects the attitude of the Church."

Mooney, seemingly emboldened by Cicognani's interest in Coughlin's talks, related that he had actually halved Coughlin's December 11, 1938, radio address but that the priest would not accept his advice to change the topic; thus the choice was between going ahead with "something which in its criticism of Jews was trivial and faultfinding" or cancelling the broadcast and causing trouble for the Church. However, when Coughlin commented on Cardinal George Mundelein of Chicago's response to the December 11 talk, Mooney warned the Royal Oak pastor. Mooney was willing to be stronger against his priest when it was a matter of an attack against a cardinal. Here is seen concretely the limits of Coughlin's free speech, something Mooney earlier had trumpeted. While Coughlin asserted his lack of anti-Semitism, Mooney charged the priest with leaving "an impression of anti-semitic feeling . . . not in harmony with the spirit of the utterances of the Holy Father in this grave crisis."[25]

Mooney's views on all this were most clearly expressed in a letter to Father Joseph Hurley, a close friend working in the Vatican. Mooney accused Coughlin of being anti-Semitic, which he defined as "one who is against the Jews as such and is obsessed with the conviction that all the evil in the world is traceable to them." Then, in a candid expression in which Mooney assigned a form of collective guilt, he added: "The Lord knows they have enough to their account without bothering about piling it up."

Mooney believed that some things "needed saying" regarding the

24. Tentler, *Seasons of Grace*, pp. 336–38.
25. AAD, MACC, Box 1, File 6, [Mooney] to Cicognani, [Detroit], December 18, 1938, copy.

Jews. Coughlin, however, was "not the one who, on account of his 'Pro-
tocol' background and his rancorous tone, [was] 'indicated' to say them
with good effect, or at least without a great admixture of bad effect."
Mooney expressed his deepest frustration

> to be connected with the vulgar cleverness of his procedure
> through this vague and inconclusive censorship business. He is
> smart enough to play up the fact that all that he says is passed by
> the censor—and to know that if I stop him for something that is
> not obviously wrong under some clear law, an agitation which he,
> of course, with all his good will, is unable to prevent or curb will
> turn Brooklyn or some other places down East upside down . . .

Mooney recognized that his censorship was ineffective. He blamed this
on weak ecclesiastical law. He requested some Vatican judgment on the
content of the anti-Semitic broadcasts to be used privately with Coughlin to tone him down.

The archbishop felt constrained not only by the limits of canon law
but also by his brother bishops, as he concluded:

> We are dealing with an unbalanced individual in a crazy age and a
> crazy country where brass counts for more than anything else—
> and where a good many people are secretly glad to see that the
> Jews have not an absolute monopoly on the brass. This feeling is so
> strong that the many bishops with whom I have talked the matter
> over have in every case counseled against any further statement on
> my part than the one I have made. But I feel that something must
> be done and this quiet papal pressure strikes me as the most practi-
> cal idea.[26]

On December 17, 1938, Mooney forwarded the talks in question to
the apostolic delegate. The archbishop and Coughlin had disagreed in
their assessment of the anti-Semitic nature of the broadcasts. Thus both
now sought the mind of the Holy See on the matter.

When Cardinal Eugenio Pacelli, the Vatican Secretary of State, sent

---

26. AAD, MAU, Box 1939 "C," Mooney to Hurley, Detroit, December 22, 1938,
copy. Hurley responded that Rome was content to let this again be a local matter; he
felt Mooney should patiently wait some of it out, of course, keeping Cicognani informed; AAD, MAU, Box 9, Hurley to "Doc," [Vatican], December 26, 1938.

a rather bland and noncommital telegram to Cicognani regarding the
materials, Cicognani urged Mooney to write directly to Pacelli. However,
a letter of the previous day, January 16, 1939, from Hurley would not
encourage Mooney to be stauncher in his opposition to Coughlin's anti-
Semitism:

> . . . Everybody agrees that C. is a dangerous person; that a way
> must be found to keep him within bounds; that it is a difficult case
> because there is no law which covers it clearly. . . . Nor has the
> Pope brought up the question on the several occasions on which I
> have been with him lately.
>
>   . . . It is felt better to go very slowly here, treating the matter
> for a time at least as a purely local problem. We are under very se-
> vere attack here for our alleged attitude of coddling Semites. . . .
> Against this background, perhaps it is felt to be more prudent to
> wait until passions cool and issues become clarified. And this may
> be the explanation if you get no answer, and are left to handle the
> problem as best you can for the time.[27]

A few days later, however, Hurley noted that the Fascists were making a stronger and more concerted attack on the Church and were also
citing and hailing Coughlin in their editorials. He also noted that the recent weakness of the Austrian hierarchy in the face of the Nazis had
made a deep impression on the Roman curia. In this context, perhaps,
there would be support for Mooney to be bolder:

> I may still be able to be of help, and you may be sure that when the
> chance comes, I shall take it, even try to create it. There are a few
> timorous spirits here who think that the storm will pass only if they
> are silent and submissive. Some of these weak sisters are strong in
> the councils of the Church, and the age and illness of the Chief
> [Pius XI] give them added importance. But they are not too popu-
> lar.[28]

Mooney, however, had already requested of Cardinal Pacelli a papal
order that Coughlin submit to his ordinary. Mooney felt that he would
otherwise have to share Pacelli's earlier telegram with Coughlin who

27. AAD, MAU, Box 9, Hurley to "Doc," Rome, January 16, 1939.
28. AAD, MAU, Box 1939 "C," Hurley to "Doc," [Vatican], January 21, 1939.

"would interpret it as an approval of the tenor of his talks on the part of the Holy See itself. . . . In such a way the meaning of Your Eminence's telegram, which I understood perfectly, would be distorted to the serious detriment of Religion. . . ."

The archbishop of Detroit's correction of Coughlin's anti-Semitism was quite limited, due to Coughlin's own personality, to a potential national reaction, and to the constraints of canon law. The archbishop saw that Pacelli's telegram would serve only to confirm Coughlin in his attitudes and preclude any deeper censorship. Mooney, therefore, suggested an alternate text dealing with priestly obedience and avoiding the content of the broadcasts.[29]

When Rome finally agreed to the idea of a statement, it recommended that it be written by the delegate. Cicognani invited a text from Mooney, who provided the one the delegate would use. Cicognani then wrote Coughlin on March 1, 1939. After recounting the background to his missive, Cicognani concluded:

> . . . His Holiness deemed it fitting that I, as Apostolic Delegate and in the name of the Holy See, should counsel you to follow the suggestions and directions of your Archbishop in a spirit of priestly docility.

The delegate then required Coughlin to submit to Mooney's censorship and be "guided by his prudent counsel in regard to the content and tenor of [Coughlin's] radio addresses." Finally, Cicognani requested that Coughlin end the mail being sent to the delegation and the Vatican "as they create only embarrassment and procure no good."[30]

Mooney now knew that he would receive support from Rome and Cicognani in upholding episcopal authority over a priest but not necessarily over the specific issue of anti-Semitism. Perhaps the whole affair was viewed by Rome as more a public relations matter than as a serious

29. AAD, MACC, Box 1, File 8, [Mooney] to Pacelli, [Detroit], January 17, 1939, copy, Italian; ". . . lo interpreterebbe come un'approvazione da parte stessa Santa Sede del tono dei suoi discorsi. . . . In tal modo il significato del telegramma di Vostra Eminenza, che ho perfettamente compreso, vorrebbe distorto a serio detrimento della causa della Religione."

30. AAD, MACC, Box 1, File 8, [Cicognani] to Coughlin, [D.C.], March 1, 1939, copy. Also see Cicognani to Mooney, Washington, February 13, 1939; and [Mooney] to Cicognani, [Detroit], February 20, 1939, copy, with attachment.

moral one. Coughlin certainly did not feel chastened concerning his prejudices.

Mooney's censors, however, were emboldened. One text was denied approval due to its blatant anti-Semitism, which led to Coughlin's famous silent broadcast of February 5, 1940.[31] In addition, since the National Association of Broadcasters had written new rules governing controversial broadcasts, clearly aimed at Coughlin, the radio orator soon found himself without stations to receive his talks. Rather than construct a new network, he ended his radio career in September 1940, though he still had, at least, some indirect ties to his newspaper, *Social Justice.* Mooney believed that it was the sustained experience of censorship and its restraints which helped to move Coughlin to cease broadcasting and to rely solely on the printed word.[32]

Mooney soon asked for a clarification of Coughlin's connection to the paper, to which he had formally severed his ties on August 18, 1939, yet which constantly mentioned his name, which had advertised on the radio broadcasts, and whose corporate secretary was one of Coughlin's secretaries. In fact, views that would not get by the censors for broadcast were being funneled into the paper and its advertisements on Coughlin's broadcasts.[33] Under pressure from his ordinary to rectify these anomalies, Coughlin resumed control of *Social Justice* on February 19, 1940.

Mooney then informed Cicognani of Coughlin's return to the editorship of *Social Justice* and of the subsequent complete censorship of the paper "for the first time in its history."[34] It was probably the resulting blander contents, subject to "the exercise of supervision," which led

31. Tentler, *Seasons of Grace,* p. 338.

32. AAD, MACC, Box 2, File 2, [Mooney] to Cicognani, Detroit, June 5, 1940, copy.

33. AAD, MACC, Box 2, File 1, [Mooney] to Cicognani, [Detroit], February 20, 1940, copy. Mooney wrote Coughlin: "I direct you, therefore, either to take control of 'Social Justice' and make it in name and in fact a Catholic paper or, as an alternative, to refrain not only, as in the last six months, from editorial collaboration regarding it but also from any cooperation which might naturally convey the impression that it is your paper . . . either you will control it as a Catholic paper under the canonical supervision of your ecclesiastical superiors or you will be entirely out of it and free of all responsibility, both in appearance and in fact, for the policies and contents of the magazine"; Mooney to Coughlin, Detroit, February 19, 1940, copy.

34. AAD, MACC, Box 2, File 2, [Mooney] to Cicognani, [Detroit], March 8, 1940, copy. Cicognani to Mooney, Washington, March 15, 1940, congratulated Mooney for gaining control over the paper.

Coughlin yet again to sever his official ties to his journal on May 16, 1940. A frustrated Mooney then ordered him to become completely disassociated from the paper. Mooney was certain that Coughlin would "comply with the letter of these instructions" though he doubted that the priest would carry out the "spirit."[35]

Donald Warren has well presented all the available archival material on the last years of Coughlin's public life, as carried out via his newspaper, *Social Justice*. With the closing of that paper in 1942 Coughlin was silent.[36] That victory was achieved by a combination of strong federal pressure to end a wartime subversive activity and an archbishop who was very willing to act now that he was not alone in confronting Charles Coughlin.

Coughlin was finally silent. It is easy, after fifty years, to judge this to have been a hollow victory for the Church. Ecclesiastical leaders never really found the courage to stop this priest from making his bigoted comments over the air or in the press. Was this because Mooney or the American hierarchy or Cicognani or the Vatican were themselves anti-Semitic? There is evidence to the contrary, including the episcopal statements mentioned above. The correspondence, however, also shows that the sensibilities about prejudice, so finely honed over the last half century, were still rudimentary in the 1930s. Dr. Leslie Tentler ascribes some of this to the "cultural isolation not only of Catholics but of Protestants and Jews as well."[37] Another factor is the internal Catholic theological development on the issue of Jewish-Christian relations which would only take place with and after Vatican II. Still, even if Mooney and his colleagues were not as fully anti-Semitic as Coughlin seemed to be, their moral leadership in this arena was almost negligible. This weakness alone played a critical role in limiting his ability to respond forthrightly and firmly to Coughlin's positions.

Nonetheless, other issues played their roles as well—so much so that the blame of a lack of moral leadership needs to be contextualized. Freedom of speech, such a hallowed treasure in American society, par-

---

35. AAD, MACC, Box 2, File 2, [Mooney] to Cicognani, Detroit, June 5, 1940, copy.

36. Warren, *Radio Priest*, pp. 224–63.

37. Tentler, *Seasons of Grace*, p. 338.

ticularly tested in the 1930s by all sorts of peoples, and completely void-
ed in Fascist and Communist Europe, was explicitly cited by Mooney as
a reason for restraint in acting against Coughlin. The Vatican's reluctance
to meddle in an American political affair affirms the ecclesial respect for
this American right. Yet, the swiftness of Mooney's response to Coughlin's attack on Cardinal Mundelein calls into question the depth of the
archbishop's commitment to Coughlin's freedom of speech. Certainly,
this right was a minor issue even if it was highly touted in public.

Mooney also clearly feared Coughlin's followers, both their reac-
tions to any episcopal censure of the priest and their potential for creating a schism in the Church. Perhaps, Mooney so feared this, that it was
only the involvement of the federal government, during a time of war,
that gave him the courage to silence Coughlin and the assurance that no
one would follow him should he attempt to lead them out of the
Church.

Finally, Mooney did not find support among his brother bishops for
stronger action against the Radio Priest. The hierarchy preferred to leave
the matter in Mooney's care. The Vatican and its apostolic delegate also
looked to Mooney to handle this priest and to provide guidance on how
best the Holy See could aid his efforts. They would not lead. Mooney
was always looking for allies to confront Coughlin and he usually found
himself alone. Alone, he would not act decisively.

If all this makes the Church's role more understandable it still does
not "exonerate the Church and its officers." The burden of this judgment
falls on Mooney, as Tentler has indicated.[38] He had the authority and the
power to censor everything that Coughlin directly said or wrote. Any of
the reasons listed above may have given him pause. None of them, however, justifies the censors' elimination of only the "manifestly wrong"
from Coughlin's output. On the one hand, Mooney himself, as is clear in
his personal correspondence, did imbibe some of the anti-Semitism of
his own day and thus was too tolerant of what was clearly "mainfestly
wrong" to others. On the other hand, more concern seemed to have
been given to public relations than to the moral evil of prejudice. For, at
least, the "wrong" should have been excised.

38. Ibid.

Christopher J. Kauffman

10. JUSTUS GEORGE LAWLER AND THE
JOURNAL OF ARTS AND LETTERS (1949–1952)

Introduction

Few, probably, would dispute the assertion that the most exciting, exhilarating, as well as the most controversial and contentious period in religious history of the last half of this century was the era of the Second Vatican Council, including its preludes in the *nouvelle théologie*, the liturgical movement, and an emerging social consciousness, and its postludes in the enfranchisement of the laity, the disintegration of many obsolete structures, and the subsequent effort on the part of conservative forces to return to the *status quo ante*.

The central focus of the half-century was the decade of the sixties, and equally few would dispute that in the English-speaking world during this period the most influential academic journal of religion and the humane and social sciences was *Continuum*, founded and edited by Justus George Lawler.[1] Launched at the time of the Cuban missile crisis (with Lawler's editorial severely critical of the Kennedy administration, and with other contributions by Archbishop Denis E. Hurley, O.M.I., of Durban—a leading opponent of apartheid—by Thomas Merton and by Ernesto Cardenal) the quarterly was terminated in the early 1970s with an issue devoted to critical theory and the Gadamer-Habermas debate.[2] The journal, though Roman Catholic in orientation and sponsorship (St.

---

1. For the poetry of Thomas Merton and Ernesto Cardenal, and articles by Denis E. Hurley, O.M.I., see *Continuum* 1 (Spring 1963): 1–125.

2. Hans-Georg Gadamer, "On The Scope and Function of Hermeneutical Reflection"; Jürgen Habermas "Summation and Response," *Continuum* 8 (Spring–Summer 1970): 77–95, 123–33, respectively.

Xavier College in Chicago), cut across confessional and political alle-giances in the name of what Jacques Maritain had called thirty years earlier an "integral humanism."

The present historical analysis will deal with its predecessor publica-tion, *The Journal of Arts and Letters (JAL)*, which was also founded by Jus-tus George Lawler in 1949 when he was emerging from the Christian Brothers' Scholasticate at St. Mary's College in Winona, Minnesota. What surprised its readers was not only the youth of the founder and editor (though he had already published in *Commonweal, Thought* and *Orate Fratres,* the forerunner of *Worship*) but the format and character of the magazine. Sponsored by the Christian Brothers, it was the successor to two earlier and randomly appearing publications, *The Latin Teacher* and *The Language Teacher,* both of which were concerned with classroom techniques and pedagogical methods.

Some idea of the radical transformation from its predecessors to the *JAL* can be seen in the subjects taken up in the first issue: Spanish Baroque, *The Waste Land,* liturgical art, the nature of the liberal arts and commentaries (mainly by Lawler) on topics in periodical literature, in religion, the arts, and philosophy, and commentaries from journals in English, French, Italian, and German. The French influences predomi-nated; frequent references to such journals as *Maison Dieu, Vie Intel-lectuelle, L'art Sacré,* and *Etudes* occurred in this first and subsequent is-sues. The Christian Brothers, who composed the principal readership of the *Journal,* were indeed surprised by the *haute culture* of the quarterly, a drastic departure from their publications on pedagogy.

Integral Humanism

Lawler was influenced by Jacques Maritain's integral humanism, which was based upon the philosopher's appreciation of the vast cultur-al changes in the Western world since the Scholastics developed "me-dieval humanism." Gerald N. McCool, S.J., captures these historical dis-tinctions:

> The medieval mind had little or no acquaintance with the multi-
> plicity of highly developed cognitive signs through which modern

man thematizes his experience of himself and his world in art, science and history. Medieval man responded to God directly on the religious level. He had not yet become aware [as Maritain and others had] of the richness, diversity and relative autonomy of God's created world and of the aesthetic and intellectual response demanded by its creative goodness and beauty.[3]

In his articles in the *JAL* Justus George Lawler represents Maritain's educated contemporary believer, one who is, according to McCool, "possessed of himself and of his world through the mediation of art, science and history. . . ." Lawler's world view also reflects Maritain's later work on "creative intuition." Integral humanism was rooted in the experience of "created goodness and beauty" not only as concepts but as creations of the human spirit in its encounter with sacred nature. Hence, Maritain's humanism stands in opposition to the ahistorical conceptual framework of the neo-scholastic manualists regnant in much theological education of the period.[4]

The stated purpose of the *JAL* may also be indebted to Maritain's views on Christian faith and modern culture. In Lawler's words the *Journal*

> seeks to present the unity existing among the arts when these are regarded through the eyes of faith. . . . In our time a complete divorce of the divine and the human has been achieved. And we have seen, as a consequence, the erection of a schizoid culture, which rather than see all ennobling human activities under the mantle of Grace, establishes artificial categories among the humanistic disciplines, labeling some "religious" and some "profane."[5]

In contrast to the Church's development of a wide-ranging modern subculture in defense of traditional ecclesiastical privileges and in opposition

---

3. Gerald N. McCool, *From Unity to Pluralism: The Internal Evolution* (New York: Fordham University Press, 1989), 151. For a clear summary of integral humanism see Jacques Maritain's 1939 article in which he states that "Such a humanism, . . . which sets no *a priori* limit to the descent of the divine into man, we may call the *humanism of the Incarnation.*" Jacques Maritain, "Integral Humanism and the Crisis of Modern Times," *Review of Politics* 1 (January 1939): 8. Note that this is the first article in the first issue of the journal published at the University of Notre Dame.

4. McCool, *From Unity to Pluralism*, 152.

5. "Foreword," *The Journal of Arts and Letters* (hereafter *JAL*) 1 (Spring 1949): 2.

to modernity, Maritain's stance was in an opposing direction; he extolled the development of modern freedom and was critical of General Francisco Franco's role in the Spanish Civil War, particularly his alliances with Nazi Germany and Fascist Italy.[6]

In the Foreword to the first issue Lawler reaffirmed the inclusive character of the *JAL:* "to show our Christian attitudes towards all elements of human culture. . . ."[7] Though the first issue's contributors were exclusively Christian Brothers, the editor invited and received the collaboration of writers outside the order and indeed outside the Roman Catholic tradition. This was not an academic journal like *Theological Studies,* nor one that was committed to publishing works on the Catholic Revival, as was *Renascence.* Not uncongenial to the character of these journals, the *JAL* was embossed with Lawler's imprint, a blend of the theological, the liturgical, the artistic, and the spiritual, and grounded in a distinctive world view of faith and culture.

To clarify Lawler's contributions to the *JAL* I have divided this essay into three parts: the intellectual life, art and religion, and spirituality and the religious life. Though the editor wrote many pieces in the commentary sections of the journal, I chose those excerpts that could easily be incorporated into these three topics.

The Intellectual Life

In his article "Meaning of the Intellectual Life" Lawler refers to the speculative intellect and how its drive for perfection influences the practical intellect. However, this scholastic rhetoric gives way to the poetic, as the intellect is most vital when it experiences the "spirit of wonder concerning the universe around us." The intellectual "perceives a little known truth, acts upon it and relates it to other truths." The subsequent enthusiasm leads toward a recreation of the relationship within, and as the process is repeated the spirit of wonderment "is what we call the intellectual life." This is quite remote from "academic cataloguing." It is not

---

6. McCool, *From Unity to Pluralism,* 153. Also see Joseph Amato, *Mounier and Maritain, A French Catholic Understanding of the Modern World* (Birmingham: University of Alabama Press, 1975), 145–47.

7. "Foreword," *JAL* 1 (Spring 1949): 1.

to be confused with the life of scholarship and research. However, by implication, if a scholar experiences the intellectual life of wonder then his
pragmatic segmentation of knowledge becomes integrated. Driven to
perceive the interrelationships among truths, intellectuals, either as
philosophers or poets, "penetrate reality" in their own distinctive modes
of insight. Lawler's own methodology appears to be more congenial to
the intuitive or poetic mode of wonderment and immersion in truth
rather than the philosopher's cerebral conceptualization of the truth,
though ideally they are complementary by their common intentions to
"penetrate reality." (The term "penetrate" is a humanist coinage in
Lawler's life of the intellect.[8])

To illustrate his preference for the poetic Lawler refers to the "cold
abstractions" of Aristotle's "ideal man," who identifies happiness as "the
good life." In contrast, an encounter with Goethe's Faust and his "won-
derings and searchings after happiness" conveys an understanding that
natural goodness is equivalent to happiness and therefore "we appreciate more concretely the meaning of the 'good life.'"[9]

The intellectual life of Christians, dependent upon the influences of
Revelation, is, according to Lawler, rooted in an understanding that the
"Christian realizes that all reality is rooted in the Divine Mind." Hence,
the Christian seeker of truth is in "close contact with the basis of all
truth." In explicating these principles Lawler probes the poetic imagery:
"The Christian thinker does not observe the Incarnation only as
achieved dogmatic fact; rather he sees there a further impulsion to re-
produce his own mental world outside the mind in the form of composition both artistic and scientific. Thus he sees in all reality the impress of
God not through any emotional conviction, but out of immanent necessity." He then quotes a lengthy passage of St. John of the Cross, who
wrote that only after the soul's "betrothal with the Spouse will she be
shown the grove and its beauty. By the grove is here understood God,
together with all the creatures that are in Him." This contemplative vision of St. John of the Cross is an extensive poetic rendering of the im-

8. The Editor, (Lawler seldom used his religious name. Since there is no list of
editors with names, only the Christian Brothers would know that he was the editor.)
"The Intellectual Life," *JAL* 1 (Winter 1950): 316–17.
    9. Ibid., 318.

manence of the Incarnation, which for Lawler is a mystic's "glimmer of the splendor" of the "impress of God," a vision that sustains the commitment of the Christian intellectual.[10]

In opposition to this graced experience of the mystic is the "Jansenistic contempt for man's natural functions . . . [that] would tend to suppress the intellectual life." Anticipating his later criticism of the negative anthropomorphism of Counter-Reformation piety, he criticized the mentality that "interprets the gospel dictum of self-abnegation, or death to self, to mean death to the faculties of man. He forgets that man operates in the supernatural order by Grace and by his own intention. Death to self means death to the egocentric element," not to the capacity to participate in the "mind of God."[11]

In his commentaries on contemporary developments, Lawler occasionally evaluated trends in the Christian intellectual life. In the Winter issue of 1951 he welcomed the appearance of *Cross Currents,* which "fills a definite need in our country." He was particularly congratulatory on its publication of several "profound thinkers of France, as well as Romano Guardini, and Waldemar Gurion's 'Humanism and Grace.' He commended an article that called for the organization of small groups "bound together by a common desire to know the true, studying the great ideas of the Christian tradition." Something needed to be done, Lawler noted, if the "fullness of Faith" is to radiate "among the shadows of ignorance and irreligion."[12] He cites Jean Daniélou, who, upon visiting the United States, criticized the "spirit of detachment on the part of Catholics from the rest of the country's cultural life." Five years before John Tracy Ellis's seminal 1955 address, "American Catholic Intellectual Life," Lawler lashed out at the "closed cosmos" with its own "standards of excellence which are maintained only by repudiating the standards of what is disdainfully termed 'the secular culture.'" Evidence of the "closed cosmos" of ghetto Catholicism was Catholic criticism of the editors of the *Oxford Anthology of American Verse* for not including the works of Father Tabb and Joyce Kilmer.[13]

In a review of Fulton J. Sheen's book *Peace of Soul,* Lawler focuses on

---

10. Ibid., 319.   11. Ibid., 320.
12. "Commentary," *JAL* 2 (Winter 1951): 339.
13. Ibid., 340.

the author's critique of the weaknesses of modern psychoanalysis and psychotherapy. In response to Sheen's contention that conscience problems are the sources of anxiety, Lawler criticizes this "euphemism for sin as the cause for mental illness," as representational of an anti-intellectual retreat from psychology. He suggests that his readers should consult the books of Dom Thomas Verner Moore, a Catholic psychiatrist, particularly his book *Driving Forces in Human Nature.* "Of the deep religious spirit and scientific competence of Verner Moore no one can doubt; why then with such studies available do we become absorbed in watered-down treatments [such as that of Sheen] which do not give the total view."[14] Though Lawler's tone was cautiously deferential to the Monsignor, he later reported to me of his superiors' criticism for tarnishing a revered icon of Catholic culture.[15]

Influenced by the works of Yves Congar, the eminent Dominican theologian, Lawler cites his article in *La Vie Intellectuelle* (March/April 1950) in which the Dominican ecclesiologist criticizes the Christian intellectuals, scholars and activists for their complicity in "the loss of the working class, the Galileo affair, the Lutheran heresy, etc." He noted that Congar does not champion nonconformism in most spheres of ecclesiastical life, such as the essential nature of the Church, its mystery, structure, and authority. However, if the Church is allied or "supports a sociological element, that of the attitudes and comportment of Catholics, both lay and clergy," then on the plane at this intersection of social-historical reality ". . . a certain non-conformity is eventually to become a right, and even a duty." Lawler's introduction to this lengthy quote by Congar is simply, "If error is tolerated, then every man who sees it as error is obliged to oppose it, even if it be an accepted element of the status quo."[16]

In a 1952 *Commonweal* article, "The Reformer in the Church," Lawler elucidates Congar's seminal *Vrai et fausse Réforme dans l'Eglise.*

---

14. Anonymous review (actually Lawler) of Fulton J. Sheen's *Peace of Soul, JAL* 1 (Autumn 1949): 265. For an analysis of Thomas Verner Moore's significance see Benedict Neenan, O.S.B., "The Life of Thomas Verner Moore, Psychiatrist, Educator and Monk" (Ph.D. diss, Catholic University of America, 1995).

15. Christopher J. Kauffman, oral interview with Justus George Lawler, October 15, 1997.

16. "Commentary," *JAL* 2 (Summer 1950): 152–53.

Closely related to the article in *Vie Intellectuelle*, Congar's larger work critically explores the principles for reform, such as the collective responsibility to remedy social evils—he gives as an example anti-semitism—endemic in Western society. In this same vein, Lawler includes repentance for "the sin of [racial] segregation" redolent in American society: "As Christians we make ourselves responsible when we fail to realize the implications of the faith in practical affairs." Lawler agrees with Congar that examples of true and false reformers would be John H. Newman and Dr. Ignaz Doellinger in their opposition to papal infallibility. The former "never avoided pastoral for intellectual pursuits" and was therefore never driven by a cerebral protest alone. On the other hand, Lawler and Congar perceived Doellinger as a false reformer driven by a knowledge "separated from charity;" he led a break from Rome and supported the "Old Catholics" schismatic movement. Newman, the authentic reformer, found his sources in the concrete "life of the church."[17]

In accord with Congar's evaluation of John H. Newman (Newman would be the subject of Lawler's later books and articles), Lawler also cited approvingly Congar's criterion of charity as an essential quality of the authentic reformer. For example, the young editor remarked on how reformers may "work and pray [for] . . . the restoration of the vernacular in certain liturgical celebrations while yet submitting to the prescriptions forbidding its use."[18]

Christian Art

Yves Congar was a principal contributor to the Dominican *La Vie Intellectuelle;* Pie Régamey parallelled him in another Dominican journal, *L'Art Sacré.* The latter was the most significant contributor to the *JAL;* Lawler later, as editor of Herder and Herder of Freiburg, edited his book on religious art and directed it through the publication process. In a *JAL* article Régamey discusses the contemporary artist's fundamental alienation and fragmentation and criticizes modern art that "tends to be either photographic banality, sentimentalism, or abstraction. Rarely is a

---

17. Justus George Lawler, "The Reformer in the Church," *Commonweal* 28 (August 15, 1952): 465.
18. Ibid.

work produced which harmoniously joins gifts of mind and of heart. . . . This state of things is particularly serious with relation to Christian art, which is the art of the Incarnation."[19]

Before the appearance of the first issue of the *JAL*, Lawler's article "The Idea of Christian Art" appeared in the June 1948 issue of *Thought*. Though this was before he encountered the work of Régamey, Lawler had developed ideas that ran parallel to those of the French scholar. He did cite two of Maritain's works: *Art and Scholasticism* and *Art and Poetry*.[20] In an earlier (1948) article in *Thought*, "Transfigured Universe," he had developed the principal idea upon which the 1949 article on art was based, "the sacramental aspect of creation."[21]

This aspect of creation is the only factor that influences the artist in "every stage of . . . creative effort." Paraphrasing M.-D. Chenu, O.P., Lawler notes that if the artist is "deprived of this sacramental vision" then he or she would be intellectually incapable of understanding the meaning of revelation and "the spiritual and physical reality it proclaims."[22] After describing several artists, poets, and musicians who are either excessively cerebral or ideologically driven, and thus fail to blend the creative spirit with the material medium, Lawler defines them as failing to perceive their created forms as sacramental. For example, he cites T. S. Eliot's "Gerontion" and "The Waste Land," and Prokofief's "micrometricly perfect" Classical Symphony as art works that are "more pronounced intellectually" and suffer from an "a-sensory" character; such works are aberrations, "resulting from a failure to realize the profound implications of the sacramental character of the material universe"; in short these art works represent a denial of the fusion of spirit and matter, the sacrament.[23]

19. Pie Régamey, O.P., "Christian Art," *JAL* 1 (Summer 1949): 107.

20. Brother Justus George, "The Idea of Christian Art," *Thought* 24 (June 1949): 311, n. 5.

21. Brother Justus George, "Transfigured Universe," *Thought* 23 (September 1948): 483–91. In this article Lawler explores several sources for the sacramentality of creation and relates it to art: "There is a mysterious dialectic which must act in the mind of the artist if his work is to attain a high degree of excellence. This movement is: detachment from creatures, attachment to God, and sublimation of creatures by regarding them sacramentally," 490.

22. Brother Justus George, "The Idea of Christian Art," 309–10.

23. Ibid., 311.

Those artists who stress the material without a guiding conceptual design—that is, spirit—descend to uninspired "gibberish," the doggerel of Kipling, the art that Coleen McDannell has called "Catholic kitsch,"[24] the *art sulpicien* sold in the galleries around the Church of St. Sulpice but not associated with the learned Sulpicians. Though the classical artist may revel in his intuitive act (which is not fully appreciated until the art work is completed), and a sense of the sacramental nature of reality, the Christian artist must be consciously focused on the Divine Artist. "The artist will devise his topic of discourse from the giant truth of religious wisdom, and . . . develop it as did Dante, after 'long study and great love.'"[25]

Not to be confused with art depicting spiritual values, Christian art must express "deific values, without being however pious or didactic." Christian art will not "bridle the creative spirit" as some anti-religious critics would lament. Among those artists who successfully entered "the realm of the deific" and have presented "themes of the greatest profundity," Lawler lists "the ascent to God (Dante); the beauty of God in creation (Hopkins), the heroicity of virtue (El Greco), the grandeur of God (Franck), . . . the simplicity of God (plain song), the struggle of good and evil (Milton)." He also includes those twentieth-century Christian artists who viewed "the weak human creature at grips with Grace (Mauriac), the fulfillment of Providence (Claudel) and the tragedy of Sin (Rouault)."[26]

Artists not intentionally infused with Christian theological wisdom, such as Beethoven, Rembrandt or Goethe, but who "manifested the sacramental vision" in the form of the art, proffer a perplexing problem for Lawler. The spiritual dimension of their art is real, yet it would not be a Christian art because the Christian artist "appreciates the intrinsic nobility of the material world when it is viewed sacramentally." Such great art, Lawler concludes, "will truly be what Dante's Virgil termed it, 'the grandchild of God.'"[27] Written when he was about twenty-one years old, Lawler's article reveals conceptual clarity, an extraordinary command of

24. Coleen McDannell, *Material Christianity* (New Haven: Yale University Press, 1997), chapter on Catholic Kitsch.

25. Justus George, "The Idea of Christian Art," 317–18.

26. Ibid., 318.   27. Ibid., 319–20.

the unity of the theological and the aesthetic, and intellectual maturity, all qualities that are foundational of the *JAL*.

In his two *JAL* articles on liturgical art the editor makes an impassioned plea for the creation of symbols that would raise our whole being to the contemplation of ". . . God Who is the *supremus artifex*," that is, an art conformable to the spirit of the liturgy. Liturgical art is not decorative religious art nor art aimed "to titillate our senses."[28] The liturgical artist must be in pursuit of a life of sanctity, given to "profound contemplation" because to create the symbolism representative of the Ineffable the artist must travel "the *via negativa*," a path infused with an understanding that the only way to capture the Infinite is by symbols derived from what God is not. An attempt to portray God directly is tantamount to banality.

To substantiate his prescription for the authentic path to symbolism, Lawler quotes St. Thomas: "Similitudes drawn from things farthest away from God form within us a truer estimate that God is above whatsoever we may think or say." Hence, authentic liturgical art "must be generated from that point where meditative reason under the influence of the Spirit comes into contact with revelation." Such notions are symbols: "they express the supernatural without implying imagery immersed in the natural."[29] Apophatic art is therefore symbolic art, congenial to the liturgy.

This plea for the creation of symbols infused with the spirit of God rather than the use of natural images should not be construed as the advocacy of an elitist art form. In a later article, "Optimism in the Arts," he stated that "Christian art must receive the stamp of approval of the Christian people. . . . As yet it seems imprudent to force upon the average Catholic, lay or cleric, art work which is so far beyond . . . [popular] powers of appreciation that the reaction is only a strengthening of irrational prejudices."[30]

In response to those scholars who lament the crisis in contemporary art, such as Pie Régamey, Lawler notes the European sources of this pes-

28. The Editor, "Towards a Liturgical Art," *JAL* 1 (Spring 1949): 52.
29. Ibid., 49–50.
30. Brother Justus George, F.S.C., "Optimism in the Arts," *JAL* 2 (Spring 1950): 48.

simism and concludes that in the United States there is a positive spirit evident: ". . . the religious ideas which were born in and which died in Europe have been taken up and followed through in America." Though many Americans decry the paganism of their society, that paganism is usually identified with widespread immorality, particularly with sexual immorality; "entirely overlooked is the core of our Christian commitment, the depth of our charity." Lawler cites the example of Eric Gill, whose ideas (if not practice) of the integration of art and the Christian community had been effectively promoted by the American Catholic Art Association. Since Gill's notion to integrate art, religion, and society did not take root in England, this association's endeavors represent a good example of the "creative American spirit of adaptation."[31]

The illustrations of Ariel Agemain for *My Daily Psalm Book* struck Lawler as another positive sign of Christian art in the United States. Far removed from "the cult of distortion which animates much pseudo modern work" Agemain's drawings "were equally remote from the hyper-sentimentality of most 'devotional' art." They elevated the popular taste by their integral Christian dimension "both in spirit and techniques without offending the average Catholic powers of appreciation." Such art represents a *"gradual modification* of the general ethos."[32]

Religious art that is too cerebral, "a picture puzzle," such as the representation of the characters of the virtues of the religious life depicted by symbols on the windows of the chapel at St. Mienrad's Abbey, "err by a sort of hyper-intellectuality." In contrast, the symbolic representation at St. Vincent's Archabbey offered, according to Lawler, "a complete spiritual notion in a single unified vision." A viable symbol in Christian art "must be completely original in its totality though it may be composed of elements in the Christian tradition." To achieve widespread popular acclaim, liturgical art must be congenial with the lived experiences of ordinary people. The advanced modern art featured among the publications of the Liturgical Arts Society, which included many excellent works with religious themes by secular artists, would not be as appropriate for the liturgical life of a parish church as would the *Missa recitata*.[33] This populist side of Lawler reveals a conscious departure from his penchant for *haute*

31. Ibid., 47.
32. Ibid., 48.
33. Ibid., 48–50.

culture. It also reveals his own experiences in parish churches in Chicago, within the daily life of ordinary Catholics.

Spirituality and the Religious Life

Central to the religious world view of the editor and the *JAL* is the sacred character of nature, essentially the sacramental presence permeating God's creation and the graced body of the Redeemer. In the new creation humanity is predisposed toward wonderment in the encounter with the sacramental character of redeemed nature. Though Lawler's incarnational spirituality permeates his vision of the intellectual life and Christian art, he captures the historical complexity of spirituality in his exploration of the French school of spirituality of Pierre Bérulle, Charles de Condren, Jean-Jacques Olier, St. Jean Eudes, and St. Jean-Baptiste de La Salle, the founder of the Christian Brothers.

In his explications of the Bérullian tradition he particularly notes the influence of the early Fathers of the Church who shaped the study of the Mystical Body of Christ and formed the predominant Neoplatonism so foundational to the school.[34] Lawler considers Augustine the principal influential figure of the Patristic Church. Because Bérulle introduced the Spanish Carmelites into France, some of whom were direct disciples of St. Teresa and St. John of the Cross, the renewal of the Carmel formed a practical stream of spirituality in the vital currents of the French school. The Flemish mystics, particularly Jan Ruysbroeck, influenced the Bérullian tradition. To illustrate these sources of spirituality Lawler critically examines Bérulle's *Short Treatise on Interior Abnegation* which "sums up the negative teachings" of the tradition. Flemish mysticism, imbued with Augustinianism, was in accord with traditional doctrine, "but it has an element of originality in that it prepared for the later concept of the French School concerning mortification." Not to be considered as formulaic techniques toward a union with God, Bérulle's dictum was "directed to emptying oneself and increasing one's capacity for an influx of Grace." His "magnificent teaching on our adherence to Christ and partic-

---

34. Brother Justus George, F.S.C., "Some Reflections on the French School," *JAL* 2 (Summer 1949): 156.

ipating in His mysteries" places him in the great Christian tradition, which Lawler interprets as the deeply humanist path where the immanence of God's presence in creation and the graced dimensions of existence permeate the environment, giving rise to continuous prayers of thanksgiving.[35]

The later writers of the French School, such as Olier, Eudes, and St. Vincent de Paul, interpreted Bérulle's doctrines in terms of "self-repression, abnegation and annihilation." "When these latter terms were coupled to the resurgence of Augustinianism and Jansenist pessimism, [they] brought about a deprecation of the concept of human nature."[36] Unlike Bérulle (a cardinal associated with ministering to the elite) the later writers were engaged in "apostolates aimed at converting the masses—the rechristianization process of the seventeenth century—and therefore stressed the need for the 'purgative way', to repress and deny the self" in order to inculcate self-control. Olier, Eudes and La Salle's self-abnegation became an end in itself and identified with Christ the Victim; there was, therefore, a tendency to depart drastically from Bérulle's emphasis upon the gratuity of God's grace. St. Jean Eudes wrote of "annihilating our offerings to testify that Love has no need of these." La Salle's early works showed a complete preoccupation with curbing our 'corrupt' nature; indeed, he wrote an entire treatise along these lines. Lawler concludes his brief encounter with his community's founder by noting his "strange" maxim, *"la nature détruit la grâce"* (nature destroys grace).[37]

The incompatibility of Lawler's sense of the sacred in nature and La Salle's projections of nature's destruction of grace is central to appreciating the editor's assessment of his founder. In a review of the book *La Doctrine spirituelle de Saint Jean-Baptiste de la Salle,* Lawler severely criticized the author, Jules Herment, for his shallow misapprehensions in identifying La Salle with the French School by linking him with "a few generalizations from the writings of Bérulle."[38] The latter's devotion to the Incarnate Word—one of Herment's links between the founder of the

---

35. Ibid.   36. Ibid.
37. Ibid.

38. Brother Justus George, F.S.C., review of *La Doctrine Spirituelle de Saint Jean Baptiste de la Salle* by Jules Herment, *JAL* 1 (Spring 1949): 83.

French school and La Salle—was, according to Lawler, not substantiated by Herment. Strands of Bérullian mental prayer, particularly the focus on the phases in the life and on the mysteries of Jesus' life, appear to be illustrative of La Salle's association with the Bérullian school of spirituality.[39] However, Lawler reiterates the significance of "Augustinian Pessimism" in La Salle's writings, to clarify his departure from the Bérullian doctrine of the Incarnate Word and the gratuity of God's grace. Lawler found Herment's proposal that Christian Brothers limit their study of the founder to those areas of his spirituality useful to "the students in the classes" to be simply "repugnant,"[40] that is, a utilitarian subversion of the integrity of the Bérullian tradition.

In his *Commonweal* piece "True and False Reform" Lawler commented on those spheres of spirituality of the Church's past conditioned by culture. Particularly concerned with the dominance of a form of contemporary prayer life that is rooted in the past, he referred to a "malnourished piety," a spirituality derived from the anthropocentrism of the Renaissance and Counter-Reformation. "A man-centered spirit was concretized . . . begotten from a fear both for personal salvation and the survival of the church." This piety, Lawler discerned, emphasized such dialectics as "the opposition between nature and grace, between knowledge and love." Against such fragmentation Lawler urges a form of contemplative prayer integrated with Christian activity. Such a synthesis—"an authentic tradition"—would liberate contemporary spirituality from an obsessive concern with one's "own soul."[41] In this same context Lawler cited the article by Régamey that appeared in the second number of the *JAL*. For those lodged in the "ancient glories" faith was simply "an individual affair" and the Church "no longer appeared as the people of God but as an exterior structure of magisterium and discipline." Christian art did not thrive in such conformity. For both Régamey and Lawler, Christian art is "the art of the Incarnation" and can thrive only in a climate of freedom.[42]

His last article on the religious life and spirituality, which was accepted for publication by *Worship* on the eve of his departure from the

39. Ibid., 84. 40. Ibid., 85.
41. Justus George, "The Reformer in the Church," 465.
42. Ibid.

Christian Brothers in 1953, is meaningfully focused by its title, "Fundamentals and Accidentals." Partially inspired by Pope Pius XII, who had called all religious communities to discern their original spirit in order to adapt to the needs of the contemporary times in tandem with fidelity to that foundational spirit, Lawler's historical/theological exploration opens with an indictment of those religious communities which reveal a "mechanical discipline . . . intent on maintaining their temporal shell apparently even at all costs."[43] He builds his case by citing Régamey and Congar, both of whom offered the spirit of self-criticism as the remedy for the abuses of obedience and the predominance of fear that stifles the free flow of ideas. Inspired by these two contemporary French Dominicans, Lawler examines the religious communities founded in the mid 1600s when the French school of spirituality was the predominant force in religious culture and discerns threads of continuity between the seventeenth-century sources of spirituality and contemporary forms of religious life. He places the French school in the general pessimism that was affecting the Cromwellian Protectorate in England, the anti-humanistic reforms of Pope Pius VI and the Jansenists of Port Royal in France: "That contempt for human nature . . . pierces through the brilliant passages of their writings and their teachings like a stream of darkness. . . ." Hence, J. J. Olier, J. Eudes, and J. B. de La Salle revealed, in varying degrees, a negative anthropology that was anti-intellectual and given to an "obsession with man's corrupt nature."[44]

Lawler juxtaposes this pessimism to the Bérullian optimism of the Incarnate Word and the life of mystical prayer, which did positively affect the writings of Olier, Eudes, and La Salle. If they were alive today they would urge their contemporary confreres to return to these vital mysteries included in their prayer life and to the "perennial piety of the Church expressed in her liturgy." It follows that these founders would severely criticize only those forms of piety characteristic of the Counter-Reformation—"emphasis on personal perfection through the exercises and the examen, low-Masses, a private liturgy aimed primarily at the apostolate."[45] The authentic La Sallian spirit of the Christian Brothers,

---

43. Justus George, "Fundamentals and Accidentals," *Worship* 27 (September 1953): 432.

44. Ibid., 439.   45. Ibid., 440–41.

derived from the richness of the Bérullian tradition, was the legitimate source of the vital tradition that the contemporary brothers should incorporate into their renewed spirituality.

There is no doubt of Lawler's commitment to the reformism of Congar and to the critique of the abuse of obedience of Régamey, commitments that ran contrary to what he perceived as "mechanical discipline" and the perpetuation of a "temporal shell." In the words of Congar cited above, Lawler inevitably incurred the "disapproval of [his] associates." The *JAL* articles on the intellectual life, Christian art, liturgical art, and the spirituality of religious life were outstanding achievements for a young brother in his late teens and early twenties. These editorial duties and his writing removed him from regular participation in community life in the schools where he taught, St. Mel's in Chicago, 1948–50, Cretin in St. Paul, 1950–51, and Christian Brothers College in St. Louis, 1951–53; on the basis of his "poor community spirit" he was dismissed from the congregation in 1953.

Thirty-five years after the *JAL*'s last issue (1988), I interviewed Lawler on the publication in the *U.S. Catholic Historian*, which I have edited since 1983. In response to my question related to the demise of the *JAL*, Lawler stated:

> . . . What finally killed the magazine was an editorial defending [General Douglas] MacArthur in the Korean War, a defense as vigorous and just as sound, I still believe, as my defense in *Continuum* and elsewhere of Soviet missiles in Cuba a decade later. The details are unimportant—in the first instance there was a mandate sanctioned by international law, in the second the U.S. was simply intent on acts of piracy on the high seas—but they serve to further explain why in the sixties I wrote my book on nuclear deterrence at the same time that I wrote my primer of religious poetics, *The Christian Image*.
>
> Its demise was a prelude to my dismissal from the Christian Brothers, which I recognized as a welcome inevitability. Like the Anglican Newman I thought this was where "providence" had placed me, and until shown otherwise, there I would stay.[46]

46. Christopher J. Kauffman, Editor, "An Interview with Justus George Lawler," *U.S. Catholic Historian* 7 (Winter 1988): 6.

Epilogue

Justus George Lawler is the quintessential intellectual-activist. To balance his commitment to elucidating the intellectual life, art and religion, and spirituality in articles and books, he brokered the writings of other intellectuals and scholars as founding editor of the *JAL* and of *Continuum,* as editor of Herder and Herder, Seabury, Winston, Harper & Row, Crossroad and Continuum books. His first book, *The Christian Imagination* (1956),[47] was a step beyond the *JAL* but derived from his articles in the journal. His latest book, *The Reconstruction of Gerard Manley Hopkins* (1998),[48] is reminiscent of those articles related to Christian art. His two other books on poetics, particularly *Celestial Pantomime,* reveal the continuity of his intuitional grasp of the poem complemented by his analysis of its structure and language. Its central thesis is a reflection of his notion of sacred nature, that is, the poet is a frustrated priest because the poem is the broken word made flesh.

47. Justus George Lawler, *The Christian Imagination* (Westminster, Md.: Newman Press, 1956).

48. Idem., *The Reconstruction of Gerard Manley Hopkins* (New York: Continuum Books, 1998).

Raymond J. Kupke

11. AN AMERICAN INTERVENTION AT ROME
Father Judge and James Norris at Vatican II

In the sacristy of the Upper Church of the Basilica of the National Shrine of the Immaculate Conception adjacent to the campus of The Catholic University of America in Washington, there is a series of stained glass windows representing the best in the American priesthood. Here are depicted some of the holiest, the most innovative, the most intrepid of the Catholic clergy who have served in the United States. Among these priest-heros is a stirring preacher and staunch proponent of the lay apostolate, Thomas A. Judge, C.M. Although most people would be unaware of it, the Judge window is closely connected to the mosaic of St. Joseph, defender of the Universal Church, in the East Apse of the basilica's Upper Church. There to the right of the central figure of St. Joseph is the image of Pope Paul VI surrounded by some of the participants in the Second Vatican Council. Just behind the pontiff's left shoulder is the figure of an American lay auditor at the Council, James J. Norris.[1] The purpose of this paper is to illuminate that connection and to trace the influence at the Council of Father Judge, American preacher and missioner, through the considerable efforts of James Norris, American in Rome.

Born of Irish immigrant parents in Boston in 1868, Thomas Judge entered the Vincentians (Congregation of the Mission) in 1890 and was

1. *The Catholic News* (December 29, 1966), news clipping, Norris Collection, University of Notre Dame Archives.

ordained a priest in 1899.[2] After a brief parish assignment in German-
town, Pennsylvania, Judge began a six-year stint in the Vincentian Mission Band, a group of itinerant preachers who conducted week-long
"missions" in parishes throughout the Northeast. It was his contact with
the laity in this capacity, as well as his concern for "leakage" from the
Church among the recent immigrants and the unevangelized, that
prompted him to organize in 1909 a group of laywomen who would become the nucleus of the Missionary Cenacle Apostolate. As Judge told
some of his earliest followers, "You are called upon to do things I cannot
do as a Priest."[3] Four decades later, James Norris would affirm this principle inherited from Judge. "I believe it will be the prevailing notion that
the priest must support and help the layman in his mission of penetrating society."[4] Although the movement eventually gave rise to two religious orders, the Missionary Servants of the Most Blessed Trinity for
women (1919), and the Missionary Servants of the Most Holy Trinity for
men (1921), it was always Judge's intention that the movement tap into
the energy and the faith of the laity and engage them more actively in
the Church's mission.

James J. Norris was born in Roselle Park, New Jersey, in 1907, but
after his father abandoned the family in 1916, he moved to Elizabeth.[5]
Active with the Columbus Cadets of New Jersey, a youth organization
sponsored by the Knights of Columbus, Norris first met Father Judge on
a weekend retreat at Stirling, New Jersey, sponsored by the Columbus
Cadets sometime in the winter of his senior year in high school. By all
accounts, a meeting with Father Judge could be the decisive moment of

2. No comprehensive biography of Father Judge has been produced. Two works
treat Father Judge within the context of the Missionary Cenacle Movement he
founded: Sister Miriam Joseph Blackwell, M.S.B.T., *Ecclesial People: A Study in the Life
and Times of Thomas Augustine Judge, C.M.* (Holy Trinity, Ala.: Missionary Cenacle
Press, 1974), and James P. O'Bryan, S.T., *Awake the Giant: A History of the Missionary Cenacle Apostolate* (Holy Trinity, Ala.: Missionary Cenacle Press, 1989).

3. Archives, Missionary Servants of the Most Holy Trinity, Silver Spring, Maryland (hereafter AST), Thomas A. Judge, C.M., Conference to Missionary Cenacle
Apostolate, November 1928.

4. Edward J. Sullivan, "The Haves, the Have-nots, and James J. Norris," *The
Sign*, August 6, 1966, 14.

5. For details on Norris's life, see Raymond J. Kupke, "James J. Norris: An
American Catholic Life" (unpublished Ph.D. dissertation, The Catholic University of
America, 1995).

a lifetime. He was a charismatic figure who, according to one contemporary account, would look you in the eye, and, "ask you right off: 'How much do you love God?'"[6] After high school, James Norris began his affiliation with the Trinitarians in September 1924.

In the ten years between 1924 and 1934 Judge and Norris developed a very close personal, spiritual, and professional relationship. It was the final decade of Judge's life, and he was playing it out against the background of the rural American South and the Great Depression, struggling with the canonical, financial, and personnel birth pangs of the two new religious communities that were emerging out of his lay apostolate movement. Conversely, the ten years were the first decade of what was to be a half-century career in church work for James Norris. In the crucible of that decade it was as if Judge was passing the torch to Norris.

Norris was an unusually mature, deeply spiritual, very talented young man with a strong organizational sense. Judge, struggling with a nascent religious community in desperate need of leadership and organizational skills, seized on Norris's ability. Despite his very young age, Norris quickly rose to the forefront of the men's branch of the Trinitarians. He was deeply involved in every aspect of the Trinitarians' early days, from their first fund-raising efforts to the process of achieving canonical recognition. He was seen by his peers as "the one singled out by Father Judge,"[7] the one who was "a favorite, a prince apparent."[8]

Like the other early Trinitarians, Norris was not allowed uninterrupted academic studies. This was due partly to Father Judge's intention "to train people by letting them do"[9] and partly to the acute personnel needs of the Trinitarians. Norris was too valuable to Judge and the Trinitarians to allow him the luxury of years solely given over to study. When the Trinitarians were allowed to open their first canonical novitiate in September 1931, Norris, even though he had seniority in the communi-

6. Paul Hendrickson, *Seminary, A Search* (New York: Summit Books, 1983), p. 134.
7. Father Timothy Lynch, S.T., interview by author, Silver Spring, Maryland, 17 July 1991.
8. Father John Baptist McCarthy, S.T., telephone interview by author, 20 July 1991.
9. Lynch interview.

ty, could not be spared to enter the novitiate. Father Turibius McCarthy, S.T., a later Trinitarian vicar, recounted the scene.

> Right after lunch, Father Judge began picking the ones who would go into the First Novitiate. All could not go; some had to continue the activities of the Congregation. Brother James Norris, Brother Joachim Benson and others would have to stay to keep the activities of the Congregation moving.[10]

Over the next several years, Judge would use Norris in many diverse efforts on behalf of the community. At various times he was prefect of the order's high school seminary, the community's agent in affairs with Toth Associates, the public relations and fund-raising company used by the Trinitarians, secretary of the Trinitarian consultors, and treasurer of the community. But primarily he was Judge's right-hand-man and trouble-shooter. As the exhausted Judge traveled the East on behalf of the community, he was constantly in contact with Norris on a wide variety of issues ranging from the purchase of material for the new habit[11] to soliciting late financial reports from recalcitrant houses.[12] Norris even dealt with personnel matters affecting those his senior.[13] When Judge was about to begin a new mission in the Caribbean, he sought out Norris's advice on the selection of personnel. "What young brothers do you think would be good for Puerto Rico? . . . work it out and send me your thought on it."[14]

In the flood of the Judge-Norris correspondence, one catches glimpses of the warmth of their relationship, which, at least for Norris, must have had some of the aspects of a missing father-son relationship.[15] Norris was only nineteen when he rather familiarly concluded a letter to

10. Quoted in Sister Mary Tonra, M.S.B.T., *Led by the Spirit: A Biography of Mother Boniface Keasey, M.S.B.T.* (New York: Garland Press, 1984), p. 314.

11. AST, Father [Judge] to Brother James, 23 August 1931.

12. AST, Father Judge, C.M., to Brother [James], 18 March 1932.

13. In 1933 Norris sent his opinion on the severance of a longtime member who had once been his immediate superior. AST, James to Father [Judge], 10 July 1933.

14. AST, [Father Judge] to Brother [James], 6 June 1933.

15. In the 1950s the Trinitarians prepared to open the cause for Judge's beatification and canonization. At the time, Norris was solicited by the his old classmate, Father Thomas O'Keeffe, S.T., who was by then the Trinitarian custodian general. Norris surrendered 128 autograph letters from Judge to the Trinitarian archives.

Judge, "This is about all for now. I'll write if anything comes up. Will be expecting you towards the end of the week."[16] Judge also could be familiar: "I remembered your birthday today and thanked the Lord for all that came out of that first birthday. You see I was afraid you might forget."[17]

After nearly ten years with the Trinitarians, Norris began to discern that his vocation lay elsewhere. The postponement of his clerical education combined with his ever deepening and successful involvement with the business world on behalf of the Trinitarians may have seemed to Norris like a sign from God that his vocation did not lie in the clerical state. He first alerted Father Judge to this possibility in January 1933. For the next year, Norris maintained an unusual in-and-out status, continuing to serve as Judge's financial agent and Trinitarian treasurer while maintaining a life apart from the community on a "leave of absence." Some of the ambivalence, and perhaps the anxiety, of the situation can be detected in an April letter to Judge, when he asked for the founder's prayers and concluded the letter with, "Your prodigal sun [*sic*], James."[18]

On August 13, 1933, an exhausted Judge returned to New York from an extended tour in Puerto Rico. Norris was among a small group of intimates who gathered around him at the Trinitarian house on Gold Street in Brooklyn, where Judge gave a reminiscence-exhortation which was subsequently enshrined as Judge's last talk to the Missionary Cenacle.[19] Later that night, Norris drove Judge to visit his sister, a nursing sister in Waterville, Maine; a week later he drove him back to the Trinitarian house in Silver Spring, Maryland. There, Father Judge was admitted to Providence Hospital in Washington, where he died on November 23, 1933. Norris, in a borrowed Trinitarian habit, was visibly moved at Judge's funeral at the Vincentian Motherhouse in Philadelphia. Colonel John Agoa, Norris's best friend from high school and a fellow former Trinitarian, described the scene.

This was the only time I ever saw Jim completely break down. When Father's casket was about to be closed, Jim rushed up, tears

16. AST, James to Father [Judge], 18 June 1927.
17. AST, Father [Judge] to Brother James, 23 August 1931.
18. AST, James to Father [Judge], 25 April 1933.
19. See Timothy Lynch, S.T., ed., *Father Thomas A. Judge, C.M. Founder, The Missionary Cenacle Family*. Mono. 2, *Early Days and Final Days* (Silver Spring, Md.: The Archives, Missionary Servants of the Most Holy Trinity, 1983), pp. 51–54.

streaming down his face. He put his hands on Father's shoulders, leaned down, and kissed him. Jim had to be helped away from the coffin.[20]

During the next nine months, Norris continued his discernment, returning to community life in June, but finally severing his ties to the Trinitarians in August 1934.[21]

After Norris's departure from the Trinitarians, he briefly worked for Automatic Electric Company, the manufacturing arm of Associated Telephone and Telegraph Company. At the end of 1936, Norris answered an advertisement for a position as administrative assistant to Father Patrick O'Boyle at the Mission of the Immaculate Virgin, an enormous childcare institution serving eleven hundred children maintained by the New York Archdiocese at Mount Loretto on Staten Island. O'Boyle quickly sized up Norris's talents, and the two men developed a close working and personal relationship that would continue as O'Boyle moved up the ecclesiastical ladder to become Cardinal Archbishop of Washington. O'Boyle officiated at Norris's wedding to Amanda Tisch on September 20, 1941, and the couple's first child, James Patrick, was named for him.

With the position at Mount Loretto came an introduction to the energetic New York Catholic Church, headed by the powerful Francis Cardinal Spellman. Norris's ability and devotion to the Church, coupled with the opportunities presented him in New York, paved the way for a career in Church work that would take him literally to every corner of the globe and to the highest corridors of power in the Church. The photographs of Norris in groups around the successive Popes Pius XII, John XXIII, and Paul VI are indicative of Norris's position: he is the only noncleric in the picture.

In May 1941 Norris accepted a position as assistant executive director of National Catholic Community Service, an agency organized by the American bishops to coordinate their efforts on behalf of Catholic servicemen during the Second World War. A year later, Norris became ex-

20. Col. John J. Agoa to the author, 27 September 1991. The details of this report were corroborated by Father Timothy Lynch, S.T., interview with author, 17 July 1991.

21. The Minutes of the Trustees of the Trinitarian Corporation (AST), formally records Norris's resignation as secretary of the corporation on August 20, 1934.

ecutive director. Norris left NCCS in June 1944 in order to accept a commission in the Naval Reserve. He served as commander of the Armed
Guard unit aboard the SS *William Windom,* a cargo ship in convoy across
the Pacific.

With the cessation of hostilities in 1945, Norris presumed he would
return to his berth at NCCS. But Patrick O'Boyle had other ideas.
O'Boyle was now the head of War Relief Services, an organization
founded by the American bishops in 1943 to coordinate their overseas
relief efforts during the war.[22] On February 15, 1946, Norris began work
at WRS as assistant to the executive director. His first assignment took
him to Europe to attend conferences of the United Nations Relief and
Rehabilitation Administration. A year later Norris moved permanently
to Europe as WRS European Director, supervising the agency's efforts on
behalf of migrants and refugees. In 1955 the American bishops acknowledged that the need for American Catholic aid had not expired with the
end of the war, and the title of the agency was changed to Catholic Relief
Services to reflect its permanent status.

On his very first visit to Europe, Norris met with Monsignor Giovanni Battista Montini, the *sostituto,* or under-secretary of the Vatican
Secretariat of State. Working with Montini and others at the behest of
Pope Pius XII, Norris was instrumental in the formation of the International Catholic Migration Commission approved by the pope in April
1951. The ICMC facilitated migration and pastoral care among Catholic
agencies in both sending and receiving countries. Norris served as president of the ICMC for the next twenty years.

In October 1958, there was a changing of the guard at Rome with
the death of Pope Pius XII and the election of Angelo Giuseppe Roncalli
as Pope John XXIII. At the same time, as CRS began to withdraw from
direct participation in migration work, Norris was recalled from Europe
to New York to assume the position of Assistant to the Executive Director at CRS headquarters.[23] On the very day that Norris departed Europe,
January 25, 1959, the new pope announced his plans to call an ecu-

22. For more on the early years of War Relief Services and its successor, Catholic Relief Services, see Eileen Egan, *Catholic Relief Services: The Beginning Years* (New
York: Catholic Relief Services, 1988).
23. In the CRS structure, both the executive director and the assistant executive
director had to be clerics.

menical council. On October 11, 1962, the Second Vatican Ecumenical Council was opened in St. Peter's Basilica. Pope John died eight months later, and on June 21, 1963, Norris's old friend, Monsignor Montini, now Cardinal Archbishop of Milan, was elected pope, taking the name Paul VI. Norris's hiatus from Rome was to be brief.

From the very beginning of the Council the absence of Catholic laity as participants was an issue.[24] The French lay philosopher Jean Guitton was named a conciliar auditor *ad personam* by John XXIII when Guitton complained that he would have to leave the Church in order to get to the Council.[25] Later, in the period between the first and second sessions of the Council, a "mixed commission" was formed from the membership of the conciliar Commissions on Theology and the Apostolate of the Laity to come up with a "schema" or document on the social order. Since the Laity Commission had lay consultors, Cardinal Fernando Cento, the president of the Mixed Commission, insisted on lay consultors for his group, and Norris was one of twenty-three lay men named to the group.[26]

With the election of Paul VI, pressure was put on the new pope to name permanent lay auditors to the Council itself. Norris very much wanted to be on the scene at the Council, and he enlisted the aid of the CRS network to advance his name should the possibility of lay auditors arise. On September 13, 1963, Norris was notified by Archbishop Pericle Felici, the conciliar Secretary-General, that he was one of ten men named by the pope as lay auditors. Monsignor Andrew P. Landi, the CRS director in Rome, commented on the appointment.

> You may be interested to know, as perhaps you have already sur-
> mised, your selection was made personally by His Holiness on the
> basis of the letter which I wrote to Monsignor Cardinal[e]. When
> this was brought to the attention of His Holiness, he said by all

24. For more on the laity at the Council, see Rosemary Goldie, "Lay Participation in the Work of Vatican II," *Miscellanea Lateranensis* (1974–75): 503–25. An Australian, Goldie was one of the first female auditors; she later worked with Norris on the Pontifical Commission "Justice and Peace."

25. The only laity present at the beginning of the Council were the non-Catholic observers.

26. See Herbert Vorgrimler, ed., *Commentary on the Documents of Vatican II* (New York: Herder and Herder, 1969), V, 15.

means to include you in the list of observers. As I have already told you, you are "solid" with the Top Person. Anything else you want?[27]

Some, like columnist John Cogley, were concerned that the role of the auditors was not much more than a gesture, "more that of a Hollywood extra than of a supporting actor."[28] While Norris defended the role of the auditors in public, in private he expressed his own doubts about their effectiveness to Mieczyslaw de Habicht, the secretary of the Conference of International Lay Organizations at Rome.

> I should like to ask whether or not you feel that the Catholic lay auditors had any influence in bringing about changes in the schemata, or in doing anything constructive to be of help in the Vatican Council. I know that a few bishops were friendly with Catholic lay auditors and consulted with them from time to time, but I have a feeling that as a group the Catholic lay auditors did more "window dressing" than productive work. If you feel that the lay auditors can show specific results, will you be good enough to let me know what you feel these results are?[29]

In just four months Norris was to provide a decisive answer to his own question.

During the Council's second session, several "focus" or "lobbying" groups emerged around such issues as world poverty, world peace, and the role of the laity. Norris had ties to two of these groups and was concerned with the proposals he had seen emanating from the Commission on the Apostolate of the Laity concerning the formation of a post-conciliar curial "umbrella" secretariat, which would coordinate the work of all the international Catholic organizations such as his own ICMC. Norris was apprehensive that such a secretariat would hamper the stature and effectiveness of the Catholic international agencies. Even more, he feared that social justice would be seen as the province of the laity alone, and not of the whole Church. Norris's ideas did not receive a ready welcome among his fellow auditors.

27. Norris Collection—University of Notre Dame Archives (hereafter NC-UNDA), Andrew Landi to Jim [Norris], 3 September 1963.

28. John Cogley, "Conciliar Rome," *America* 112 (March 27, 1965): 420–22.

29. NC-UNDA, James J. Norris to Mieczyslaw de Habicht, 8 July 1964.

When I began to present my ideas in the weekly meetings of the Lay Auditors about a secretariat for World Justice and Development, the proposal for a secretariat to promote world justice was received without much enthusiasm. The Auditors were understandably trying to promote the Secretariat for the Laity, and therefore they did not understand the type of organ that we were talking about, namely, a secretariat which would not be for the Laity alone, but would involve the total Church at all levels.[30]

Striking out on his own, Norris aligned himself more closely with the "poverty group."

At the Council's second session, numerous bishops had made interventions on the issue of world poverty. Cardinal Benjamin de Arriba y Castro of Tarragona, Spain, had even called for a poverty secretariat in the Roman Curia. These speeches had the effect of bringing together a loose federation of those interested in lobbying the Council for some concrete proposal with respect to the social order. The group often held informal meetings at the Belgian College. Included in this "poverty group" were two English Mill Hill Missionaries, Fathers Gerald Mahon and Arthur McCormack, and two Americans with backgrounds in rural social justice, Monsignors Luigi Ligutti of Iowa and Joseph Gremillion of Louisiana.[31] The group set as its immediate goal a "world poverty day" at the next session of the Council, to focus the attention of the conciliar fathers on social justice issues.

Independently of this group, Cardinal Leo-Joseph Suenens of Brussels, who had also called for a social problems secretariat at the first session of the Council, had solicited the brilliant English Catholic economist Barbara Ward (known in private life as Lady Jackson) to write a memorandum on this topic for circulation at the next session of the Council.[32]

30. NC-UNDA, Sister Mary Evelyn Jegen, S.N.D., transcript of interview with James J. Norris, 6 June 1973, p. 9.

31. Mahon (1922–92), as superior general of his congregation, was a full Council participant and would later be named Auxiliary Bishop of Westminster. McCormack (1911–92), a prolific writer, was present in Rome as his advisor. Ligutti (1895–1984), founder of the Catholic Rural Life Conference, was the Holy See observer at the U.N. Food and Agriculture Organization. Gremillion (1919–94) was the head of the CRS Office for Socio-Economic Development.

32. For more on Ward (1914–81), see Pamela Martin Pelzel, "Barbara Ward, Advocate for Social Justice," *Living Light* 28 (Fall 1991): 60–69.

By the end of August 1964, Norris had seen a copy of the Ward memorandum. That summer Norris and McCormack discussed it with Father Bernard Häring, C.Ss.R., the secretary of the Mixed Commission on what was now known as "Schema XIII." Häring urged them to pursue the idea of a "world poverty day" at the third session. Meanwhile, McCormack, a friend of Ward's, was also making her aware of the intentions of the poverty group.

> I have suggested to Mr. Jim Norris of Catholic Relief Services that he contact you: I told you about him: he is a very fine man and a good friend of mine. He is very interested in a short-term, dramatic gesture against poverty from the Council but is wholeheartedly for the long-term approach which you outline.[33]

On September 30, 1964, McCormack facilitated a luncheon meeting with Ward, Norris, Mahon, Gremillion, and himself at the *Tre Scalini* Restaurant in the Piazza Navona. The meeting coalesced the energies of the group, including the absent Ligutti, and helped them clarify their goals. In particular, there was an immediate connection between Ward and Norris, a sense of shared awareness of and commitment for the poor.[34] That very day Norris and the others began to lobby more intensively. They prepared a *pro-memoria,* or proposal, which called for a world poverty day at the Council, during which interventions would focus on the creation of a permanent organism for social justice in the Roman Curia.[35]

While most everyone lobbied by the group was receptive, the four Council moderators[36] did not feel they could assign a specific date because the discussions on Schema XIII had not yet reached the appropriate section of that document. With time running out on the third session, Norris began to sense a stalling action, and using all his knowledge of ecclesiastical personalities and ways of operating, he made his move.

---

33. NC-UNDA, Arthur McCormack to Lady Jackson, 8 September 1964.

34. I am indebted to Monsignor Joseph Gremillion, who described this luncheon meeting to me during an interview in August 1992.

35. NC-UNDA, Pro-Memoria for His Excellency Archbishop Dell'Acqua, 30 September 1964.

36. Cardinals Gregory Peter Agagianian (Armenia), Julius Doepfner (Germany), Giacomo Lercaro (Italy) and Suenens.

At a certain point, I learned that Cardinal Koenig of Vienna was to have an audience with Pope Paul VI, and I got my good friend Cardinal Meyer of Chicago, to meet with Cardinal Koenig and myself to lay out the proposal and ask Pope Paul's approval. This was going over the head of Archbishop Felici, Secretary of the Council, as well as the President's, but by this time, we felt that direct action was needed. Inasmuch as I have been for many years a personal friend of Pope Paul VI, because of my years of working with him during my stay in Europe, I think that the proposal received a warm response, and he told Cardinal Koenig that he would approve the idea.[37]

While the pope had agreed that the intervention could be made by a lay expert, Paul VI balked at the suggestion that Lady Jackson be the presenter. Despite lobbying efforts by Cardinal Suenens, the pope was firm in his decision that an address by a woman was inopportune and suggested that Norris himself make the presentation.[38]

On October 31 Archbishop Felici informed Norris that he was to prepare an intervention, which must be submitted to the Council Secretariat by November 2, for presentation in the Council aula on November 5. In anticipation of a speech by herself or one of the poverty group lobbyists, Barbara Ward had written a ten-page preliminary presentation for the Council.[39] In an interview nine years later, Norris stated that this Ward draft was essentially the intervention he delivered at the Council.

The speech that I gave was essentially material that Lady Jackson had written out. When we were talking about having her give a talk, she one day wrote out these ideas. Since she was able to write and say them better than I, it seemed appropriate that I should just take the material and use it for my intervention. There has never been any question but that these were Lady Jackson's ideas and that we drew very heavily on them in preparing the intervention.[40]

---

37. Jegen interview, pp. 6–7.
38. It is not clear whether Barbara Ward's marital status—she was separated from her husband, Commander Sir Robert Jackson—influenced the pope's decision.
39. The original draft document in Ward's own hand can be found in NC-UNDA.
40. Jegen interview, p. 7.

But, Norris's statement too easily dismisses his own contribution to the intervention, "World Poverty and the Christian Conscience," and the clear influences of his early mentor, Thomas Judge. When Norris left the Trinitarians in 1934, he seemed to want to close the door on this chapter of his life. His motives are not entirely clear. Perhaps he struggled with a feeling of having disappointed Judge, or a sense of disloyalty in leaving the Trinitarians just when the community seemed to need him most, at the time of the founder's death. Or, more practically, in a long Church career, constantly working with and for priests, he may have felt it would hamper his effectiveness if he was seen as "one who could not make it" in the seminary. Whatever the motives, Norris in later life was silent about the relationship.

In an ever expanding series of Norris *curriculum vitae* over the course of thirty years, the Trinitarian decade is always omitted, even when his high school founding membership in the Columbus Cadets is mentioned. The community is not mentioned in the Norris obituary carried in *L'Osservatore Romano* at the time of his death,[41] nor in Cardinal O'Boyle's statement at the time in the Washington archdiocesan newspaper,[42] nor in the entry on Norris in a supplemental volume of the *New Catholic Encyclopedia*.[43] Monsignor Andrew Landi, a co-worker of three decades in CRS, and Monsignor Joseph Gremillion, one of the fellow *cospiritori* in the lobbying effort for the Pontifical Justice and Peace Commission, were aware that Norris knew Judge, but had no idea that there was once a "Brother James Norris."

Despite Norris's silence on his association with Father Judge, one can clearly detect Judge's influence on Norris in the latter's activity within the Church as a layman. Even more, one can hear the echo of Judge's thought and words in the intervention Norris delivered on the floor of the Second Vatican Council. The first half of the Norris speech, minus references to specific countries and to the eradication of communism, is indeed taken almost verbatim from the Ward document. However, in

41. "In the United States: Death of James J. Norris," *L'Osservatore Romano*, English Language Edition, 15 November 1976.

42. *Catholic Standard*, November 25, 1976, p. 4.

43. Thomas C. O'Brien, ed., *New Catholic Encyclopedia* (Washington: McGraw-Hill Book Co., 1979), vol. XVII "James Joseph Norris," by J. C. O'Neill.

the second half of the speech, Norris writes from his own experience, and it is here that one can detect the influence of Father Judge.

Father Dennis Berry, S.T., in a study of Judge's spiritual theology, describes a number of principles of action, or "Cenacle methods," which are characteristic of Judge's apostolic activity.[44] The first of these principles for Judge was "to go to the laity." In answering questions from Boston's Cardinal William O'Connell about the Missionary Cenacle, Judge described the potential in the laity.

> There are in every locality many hidden saints who need but a word of encouragement to do and suffer much for souls.[45]

Again, in a talk Judge gave to a meeting of the National Council of Catholic Charities in 1923, he elaborated on this principle.

> It is necessary to make each of them [the laity] realize that indeed he is his brother's keeper. To thus arouse the interest of the laity is the duty of every priest no matter in what particular line he is engaged.[46]

Norris mirrored this Judge principle in his Council intervention.

> But the goal will be reached if in each wealthy country there is brought into being a strong, committed, well-informed and courageous group of men of good will who are prepared to see world poverty as one of the great central concerns of our time and press steadily and vocally for the policies in aid, in trade and in the transfer of skills that will lessen the widening gap between the rich and the poor.[47]

Another of Judge's principles is his emphasis on work within the Catholic community. Judge saw the power of the laity working in con-

44. Dennis Berry, S.T., "God's Valiant Warrior: A Study in the Spiritual Theology of Thomas Augustine Judge, C.M." (Ph.D. diss., Union Graduate School, 1989), pp. 214–46.

45. AST, Thomas A. Judge, C.M., to William Cardinal O'Connell, 27 September 1913.

46. AST, Thomas A. Judge, C.M., "Address Given before the National Council of Catholic Charities," October 1923.

47. NC-UNDA, James J. Norris, "World Poverty and the Christian Conscience," Speech at Vatican Council II, 5 November 1964.

cert within the Church. Norris was even more insistent on working within the framework of the Church, and by extension the broader ecumenical community, because he saw it as the only realistic vehicle for the sustained effort that would be needed in waging the campaign against poverty.

> A number of Church, private, governmental and international agencies have been attempting to alleviate the problems of poverty and hunger in the world: nevertheless, the constantly widening gap between the rich and the poor demands now a sustained, realistic dedicated campaign to bring full Christian activity to bear upon these problems. No other group is likely to have the staying power needed for this long, arduous and often disappointing work.[48]

His sentiments echo the words that Norris heard Father Judge preach at a church dedication in the South in 1931.

> The world knows that the Church was and is and gives invincible proof of going on in her vigor and abundant life. Other bodies, movements and states have been admirably organized. Yet, eventually decay and disintegration have accompanied them and they have disappeared. We of the family of the Church know the secret of the divine life of the Church to be that living promise of her divine Founder that He will be with her all days even to the consummation of the world.[49]

Still another of Judge's Cenacle methods was working with those who were considered "abandoned." He was always drawn to situations that were deemed "impossible" or had been withdrawn from by others because they had not borne fruit. He had even written out instructions for the Cenacle members for the "discernment about accepting a spiritually abandoned work."[50] Judge considered it "a particular grace to work

48. Norris, "World Poverty."

49. Thomas A. Judge, C.M., "Sermon at Church Dedication," 15 November 1931, quoted in Timothy Lynch, S.T., *Missionary Cenacle Meditations from the Writings of Father Judge* (Silver Spring, Md.: Archives, Missionary Servants of the Most Holy Trinity, 1972), p. 77.

50. Father Timothy Lynch, S.T., ed., *Father Thomas A. Judge, C.M., Founder, The Missionary Cenacle Movement.* Mono. 4, *Writings of Father Judge: Key Documents* (Silver Spring, Md.: The Archives, Missionary Servants of the Most Holy Trinity, 1984), pp. 87–94.

for those who are destitute and poverty stricken in religious and spiritual opportunities."[51] Judge wrote to an associate:

> You know the stress we put on that word "abandoned". You know what it means to be rejected, left alone, overlooked, worthless. What a life it is to seek such! The people we are discussing are objects of compassion that can only be of Christ.[52]

In one of the longest paragraphs of his Council speech, Norris echoed Judge's thoughts, as he described for the Council fathers, from his own observations, the sense of abandonment brought on by poverty.

> "The first is hunger. . . . Poverty brings diseases. . . . Poverty brings illiteracy. . . . Poverty brings bad housing. . . . Poverty means that a mother looks at her newborn infant knowing that it will probably die before the year is out. For millions of people, living in this kind of poverty, death is a sweet release."[53]

More than half a century before Norris's Council speech, Father Judge had spoken to a group of New York City Catholic businessmen on the responsibility that the Christian incurred because of the gifts that God had blessed him with.

> I am addressing an assemblage of Catholic laymen, representatives in our midst, men whom God has blessed with success in their different walks of life, and who because of this success are in a position to do much in the noble and uplifting work of Catholic influence. I will even say more than this: these men who because of this success, God given, are obligated to do much for such an influence. I use that strong word "obligated" advisedly for I am persuaded that talent, prosperity in material or commercial endeavor, the possession of some of the conveniences of life, are given by Providence to men not for self aggrandizement or personal interest or luxurious surfeit but to furnish those thus favored with an opportunity of helping the less fortunate . . .[54]

51. AST, Father Judge to Father Bede [Hermann, O.F.M.Cap.], 30 January 1932.

52. AST, Thomas A. Judge, C.M., to an Associate, 10 February 1930.

53. Norris, "World Poverty."

54. AST, Thomas A. Judge, C.M., "The Catholic Layman's Responsibility to His Generation," Conference to the Catholic Business Men of New York City, undated.

What Judge applied to American Catholic businessmen, Norris univer-
salized in his Council speech, following the lead that he had heard from
Judge a half-century earlier.

> There will be no meaning to their Christian profession or humane
> traditions if they forget that wealth is a trust and that property car-
> ries social obligations and that riches on the scale of the West's
> modern riches must be redeemed by generosity.[55]

Norris understood that the war on poverty would not be concluded in
one decisive battle, and that a sense of perseverance would be required
of those who enlisted in the cause.

> World poverty will not be wiped out speedily, nor will the problem
> of development be solved in anything short of several generations.
> Our Christian peoples must not become weary of well doing.[56]

Father Judge had advised Norris and the other early Trinitarians in a
similar vein.

> We are encouraged not to fail in doing good. We are encouraged by
> the promise that we shall reap. No doubt about it, there is a tedium
> in the application to duty.[57]

Judge was very suspicious of a faith that was not lived out in good
works. "He questioned the love of God that was not restless in its desire
to be a power of good in the lives of others."[58] In a conference Judge
gave to the original Cenacle members in Brooklyn in 1913, he expounded on this theme.

> In the light of our Blessed Lord's teaching, if there be anguish in
> this world and we are indifferent to it, we are not right with God. If
> our neighbor be in need, this cannot be an impersonal matter to us.
> Our Lord has heaped curse upon curse against those who have
> hardened their hearts to a cry of distress as He has heaped blessing
> upon blessing upon those who are swift to relieve distress. Our

55. Norris, "World Poverty."
56. Ibid.
57. Thomas A. Judge, C.M., "Letter to Missionary Servants in Puerto Rico," 28
August 1932, quoted in Lynch, *Missionary Cenacle Meditations*, p. 47.
58. Lawrence Brediger, S.T., lecture notes on the Trinitarian charism, quoted in
O'Bryan, *Awake the Giant*, p. 4.

Lord is dreadfully personal in this matter of our exercising ourselves in corporal and spiritual works of mercy, saying what we do
to the least of His little ones, we do unto Him.[59]

Norris was just as direct, but also succinctly optimistic, about the role
Christians must play in the war on poverty in his Council speech.

A loving family does not permit its members to suffer in this way.
When all the members of the Christian family become aware of the
extent of suffering and privation among the poor of the world,
surely they will make certain that their wealthy lands will not fail
to respond to their Christian obligation.[60]

Norris worked furiously over the weekend on the text of his intervention, and on its translation into Latin. On the morning of November
5, 1964, Norris came early to the Council aula in St. Peter's Basilica and
attended the daily Mass. The celebrant of the Mass that day was a native
bishop from Zambia, the former British colony of Northern Rhodesia,
which had just become independent the previous week. It was the 115th
General Congregation of the Council, and the day's deliberations began
with the concluding debate of Paragraph 23 of Schema XIII and a preliminary report on the Schema on Bishops. An accomplished linguist,
Norris had excelled at Latin while a student at Battin High School in
Elizabeth, New Jersey, and had remained fluent in the ancient language
all his life.[61] Nonetheless, while these preliminary deliberations were
taking place, Norris went over his seven typed half-pages of Latin text
with a young American *peritus* from Chicago, Robert F. Trisco, who suggested a few changes in style and emphasis, which were penciled into
the text.[62]

At 11:30 A.M., Norris mounted the rostrum into Church history as
the only layman to participate in the debates of the Second Vatican

59. Thomas A. Judge, C.M., "Retreat Conference to Pioneer Cenacle Members,"
17 August 1913, quoted in Lynch, *Missionary Cenacle Meditations,* p. 76.

60. Norris, "World Poverty."

61. "I used to take a book of Latin poetry with me on the train when I was commuting between New Jersey and New York," "Rumson's James J. Norris Lay Auditor
at Council," *The Monitor* (October 4, 1963): 1, press clipping in NC-UNDA.

62. Francis X. Murphy, C.Ss.R. [Xavier Rynne], interview with the author,
22–23 September 1993. Like Trisco, Father Murphy was a *peritus* at the Council. The
original rostrum copy of Norris's intervention with corrections is in NC-UNDA.

Council.[63] "Although Norris spoke at an hour when many Council fathers usually step out of the Council hall for a cup of coffee and a brief chat, the benches of the vast basilica were full."[64] He "delivered his talk in excellent, clearly enunciated Latin and he was listened to with marked attention until the end."[65] Although the fathers had a printed copy of Norris's text at their seats,[66] Norris departed from the text at the outset in order to present a good-natured joke at the expense of Archbishop Felici.

> I beg the fathers to excuse me, but I dare to speak in an ancient
> tongue about modern problems, not because of my knowledge of
> the Latin language, but on account of my great reverence for this
> Sacred Council and because of the ardent desire of our most excel-
> lent and loveable Secretary General.[67]

Then he proceeded with his text, *"In ultimis duobus decennis problema pau-pertatis . . . ,"* and concluding with a ringing call to the fathers for action on behalf of the world's poor, *"Audeo proponere: ut ex hoc Concilio Oecu-menico edatur vox clamans ad actionem . . . "*

> I make bold to propose that from this ecumenical council there
> come a clarion call for action which would involve the creation of a
> structure that would devise the kind of institutions, contracts,
> forms of cooperation and policy, which the Church can adopt, to
> secure full Catholic participation in the world-wide attack on
> poverty.[68]

63. Three weeks before Norris's intervention, the British auditor, Patrick Keegan, had spoken in English on behalf of all the auditors, but Keegan's address was not part of the Conciliar debate. Norris was actually introducing Chapter 4, Paragraph 24 *"De Paupertate Mundiali,"* in Schema XIII, "On the Church in the Modern World."

64. Floyd Anderson, ed., *Council Daybook*, vol. 2 (Washington, D.C.: National Catholic Welfare Conference, 1965), p. 221.

65. Xavier Rynne [Francis X. Murphy, C.Ss.R.], *Vatican Council II* (New York: Farrar, Strauss and Giroux, 1968), p. 377.

66. *Relatio Iacobi I. Norris De Paupertate Mundiali in Schemate de Ecclesia in Mundo Huius Temporis, Cap. IV, Par. 24,* original in NC-UNDA.

67. *"Faveant Patres me excusatum habere . . . "*

68. For the official Latin text of Norris's speech, see *Acta Synodalia Sacrosancti Concilii Oecumenici Vaticani Secundi*, vol. III, pars VI (Rome: Typis Polyglottis Vaticanis, 1975), pp. 316–32. For the English version, see Anderson, vol. 3, p. 221.

Norris spoke for about fourteen minutes, and was followed in the rostrum, as planned by the poverty group, by a number of supporting interventions by various Council fathers. Norris received congratulatory messages from around the world, ranging from his old summer camp tentmate and Trinitarian confrere, John Agoa ("We were all pleased and proud when Chet Huntley announced over the T.V. that you had addressed the Council in fluent Latin"),[69] to Pope Paul VI, who sent a personally written longhand note thanking Norris "for his beautiful Christian witness."[70]

The immediate aftermath of Norris's speech took form one week later when Paul VI, after a conciliar Mass celebrated in the Byzantine Rite, placed his coronation tiara, a gift from the Catholics of Milan, on the altar of St. Peter's as a gift for the poor of the world, "in response to the many grave words spoken in this Ecumenical Council on the misery and hunger in the modern world."[71] The "clarion call" that Norris issued was enshrined by the Council fathers in Paragraph 90 of *Gaudium et spes*, the "Pastoral Constitution on the Church in the Modern World." The long term result was that Norris and the other members of the poverty group remained in Rome after the close of the Council, lobbying intensely for the implementation of Paragraph 90 and striving to insure that the call would not be buried in a curial group focused on the laity. In April 1966, Norris was named to the *"Gaudium et spes* 90 Working Group" entrusted by the pope with making a proposal for the concrete implementation of that paragraph's call for a dicastery or commission in the Roman curia, the heart of the Church's organizational structure, which would be focused on the needs of the poor.[72] At the same time, Norris was also a member of a similar working group charged by the pontiff with making a proposal to implement a similar call in Paragraph 26 of *Apostolicam actuositatem*, the "Decree on the Apostolate of Lay People."[73]

---

69. NC-UNDA, John Agoa to Jim Norris, 11 November 1964.

70. NC-UNDA, Paulus P.P. VI to *Al nostro diletto Figlio Giacomo Norris,* 6 November 1964.

71. Ernest Sakler, "Pope Paul Gives Crown to the Poor," *New York World Telegram* (November 13, 1964), press clipping in NC-UNDA.

72. Austin Flannery, O.P., ed., *Vatican Council II: The Conciliar and Post Conciliar Documents* (Northport, N.Y.: Costello Publishing Co., 1975), p. 999.

73. Ibid., p. 792.

On January 6, 1967, Pope Paul VI issued the *motu proprio, Catholicam Christi Ecclesiam,* which established two new organisms in the Roman Curia: the Council on the Laity and the Pontifical Commission for Studies on Justice and Peace.[74] Norris, Ligutti, and Ward were named full members of the new commission. Mahon was named a consultor, Gremillion was named secretary, and McCormack was brought on as a staff member. Monsignor Pio Laghi, a member of the staff of the Secretariat of State who had counseled Norris, penned a letter of congratulations and recognition.

> You are the first to be congratulated for the establishment of the Pontifical Commission *Iustitia et Pax:* you have been the pioneer and sponsor of the proposal on the Council and out, *in spem, contra spem.*[75]

Four years later in the summer of 1971, Paul VI, by the papal letter *Amoris officio,* established the Pontifical Council *Cor Unum* to coordinate the activities of Catholic aid and development agencies. Norris was also named a member of this new curial body.[76]

Norris saw the Second Vatican Council as "an act of faith in the laity's capacity to animate the temporal order in a Christian spirit."[77] His own role as a layman at the Council was a strong validation of the confidence that Father Judge had in the laity's ability, a confidence that Judge instilled in Norris and to which Norris gave tremendous witness by his whole life. As Judge once prophetically commented to his early associate Amy Marie Croke: "You would be astonished what can be accomplished by simple hearted servants of God if they be encouraged."[78] Father Judge provided the encouragement, and in a ground-breaking way, James Norris's witness at Vatican II provided the astonishing accomplishments.

---

74. See *Acta Apostolicae Sedis* 59 (1967): 25–28. In a later reorganization of the curial structure, the name of the new organism was changed to Pontifical Council for Justice and Peace.

75. Gremillion Collection, University of Notre Dame Archives, Pio Laghi to James J. Norris, 25 January 1967.

76. See *Acta Apostolicae Sedis* 63 (1971): 669–73.

77. NC-UNDA, James J. Norris, "Lay Apostolate Vocation," New Jersey Holy Name Society Convention, notes, 5 November 1966.

78. AST, Thomas A. Judge, C.M., to Amy Marie Croke, 18 April 1913.

While commuting by train from his home in Rumson, New Jersey, to his CRS office in New York City on the morning of November 15, 1976, Norris was struck by an aneurysm of the aorta while the train lumbered past his childhood home in Elizabeth. He was removed from the train and taken first to St. James Hospital and then to the larger St. Michael's Hospital, Newark, where he died two days later. Lest anyone doubt the enduring effect of Father Judge on James Norris, among the personal effects found in Norris's wallet that day were a prayer to the Holy Spirit, composed for him personally four decades earlier by Father Judge, as well as a lock of Judge's hair.[79]

Today, pilgrims who visit the National Shrine of the Immaculate Conception in Washington often pause on the Shrine's lower level to admire the coronation tiara of Pope Paul VI, displayed in a special case in Memorial Hall just outside the entrance to the Shrine's Crypt Church. In the process, they may overlook the monument immediately opposite the tiara. There, in a bronze portrait-bust, the image of James Norris gazes across at the papal insignia, which was once offered up for the poor of the world in response to the words Norris spoke at the Second Vatican Council. Carved on the green marble pillar on which the bust rests is a quote from the speech Norris was writing the morning of his death: ". . . keep holding high the torch of charity that tells our brother in need that we stand, in love, at his side."

But the real monument to James Norris and to his living out of Father Thomas Judge's vision of the power of the laity in the Church is found in Paragraph 90 of *Gaudium et spes:*

> . . . the Council suggests that it would be most opportune to create some organization of the universal Church whose task it would be to arouse the Catholic community to promote the progress of areas which are in want and foster social justice between nations.

79. I am grateful to the late Brother James McPike, S.T., former Trinitarian archivist, for explaining Judge's custom of composing individually tailored prayers for his associates and friends.

Joseph P. Chinnici, O.F.M.

12. TRADITIONS OF PRIESTLY IDENTITY AND SPIRITUALITY IN THE UNITED STATES

In 1989 a group of bishops and theologians gathered together to discuss the possibilities of issuing a pastoral statement commemorating the twenty-fifth anniversary of Vatican II's *Presbyterorum Ordinis*. Many different aspects were considered. Certainly there existed a backlog of books and articles, some of them issuing from the National Conference of Catholic Bishops, which provided an outline for an identity and spirituality of the priesthood inculturated within the American experience. For examples, in the late 1960s the bishops had commissioned studies of the priesthood from ecclesiological, sociological, psychological, and historical perspectives.[1] In 1973 *Spiritual Renewal of the American Priesthood* appeared; in 1977, *As One Who Serves;* and in 1981, *The Program of Priestly Formation,* revised in succeeding years, set the structures for the development of priestly life.[2] Important documents on stress, sexuality, the

1. John Tracy Ellis, ed., *The Catholic Priest in the United States: Historical Investigations* (Collegeville, Minn.: Saint John's University Press, 1971); Andrew Greeley, *The Catholic Priest in the United States: Sociological Investigations, The National Opinion Research Center, the University of Chicago* (Washington, D.C.: United States Catholic Conference, Publications Office, 1972); Eugene C. Kennedy with J. Heckler, *The Catholic Priest in the United States: Psychological Investigations* (Washington, D.C.: United States Catholic Conference, Publications Office, 1972). To the best of my knowledge, the ecclesiological investigation was never published.

2. Ernest E. Larkin, O.Carm., and Gerard T. Broccolo, *Spiritual Renewal of the American Priesthood* (Washington, D.C.: United States Catholic Conference Publication

changing role of the pastor, and the morale of priests followed.[3] In addition to these official publications, numerous theologians had tackled the vexing issue of the identity of the priest within the context of the modern American world.[4]

Yet, despite all of these reflections, in 1989 the "opportuneness" of publishing a pastoral letter on the priesthood seemed questionable. The cultural and ecclesiastical situation was too volatile, the theological opinions too divisive, the underlying ecclesiological issues irresoluble within the present Roman and American contexts. Could there be in such a situation any unifying view of the spirituality of the priesthood? Or would any statement about priestly identity simply encourage more division? Eventually, it was hoped, the ministerial priesthood would be strengthened by the development of a large-scale program of video presentation, audio tapes, and written materials in an attempt to encourage priests to share their experience of God, the Church, and their ministry.[5]

These debates about priestly identity and spirituality which surfaced so clearly in the late 1980s, twenty-five years after the Council, have continued unabated since that time; if anything, they have become more "popularized." Theologically, there are still major disagreements over the relationship between the priesthood of all believers and the ministerial priesthood, the necessity of celibacy, the pastoral nature of priestly spirituality, the admission of women to Orders, and the interpretation of how sin and grace coexist within the experience of the priest.[6] The reve-

---

Office, 1973); *As One Who Serves* (Washington, D.C.: United States Catholic Conference Publications, 1977); *The Program of Priestly Formation* (Washington, D.C.: United States Catholic Conference Publications, 1982).

3. "The Priest and Stress" (Washington, D.C.: United States Catholic Conference, Office of Publishing and Promotion Services, 1982); "A Reflection Guide on Human Sexuality and the Ordained Priest" (Washington, D.C.: United States Catholic Conference, Office of Publishing and Promotion Services, 1983); "A Shepherd's Care: Reflections on the Changing Role of Pastor" (Washington, D.C.: United States Catholic Conference, Office of Publishing and Promotion Services, 1987); Priestly Life and Ministry Committee, "Reflections on the Morale of Priests," *Origins* 18 (January 12, 1989): 497–505.

4. See, for examples, David N. Power, *The Christian Priest: Elder and Prophet* (London: Sheed and Ward, 1973); Kenan B. Osborne, *Priesthood: A History of Ordained Ministry in the Roman Catholic Church* (New York: Paulist Press, 1988); Avery Dulles, S.J., "Models for Ministerial Priesthood," *Origins* 20 (October 11, 1990): 284–89.

5. See "Priests' Spirituality," *Origins* 20 (November 29, 1990): 408.

6. For examples, see Peter Drilling, *Trinity and Ministry* (Minneappolis: Fortress

lations of sexual abuse have led to a searching examination of the relationship between the priest and institutional power, but from many different perspectives.[7] The pastoral implications of differing views are now
apparent, with the open discussion of liturgical styles, two Latin rites,
different diocesan models, and the distinction between religious and
diocesan priests.[8] Our current situation is clearly one marked by a pluralism of viewpoints.

As an historian, I cannot help but reflect that different views of the
identity and spirituality of the ministerial priesthood have been present
in the American Catholic community from the very beginning of its institutional establishment at the first synod in 1791. At times, when the
community was in the process of social mutation, these debates reached
epidemic proportions, as for example in the last quarter of the nineteenth century. In what follows, I would like to present some background to the current situation, first, by detailing two different approaches to priestly identity in the historical experience of the community, and second, by examining in brief fashion part of the history of the
Sulpician tradition of priestly spirituality. My simple hope is that what is
presented will help our community today discuss the issues involved
with the knowledge that they are joining a long line of predecessors who

---

Press, 1991); Thomas P. Rausch, S.J., *Priesthood Today: An Appraisal* (New York: Paulist
Press, 1992); Tim Unsworth, *The Last Priests in America, Conversations with Remarkable
Men* (New York: Crossroad, 1993); Bishop Anthony Pilla, "Expressing Support and
Respect for Priests," *Origins* 26 (November 21, 1996): 366–70.

7. Jason Berry, *Lead Us Not into Temptation: Catholic Priests and the Sexual Abuse of
Children* (New York: Doubleday, 1992); Elinor Burkett, Frank Bruni, *A Gospel of
Shame: Children, Sexual Abuse and the Catholic Church* (Viking, 1993); A. W. Richard
Sipe, *Sex, Priests, and Power: Anatomy of a Crisis* (New York: Brunner/Mazel Publica-
tions, 1995); Stephen J. Rossetti, *A Tragic Grace: The Catholic Church and Child Sexual
Abuse* (Collegeville: The Liturgical Press, 1996); Philip Jenkins, *Pedophiles and Priests:
Anatomy of a Contemporary Crisis* (New York: Oxford University Press, 1996).

8. Monsignor M. Francis Mannion, "Agendas for Liturgical Reform," *America*
165 (November 30, 1996): 9–16; Michael W. Cuneo, *The Smoke of Satan: Conservative
and Traditonalist Dissent in Contemporary American Catholicism* (New York: Oxford University Press, 1997); Rembert G. Weakland, "Liturgical Renewal; Two Latin Rites,"
America 176 (June 7–14, 1997): 12–15; Charles R. Morris, "A Tale of Two Dioceses,
From Lincoln to Saginaw," *Commonweal* 124 (June 6, 1997): 11–18; Paul K. Hennessy, C.F.C., ed., *A Concert of Charisms, Ordained Ministry in the Religious Life* (New
York: Paulist Press, 1997); John O'Malley, S.J., "Priesthood, Ministry, and Religious
Life: Some Historical and Historiographical Considerations," *Theological Studies* 49
(1988): 223–57.

also witnessed to the vitality of the faith in its attempts to inculturate in the American environment.[9]

I. Corpus Christi, Corpus Ecclesiae, Corpus Mariae: *Images for Priestly Identity*

Ever since the fourth Gospel pictured Mary and John at the foot of the crucified Christ, out of whose side flowed sacramental blood and water, there has been a deep theological and analogous relationship between the body of Christ the Priest, the body of Mary, his mother, the body of the Church, and the identity of the ministerial priest. To begin these reflections, I would like to examine how in the history of Catholicism in the United States the understanding of the spiritual identity of the priest has changed depending on the different images of Christ, Mary, and the Church. The identity of the priest can be best understood by addressing the questions: What is the image of Christ? What is the image of Mary? What is the image of the Church? In approaching the subject in this way, I hope to delineate two different emphases in priestly identity which have been present in the community, thus indicating that there has been no one single view which can be exhaustive.

1. The Sermons of John Carroll (1735–1815)

The journey to examine the history of priestly identity in the United States can begin with John Carroll's sermons on Holy Orders. As the first bishop of the United States (1790–1815) and a friend of the Sulpicians, whom he invited to establish St. Mary's Seminary, Carroll was in a unique and representative position in the early years of the republic. Two of his reflections are particularly revelatory, one given possibly at the first synod in 1791 and the other at an ordination.[10] In these sermons

9. The substance of this study was first presented at St. Mary's Seminary, Baltimore, for the International Reunion, July 7–8, 1991, celebrating the bicentennial of the Society of Saint-Sulpice in the United States. I am indebted to the Sulpicians for their invitation and to Father John Bowen, the archivist, for his help. It is with gratitude that this study is offered for a publication honoring Father Robert Trisco.

10. See "Holy Orders: John XV, 16," and "Holy Orders: Hebrews V," printed in Thomas O'Brien Hanley, S.J., *The John Carroll Papers, Volume 3, 1807–1815* (Notre Dame: University of Notre Dame Press, 1976), pp. 408–15.

the bishop concentrated on two biblical texts: "I have chosen you; and have appointed you, that you should go, and should bring forth fruit, and your fruit should remain" (John 15.16). "Every priest, taken from among men is appointed for men in the things, that appertain to God, that he may offer up gifts and sacrifices for sins: who can have compassion for those, that are ignorant and err; because he himself also is encompassed with infirmity . . . neither doth any man take the honour to himself, but he who is called by God, as Aaron was" (Heb. 5.1–4).

The bishop begins his sermon on Hebrews by indicating that Christ is high priest and Lord of a visible society; he willed his work to continue in a ministry "subordinate to & associated with him in the performance of the most sacred duties." Carroll stressed above all Christ's ministry of reconciliation, which offers sacrifice, teaches the ignorant, redeems the erring, and sympathizes with all. "Elevated to a participation of the ministry of Christ," the priest is to ask the people to join their prayers with his.[11] When commenting on John 15.16, Carroll expanded this notion of reconciliation by arguing that the priest is an example to all Christians of their duty to save their own soul and cooperate in the salvation of others, "by example, by persuasion, by influence, and by authority." As "coadjutors of God," "ambassadors of Christ," followers of the "good Shepherd," priests instruct, reconcile, and follow "our desolate Brethren into the uncultivated wilderness, whither they betake themselves for Sup (po) rt."[12]

Carroll was certainly aware of the hierarchic functions of the priest, but the sermons indicate that at the heart of his priestly identity was the whole Church's participation in the ministry of Christ. He admonished the ordinand:

> Remember, that in every act of your ministry, you will have him invisibly present, acting through you; that the functions, which you will perform before men, are his functions, & that he will present them to his eternal Fr., as his own: that the doctrines, which you are to teach, are his doctrines; that the reconciliation of sinners, which you will pronouce with your lips, is a reconciliation

11. "Holy Orders: Hebrews V," pp. 413, 414,
12. "Holy Orders: John XV, 16," pp. 410, 411.

perfected by him; that the solemn & most awful Sacrifice, which you will offer on his altars here, is the Sacrifice, which he offers on the cross, & continues for ever to represent before the throne of his heavenly Fr. to glorify him, & to perfect the redemption of mankind.[13]

In the fashion of Bérulle, Carroll described the priest as representing an angel on the mystical ladder. He detailed the priest's action as clearly imitative of the Incarnate and Risen Christ:

He descends to carry up with him the petitions and necessities of the people; and he mounts upwards, when by prayer he lays their supplications before the throne of the Almighty. Observe, that I speak not here of the prayers and vows of a private individual, who addresses heaven in his own name without any delegated title or commission: but the prayers of the priest are the prayers of a public minister, of an appointed mediator and agent with God for his people; of one, who prays officially, who pleads in the name of the whole church, in the name of the Society of the Just.[14]

It should be noted that the action of the priest, in Carroll's view, is first *descending* and only then *ascending:* both identification with the people through compassion, sympathy, and sharing of weakness, and also supplication with and for them by virtue of the priest's close union with Christ.[15]

In his sermons on "Charity" and the "Eucharist," Carroll reiterated his central image of the incarnate Christ *(corpus Christi)* acting for the people precisely because he is one with them: ". . . He humbled and debased himself, and made himself as it were, of no account: and yet through the darkness of his humiliations, rays of divinity are continually breaking forth and manifesting his greatness & the sanctity of his ministry by astonishing instances of his power over all the works of creation."[16] In an extensive reflection on the Eucharist, Carroll gave a

13. "Holy Orders: Hebrews V," p. 415.

14. "Holy Orders: John XV, 16," p. 412.

15. For the larger context of this interpretation see Joseph P. Chinnici, O.F.M., *Living Stones: The History and Structure of Catholic Spiritual Life in the United States* (New York: Macmillan Publishing Company, 1989), pp. 20–34.

16. "Charity: Mark VIII, 2," in Hanley, *The John Carroll Papers, III,* pp. 436–43, with quotation from page 437.

supreme example of what it means to be a priest. "The Son of God," he
preached,

> Priest forever of a much higher order than Aaron and destined to
> introduce a far more perfect dispensation of grace and religion,
> comes down from heaven, and by the wonderful and omnipotent
> operation of the Holy Ghost, assumes and is united to a body,
> formed of the same materials, as our own. During the course of his
> mortal life, he remains in this tabernacle of his body, inviting us to
> the practice of virtue by his examples, confirming our faith by his
> miracles, enlightening our ignorance by his doctrines, protecting us
> by his prayers, & devoting himself daily for our sakes, to humilia-
> tions, to sufferings, to poverty, to reproach & injuries: and after ful-
> filling these functions of a Pastor, & prophet, & Legislator, he con-
> cludes his life in the office and exercises of a Pontiff, & victim; for
> our iniquities, he is covered with his own sacred blood . . .[17]

The bishop believed that this priesthood of Christ was shared by all who
made up the Church *(corpus ecclesiae)*. The savior offered an example to
teach "in what manner we are to exercise charity on behalf of our fel-
lowmen, by extending our solicitude to lighten their miseries both corporal and spiritual," to assuage "the evils of poverty and disease," and to
deliver people from ignorance.[18] The vocation of the ministerial priest
was in direct continuity with the call of everyone to imitate the priesthood of Christ; his functions were united with exemplarity, reconciliation, and duty; his privilege came from his closer identification with
Christ. When the bishop spoke of Holy Orders, he could be moralizing,
but he also emphasized "responsibilities" and a contractural arrangement between the minister and the people. "Will you not add your en-
deavours to mine," he asked his listeners?[19] For Carroll the *corpus Christi*
took shape in the *corpus ecclesiae;* the action of the priest was rooted in his
participation in this one body.

It should be noted that when Carroll preached about Mary, the
source of Christ's human body, he paralleled the grace given her at con-

17. "Eucharist: The Old Law and the New," ibid., pp. 404–7, with quotation
from p. 405.
18. "Charity: Mark VIII, 2," p. 436.
19. "Holy Orders; Responsibilities," in Hanley, *The John Carroll Papers, III*, pp.
415–17, with quotation from page 416.

ception with the grace of adoption and reconciliation given to the Christian in the sacraments of Baptism and Penance.[20] Mary's fidelity to her first grace came to completion in the assumption of her body into heaven; she exemplified for all the "indispensable obligation of using our earnest endeavor to preserve the grace of justification conferred on us in either of the above mentioned Sacraments." Mary, by the grace given her, her faithfulness and her assumption into heaven, stood as the model for the Christian, and hence for the priest. *Corpus Christi, corpus ecclesiae, corpus Mariae:* these images at the heart of Carroll's spirituality unified his christology, ecclesiology, and anthropology in a single field, and placed at the heart of his image of the priest the values of participation, reconciliation, unity within the one body, mutual exemplarity and responsibility. These coalesced well with the personal, social, and republican values Carroll found embedded in the mystery of Christ's priesthood—and the values he wanted fostered through priestly leadership in the community.

2. The Sermons of William Henry Elder (1819–1904)

The sermons of William Henry Elder, archbishop of Cincinnati from 1883 to 1904, may be taken to exemplify the second pole of priestly identity in the history of the Catholic community in the United States. Educated at Mount St. Mary's, Emmitsburg, Maryland, Elder's life in leadership spanned the second half of the nineteenth century, and his views generally reflected those of his contemporaries. The archbishop delivered sermons at both the Second (1866) and Third (1884) Plenary Councils of Baltimore, one on Mary and the other on the priesthood.[21] The differences between his views and those of Carroll are immediately apparent.

As the basis of his sermon at the Third Plenary Council, Elder chose the same text Carroll had selected in 1791, John 15.16. He began by de-

20. "On the Assumption of Mary," in Hanley, *The John Carroll Papers, III,* pp. 402–3, with quotation from page 403.
21. See "Devotion to the Blessed Virgin Mary," in *Sermons on Subjects of the Day Delivered by Distinguished Catholic Prelates and Theologians at the Second Plenary Council of Baltimore, United States, October 1866* (Dublin: W. B. Kelly, 1868), pp. 126–37; "The Priesthood," in *The Memorial Volume: A History of the Third Plenary Council of Baltimore* (Baltimore: The Baltimore Publishing Company, 1885), pp. 43–58.

scribing the assembly seated before him. It is, in his mind, "a compendium of what is seen over the entire world—Christ living in those whom he has sent, and through them living in the civilized world and infusing life into the uncivilized." Bishops and priests are, above all, spiritual teachers and rulers surrounded by "faithful children in the Church" and by the many people who do not acknowledge "those teachers as their own, and yet [are] enlightened by the truths which He commissioned His Church to teach."[22]

In this context, the archbishop imaged priests as civilizing agents in the midst of "men's earthly inclinations, their sensuality, their pride and their passions." He focused preeminently on their authority, their influence for order, and linked the priesthood with the Church's hierarchical constitution. It is the duty of the ordained, he argued, to communicate the office of Christ's priesthood which is present in the bishops, "who hold it in all its fullness: and the priests of the second order, who hold not indeed its fullness, but its sublimest powers and those most needed for each individual soul." In his view, "power" characterized the priest: power to preach; power to offer the Holy Sacrifice; power to purify souls; "the power to sanctify them by blessing and by all the other means of grace." It is the priest, Elder concluded, who gives on earth all those things which make life worth living.[23]

Elder, like Carroll, rooted the identity of the priest in the one Priesthood of Christ, which comes to its deepest expression in the Incarnation, a condescension on the part of the Lord so that "he might raise us up to be His brothers in the Kingdom of His Father." However, in contrast to Carroll's emphasis on the Son's assumption of human nature and his sympathy for its weakness, the Cincinnati prelate presented the following analogy for the central mystery of the faith. "Man is composed of body and soul," he preached,

> of spirit and matter each in its nature utterly and entirely distinct from the other. His body is matter, utterly incapable of thinking or willing or of any act of consciousness. The soul is spirit, having neither shape nor weight nor any other property belonging to matter. And yet as constituted man is one single human person. All our

22. "The Priesthood," p. 43.   23. Ibid., p. 51.

acts, whether done through the soul or through the body, are equally human acts. In like manner our divine Lord, being one divine Person with two natures, divine and human, all His acts were divine, whether done through His divine or His human nature. When, therefore, our Lord, God and man, made acknowledgment of the subjection of His human, created nature to Almighty God and declared the supreme dominion and majesty of God, His absolute right of life and death over Himself and all creatures—this confession and homage was a perfect and adequate act of sacrifice.[24]

For Elder, Christ's priesthood came to its fullest expression in sacrificial acts which confirmed the absolute dominion of God: "He lived all his human life in obedience to it [God's will], and he filled up the measure of all possible obedience by suffering every pain of body, every anguish of soul that His human nature was capable of suffering; consummating His homage to His Father by laying down His life itself—the highest possible confession of God's dominion."[25] Here the incarnate *corpus Christi* as the model of priesthood signified the sacrificial submission of humanity to divinity, body to soul, man to God, world to Church—all of this to remedy the original sin of disobedience. It was not accidental that Elder framed his view of priestly identity in the context of the excesses of the French Revolution and the Paris commune. Rebellious people had rejected the "truths which our Lord commissioned His priests to teach: the fear of God; the obligations we all owe to our fellow-men, and the obligation to subdue our passions . . ."[26]

In the remainder of his sermon, Elder narrated the implications of this view of the Incarnation for the operations of the ministerial priesthood. He made no equation, as Carroll had done, between the *corpus Christi* and the *corpus ecclesiae*. Instead, although acknowledging that all the faithful participate in the priesthood of Christ ("Each one of us can claim the Victim as our own, and thus, in the Mass, each one of the faithful present becomes himself in a secondary manner a priest, because each of us offers the divine Victim"),[27] Elder drew attention to the dis-

---

24. Ibid., p. 44, with long quotation from pages 45–46.
25. Ibid., p. 46.   26. Ibid., p. 54.
27. Ibid., p. 49.

tinctive hierarchical role of the ministerial priest. In a way similar to his explanation of the divine person ruling the human nature of Christ, the prelate viewed the priest as carrying Christ's power and leadership within the *corpus ecclesiae*. "But the Christian priest has Christ living in him," he noted,

> speaking by his lips and giving divine efficacy to his words. "He that heareth you heareth Me." Hence it is by the priests His truths have been handed down to our day with the same clear sound, and the same certain meaning, and the same exactness, and the same intrinsic, living energy that they had from the mouths of the Apostles: because they are always the words of the same priest, Jesus Christ, having all the attributes which His divine priesthood gives to them.[28]

The place of the faithful in this conception of Church is one of subordination, obedience, passive receptivity. Elder's priest was marked by separation, distinction, institutional role, and cultic holiness.

Significantly enough, when the archbishop spoke about the *corpus Christi* within the Church, he emphasized not the social action of Christ feeding the multitude, as had Carroll, but the consecratory action of the hierarchical priesthood which made the Body of Christ present in the Mass: "By the hands of His priest He is elevated for the people's adoration; by the hands and lips of His priests, He is offered to the Father in behalf of all the people; by His priest He gives Himself to his faithful disciples, to be the food of their souls, their strength and their life on earth and the pledge of their eternal life in heaven."[29] *Corpus Christi* meant for Elder the Eucharist, food given to the people through the power of the priesthood.[30]

Given these views of the *corpus Christi* and the *corpus ecclesiae*, it was not surprising that Elder's understanding of the *corpus Mariae* developed in a similar fashion. "Mary and the Church are so associated, or rather identified," he preached at the Second Plenary Council of Baltimore in

---

28. Ibid., p. 52.   29. Ibid., p. 48.

30. For the important development which this viewpoint represents see Henri de Lubac, *Corpus Mysticum, L'Eucharistie et l'église au moyen âge* (Paris: Aubier, 1949), chap. 4.

1866, "that what is true of one may be said of the other."[31] In contrast to Carroll, Elder's central image was not the Assumption of Mary as the model of fidelity and completion for all Christians, but rather the Virgin's intercessory role, her distinction as the "greatest of His creatures." In an age of pride, she engendered humility; in an age of incredulity, she drew people to her Son. Mary, he noted,

> is given to us; all her glories and virtues are for our use and benefit; and we are ungrateful to God and rob Him of the glory that is due to Him, if we do not freely and abundantly make use of her glories to give Him praise, and avail ourselves of the power which He has granted to her prayers, to draw down on earth the blessings that He desires to send through her.[32]

At the end of the sermon, Elder mentioned the prevalence of the medals of the Immaculate Conception and the devotions of the month of May. December 8th was now the patronal feast for the Church in the United States.[33] Thus, although he adverted to the Church's Marian continuity with the Church of Carroll's time, Elder shared with many of his contemporaries a different symbolic equation between the Church and Mary, one centered not on the Assumption but on the Immaculate Conception. Free from sin, pure and unspotted, the supreme advocate, extraordinarily filled with grace, Mary stood removed from the changing and materialistic forces of the world. Elder's image of priestly identity followed suit and as an institutional symbol his priest represented the many different social and theological changes that had taken place in the Catholic community after the death of the first archbishop of Baltimore.

In summary, the different images of Carroll and Elder representing two different tendencies in priestly identity in the United States might be presented in schematic fashion (see Table).

This sketch is oversimplified and the views of Carroll and Elder were certainly not mutually exclusive. They shared a common Roman Catholic, post-Tridentine inheritance, which highlighted the role of the hierar-

31. "Devotion to the Blessed Virgin Mary," p. 127.
32. Ibid., p. 132.
33. For a description of the Marian background to Elder's views see John D. Bryant, *The Immaculate Conception of the Most Blesssed Virgin Mother of God; A Dogma of the Catholic Church* (Boston: Patrick Donahoe, 1855).

TABLE

John Carroll	William Henry Elder
The Incarnation as assuming humanity into divinity.	The Incarnation and redemption as establishing the dominion of divinity over humanity.
Corpus Christi: corpus ecclesiae	*Corpus Christi:* Eucharist
Corpus ecclesiae: "congregation of believers"	*Corpus ecclesiae:* hierarchical body
Corpus Mariae: Assumption	*Corpus Mariae:* Immaculate Conception
The Priest: sympathizing with weakness imitating Christ's ministry of reconciliation fulfilling Christian vocation teaching duties of religion promoting social charity	*The Priest:* receiving power at Orders mediating between God and man a separate holiness consecrating/forgiving directing civilization

chy and the centrality of the sacraments of Eucharist and penance. In the context of the French Revolution and the Protestant ascendancy, both were well aware of the importance of authoritative structures in the Church. Yet, their presuppositions about the relationship between the Church and society, the theological tendencies and emphases of their reflections, the way they attempted to shape the Catholic body through their sermons on the identity of the priest, and their basic orienting images of Christ and Mary differed profoundly. As twin poles of a common inheritance, these two typologies in various forms wove themselves like threads throughout much of the history of the Church in the United States. During some of that history they entered into direct tension with each other, not on the level of systematic belief about the priesthood, but in arguments about the priest's role in society, his formation, and his attitude toward the intellectual culture of the times. The language of the argument was popular, not abstract.[34] Perhaps a more specific indication

34. Confer for some examples, the arguments of the late nineteenth century summarized in John B. Hogan, *Clerical Studies* (Boston: Marlier, Calanan & Co., 1898); John Talbot Smith, *The Training of a Priest* (New York: William H. Young &

of how these views tended to interact and the complexity of the history of priestly identity in the United States can be discovered through a brief examination of the fortunes of the Sulpician tradition of spirituality.

II. The Sulpician Tradition of Priestly Spirituality

The Society of St. Sulpice, or Sulpicians, founded by Jean Jacques Olier (1608–57), came to the United States with the foundation of St. Mary's Seminary, Baltimore, in 1791, and through the seminary system exercised a profound impact on the course of priestly spirituality.[35] All of the elements that have been examined in the first part of this essay were present in some form or other in the history of priestly spirituality in the Sulpician tradition: emphasis on the Incarnation, sacrificial action, the Eucharist, the role of Mary, view of the Church. Yet it is also true that the interpretation of the vision of Jean Jacques Olier has undergone some modification, often within the larger context of the typologies which have been outlined.[36] The key areas have been the relationship between the priest and the people and the understanding of "incorporation into Jesus Christ." Here, only some brief indications of these different views can be delineated.

Olier's method of prayer, which focused attention on the Incarnation of Christ in mind, heart, and hands (adoration, communion, coop-

Company, 1897); James Cardinal Gibbons, *The Ambassador of Christ* (Baltimore: John Murphy & Company, 1896). Compare these views with the description of priestly identity in Right Rev. John Hennessy, "The Sanctity of the Church," in *The Memorial Volume: A History of the Third Plenary Council of Baltimore* (Baltimore: The Baltimore Publishing Company, 1884), pp. 224–44, especially 227–34. This institutional understanding was popularized in, for example, Joseph Wissel, C.Ss.R., *The Redemptorist on the American Missions*, 3d ed. (privately printed, 1920), II, pp. 274–84. For a continuation of the tension into the twentieth century see Bruce H. Lescher, C.S.C., "The Spiritual Life and Social Action in American Catholic Spirituality: William J. Kerby and Paul Hanly Furfey" (dissertation, The Graduate Theological Union, 1990).

35. For a very fine overview of their history and influence in the United States see Christopher J. Kauffman, *Tradition and Transformation in Catholic Culture: The Priests of St. Sulpice in the United States: 1791 to the Present* (New York: Macmillan, 1988).

36. See for background Eugene A. Walsh, *The Priesthood in the Writings of the French School: Berulle, De Condren, Olier* (Catholic University of America, Ph.D., 1949); Lowell Martin Glendon, "Jean-Jacques Olier's View of the Spiritual Potential of Human Nature: A Presentation and an Evaluation" (dissertation, Fordham University, 1983).

eration) was meant for everyone: priests, pastors, religious, penitents.[37] His prayer, "O Jesu, vivens in Maria," from the *Catéchisme chrétienne,* was designed for priests and laity alike. As Eugene Walsh would later write, "The form of prayer of the French school is a perfect summary of the Christian way of life." James Keller (1900–1977) would incorporate this tradition into his own democratic spiritual vision.[38] This prayer and method at the base of the Sulpician tradition stressed union with Jesus and presupposed an alliance between incarnational Christology and ecclesiology.[39] The Church was the Mystical Body through which Jesus acted in the world; priests were "experienced Christians," examples who reflected the participation of all in the priesthood of Christ. Olier's practice of spiritual direction for the laity correlated well with this general orientation. Although there were basic differences in their views of human nature, there were also similarities between Olier's view and that of John Carroll.[40] Carroll was firmly grounded in the Ignatian meditative tradition and an enlightenment anthropology, but both he and Olier had profound roots in the sixteenth-century Catholic reform and shared at least a common equation between the *corpus Christi* and the *corpus ecclesiae.* This presupposition argued for an organic vision of Church; combined with Carroll's vision of the person, the unity between the body of Christ and the Church provided a strong foundational synthesis for an American priestly spirituality.

However, in the course of the nineteenth century, not only was Carroll's vision of the person lost, but Olier's more unified synthesis between an incarnational Christology and ecclesiology, which joined priest and people in one body, split apart as the sacral character of the priesthood came to be emphasized. For example, Olier's basic synthesis was

37. See Jean-Jacques Olier, *Introduction à la vie et aux vertus chrétiennes, pietas seminarii* (Paris, 1954), IV, pp. 22–26.

38. Jean-Jacques Olier, *Catéchisme chrétien pour la vie intérieure et journée chrétienne* (Paris, 1954); Walsh, "The Priesthood," p. 17; James Keller, *To Light a Candle: The Autobiography of James Keller, Founder of the Christophers* (Garden City, N.Y., 1963), pp. 50, 87.

39. For background see William M Thompson, ed., *Bérulle and the French School, Selected Writings* (New York: Paulist Press, 1989), "Introduction," especially pp. 54–66.

40. For an analysis of the French school in the area of its view of human nature see Justus George Lawler, "Religious Life, Fundamentals and Accidentals," *Worship* 27 (September 1953): 437–51.

centainly present at mid-century in the American *Manual of Piety for the Use of Seminaries*.[41] Here priests were encouraged to be models and guides for the faithful, and the Sulpician method was presented for the laity. Stressing the priest's incorporation into Jesus, the *Manual* read: "There should be no *self* in a priest; for the *myself* of the priests should be changed into Jesus Christ, who makes them say at the altar, *This is my body;* priests should have no other interior life, than that of the Son of God, which will enable them to say with St. Paul: *I live, now not I; but Christ liveth in me.*"[42] But how this tradition was understood marked a clear mutation in the synthesis. The change can be seen in one of the key figures of the mid-nineteenth century, Martin John Spalding (1810–72), bishop of Louisville and later archbishop of Baltimore.[43]

Olier's stress on the interior identification with Jesus had been passed on to Martin John Spalding by two Sulpicians, Benedict Joseph Flaget (1763–1850) and John Baptist David (1761–1841). David's *True Piety,* a popular prayer book for priests and laity alike, his more systematic *Spiritual Retreat of Eight Days,* and Flaget's personal example modeled meditative identification with the incarnate Christ: "But penetrate into his sacred interior," *True Piety* reads, "and contemplate him offering himself to his Father in his temple, to be substituted to the ancient victims, and accepting all the sufferings and ignominies which were to attend his immolation on the altar of the cross."[44] Spalding praised David's and Flaget's lives as "models for the flock and mirrors of the clergy."[45] He admonished his priests:

41. *Manual of Piety for the Use of Seminaries* (Baltimore: John Murphy & Company, 1856).

42. Ibid., p. 341; the section on mental prayer, clearly including the laity, is pp. 69–100.

43. The standard work on Spalding remains Thomas W. Spalding: *Martin John Spalding: American Churchman* (Washington, D.C.: The Catholic University of America Press, 1973).

44. A Catholic Clergyman, *True Piety, or the Day Well Spent, Being A Catholic Manual of Chosen Prayers, Devout Practices, and Solid Instructions. Adapted to Every State of Life* (Baltimore: Warner & Hanna, 1809), p. 236. See also John Baptist David, *A Spiritual Retreat of Eight Days,* edited with additions and introduction by Martin John Spalding (Louisville: Webb and Levering, 1864).

45. See J. L. Spalding, *The Life of the Most Rev. M. J. Spalding, D.D., Archbishop of Baltimore* (New York: Christian Press Association, n.d.), p. 220; M. J. Spalding, *Sketches of the Life, Times, and Character of the Rt. Rev. Benedict Joseph Flaget, First Bishop of Louisville* (Louisville: Webb & Levering, 1852), "Appendix."

Our Blessed Lord came to send fire on the earth, and what does he wish more than that it be enkindled in the hearts of all men? In order that we may be able to scatter this heavenly fire over the earth, we must take care to keep it always burning in our own hearts; for if we be cold ourselves, how shall we be able to warm others? Happy shall we be if, by a constant and living union with Jesus Christ, the Source of the divine fire, we maintain ourselves in the fervor of the holy priesthood, and thus become, like St. John the Baptist, burning and shining lights in God's sanctuary.[46]

The depth of Spalding's piety, his priestly union with Jesus, came out very clearly in this description of Flaget's final illness:

He was willing to die, he was willing to get well, or he was willing to live and suffer, as it might please his divine Master. He united each pain with the different stages of our Lord's passion. When able to speak, he gave frequent utterance to acts of faith, hope, and resignation. "Not only will I suffer patiently and cheerfully," he would often say, "but, oh,! How lovingly, my sweet Jesus! May thy holy will be done for ever and ever!" "Grant me, O My God! Patience and resignation, but, above all, thy love; for patience and resignation may be pagan, but *love* is Christian."[47]

Clearly, the archbishop of Baltimore had drunk deeply at the wells of both the Sulpician and the Ignatian traditions.[48]

Yet, the structure of Spalding's thought was such that the unity between the clergy and the laity in the one Priesthood of Christ was lost and incorporation into Christ meant primarily institutional allegiance to the Church. The ecclesiological underpinnings of Olier's vision (and also that of Ignatius Loyola and John Carroll) disappeared. The American apologist defined the Church primarily as "an external, organized body or society of men, professing the one true religion of Jesus Christ." Only tangentially did he refer to the Church as "spouse of Christ," "kingdom of heaven," or "house of God."[49] He argued instead that, just as the per-

---

46. Ibid., p. 221.   47. Ibid., p. 454.

48. For Spalding's use of the Ignatian tradition, as it was passed on to him, see David, *A Spiritual Retreat of Eight Days*, pp. 37ff., and *Manresa: or the Spiritual Exercises of St. Ignatius* (New York: The Catholic Publication Society, n.d.).

49. See, for example, Martin John Spalding, *Lectures on the Evidences of Catholicity*, 5th ed. (Baltimore: John Murphy, 1870), pp. 50, 197–98 in section on "Sanctity," pp.

son is composed of two distinct parts, body and soul, so the Church has
an external body united to its spiritual soul; it is divided into officers and
subjects, those who rule and those who hear and obey; it is a divine institution with governing power to restrain men's passions and interests.[50]
Struggling against Protestant sectarianism and the bigotry of anti-
Catholicism, Spalding equated the priesthood almost exclusively with its
cultic manifestations.

The archbishop took a leading hand in the theological synthesis that
was adopted at the Second Plenary Council of Baltimore in 1866. The
section of its decrees entitled "De Ordine" emphasized an external and
visible priesthood. Relying on the Tridentine inheritance, the Baltimore
Council defined Orders as a *"munus et officium"* intrinsically joined to sacrifice. Clerics were distinguished from others not only by station and
condition but also by dress, physical appearance, gestures, and participation in the life of society: "Quoniam uniformitas etiam in rebus minimis
maxime optanda Ecclesiae semper visa est."[51] As men preoccupied with
God and divine things, bound by no bodily ties, and separated from
women, priests were to be sharply distinguished from the laity.[52] In this
fashion, priestly spirituality, shorn of its roots in Olier's more organic
Christian vision, became highly personalized. The "sanctity of the
Church" in Spalding's view related to doctrine, unchanging moral principles, and sacramental ordinances, all commissions, functions, of the hierarchical and ministerial priesthood.[53] Spalding exemplified the American Church's transition from Carroll's communal pole to Elder's hierarchical pole as the dominant typology controlling the "thought style" of
priestly spirituality.[54]

194–228; for context, M. J. Spalding, *Miscellanea; Comprising Reviews, Lectures, and Essays, on Historical, Theological, and Miscellaneous Subjects,* 2 vols. (Baltimore, 1862), "Influence of Catholicity on Civil Liberty" (1844), 1:131–50; "The Philadelphia Riots"
(1845), 2:596–618.

50. See *Lectures on the Evidences of Catholicity,* pp. 39, 51–52, 319–21, and "Pastoral Letter of 1866," in Peter Guilday, ed., *The National Pastorals of the American Hierarchy (1792–1919),* pp. 198–225, passim.

51. *Concilii Plenarii Baltmorensis, II, Acta et Decreta* (Baltimore: Joannes Murphy,
1868), Title V, Chapter VIII, "De Ordine," pp. 165–70; Title III, Chapter VI, "De Vita et
Honestate Clericorum," pp. 93–105.

52. Ibid., nos. 163, 164, 165.

53. See Spalding, *Lectures on the Evidences of Catholicity,* pp. 194–228.

54. For "thought style" and its anthropological functions see Mary Douglass,

In the latter portion of the nineteenth century many Sulpician teachers labored for a wider understanding of incarnational Christology, ecclesiology, and spirituality, and their efforts can be read against this backdrop of the dominant typology's tendency toward formal, objectified structures and its separation of the ministerial priesthood from the baptismal priesthood of the faithful.[55] Paul Francis Dissez (1828–1908) was known for his appreciation of the different forms of the one Christian life. He stressed the formation of the gentleman-Christian-priest by arguing that "sacerdotal virtues are Christian virtues carried to a high degree of perfection."[56] Could it be that this director of Bishop John Joseph Keane and friend of James Cardinal Gibbons contributed to the Americanist vision of the Church as the extension of the Incarnation? John Hogan (1829–1901), a leading seminary educator and reformer, consistently recalled the "natural" foundations of the priestly vocation. "The truth is," he wrote in *Daily Thoughts for Priests,* "all the normal, natural affections remain; the Christian virtues inferior to charity continue to play their part; but they are all informed and regulated by the principle of love, and the nearer the soul approaches to God, the more love predominates as the animating principle of action." Using metaphors from daily life, Hogan tried to place personal experience, reflection on the Scriptures, and the example of Christ at the center of priestly spirituality and action.[57]

Other teachers supported this direction. Joseph Bruneau (1866–1933) published *Our Priesthood* in 1911. Dedicated to James Gibbons, these previously delivered lectures began with a general consideration of the title "Christian": "To bear the name of son of God, but to be also the son of God! To judge as a Christian; to speak as a Christian; to live as a

---

How Institutions Think (Syracuse, N.Y.: Syracuse University Press, 1986). For a review of the more general developments see Patricia Byrne, C.S.J., "American Ultramontanism," *Theological Studies* 56 (June 1995): 301–26.

55. For general background see Christopher J. Kauffman, *Tradition and Transformation in Catholic Culture.*

56. See Rev. P. Dissez, S.S., "On the Spiritual Formation in Seminaries of Candidates to the Holy Priesthood," *Catholic Educational Association, Bulletin,* 1 (1906): 1–20, p. 3, as found in Sulpician Archives, Baltimore, RG 10, Box 4; *Paulinus Francis Dissez, August Mary Chéneau, A Memorial* (St. Mary's Seminary, Baltimore, 1908).

57. John B. Hogan, *Daily Thoughts for Priests,* 4th ed. (Boston, 1903), p. 33 and passim.

Christian; to act as a Christian; to give in a thoroughly Christian life a vivid commentary on the divine Gospel! But, mind, gentlemen, that your grace presupposes nature." In a later work, *Our Priestly Life*, Bruneau based his reflections on Olier's ideal *vivere summe Deo in Christo Jesu*, noting the formula: *Christianus alter Christus, Sacerdos alter Christus*. "In fact," he wrote, "the only reason why Father Olier proposed this ideal to seminarians and priests is that he considered it the essence of the Christian life. *Christianus alter Christus*."[58] Lastly, Gabriel André (1848–1931), who taught at St. John's Seminary, Brighton, published a French translation of Gibbons's *Ambassador of Christ* and argued for a closer relationship between priest and people in addressing the social questions of the time. André had a profound effect on James Anthony Walsh (1867–1936), one of the founders of Maryknoll. Walsh's union between ecclesiology and mission supported a more radical emphasis on an incarnational priestly spirituality and was aligned with a new understanding of Church.[59]

Yet all of these teachers labored within an intellectual framework and tradition that structured priestly spirituality in a sacral and cultic direction. Symptomatic of the approach was Bruneau's attempt to fit his thoughts into a commentary on the *ritus ordinationis*.[60] The perduring effects of the tension can be seen in the work of Francis Havey (1864–1945), one of the most popular expositors of the spirituality of the priesthood in the first half of the twentieth century. Inheriting the wide vision of his predecessors, Havey still presupposed the ecclesiastical world shaped by Spalding and Elder and signficantly strengthened in the struggles over Americanism and the condemnation of modernism. The broader implications of "incorporation into Jesus Christ" received little attention. In the best fashion, Havey continued the tradition by personalizing "O Jesu vivens in Maria." He admonished the seminarians:

58. Joseph Bruneau, S.S., *Our Priesthood*, B. Herder, 1911, p. 14; *Our Priestly Life* (Baltimore: John Murphy Company, 1928), p. 3.

59. See James Cardinal Gibbons, *L'Ambassadeur du Christ*, traduit de l'anglais par l'abbé André (Paris: P. Lethielleux, 1897), "Introduction," v–xxxix. For the impact on Walsh see Robert E. Sheridan, *The Founders of Maryknoll* (Maryknoll Fathers, 1980), p. 33. I am indebted for these references to the unpublished study of Sr. Angelyn Dries, O.S.F., "The Sulpician Mission Legacy and the Foundations of Maryknoll."

60. See Bruneau, *Our Priesthood*, passim.

What we see in Mary we desire for ourselves. We stretch out our hands towards Jesus whom we behold living so wonderfully in Mary; we beg Him to come also and live in us; not as in a church or in the tabernacle, but as He lives in Mary, that is to say, by uniting ourselves perfectly to Himself, by animating our most intimate actions, by becoming the principle of all our movements, by pouring out into us all His gifts and all His graces, to such an extent that all our actions, feelings, thoughts, and all the movements of our will, and in general, all our vital operations, may come solely from Jesus living in us, and communicating to us His life, thoughts, affections, desires, and actions; and that thus our life may be no longer our own, but the life of Jesus, who was also the lofe [sic] of Mary. "Vivo jam non ego, vivit vero in me Christus." Our desire is the more ardent, the greater is our need.[61]

Havey also recognized the call of the laity for a deeper spiritual life. But within his thinking the cleric and laic vocations within the one priesthood of Christ remained significantly separated by an emphasis on priestly "holiness," "ministry," "power," and "office." Pauline identification with Christ was interiorized and individualized. Priestly spirituality related to the other person primarily though its emphasis on apostolic mission.

The limitations of this view came to be severely criticized as the liturgical and theological reforms of the mid-twentieth century developed. In 1949 Eugene Walsh published his study *The Priesthood in the Writings of the French School: Berulle, De Condren, Olier.*[62] The book drew great attention to Olier's roots in the Pauline teaching on the Mystical Body of Christ. Concentrating on the incorporation into Christ that occurs in Baptism, Walsh reunited Christology, ecclesiology, and spirituality in a dynamic fashion. Yet his work was considered progressive; its implications far reaching. One anonymous reader went to the theological

---

61. Havey, "Meditations: O Jesu Vivens in Maria," in Sulpician Archives, Baltimore, RG 11, Box 4. For Havey see also *American Necrology of the Society of St. Sulpice,* pp. 352–55, and other materials in the archives, all in RG 11, Box 4; "Notes on Early Prayer Books I & II"; "Sulpician Spiritual Direction, Notes"; "Knowing Christ"; "Notes on Asceticism"; "Meditation, Notes on Various aspects"; and "Ecclesiastical Seminaries," *Messenger of the Sacred Heart* 12 (July 1908): 365–70.

62. Ph.D. dissertation, The Catholic University of America, 1949.

heart of the problem when he criticized Walsh for emphasizing Christ's humanity. He leveled the same criticism at the book that had been leveled at St. Irenaeus:

> St. Irenaeus' doctrine of recapitulation is criticized for making the *Incarnation* rather than the *Redemption* the central mystery of Christ's life. The Berullian school apparently is open to the same objections.
>
> This seems to imply that Christ's humanity is the soul or life-principle of the Mystical Body (as Mersch held). But *Mystici Corporis* makes it clear that the Holy Spirit is the soul.[63]

At first glance these comments might appear cryptic. But they summarize the contrast between two different approaches to priestly spirituality and identity. Coming as they did just a few years before the Second Vatican Council, Walsh's book and the criticisms of the unknown reader pointed to a divergence of views that would move out of the textbooks and into the congregation in the years to come. From the historical point of view, the contemporary debate reflects in some measure this dual inheritance. It seems to have marked the Catholic community from its beginnings, and at its symbolic center are slightly divergent but very Catholic understandings of the priesthood.

63. The criticisms are in the margin of Walsh's *The Priesthood* contained in the Sulpician archives library, p. 11.

PUBLICATIONS OF
MONSIGNOR ROBERT TRISCO

Books
Author

The Holy See and the Nascent Church in the Middle Western United States 1826–1850
("Analecta Gregoriana," No. 125 [Rome: Gregorian University Press, 1962]).
Bishops and Their Priests in the United States ("The Heritage of American Catholicism" [New York and London: Garland Publishing, Inc., 1988]).

Editor

Catholics in America, 1776–1976 (Washington, D.C.: National Conference of Catholic Bishops, Committee for the Bicentennial, 1976).

Co-author (with John Tracy Ellis)

A Guide to American Catholic History, 2d ed., revised and enlarged (Santa Barbara, Calif.; Oxford, Eng.: American Bibliographical Center—Clio Press, 1982).

Co-editor (with Nelson H. Minnich and Robert B. Eno, S.S.)

Studies in Catholic History in Honor of John Tracy Ellis (Wilmington, Del.: Michael Glazier, 1985).

Articles

"The Catholic Church in the United States," *Dictionary of American History,* Supplement (vol. 6) (New York: Charles Scribner's Sons, 1962).
"Vatican City," *Encyclopedia Americana* (1964 edition).
"Papal Elections" and "Vatican City," *Catholic Encyclopedia for School and Home* (New York, 1965).
"Feehan, Patrick Augustine," *Dictionnaire d'Histoire et de Géographie Ecclésiastiques,* Fascicle 93 (1966), cols. 812–15.
"Second Vatican Council" (under "Vatican Councils"), *Encyclopaedia Britannica* (1967), 23:912–18.

"American Board of Catholic Missions," *New Catholic Encyclopedia* (New York: Mc-
Graw-Hill Book Company, 1967), 1:398.

"Apostolic Delegation in the U.S.," ibid., 1:690–93.

"John XXIII, Pope," ibid., 7:1015–20.

"Meyer, Albert Gregory," ibid., 9:785–88.

"Paul VI, Pope," ibid., 11:16–23.

"Stritch, Samuel Alphonsus," ibid., 13:740–42.

"Vatican Council II," ibid., 14:563–72.

"The Synod of Bishops and the Second Vatican Council," *American Ecclesiastical
Review* 157 (September 1967): 145–60.

"Christian Freedom and Ecclesiastical Authority," *Foundations* (A Baptist Journal
of History and Theology), 11 (July–September 1968): 207–26.

"An American Anomaly: Bishops without Canons," *Chicago Studies* 9 (Summer
1970): 143–57; reprinted in *Shared Responsibility in the Local Church*, edited by
Charles E. Curran and George J. Dyer, a project of the Catholic Theological
Society of America (1970), pp. 31–45.

"The Variety of Procedures in Modern History," in *The Choosing of Bishops*, edited
by William W. Bassett (Hartford, Conn.: The Canon Law Society of America,
1971), pp. 33–60.

"Bishops and Their Priests in the United States," in *The Catholic Priest in the United
States: Historical Investigations*, edited by John Tracy Ellis (Collegeville, Minn.:
Saint John's University Press, 1971), pp. 111–292.

"Fitton, James," and "Fitzpatrick, John Bernard," *Dictionnaire d'Histoire et de Géographie Ecclésiastiques*, Tome XVII (1971), cols. 285–87, 295–99.

"Democratic Influence on the Election of Bishops and Pastors and on the Administration of Dioceses and Parishes in the U.S.A.," in *Election and Consensus in
the Church*, edited by Giuseppe Alberigo and Anton Weiler (*Concilium*, Vol.
77—Church History [New York: Herder and Herder, 1972]), pp. 132–38.
Also published in a British edition and in Dutch, French, German, Por-
tuguese, and Spanish translations.

"The Catholic Theology of the Local Church," *Foundations* 15 (January–March
1972): 53–71.

"Church History and Ecumenism," *Seminarium* 25 (January–March 1973):
102–15.

"The Debate on the Election of Bishops in the Council of Trent," *The Jurist* 34
(1974): 257–91.

"McGuire, Martin R. P.," *New Catholic Encyclopedia*, 16 (Supplement 1967–74),
268.

"American Catholicism: The Voice of Conscience and Culture," *Columbia* 55
(April 1975): 6–15.

"Catholicism," *Dictionary of American History*, rev. ed., 8 vols. (New York: Charles
Scribner's Sons, 1976), 1:466–70.

"Die Länder des englischen Sprachbereichs," chap. 23 in *Handbuch der
Kirchengeschichte*, edited by Hubert Jedin and Konrad Repgen, Band VII: *Die
Weltkirche im 20. Jahrhundert* (Freiburg: Herder, 1979), pp. 625–85. "I paesi
di lingua inglese," chap. 21 in *Storia della Chiesa*, vol. X/2 (Milan: Jaca Book,

1980), pp. 574–632. "The Countries of the English-Speaking Area," chap. 23 in *History of the Church,* edited by Hubert Jedin, Konrad Repgen, and John Dolan, vol. 10: *The Church in the Modern Age* (New York: Crossroad, 1981), pp. 614–71.

"Reforming the Roman Curia: Emperor Ferdinand I and the Council of Trent," in *Reform and Authority in the Medieval and Renaissance Church,* edited by Guy F. Lytle (Washington, D.C.: The Catholic University of America Press, 1981), pp. 143–337.

"American Catholic Lay Movements in the XIXth and XXth Centuries," in *Miscellanea Historiae Ecclesiasticae,* vol. 7: Congrès de Bucarest, Aout 1980 ("Bibliothèque de la Revue d'Histoire Ecclésiastique," Fascicle 71 [Brussels: Éditions Nauwelaerts, 1985]), pp. 346–78.

"The Holy See and the First 'Independent Catholic Church' in the United States," in *Studies in Catholic History in Honor of John Tracy Ellis,* edited by Nelson H. Minnich, Robert B. Eno, S.S., and Robert F. Trisco (Wilmington, Del.: Michael Glazier, 1985), pp. 175–238.

"Carlo Borromeo and the Council of Trent: The Question of Reform," in *San Carlo Borromeo: Catholic Reform and Ecclesiastical Politics in the Second Half of the Sixteenth Century,* edited by John M. Headley and John B. Tomaro (Washington, D.C.: The Folger Shakespeare Library; London and Toronto: Associated University Presses, 1988), pp. 47–66.

"Giovanni XXIII ed il card. Amleto Giovanni Cicognani," in *Giovanni XXIII: Transizione del Papato e della Chiesa,* edited by Giuseppe Alberigo (Rome: Edizioni Borle, 1988), pp. 79–104.

"Cody, John Patrick," *New Catholic Encyclopedia,* 18 (Supplement 1978–88), 101.

"The Church's History in the University's History," *Catholic Historical Review* 75 (October 1989): 658–76.

"Ellis on Gibbons," *Records of the American Catholic Historical Society of Philadelphia* 104 (SpringWinter 1993): 4–7.

"After Columbus: Spanish Missionaries and American Indians," *Delta Epsilon Sigma Journal* 38 (Fall 1993): 40–54.

"Building a New Home for the Apostolic Delegate in the Decade of the Great Depression," *U.S. Catholic Historian* 12 (Spring 1994): 107–29.

"Nord-Amerika" (colonial period), *Lexikon für Theologie und Kirche,* 3d ed., vol. 1 (Freiburg im Breisgau: Herder, 1994), cols. 503–5.

"Carl Joseph Peter: In Memoriam," in *Church and Theology: Essays in Memory of Carl J. Peter,* edited by Peter C. Phan (Washington, D.C.: The Catholic University of America Press, 1995), pp. 3–20.

"Bayley, James Roosevelt," "Keane, John Joseph," and "Catholic University of America," *The HarperCollins Encyclopedia of Catholicism,* general editor Richard P. McBrien (San Francisco: Harper-Collins, 1995), pp. 145–46, 287–88, 733.

"Melville, Annabelle M.," *New Catholic Encyclopedia,* vol. 19 (1995), p. 256.

"Gibbons, James," *Lexikon für Theologie und Kirche,* 3d ed., vol. 4 (Freiburg im Breisgau: Herder, 1995), col. 641.

"Borromeo, Carlo, Cardinal," *Encyclopedia of the Reformation* (New York: Oxford University Press, 1996), 1:203–5.

"Pius IV, Pope," ibid., 3:277–78.

"Hughes, John," *Lexikon für Theologie und Kirche,* vol. 5 (Freiburg im Breisgau: Herder, 1996), col. 303.

"Ireland, John," ibid., col. 583.

"Archbishop Cicognani, Apostolic Delegate, Apostle of the Word Spoken and Printed," in *The Church's Mission of Evangelization:* Essays in Honor of His Excellency, the Most Reverend Agostino Cacciavillan, Apostolic ProNuncio to the United States of America, on the Occasion of His Seventieth Birthday, August 14, 1996, ed. William E. May (Steubenville, Ohio: Franciscan University Press, 1996), pp. 371–86.

"American Catholic Historical Association," *The Encyclopedia of American Catholic History,* edited by Michael Glazier and Thomas J. Shelley (Collegeville, Minn.: Liturgical Press, 1997), pp. 42–43.

"Missions in Colonial America, English," ibid., pp. 939–46.

"American Catholic Historical Association," *Encyclopedia USA,* Supplement, vol. 2 (Gulf Breeze, Fla.: Academic International Press, 1998), pp. 140–43.

"Cody, John Patrick," *American National Biography* (New York: Oxford University Press, 1999), 5:133–34.

"Crowley, Patrick Francis," ibid., pp. 805–6.

"Kerby, William Joseph," ibid., 12:620–21.

"Pace, Edward Aloysius," ibid., 16:878–79.

"Shahan, Thomas Joseph," ibid., 19:701–2.

Reports

"Report of the Secretary [of the American Catholic Historical Association and of the Editor]," *Catholic Historical Review,* annually in the April issue, XLVIII–LXIX (1962–83).

"Report of the Secretary and Treasurer [of the American Catholic Historical Association and of the Editor]," *Catholic Historical Review,* annually in the April issue, 70– (1984–).

"Religious History at the Twelfth International Congress of Historical Sciences, Vienna, August 29–September 5, 1965," *Catholic Historical Review* 51 (January 1966): 539–58.

"Religious History at the Thirteenth International Congress of Historical Sciences, Moscow, August 16–23, 1970," *Catholic Historical Review* 56 (January 1971): 649–60.

Book Reviews

American Ecclesiastical Review
American Historical Review
Catholic Historical Review
Church History
International Migration Review
The Journal of Religion
The Jurist

DOCTORAL DISSERTATIONS DIRECTED BY
MONSIGNOR ROBERT TRISCO

Department of History

1969   William Barry Smith, "The Attitude of American Catholics toward Italian Fascism between the Two World Wars"

1971   Thomas William Spalding, C.F.X., "Martin John Spalding, Bishop of Louisville and Archbishop of Baltimore, 1810–1872"; published as *Martin John Spalding: American Churchman* (Washington, D.C.: The Catholic University of America Press, 1973)

1971   Henry A. Szarnicki, "The Episcopate of Michael O'Connor, First Bishop of Pittsburgh, 1843–1860"; published as *Michael O'Connor, First Catholic Bishop of Pittsburgh, 1843–1869* (Pittsburgh: Wolfson Publishing Co., 1975)

1972   Blase Robert Dixon, T.O.R., "The Catholic University of America, 1909–1928: The Rectorship of Thomas Joseph Shahan"

1975   Mary Griset Holland, "The British Catholic Press and the Educational Controversy, 1847–1865"

1976   Frances Panchok, "The Catholic Church and the Theatre in New York, 1890–1920"

1979   Thomas W. Tifft, "Toward a More Humane Social Policy: The Work and Influence of Monsignor John O'Grady"

1980   Barbara Misner, S.C.S.C., "A Comparative Social Study of the Members and Apostolate of the First Eight Permanent Communities of Women Religious within the Original Boundaries of the United States, 1790–1850"

1981   Douglas James Slawson, C.M., "The Attitudes and Activities of American Catholics Regarding the Proposals to Establish a Federal Department of Education between World War I and the Great Depression"

1982   Thomas Joseph Peterman, "Thomas Andrew Becker: The First Catholic Bishop of Wilmington, Delaware, and the Sixth Bishop of Savannah, Georgia, 1831–1899"; published as *The Cutting Edge: The Life of Thomas Andrew Becker* (privately printed, 1982)

Department of Church History

1981   Fergus M. O'Donoghue, S.J., "The Jesuit Mission in Ireland, 1598–1651"

1985   Timothy Michael Dolan, "To Teach, Govern, and Sanctify: The Life of Edwin Vincent O'Hara"; published as *"Some Seed Fell on Good Ground": The Life of Edwin V. O'Hara* (Washington, D.C.: The Catholic University of America Press, 1992)

1985   Takako Frances Takagi, S.N.D., "A History of the Sisters of Notre Dame de Namur in Japan, 1924–1978"; published under the same title (Washington, D.C.: Port City Press, Inc., 1987)

1987   Earl Boyea, "The National Catholic Welfare Conference: An Experience in Episcopal Leadership, 1935–1945"

1989   Martin Zielinski, "Doing the Truth: The Catholic Interracial Council of New York, 1945–1963"

1989   Joseph S. Rossi, S.J., "American Catholics and the Formation of the United Nations"; published under the same title (Lanham, Md.: University Press of America, 1993)

1992   Joseph Hubbert, C.M., "'For the Upbuilding of the Church': The Reverend Hermann Heuser, D.D., 1851–1933"

1995   Raymond J. Kupke, "James J. Norris: An American Catholic Life"

1995   Joseph C. Linck, C.O., "'Fully Instructed and Vehemently Influenced': Catholic Preaching in Anglo-Colonial America"

1996   Rory T. Conley, "Arthur Preuss, Journalist and Voice of German and Conservative Catholics in America, 1871–1934"; published under the same title (New York, etc.: Peter Lang, 1998)

1996   Ruth L. O'Halloran, "Organized Catholic Laywomen: The History of the National Council of Catholic Women"

1999   Brian Van Hove, S.J., "The Life and Career of François Annat, S.J.: The Failure of His Anti-Jansenism, May 1641–October 1668"

1999   Floyd McCoy, "Bishop William Jones, O.S.A.: His Background in the United States and Cuba and His Work in Puerto Rico (1907–1921)"

In progress: Thomas A. Lynch, "Francis Cardinal Spellman: American and Catholic Leader between New York, Washington, and Rome, 1939–1967"

In progress: James Garneau, "'Commandoes for Christ': The Foundation of the Missionary Society of St. James the Apostle and the 'Americanism' of the 1950's and 1960's"

CONTRIBUTORS

Earl Boyea, a priest of the Archdiocese of Detroit, has authored numerous articles on the history of the Catholic Church in Michigan for the *Catholic Historical Review,* the *Michigan Historical Review,* and the *Encyclopedia of American Catholic History.* He currently serves as Professor of Church History and Dean of Studies at Sacred Heart Major Seminary, Detroit.

Joseph P. Chinnici, O.F.M. (CDA 1987),* the author of several books and numerous articles, including *Living Stones: The History and Structure of Catholic Spiritual Life in the United States* (New York: Macmillan, 1989), currently teaches the history of the Church at the Franciscan School of Theology, Berkeley, California. He is a Franciscan priest of the Order of Friars Minor, Province of Saint Barbara.

Rory T. Conley was ordained a priest of the Archdiocese of Washington in 1989 and works in parish ministry. He has published a variety of articles on subjects related to the history of the Catholic Church in the United States as well as *Arthur Preuss: Journalist and Voice of German and Conservative Catholics in America, 1871–1934* (New York: Peter Lang, 1998). From 1993 until 1996 he served as president of the Catholic Historical Society of Washington, and has been editor of the Society's quarterly *NEWSLETTER* since 1996.

Robert Emmett Curran (CDA 1986) is Professor of History at Georgetown University. He is the author of *Michael Augustine Corrigan and the Shaping of Conservative Catholicism, 1878–1902* (New York: Arno, 1978), *American Jesuit Spirituality: The Maryland Tradition, 1634–1900* (New York: Paulist Press, 1988), and *Georgetown University: A Bicentennial History* (Washington, D.C.: Georgetown University Press, 1993), as well as numerous articles on American Catholic history.

---

*CDA: A number of the contributors to this volume held the Catholic Daughters of the Americas Chair in American Catholic History at The Catholic University of America, which until the fall of 1991 was a visiting chair.

Gerald P. Fogarty, S.J. (CDA 1985), a member of the Maryland Province of the Society of Jesus, received his doctorate from Yale University and is presently William R. Kenan Jr. Professor of the History of American and Modern European Catholicism at the University of Virginia. His publications include *The Vatican and the American Hierarchy from 1870 to 1965* (Collegeville, Minn.: Liturgical Press, 1985) and *American Catholic Biblical Scholarship: A History from the Early Republic to Vatican II* (San Francisco: Harper, 1989).

Philip Gleason (CDA 1982) graduated from the University of Notre Dame in 1960 and is currently on the faculty of his alma mater as professor emeritus of religious history and the history of ethnicity in America. Among his many publications are *The Conservative Reformers: German-American Catholics and the Social Order* (Notre Dame: University of Notre Dame Press, 1968) and *Contending with Modernity: Catholic Higher Education in the Twentieth Century* (New York: Oxford University Press, 1995).

Charles Edwards O'Neill, S.J. (CDA 1989), a New Orleans Province Jesuit, has specialized in the history of French colonial Louisiana. He has taught at Loyola University in New Orleans and served as director of the Jesuit Historical Institute in Rome. He is the author of *Church and State in French Colonial Louisiana* (New Haven: Yale University Press, 1966); his latest book, entitled *Séjour: Parisian Playwright from Louisiana*, was published by the University of Southwestern Louisiana's Center for Louisiana Studies.

Christopher J. Kauffman (CDA 1990), editor of *U.S. Catholic Historian* and distinguished Catholic Daughters of the Americas Professor of American Catholic History (1991–) at The Catholic University of America, has authored numerous works on the history of the Church in America, including *Faith and Fraternalism: The History of the Knights of Columbus 1882–1982* (New York: Simon & Schuster, 1992), and *Ministry and Meaning: A Religious History of Catholic Healthcare in the United States* (New York: Crossroad, 1995).

Raymond J. Kupke, a priest of the Diocese of Paterson, N.J., was ordained in 1973. He currently serves as pastor of Holy Family Parish, Florham Park, and as diocesan archivist. He is an adjunct instructor in Church History at Immaculate Conception Seminary, Seton Hall University, South Orange, N.J., Immaculate Conception Seminary, Huntington, N.Y., and in the Education for Parish Service program headquartered at Trinity College in Washington. He is the author of *Living Stones. A History of the Catholic Church in the Diocese of Paterson* (Clifton, N.J.: Diocese of Paterson, 1988), as well as several articles.

Joseph C. Linck, C.O., a member of the Oratory of Saint Philip Neri in Pittsburgh, was ordained in 1994. He serves as campus chaplain at the University of Pittsburgh and Carnegie Mellon University, as well as a lecturer in Church History at Saint Vincent's Seminary in Latrobe, Pennsylvania. He has published articles on the history of the colonial Church in the United States and co-edited an earlier volume with Raymond Kupke entitled *American Catholic Preaching and Piety in the Time of John Carroll* (Lanham, Md.: University Press of America, 1991).

Thomas J. Shelley, a priest of the Archdiocese of New York, is associate professor of historical theology at Fordham University. He is the author of *Paul J. Hallinan, First Archbishop of Atlanta* (Wilmington, Del.: Glazier, 1989), *Dunwoodie: The History of Saint Joseph's Seminary* (Westminster, Md.: Christian Classics, 1993), and editor of *The Encyclopedia of American Catholic History* (Collegeville, Minn.: Liturgical Press, 1997).

Douglas J. Slawson is a native of Southern California. He has been associate professor of Church History at Saint John's Seminary in Camarillo, California, and at Saint Thomas Theological Seminary in Denver, Colorado. Most recently, he has served as professor of history, and an administrator, at National University in San Diego, California. His most recent book is the *Foundation and First Decade of the National Catholic Welfare Council* (Washington, D.C.: The Catholic University of America Press, 1992). His articles have appeared in the *Catholic Historical Review, The Americas,* and *Vincentian Heritage.*

Thomas W. Spalding, C.F.X. (CDA 1991), a Xaverian Brother, is professor emeritus in history at Spalding University, Louisville, Kentucky. A native of Bardstown, Kentucky, he has published *Martin John Spalding: American Churchman* (Washington, D.C.: Catholic University of America Press, 1973), for which he received the John Gilmary Shea award, *The Premier See: A History of the Archdiocese of Baltimore, 1789–1989* (Baltimore: Johns Hopkins University Press, 1989), a parish history, and articles for encyclopedias and historical journals.

INDEX